Hinweise zum Lehrwerk

Das neue *Focus on Success* ist konzipiert für Lernende und Unterrichtende an Fachoberschulen, Berufsoberschulen, Höheren Berufsfachschulen und Beruflichen Gymnasien. Es setzt Englischkenntnisse auf dem Niveau des mittleren Schulabschlusses voraus und führt zur Fachhochschulreife sowie zur (fachgebundenen) Hochschulreife.

Das neue *Focus on Success* ist keine Überarbeitung, sondern ein neues Lehrwerk, das auf die Bedürfnisse von Lernenden und Unterrichtenden in der beruflichen Oberstufe eingeht. Das Lehrwerk wurde überwiegend von Lehrer/Innen und Berater/Innen aus Bayern mit konzipiert.

Das Lehrwerk besteht aus 15 auf Lehrplan und Abschlussprüfung abgestimmten Kapiteln, Hinweisen zu Spracherwerb, Lerntechniken und Lösung von Prüfungsaufgaben. Hinzu kommen eine lernerorientierte Zusammenstellung der englischen Grammatik, ein ausführlicher Wortschatzteil zu jedem Kapitel und eine alphabetische Wortschatzliste. Texte und Übungen innerhalb eines Kapitels sind von unterschiedlichem Schwierigkeitsgrad, wodurch auf die Bedürfnisse der jeweiligen Lerngruppe besser eingegangen werden kann. *Focus on Success* enthält aktuelle, frische Materialien, die in einem zeitgemäßen, lebendigen Layout präsentiert werden.

Jedes Kapitel des Lehrwerks beginnt mit einer meist visuellen Hinführung zum Thema (*Focus*). Im Mittelpunkt stehen zwei Texte unterschiedlicher Länge, Textsorte und Perspektive, wobei darauf geachtet worden ist, dass sie sowohl Motivation für die Lernenden bieten als auch einen klaren Lehrplanbezug besitzen. Die mit den Texten verbundenen Aufgaben dienen dazu, das Leseverstehen zu verbessern und auf die Anforderungen der neuen Abschlussprüfung vorzubereiten; außerdem werden verschiedene interkulturelle Aspekte behandelt, welche die Texte und ihr Umfeld beleuchten. Natürlich sind auch vielfältige Übungen enthalten, die den Wortschatz festigen und am Ende jedes Kapitels wiederholen.

Zur Schulung der Schreibfertigkeit dienen einerseits aktuelle Bilder, Cartoons, Statistiken und Graphiken, andererseits motivierende Schreibanlässe mit realistischem Situations- und Adressatenbezug. Jedes Kapitel enthält zudem Themenstellungen zur Förderung der Sprechfertigkeit und Vorbereitung auf die mündliche Gruppenprüfung sowie abwechslungsreiche Aufgaben zur Schulung des Hörverstehens. Zur Festigung der Grammatik dienen Übungen zum selbstgesteuerten Lernen, das eigenständige Verbessern von Fehlern und Hinweise auf Probleme, die bei deutschsprachigen Lernenden häufig auftreten. In jedem Kapitel finden sich zahlreiche Querverweise zum Anhang, um den Lernprozess zu unterstützen.

Autoren und Redaktion, 2006

Dieses Symbol weist darauf hin, dass sich der Text auf CD befindet.

Table of contents

Years 11 and 12

Table of contents

Reference section

LANGUAGE STUDY SKILLS

1 Happiness is ...

FOCUS

1 Choose one photo which expresses 'happiness' best. Explain why you have chosen it.

a

b

c

d

2 Talk with other students who have chosen the same photo as you.

Talk about
a what makes you happy,
b what you spend your money on.

Make two lists of your top five ideas and report to the class.

TEXT 1

Reading skills p170/171

CD1/2

What is the price of happiness?

You are going to read a report on how British people try to find happiness. The report was sponsored by Cadbury, an international chocolate and drinks company. Why do you think Cadbury wants to know what makes people happy?

http://www.cadburys.co.uk

Search | Text Only | Legal | Rate Our Site | Site Map | Contact Us | My Account

Cadbury

Money might make the world go round but does it really make us happy? A study carried out by Cadbury has revealed that the average adult in Britain spends £2,050 a year on increasingly complex methods to boost their happiness levels. This adds up to a massive £96 billion spent by the nation every year.

The report reveals that 48% of the people who completed the survey regularly splash the cash on nights out on the town with friends, 34% like to spend money on new clothes, and 27% go on holiday – all in the hope of finding a quick happiness fix. However, the report reveals that the key to long-term happiness rests with the everyday pleasures that are often taken for granted: family, friendship and having a laugh. Thirty per cent of the 18 –20-year-olds questioned said they were happiest when they were in bed.

The study listed the top five happiness boosters as:

1. Family
2. Friends
3. Food
4. Time off work
5. Relaxing – 'me' time

In an interview, psychologist Dr Dylan Evans who helped on the report said, 'Our study shows that people are aware that money is not the key to happiness. Some of the simplest routes to happiness include time off work and close relationships with friends and family. On the other hand,' he went on, 'people are also adept at spending money on short-term pick-ups including mood enhancers like chocolate.'

It seems that people are always in search of something more. This may be due to the fact that we tend to get used to sources of happiness that are always present in our lives and take them for granted. This means that we rapidly get used to improvements in well-being. To be continually happy, we would need constant improvements, as the joys of one improvement quickly wear off.

A Cadbury spokesperson commented, 'As a company with a heritage of bringing smiles to people's faces, we wanted to identify the mood of the nation to see just how happy we all are. The report shows that it's the simple things in life like family and friends that matter most, and for times when we need a boost, then a little of what we fancy can do us the world of good.'

384 words, adapted from http://www.cadbury.co.uk

1 Looking at the text

A Compare your top five lists with the results in Britain. What are the differences? How do you explain them?

B Which of these statements summarizes the text best?

1 Although many good things in life are free, Britons do not achieve true happiness without spending a lot of money.
2 Only money can buy happiness and that is why British people spend a lot on going out, clothes and holidays.
3 Although a lot of people in Britain spend money on having a good time, it is the simple things in life that make people happy.
4 British people don't spend a lot of money on themselves.

C True or false? Correct the false statements.

1 The average British adult spends more than £2,000 a year on nights out, clothes and holidays.
2 For most Britons, being alone is more important than spending time with friends.
3 According to the report, eating chocolate makes some people depressed.
4 People are never satisfied with what they have for long. They always need something better to make them happy.
5 The report shows that rich people are usually happier than poor people.

Now work with a partner and write two additional statements (true or false) about the text. Read your sentences to the class. They should decide if they are true or false and correct the false statements.

D Match sentences (1–5) from the text with five of the explanations (a–g). Two explanations do not match.

1 People ... regularly splash the cash on nights out on the town. (lines 5/6)
2 The key to long-term happiness rests with the everyday pleasures that are often taken for granted. (lines 8/9)
3 People are also adept at spending money on short-term pick-ups. (lines 15/16)
4 To be continually happy, we would need constant improvements. (lines 21/22)
5 A little of what we fancy can do us the world of good. (lines 26/27)

a It's the nice moments in our daily lives, that we don't think about very much, which really make us happy in the long run.
b An occasional treat is good for us.
c People spend a lot of money in restaurants, bars, clubs, etc.
d We can only stay happy if we find new pleasures.
e People manage to find things to buy which lift their mood for a short time.
f People can only be happy when they are surrounded by their family and friends.
g A lot of people think money is very important.

2 Working with words

A Find words and phrases in the text for the German words and phrases below.

1 eine Untersuchung
2 zunehmend
3 Milliarde
4 kurzlebiges Glückserlebnis
5 Leute sind sich bewusst
6 Wege
7 Quellen
8 ständig(e)
9 Stimmung
10 Auftrieb

B Find a word from the text which fits all the expressions in each list.

EXAMPLE save … for something • make a lot of … • spend … on something
lend a friend some … • borrow some … from the bank
be rolling in …

The correct word is *money*.

1 be … about/with something • make somebody …
keep somebody … • look … • a … ending • a … coincidence
2 find … • make … with somebody • be … with somebody
spend an evening with … • one of my best … • everybody needs …
3 travel all over the … • live in a dream … • have little contact with the outside …
have the … at your feet • have all the time in the … • the … Wide Web
4 a feeling of … • give somebody new … • give up … • lose …
in the … of doing something
5 be in a good … • be in a bad … • not be in the … for something
put somebody in a good … • a foul …
6 be on … • go on … • get four weeks' … a year • get a … job • a camping …
a … romance

Now choose one expression from each list. Use them to write six sentences.

3 Writing

Text production p180

'Money might make the world go round, but it does not really make us happy.'

Write about 150 words saying why you agree/disagree with this statement.

4 Happy learning

The only 'right' way to learn anything is to adopt a positive, pro-active attitude and take responsibility for your own learning. Find out which ways you learn best and set aside a learning time-slot every day for your English. Use the **Language Study Skills** in the Appendix starting on p163.

Language Study Skills p163

Talk in groups about ways you learn English.

CROSS-CULTURAL SPOTLIGHT

Happiness around the world
A study of 65 countries suggests that the happiest people live in Nigeria – and the least happy in Romania. The things that make people happy vary around the world. Personal success and self-expression are most important in the USA; in Japan, family values and being a good member of society come tops.
It's important to remember this when you are making small talk with people from other cultures. Don't be surprised if an American tells you how successful he or she is. And remember to ask about the family when you are talking to someone from Japan.

The study found out that these things make people happy
- *Having friends and valuing them*
- *Wanting less*
- *Doing someone a good turn*
- *Having faith (religious or not)*
- *Not comparing your looks with others*
- *Not worrying if you're not a genius*

5 Project – boosting your happiness at school

Doing projects p189

In groups, find some ways to make your school life happier.

Here are some ideas:

- make the classroom more attractive
- help each other with schoolwork (homework, exam preparation, etc.)
- plan an excursion in your town or area.

Present your results to the class. Together, put some of your ideas into practice.

6 Listening and talking

Listening skills p185

A Listen to three high school students talking about their future plans.

CD1/3

1 Take notes about the job each student wants to do in the future.
2 Listen again and take more notes. Why does each student want to pursue his or her particular career?

B Work in pairs. Find out what each of you wants to do when you finish school.

TEXT 2

Reading skills p170/171

CD1/4

'It's you we're talking about. Your future.'

The quotation above is from the text you are going to read. In groups, discuss the following questions:

- *Who do you think said this? Who might they be talking to?*
- *What might the situation be?*

Banks walked into the kitchen and put the kettle on for a cup of tea.

The telephone rang. Banks turned off the stereo and picked up the receiver.

'Dad?'

'Brian, is that you? I've been trying to get in touch with you.'

'Yeah, well ... we've been on the road. I didn't think you'd be in. Why aren't you at work?'

'If you didn't expect me to be in, why did you call?'

Silence.

'Brian? Where are you? Is anything wrong?'

'Nothing's wrong. I'm staying at Andrew's flat.'

'Where?'

'Wimbledon. Look, Dad ...'

'Isn't it about time your exam results were out?'

More silence. Christ, Banks thought, getting more than a few words out of Brian was as tough as getting the truth out of a politician.

'Brian?'

'Yeah, well that's why I was calling you. You know ... I thought I'd just leave a message.'

'I see.' Banks knew what was going on now. He looked around in vain for an ashtray and ended up using the hearth. 'Go on,' he prompted.

'About the exams, like ...'

'How bad is it? What did you get?'

'Well, that's it ... I mean ... you won't like it.'

'You *did* pass, didn't you?'

'Course I did.'

'Well?'

'It's just that I didn't do as well as expected. It was really hard, Dad. Everyone says so.'

'What did you get?'

Brian almost whispered. 'A third.'

'A *third*? That's a bit of a disappointment, isn't it? I'd have thought you could have done better than that.'

'Yeah, well it's more than you ever got.'

Banks took a deep breath. 'It doesn't matter a damn what I did or didn't get. It's you we're talking about. Your future. You'll never get a decent job with a third-class degree.'

'What if I don't want a *decent* job?'

'What do you want to be then? Another statistic? Another cliché? Another unemployed yobbo?'

'Thanks a lot, Dad. Nice to know *you* believe in me. Anyway, as a matter of fact, I'm not on the dole. We're going to try and make a go of it. Me and the band.'

'You're *what*?'

'We're going to make a go of it. Andrew knows this bloke who runs an indie label, and he's got a studio, like, and he's said we can go down and make a demo of some of my songs. You might not believe it, but people actually like us. We've got gigs coming out of our ears.'

'Have you any idea how tough it is to succeed in the music business?'

'The Spice Girls did it, and look how much talent they've got.'

'So did Tiny Tim, but that's not the point. Talent's got nothing to do with it. For every one that makes it, there are thousands who get trampled on the way.'

'We're making plenty of money.'

'Money's not everything. What about the future? What are you going to do when you've peaked at twenty-five and you don't have a penny in the bank?'

'What makes you an expert in the music business all of a sudden?'

'Is that why you got such a poor degree? Because you were too busy wasting your time rehearsing and going out on the road?'

'I was getting pretty bored with architecture anyway.'

Banks flicked his cigarette butt in the hearth. It scattered sparks against the dark stone. 'Have you talked to your mother about this?'

'Well, I sort of thought, maybe ... you know ... you could do that.'

That's a laugh, Banks thought. *Him* talk to Sandra? They couldn't even discuss the weather these days without it turning into an argument.

'I think you'd better ring her yourself,' he said. 'Better still, why don't you pay her a visit? She's only in Camden Town.'

'But she'll go spare!'

'Serves you right. You should have thought of that before.'

The kettle started whistling.

'Thanks a lot, Dad.' Brian said, his voice hard-edged with bitterness. 'I thought you'd understand. I thought I could depend on you. I thought you *liked* music. But you're just like the rest. Go see to your *fucking* kettle.'

'Brian ...'

But Brian hung up. Hard.

692 words, from Peter Robinson: *In A Dry Season*, Macmillan, London, 2000

7 Looking at the text

A Were the ideas you had before you read the text right or wrong? Explain what made you think the way you did.

B Complete the sentences with the most appropriate ending.

1 Brian phones his father
  a at a time when he knows that his father will be at home.
  b hoping to be able to leave a message on his answering machine.
  c because his mother has asked him to phone.

2 Brian tells his father that
  a he has failed his university exams.
  b he has got very good exam results.
  c he has passed his exams but did not get very good results.

3 Banks himself
  a did well at university.
  b got a first in his university exams.
  c hopes that his son will achieve more in life than he has.

4 At university, Brian
  a studied architecture, but did not find it very interesting.
  b studied music and loved it.
  c wanted to drop out after one year.

5 At the moment, Brian is
  a looking for a job as an architect.
  b thinking about working in the USA.
  c planning a career in the music business with some friends.

6 When Banks hears about Brian's plans, he is
  a happy because he thinks Brian will make a lot of money.
  b worried about Brian's future.
  c angry because he thinks that Brian should have studied music.

7 Finally, Brian hangs up because
  a he wants to call his mother and tell her about his plans.
  b the kettle is boiling.
  c he is angry and disappointed at his father's reaction.

8 Talking

Group discussions p186

Talk in groups.

1 Who do you think is right, Brian or his father? Explain why.
2 Think up a suitable title for the text.

9 Writing

Text production p175

Choose <u>one</u> of these tasks and write about 150 words.

1 Shortly after Brian hangs up, Banks writes him a letter. Write the letter.
2 The next day, Brian sends an email to his mother. Write the email.

10 Language – the simple present and the present progressive

SPOT THE MISTAKES

Spot the mistakes and correct them. Explain why they are wrong.

1 ~~Brian live and work in Wimbledon, but he work in Chelsea today.~~
2 ~~Do Mark like his new job?~~
3 ~~Lucy is cycling to work every day.~~
4 ~~In this photo, David plays football with his friends from Scotland.~~
5 ~~I'm going swimming on Saturdays.~~
6 ~~Iris always go to a club on Fridays.~~
7 ~~Are you liking tennis?~~
8 ~~I look for my pen. You know where it is?~~

The simple present

I **teach** him English.
Does he **need** a written excuse?

Language check p192

The present progressive

I'**m calling** to say that Ben's ill.
Who'**s speaking,** please?

Language check p192

1 The simple present

1 Write three sentences about your habits. Say what you do every day/week or once a month/year.
2 Write three things that you do not do.
3 Write three questions about habits which you can ask another student.
4 Now ask another student the questions.

2 The present progressive

Complete the conversation between Brian and his old school friend, Sarah, using the present progressive.

Brian: Hi, Sarah. Nice to see you. What …[1] (you/do) these days?
Sarah: I …[2] (work) in a bank. What about you? …[3] (you/work)?
Brian: Well, I …[4] (not/really/work) at the moment. I …[5] (practise) with a band. We …[6] (try) to set up some gigs.
Sarah: Cool. Who …[7] (you/play) with?
Brian: Nick, Oliver and Andrew.

3 The simple present and the present progressive

Put the verbs in brackets in the correct form.

1 Sarah …[1] (spend) her holidays in London at the moment. She …[2] (go) there once a year. She …[3] (usually/stay) with her cousin Joe who …[4] (live) in Wimbledon.

2 …[1] (you/need) any help with the preparations? Why …[2] (you/not ask) Oliver? He …[3] (not work) today. I …[4] (be) sure he …[5] (have) time. And he …[6] (like) parties and cooking and all that.

WATCH OUT!

Word order – position of adverbs

Language check p204

People ~~like to eat often~~ a bar of chocolate. ➤ People often like to eat a bar of chocolate.
We ~~go always~~ on holiday in July. ➤ We always go on holiday in July.
Some people ~~never are~~ happy. ➤ Some people are never happy.

Put the words in the correct order to make sentences. Change the verb and add a capital letter where necessary.

1 practise / in his room / Brian / usually
2 his band / once a week / play in a club
3 eat a chocolate biscuit / Banks / sometimes / with his tea
4 drink more coffee than tea / last year / british people
5 glad / they / when they have time off work / always / be
6 Nick / in London / twice / played / last week

VOCABULARY REVIEW

A Unscramble these words from the two texts and put them into two lists – good things in life / bad things in life. The first letter of each word is given below.

1 u 2 a 3 l 4 s
5 b 6 j 7 t 8 w-b

1 eeoudlmnpy
2 aeugmnrt
3 aughl
4 eilmss
5 eobdr
6 ojsy
7 uohgt
8 ellw-eibgn

B Continue to add good/bad things to your lists as you expand your English.

2 Going places

FOCUS

1 **In groups, talk about these cartoons.**

a

b

c

2 **Make up captions for the cartoons. Tell the class. Which captions are the funniest?**

TEXT 1

Reading skills p170/171

Online holiday advertisements

Read the holiday advertisements. Which holiday would you choose? Why? Tell the class.

a

City breaks

Prague £139
This 'City of Spires' is clean, romantic, relaxed, easy to discover on foot and brims with architectural treasures.

New York £339
Take a bite out of 'The Big Apple', the home of the Statue of Liberty, the Hudson river and Manhattan.

Las Vegas £799
This city is famous for sparkling showgirls and crazy casinos. It's a place of wonder and delight.

www.holiday.co.uk/shortbreaks

d

Family Active Holidays

The English Lake District

A fantastic family holiday at the beautiful English Lakes in one of Britain's most famous National Parks. The lakes and mountains create a perfect natural adventure park and with a different activity every day, we guarantee that you will make the most of your stay.

There will be
- mountain trekking
- Canadian canoeing
- dinghy sailing
- rock climbing
- mountain biking
- swimming

www.activitiesabroad.com

b

Get the best from your holiday!

Photography, painting and cookery courses are offered with visits to stunning and varied locations in the Languedoc region of France. Relax in the luxurious and tranquil surroundings of a chateau or cottage with gourmet food. Have fun developing skills you never knew you had and return home refreshed and invigorated.

www.goholidayfrance.com

e

Travel-to-Teach

TTT

- Travelling for Personal Development
- International Volunteering Opportunities
- Teach English or web design in north eastern Thailand.

f

Discover India – Discover Yourself

Welcome to Tiger Travel Specialist in Women's Holidays in India

Whatever your reasons for travelling solo as a female, you need never feel lonely or vulnerable again if you travel with us.

Rajasthan Pushkar Festival Tour

www.tigertravel.co.uk

c

EARTHWATCH INSTITUTE

Earthwatch Expedition – Cheetahs and Ranchers

Research mission in North Central Namibia finding common ground for cheetahs and ranchers.

€2,830

90% of Namibia's cheetahs live on farmlands where their survival is threatened by farmers. You will support a project organized by the Cheetah Conservation Fund (CCF) and participate in wildlife surveys, feeding and caring for captive cheetahs on-site and informing local farmers about cheetah conservation.

www.earthwatch.org

330 words, adapted from websites given

1 Looking at the texts

Read what these people say and choose a suitable holiday for each of them. Give reasons for your choice.

1

Anita Parson
Although we've got two small children, we would like to go on an active holiday with lots of different things to do. My husband loves all kinds of water sports while I prefer walking and hiking. Last year we went to Switzerland and it was great fun.

Mathew Scott
I went to Spain last summer and did not enjoy it at all. There was nothing to do all day but lie on the beach. It was cheap, but I'd rather spend more money and have a real adventure holiday this year, perhaps India or another faraway country.

2

3

Jasmine Chopra
We spent two weeks camping in Scotland last August. It rained most of the time so this year we want to go to a place where there's plenty to do even if the weather is bad. Unfortunately, we can't take a long holiday because my husband started a new job two months ago, but I think we can get away for a long weekend.

Claire Campbell
Well, I want a lazy holiday where I can relax and enjoy good food. But on the other hand, I always need something to do too. A few months ago I took a painting course, so I would like to spend my next holiday in a place with beautiful scenery where I can paint out in the open. Somewhere warm would be nice.

4

5

Oliver Shaw
I am a student and can't afford an expensive holiday. Last year I went on a working holiday on Malta. In the mornings I taught English at a language school. As I was free in the afternoons and evenings, I had enough time to explore the island. It was a great holiday. It didn't cost much and I enjoyed the teaching too.

2 Working with words

A **Work in groups. Use these words to make five word spiders to do with holidays. Add more words to each spider.**

on • around • by • for • to • holiday • abroad • trip • journey • bike • motorbike • bus • train • car • plane • camel • the world • the USA • India

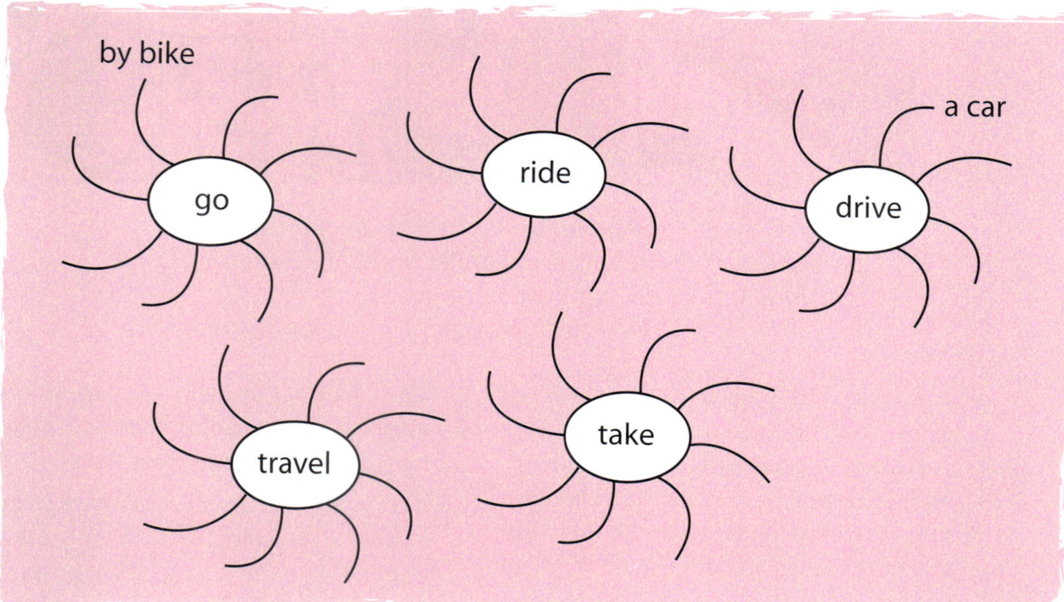

B **Use some of the expressions above to write about your dream holiday. Write about 180 words.**

Text production p180

3 Talking

Group discussions p186

Work in groups. Look at the advertisements on page 19 again and decide which holiday to go on together. Tell the class, giving reasons.

CROSS-CULTURAL SPOTLIGHT

Non-verbal communication

Different cultures often interpret the same non-verbal behaviour in different ways. Here are some points to remember.

Eye contact: In some countries, people may avoid looking at you while they are talking. In Japan and other Asian countries, for example, this is a sign of respect.

Space around you: While Britons like to keep more space around them than Americans when talking, both nationalities might feel uncomfortable in Arab and African countries where people stand much closer together.

Greeting and touching: In most countries, business people shake hands when they meet. In the UK, people do not normally shake hands in informal situations.

TEXT 2

Reading skills p170/171

CD1/5

Are you a tourist or a traveller?

You are going to read a text which compares tourists and travellers. First look at these drawings. Which drawing best fits which of the sentences below?

1 They avoid hotels and prefer to stay in tents or cabins.
2 They book package holidays and prefer popular destinations.
3 They often destroy the natural environment.
4 They sometimes do volunteer work at their holiday destination.

a One day, there will be no more tourists. There will be 'adventurers', 'fieldwork assistants', 'exploraholics', 'volunteers' and, of course, 'travellers'. But the term tourist will no longer exist. There might still be those who quietly travel to foreign countries for nothing other than pure pleasure, but it will be a secretive activity. No one will want to admit to being one of those. It might even be illegal.

b The list of territories which have been negatively affected by tourism is getting longer. Tourism Concern lists areas in China, Botswana, Belize, Zanzibar, East Africa, Peru and Thailand which tourists are not allowed to enter. Tourists only destroy the natural environment. Tourists do not respect local cultures. Tourists bring with them nothing but their money. They must be stopped at any price.

c Less than 40 years ago, tourism was considered a positive development. With the arrival of package holidays and charter flights, the masses could at last enjoy tourism. By the 1980s, tourism was the largest and fastest-growing industry in the world. Today there are more than 700m tourist arrivals each year. The World Tourism Organization (WTO) forecasts that, by 2020, there will be 1.56 billion tourists travelling at any one time.

d It won't be easy to stop more than a billion tourists from going where they want to go. It is impossible to convince a billion people that mass tourism is harmful to the welfare of the world. It is also clearly absurd to say it is very selfish and totally irresponsible to continue going on holiday. Tourism is not evil, even though it can cause harm.

e The tourist is being attacked by more subtle methods. The tourist is no longer called a 'tourist'. As the tourist is re-branded, so the holiday has to follow. Adventurers, fieldwork assistants, exploraholics, volunteers and travellers don't go on holidays. Un-tourists (as I will call them) go on things called 'cultural experiences', 'expeditions', 'projects', 'mini-ventures' and 'missions'. The modern un-tourist believes that the main motivation for travelling should be to help others. Environmental charity Earthwatch, which organizes holidays for 'volunteers', assures their clients that their trips will 'offer life-changing opportunities for the volunteers and be of great benefit to the environment.' Their motto is: 'See the world and give it a future.'

f The new kind of un-tourism excludes the masses. Un-tourists pretend they are not doing what they actually are doing – going on holiday. The brochures for the un-tourist industry look like magazines with articles on ecological and cultural issues. The price of the holiday is usually well hidden. There is something unpleasant about having to pay to do good.

g Naturally, un-tourists feel morally superior to tourists. They avoid tourist infrastructures such as hotels. They prefer to stay in a tent, a cabin or local-style houses (yurts, thatched huts, etc.). These, they believe, are somehow part of the local culture. Local culture is very important for the un-tourist. However, it only seems to apply to the Developing World, where un-tourists go on organized trips to meet hill tribes in Northern Thailand or the tattooed Ifugua of the Philippines. When the tourist travels to other parts of the world, the locals are not so attractive and there are even warnings to avoid them. When visiting New York no one wants to check out a housing project in the Bronx.

h All tourism should be responsible towards and respectful of the environment and the local people. Some tourist developments as well as individual tourists have not been so careful in the past and this should be stopped. But the division between those few privileged, high-paying un-tourists and the masses is absurd. The un-tourists are doing the same thing as the tourists – they are just being called something different. So do you really want to be a 'volunteer' on a 'mission' rather than go on holiday? Isn't it time to speak out against re-branding? Next time you're staying in that two-room local hotel in Oaxaca, Mexico's town for alternative travellers, say what you really are. When asked by an adventurer, fieldwork assistant, exploraholic or volunteer if you know where the other travellers are staying, say, 'How should I know? I'm not a traveller, I'm a tourist.'

700 words, adapted from *The Guardian*, 24 August 2002

4 Looking at the text

Match eight of the statements with the appropriate paragraph (a–h) from the text. There are two more statements than you need.

1. Some countries have closed their borders to tourists.
2. A new term has been invented to emphasize that tourism can have a positive effect on foreign cultures: there are no longer tourists going on holidays, but travellers or volunteers going on a mission and helping others.
3. In the future, some of today's tourists will be called 'travellers'.
4. In the past 40 years tourism has developed into a large and fast-growing industry.
5. Saying that tourists who destroy the environment are bad people won't halt mass tourism.
6. Since many places have been damaged by tourism, some countries no longer allow tourists to visit certain areas.
7. The brochures for the new kind of travellers look like magazines.
8. Travellers should stop thinking they are better than tourists just because they feel more concerned about environmental issues. After all, tourism in general should respect the natural environment.
9. Un-tourists believe they are better than tourists because they are interested in local culture and try to meet local people, but usually only in locations in the Developing World.
10. Some tourists are afraid of being attacked when they go abroad.

5 Mediation

Mediation skills p174

Work in pairs. You are going to tell each other in German about parts of the text. Do not translate word for word, just get the contents across.

Partner A, tell your partner about paragraph b.
Partner B, tell your partner about paragraph c.

6 Talking

A In groups, look at the map and answer the questions below and on the opposite page.

from *Tourism and Market Trends*, World Tourism Organization, 2003

1 How many trips did tourists worldwide take last year?
2 Which region had
   a the highest number of visitors?
   b the lowest number of visitors?
3 How much money did they spend in total?

4 How much money did tourists spend on average per trip
   a in Europe?
   b in the Americas?
   c in the Asia/Pacific region?
5 Which regions
   a earn less than average through tourism?
   b earn more than average through tourism?
6 What might be the reasons for low tourism receipts in some regions?

B Using the information from the map and the text, discuss these questions. Make notes and tell the class.

1 What are the positive effects of tourism?
2 What are the negative effects of tourism?
3 What might the negative effects of un-tourism be?

7 Listening

Listening skills p185

Sue works for the tour operator *Go!* She talks about her work to Ken Hall.

A Here are some of the things she says. Guess the questions Ken asked her.

1 I've visited quite a number of countries around the world.
2 I think my favourite country is India.
3 *Go!* specializes in taking people to exotic places.
4 I studied anthropology at university and spent a lot of time abroad.
5 *Go!* is one of the few tour operators that looks for employees with extensive travel experience.
6 The position in marketing became vacant and I applied for it.

CD1/6

B Now listen. How many questions did you get right? (You do not need to have guessed the exact words.)

8 Writing

Text production p180

Write around 180 words about something that happened to you on holiday. Use some of these words.

romantic	adventure	relax
famous	experience	discover
charming	weather	enjoy
foreign	food	explore
unpleasant	people	travel

9 Language – the simple past

SPOT THE MISTAKES

Spot the mistakes and correct them. Explain why they are wrong.

1 ~~In August Mark were on a camping holiday in France.~~
2 ~~Oliver start learning French when he was in France.~~
3 ~~David go to New Zealand last summer.~~
4 ~~Where you spent your last holiday?~~
5 ~~I enjoyed not my holiday in Spain two years ago.~~

The simple past

Did your son go to the USA?
He wanted to go to the USA.
His last postcard came from Japan.
He was always bad at geography.

Language check p193

The simple past

1 Complete the text by putting the words in brackets into the simple past.

A few years ago Joni Andrews took a gap year and …[1] (travel) round the world. She spoke to her friend, Richard, about her trip.

Richard: …[2] (you/go) by yourself?
Joni: No, I …[3] (not/travel) alone. My friend Penny …[4] (come) with me.
Richard: Where …[5] (you/start out)?
Joni: We …[6] (fly) from London to Los Angeles. We …[7] (stay) in California for three weeks then we …[8] (discover) the rest of America by Greyhound bus. That …[9] (be) the cheapest way to travel. We …[10] (meet) lots of friendly people on the buses. We really …[11] (enjoy) ourselves in America. We …[12] (see) such a lot of interesting things.

2 Work with a partner. Ask and answer questions about your holidays. The first one has been done for you.

1 Where / holidays?

Where did you go for your holidays?
I went to Hawaii.

2 When / go?
3 What / see?
4 What / do?
5 How / get there?
6 You / enjoy it?
7 Who / go with?
8 Where / stay?

WATCH OUT!

Language check p210

Problem words (1)

He was nervous when the aeroplane ~~started off~~. ➤ He was nervous when the aeroplane took off.

Choose the correct word or phrase so that each sentence makes sense.

1 *For two days* / *Two days ago* I was really annoyed because I had lost my passport.
2 The *latest* / *last* surveys show that some developing countries are being damaged by tourism.
3 Unfortunately, not everyone *has enough luck* / *is lucky enough* to find a beautiful place to stay on holiday.
4 If you are looking *for* / *after* a way to go abroad without paying too much, a job in a language school can be a good opportunity.
5 The travel *brochures* / *prospects* always make the hotels sound perfect.
6 Some *handys* / *mobile phones* don't work abroad.
7 They were *discussing* / *discussing about* where to go on holiday next year.
8 She said she could *possibly* / *eventually* go on holiday next month, if she finished her project on time.

Vocabulary review

Choose the correct words from the brackets to complete this text.

A lot of people who (travelling/travel/travellers)[1] abroad simply want to (relaxed/relaxing/relax)[2] in a nice (hotels/environment/holiday)[3]. Other people prefer (active/activity/activate)[4] and book an (expedition/adventure/trekking)[5] holiday in an exciting (locate/local/location)[6]. Whatever kind of (tourist/trip/travel)[7] people choose, most of us don't want to be with the (masses/massive/mass)[8]. It goes without saying that all (tourism/tourists/tours)[9] should always respect local people and the (environmental/environmentally/environment)[10].

3 Keeping fit

FOCUS

The Fit & Fun Centre offers a wide range of activities to people of all ages.

Use the Fit & Fun flow chart to find out which activities suit you. Tell another student why you have chosen these activities.

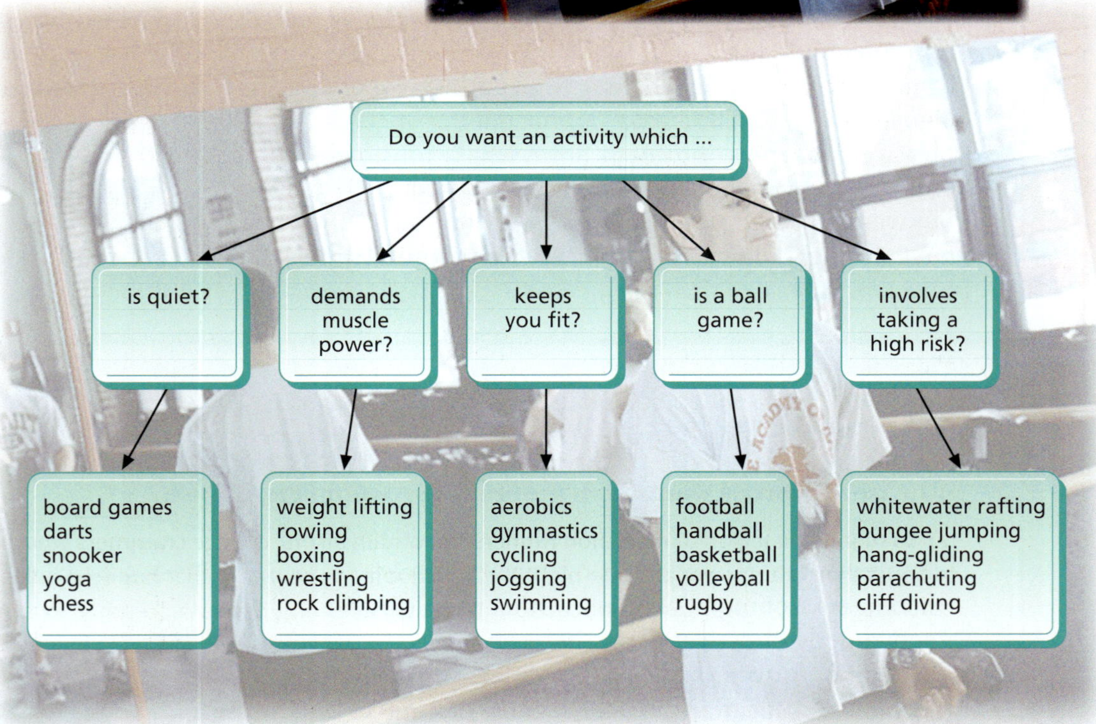

I'm interested in aerobics but I'm not interested in boxing because … .
I'm enthusiastic about darts because … .
I'm keen on trying out hang-gliding.
I don't mind playing board games but I'm not keen on chess.
I enjoy going cycling and I also like … .
I prefer … to … .

TEXT 1

Reading skills p170/171

CD1/7

Staying fit all night long

Disco, club or party time? What's the best way to keep going through the night?
In the late '80s, Dietrich Mateschitz, invented the energy drink, Red Bull. The target market for the drink was the educated, vigorous and well-paid European youth culture – people who spent long days in fitness studios and long nights at downtown clubs, dancing and drinking till dawn. Mateschitz came up with some great advertising lines for his product. 'You've got better things to do than sleep,' one ad proclaims, while another promises, 'Red Bull gives you wings.' Read about Red Bull drinkers at a London club.

It's 4:45 a.m. at the popular London club, Egg, and a few of the dancers have collapsed on the sofas or taken refuge at the bar. But after a long night of booze, drugs, tobacco and earth-shaking noise, most people are still vigorously, and happily, strutting their stuff across that trembling wood floor. How do they do it?

'Actually, we usually see a revival around half past four in the morning,' says Egg night manager Simon Patrick. 'That's when we get the real rush at the bar for Red Bull. The kids say, "I've had eight Red Bulls – I'm flying!" They'll dance right round the clock. At seven in the morning we have trouble getting them out the door.'

'It's like putting your whole system on fast-forward,' Lee Murphy shouts above the din as he glides across the dance floor holding a slender silver and blue can of Red Bull energy drink in each hand. 'By four or five in the morning, you're totally blotto,' the 29-year-old London nurse explains. 'That's where the Red Bull comes in. I just need two cans. It's like drinking a pint of speed.'

For Lee Murphy and other regular customers of the all-night club scene around the world – not to mention a legion of marathon runners, mountain bikers, college crammers who need to boost their brainpower and late-night truckers hoping to cover another hundred miles before turning in – the canned concoctions marketed as energy drinks represent a fizzy new manifestation of one of mankind's oldest stimulants: caffeine. The active ingredient in the hugely successful Austrian product Red Bull is a solid jolt of the stuff you find in coffee, blended with a handful of other ingredients. One 8.3-ounce can has two to three times the amount of caffeine as a 12-ounce can of other soft drinks.

The dual power to counter physical fatigue and increase alertness is part of the reason caffeine ranks as the world's most popular mood-altering drug, eclipsing the likes of nicotine and alcohol. Caffeine's pervasiveness is a cause for concern among some scientists and public health advocates, but that hasn't dampened its popularity. Sales of Red Bull and copycat energy drinks with names like Red Devil, Roaring Lion and Whoop Ass are booming.

373 words, adapted from *National Geographic*, January 2005

1 Looking at the text

A Choose the most suitable answer.

1 The main intention of the author is to inform the reader about
   a the potential dangers of using energy drinks.
   b the fact that people can only enjoy themselves if they use energy drinks.
   c the new trend of dancing round the clock in London discos.
   d the need of some people to consume energy drinks in order to keep going.

2 Which of the following effects of energy drinks is **not** mentioned in the text?
   a They make you feel wide awake.
   b They help you think better.
   c They make you more creative.
   d They make you feel more energetic.

3 The expression 'dancers have taken refuge at the bar' (lines 1/2) means that the dancers
   a are so exhausted that they need to recover with a drink.
   b are disappointed with the range of drinks offered at the bar.
   c are trying to forget their personal problems by having a drink at the bar.
   d have been frightened by other, aggressive dancers so they need a drink.

4 The author suggests that
   a the stimulants used in the new energy drinks are relatively new.
   b truck drivers probably don't like energy drinks.
   c runners and mountain bikers are worried about consuming new energy drinks.
   d energy drinks are like coffee in a can.

5 In saying that caffeine is 'eclipsing the likes of nicotine and alcohol' (lines 23/24), the author means that people
   a who use caffeine find it relatively easy to stop smoking and give up alcohol.
   b who use caffeine also enjoy smoking and drinking alcohol.
   c use caffeine now when they need a boost, rather than cigarettes and alcohol.
   d use caffeine, cigarettes and alcohol in equal measures.

6 What attitude to energy drinks comes over in the text? The author
   a thinks they are great.
   b is neutral about them.
   c is critical of them.
   d doesn't understand the fuss being made about them.

B Match these nouns from the text (1–7) with seven of the phrases (a–i) which have the same meaning. Two phrases do not match.

1 refuge	(line 2)	a	person who is in favour of something
2 revival	(line 5)	b	a mixture of various substances
3 concoction	(line 17)	c	a very clear sign of
4 manifestation	(line 18)	d	bodily organisms
5 alertness	(line 22)	e	universal availability
6 pervasiveness	(line 24)	f	adviser in legal matters
7 advocate	(line 25)	g	process of becoming active again
		h	place that provides safety or shelter from danger
		i	state of being wide awake / state of utmost concentration

C Erläutern Sie die Bedeutung der folgenden Ausdrücke bzw. Sätze auf Deutsch. (Keine wortwörtliche Übersetzung.)

a It's like putting your whole system on fast-forward. (line 9)
b Truckers hope to cover another hundred miles before turning in. (lines 16/17)
c The dual power to counter physical fatigue and to increase alertness. (line 22)
d It hasn't dampened its popularity. (line 25)

2 Talking

Group discussions p186

A What problems might people have when they drink energy drinks?

B What do you think of the trend shown in these pictures?

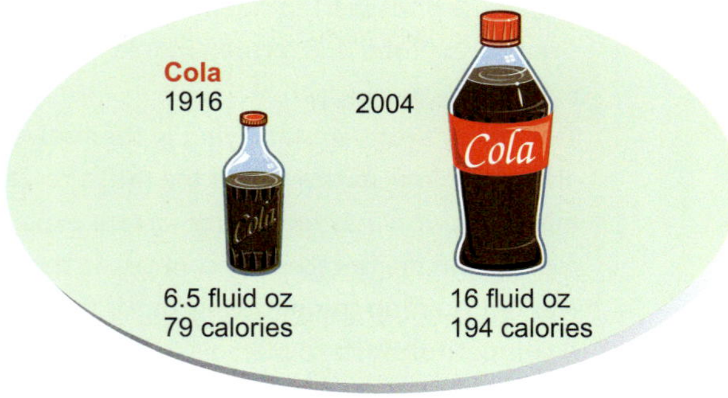

3 Writing

Text production p180

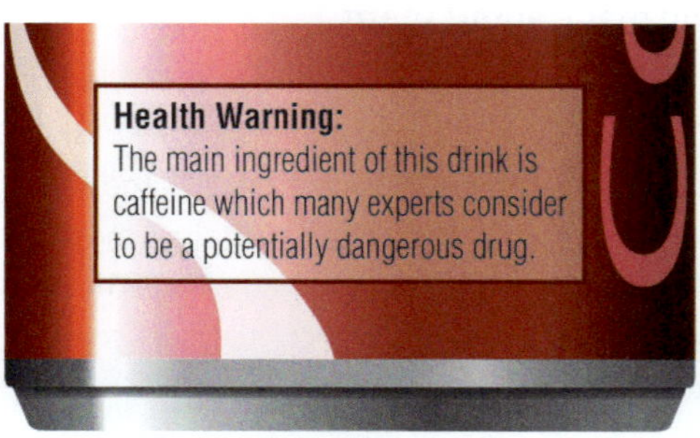

Someone has suggested putting warnings on some types of food and drink. Do you agree / disagree with this idea? Write 180–200 words.

TEXT 2

Reading skills p170/171

The joy of running

CD1/8

Running has become a very important part of Jeff Galloway's life. Here is an extract from his book, 'The Five Stages of a Runner'.

http:www.fivestagesofarunner.com

Apple .Mac Amazon eBay Yahoo! News

I started running when I was 13. I was immediately intoxicated with a beginner's enthusiasm: the very special thrill of exertion, and the feeling that my body had vast capabilities. Of course, I tried to maximize every step on that first run and then had to hobble around for a week, almost too sore to move. But once the soreness decreased, I was back out there, running again. I was hooked.

As is the case with many things, the energy of beginning wore off. I found it harder to motivate myself to go out for that daily run. It was all too easy to stop when the weather turned cold or when it rained or snowed. Fortunately, I discovered that one good approach to overcome that problem was to make a pact with a friend who dragged me out on bad days and vice versa. As I made progress, I found within myself the strength and security to keep going. My body started cleaning itself up, establishing muscle tone, circulating blood and oxygen more vigorously. I had turned from a beginner into a jogger.

The jogger's runs are satisfying in themselves. There is almost always a 'glow' at the end of the run, a reward for the effort. If you miss a run, you may feel guilty – a rare experience for the beginner. I now started taking part regularly in major races – in contrast to the few 'fun runs' I had attended as a beginner. Although I was not running competitively or for time improvement, a sense of competition began to develop.

A competitor starts to plan his or her running around racing goals. With me, it all started rather innocently. After a few races, I began to wonder how fast I might run if I really trained. Before I knew it, I was caught in a compulsive drive to run faster at the expense of running enjoyment. I no longer valued my daily runs for their own worth, but thought only of how well they prepared me for races and better times. Missing a run seemed to spell racing doom. I could almost feel the fat being deposited on my body and see the seconds I had fought hard to erase ticking back on the clock. When I heard of a friend clocking up a record time, I had to match it or die trying.

Once the competitive spirit had taken over, I almost lost sight of my limitations. Although I had read many times about the need for rest, I felt that mine was a special case and that I didn't need as much recovery time as other mortals. Yet, at that stage, I felt tired most of the time, but still had trouble sleeping at night. I became irritable and made life difficult for my family and friends. However negative this phase may seem in retrospect, there are some very positive lessons to be learned from competition. Pushing through tiredness and discomfort in a race is not only rewarding in itself but gives you an idea of what you can do in other areas of life. Being challenged to our limits through competition helps bring forth strengths that lie buried in each of us. Moreover, we can learn from our mistakes and move on to new heights. And that's what I did. I worked my way up the ladder again and passed into the stage of 'runner'.

Today, running is a natural part of my daily program – as is eating, sleeping or talking. Now, however, if I miss a run, I don't panic. (I actually don't miss many days over the span of a year.) If scientists announced tomorrow that running was harmful, I'd read the news with interest and go out on my daily run. I know about the positive effects of exercise, but that alone doesn't get me out on the roads. I get so much satisfaction from the experience itself that running has become a necessary and stable part of my lifestyle. It's a great activity. I am a happy person.

680 words, adapted from http://www.shelterpub.com/_fitness/_running/run_5_stages.html

4 Looking at the text

A Match the beginnings of the sentences (1–6) with the corresponding endings (a–g). There is one more ending than you need.

1 The challenge that running posed
2 After overexerting himself on his first run, he
3 Jeff didn't always fancy running, especially
4 Luckily he found a friend who
5 The positive physical effects showed Jeff that he
6 When Jeff forced himself to compete with other athletes, he

a made him go out when he didn't feel like it.
b immediately fascinated Jeff Galloway.
c couldn't stop running.
d was no longer a beginner.
e didn't enjoy running as much as before.
f was stiff.
g when the weather was bad.

B Find words or phrases in the text that have the same meaning as the ones below.

lines 1–17
addicted • cope with
extremely excited about
gradually became less intense
kick you get from pushing yourself very hard

lines 18–28
be a bad omen • eliminate
naively / unintentionally
obligatory
perform equally well

lines 29–44
agitated • in hindsight
ordinary people • pain

C Answer the following questions, based on the text, in your own words.

1 What are the differences between a 'beginner' and a 'jogger'?
2 How did the compulsive drive to run that Jeff mentions show in his case?
3 According to Jeff, what advantages can be gained from competition?

5 Talking

Group discussions p186

Your school is thinking about offering extra activities to help students relax and improve their physical well-being. These options have been suggested.

table tennis

gymnastics and aerobics classes

chess club

jazz dance lessons

jogging

In groups, discuss the options and try to reach an agreement regarding the most suitable idea.

6 Listening and talking

Listening skills p185

A **Have you (or has someone you know) ever had a negative experience involving a high-risk sport? Tell the class.**

CD1/9

B **You are going to hear part of a phone-in programme about snow sports. Listen and decide if these statements are true or false.**

1 The discussion deals with accidents which occur in high-risk sports.
2 Alan Hall is a relatively inexperienced snowboarder.
3 He wants to tighten safety rules to reduce the number of accidents.
4 Helen Davis thinks that people almost always follow safety rules.
5 She believes that most accidents are caused by families with children.
6 She suggests that some people be banned from ski slopes.
7 Jack would like cameras and professional supervision on ski slopes.
8 He says that it is cheaper to introduce safety measures than to treat injured skiers in hospital.

C **Which of the speakers do you agree / disagree with? Why?**

7 Writing

Text production p180/183

Choose <u>one</u> of these tasks.

1 Some schools have reduced the number of sports lessons.
How do you feel about this? Write approximately 200 words.

2 Describe the cartoon and the message it conveys. Write about 100 words.

CROSS-CULTURAL SPOTLIGHT

British schools and qualifications

Here are the approximate British equivalents of German schools and qualifications. In an interview you can describe your education with sentences like, 'I went to a Realschule. That's like going to a comprehensive and leaving with good GCSEs.' Remember, there are no exact British equivalents of the *Gesamtschule, Realschule* or *Hauptschule*. They are all different types of secondary school.

Gesamtschule	Comprehensive School
Gymnasium	Grammar School
Realschule	Comprehensive School
Fachoberschule	Further Education College (FE College)
Berufsschule	Further Education College (FE College)
Berufsoberschule	Further Education College (FE College)

mittlerer Bildungsabschluss GCSE[1]
Abitur, Hochschulreife A-level[2]

[1] GCSE = General Certificate of Secondary Education

[2] A-level = Advanced level. Entitles British students to study at a British university.

8 Language – the simple past and the present perfect

SPOT THE MISTAKES

Spot the mistakes and correct them. Explain why they are wrong.

1 ~~At the beginning of the year, you have suggested that I lose weight.~~
2 ~~I am a member of a fitness club since three months now.~~
3 ~~My fitness coach has told me a month ago to stay away from fast food.~~
4 ~~I didn't go to a fast food restaurant since several weeks now.~~
5 ~~I only ate salad for the beginning of the month.~~
6 ~~Last week when I have weighed myself, I saw that I had lost 5 kg.~~

1 The simple past

Complete this conversation with the verbs in the simple past.

The simple past	The present perfect
I had it last year.	How long have you had it? I've had it for two weeks. Have you had it before?
Language check p193	Language check p194

Annie: I ...[1] (try) to call you yesterday but you ...[2] (not/be) at home.
Rob: What time ...[3] (you/call)?
Annie: 7.30. Where ...[4] (you/be)?
Rob: I ...[5] (be) at the gym.
Annie: Oh. ...[6] (you/go) to the new gym, the one which ...[7] (open) last month?
Rob: Yes, but I ...[8] (not/like) it. The equipment ...[9] (not/be) very good.

2 The present perfect

Make sentences using these words. Put the verbs into the present perfect.

1 We / just / finish / running a marathon.
2 I / not be to the gym / since last February.
3 Tony / start training / again.
4 you / see / my football boots?
5 How many lengths / Sandy / swim / so far?
6 How long / they / be / members of the volleyball team?

3 The simple past and the present perfect

Complete this postcard. Put the verbs in brackets into the correct form.

Hi Jacky,
Yesterday I suddenly …[1] (realize) that I …[2] (not/hear) anything from you since you …[3] (open) your new gym last Easter. …[4] (it/be) successful so far? In your last email, you …[5] (tell) me that you were also looking for a bigger flat. …[6] (you/find) one yet? As for me, I'm still working on Fifth Avenue, though life …[7] (not/be) particularly exciting since you …[8] (leave). The big news with me is that I …[9] (write) several magazine articles on health and fitness over the last few months. So, lately, my career as a journalist …[10] (finally/take off). I …[11] (do) a couple of articles for Gotcha!, the youth magazine, last summer and now they …[12] (ask) me to do a regular column for them. What do you think of that?
Hope to hear from you soon.
Yours,
Becky

WATCH OUT!

Language check p194

since / for

They have had snow ~~since~~ two weeks. ➤ They have had snow for two weeks.

Translate these sentences into English.

1 Jo ist seit Dienstag im Krankenhaus. Er hat sich das Bein bei einem Skiunfall gebrochen.
2 Lucy ist seit zwei Monaten Mitglied im Tennisverein.
3 Er ist nun schon seit über zwei Stunden im Schwimmbecken.
4 Seit 2004 haben wir eine Bowlinghalle in unserem Dorf.
5 Seit März bin ich nicht mehr im Fitness-Studio gewesen.

Vocabulary review

Copy and complete this word families table without looking back at the texts.

noun	adjective	adverb
***	***	popularly
happiness	***	***
regularity	***	***
***	***	sorely
***	***	actively
*** ***	competitive	***

4 Point of sale

FOCUS

1 **Think of an advertisement that you particularly like or dislike. Tell other students about it and explain why you find it appealing or annoying.**

a

b

c

d

2 **How do these adverts appeal to the conscious and subconscious desires of the consumer? Match two of the following attributes to each ad. There are two more attributes than you need.**

1 fun and freedom
2 constant availability
3 an unspoiled environment
4 coolness/style
5 yearning for Paradise
6 getting away from it all
7 political correctness
8 eternal youth and beauty
9 mobility
10 social climbing

3 **What do you think about the pictures and the slogans used in the adverts?**

I think the slogan for the SUV is funny.

That one is ambiguous.

It's exaggerated.

TEXT 1

Reading skills p170/171

CD1/10

Online ads finally come of age

14 | International Herald Tribune
January 10 2005

As advertising industry gurus fine-tune their spending forecasts for this year, there is one area in which a sense of caution bred by several years of disappointment doesn't apply: online ads. Even though one leading ad agency predicted last week that global ad spending would only expand this year by 4.9% – a modest increase, given that expenditures rose 6% last year – the firm added that online ad spending would surge 22%, to $15.5 billion. While that is still less than 2% of overall global ad spending, there are signs that online advertising has come of age.

The main reason for this is the fact that the Internet, where advertising used to be dominated by other Internet companies, is now attractive for mainstream marketers like Coca-Cola, Procter & Gamble and Volvo. Concerned that consumers are becoming more and more immune to sales pitches made via traditional media like television and print, these companies are also advertising online. In addition, the spread of broadband technology has fuelled online commerce and allowed agencies to develop more creative, engaging ads aimed at Internet users. Perhaps most important for the global growth of Internet advertising, spending is increasing most rapidly in Europe and Asia; it rose 31% in Europe last year and 42% in Asia. At the beginning of the millennium, there was relatively little online advertising outside the United States.

'If you want to reach the consumer in a fragmented media world, you have to go where the consumer is,' Nigel Morris, an Internet expert, says. 'The market is catching on to that.' Indeed, more and more marketers find that it's well worth considering larger investments in online advertising.

Surveys show that in many developed countries, more than 10% of media consumption, measured in terms of time, is online. In contrast to that, the share of Internet advertising spending is still less than 2% of overall ad spending. It's therefore clear that online advertising represents a fabulous deal for marketers. However insignificant those 2% may seem, the trend clearly shows that investments made in Internet advertising will soon rival the relatively high expenditures on radio and outdoor advertising, analysts say.

Online ads offer some advantages over traditional media, including the ability to aim sales pitches directly at those consumers who are most likely to respond, and then to observe if and how they react. That helps solve one of the biggest complaints about television advertising – that much of the spending is wasted, particularly among consumers who use video recorders that let them skip the adverts.

The growth of Internet advertising is also causing users to react as they seek ways to avoid online spots, however. The Mozilla Firefox Web browser, which is gaining users, includes a feature that blocks annoying pop-up ads. The Google toolbar also blocks pop-ups. Even before Firefox, pop-ups were on their way out, as the spread of broadband Internet access permits advertisers to use more sophisticated ads that combine video, audio and interactive features. The problem, analysts say, is a lack of standardization. On the Internet, there is nothing comparable to the traditional 30-second TV spot. Instead, there are thousands of formats, sizes, shapes and styles. 'It's still the Wild West,' says Morris. 'It's difficult to come to terms with this confusing variety because people keep creating new formats and styles.'

553 words, adapted from *The International Herald Tribune*, January 10 2005

1 Looking at the text

A Choose the most suitable answer.

1 The main intent of the author is to inform the reader about
  a the growth of the advertising industry around the globe.
  b how broadband technology functions.
  c how to avoid pop-ups.
  d why internet advertising is expanding so rapidly.

2 Why are mainstream marketers justified in turning to the internet?
  a Consumers are hardly interested in ads in other media.
  b Not as many ads appear in other media these days.
  c Fewer people read newspapers and magazines than before.
  d Cinema ads don't attract as much attention as they used to.

3 With 'fragmented media world' (line 34), the author is referring to the
  a huge variety of different media available today.
  b sections of the media which play an increasingly minor role in our lives.
  c fact that many people can't make sense of some types of media.
  d news provided by the media which comes in very small bits and pieces.

4 Which of the following is **not** expressly mentioned in the final paragraph?
  a There are lots of ways to avoid seeing ads while online.
  b Experts dislike the fact that there are no standards for online adverts.
  c Pop-up ads were popular until broadband technology was introduced.
  d Pop-ups began to be replaced as a result of the spread of broadband.

5 What is the author's attitude towards the growth of internet advertising? He/She
  a thinks that it hampers the growth of other industries.
  b doesn't have anything against it.
  c is extremely enthusiastic about it.
  d is prejudiced against it.

B Match the beginnings of the sentences (1–6) to the correct endings (a–h) to make true statements based on the text. There are two more endings than you need.

1 There is no reason to be pessimistic about the future of online ads
2 It's obvious that online advertising
3 Big international firms are worried about
4 Until a few years ago, online advertising
5 One big benefit of advertising online is that
6 Nowadays more and more consumers try to get round watching TV ads

a was virtually restricted to the United States.
b with the help of new technology which blocks out commercials.
c expenditure on ads on the internet will go up by 22 per cent this year.
d people not showing enough interest in their ads presented on TV.
e companies can reach consumers better than with other media.
f showed their commercials online.
g is now playing an important role.
h just because the advertising industry didn't grow as fast as expected over the past years.

2 Working with words

Match these phrases from the text (1–6) with six of the explanations (a–h).

1 come of age (line 14)
2 immune to sales pitches (lines 20/21)
3 fuel online commerce (line 24)
4 rival the expenditures (line 49)
5 aim sales pitches directly at consumers (lines 52/53)
6 a lack of standardization (lines 70/71)

a resistant to influence by TV commercials
b well-known cartoon figures
c establish itself as a factor to be reckoned with
d try to reach a select group of customers
e failure to provide a common format
f cause more people to buy things on the internet
g provide the energy needed to convince people to gain access to the Web
h spend just as much money as

3 Writing

Text production p180

Comment on one of these statements. Write about 250 words.

1 Pop-up ads make using the internet more entertaining.
2 Advertising manipulates consumers more than it informs them.

TEXT 2

Reading skills p170/171

CD1/11

Latinos and the lust for profit

FOUR LATINOS - a Dominican, a Mexican, a Cuban and an Argentine - walk up to the bar in a New York pub. Each asks for the best beer in the house in his own colloquial Spanish, and the bartender who is a maestro de idiomas (master of languages), serves up four Heinekens. No, this isn't the beginning of a bad joke, it's one of the hottest Hispanic ads of the year, praised as a masterpiece in marketing circles for its ability to appeal directly to various Latino subgroups in the United States.

'The Heineken ad celebrates the differences,' says Tony Ruiz of the New York-based advertising agency that produced the spot. At the same time, it makes members of these ethnic groups realize that they do matter to advertisers and that they are being taken seriously.

At the start of the 21st century, Hispanic marketing was little more than an afterthought to most major corporations in America. 'When companies considered Latinos, they thought, "Sombreros and no money",' says Isabel Valdés, a California-based Hispanic marketing expert. 'They simply didn't feel like investing large sums of money in a market that didn't look particularly promising.' Lately, however, corporate America has come to realize both the diversity and spending power of Hispanic consumers.

Latino consumers now range from Argentine investment bankers in New York to poor Mexican immigrants in California. The sheer growth of the market is undeniable. America's 39 million Latinos spent nearly $700 billion last year and are the fastest growing consumer group in the country. By the end of the first decade of the 21st century, Hispanic consumer spending is expected to top $1 trillion. Faced with these astounding figures, the US business community is trying to win over Latinos in an unprecedented way, changing how mainstream American society sees its largest minority - and itself - in the process.

In the 80s and 90s, Hispanic marketing consisted mainly of US ad agencies translating their mass-market, English-language ads and TV spots into Spanish. But US businesses now realize they need creative strategies aimed at specific Latino subgroups. To do this, they've turned to Hispanic ad agencies that employ what Valdés calls 'in-culture' marketing techniques. That means using key values and cultural characteristics - for example, family values, music and food - to connect with the Puerto Ricans who live along America's East Coast or the Mexicans in the American Southwest.

Ironically, language isn't such a key issue any more. In a recent poll of third-generation US

Latinos, 78% of the respondents said English was their primary language. 'It doesn't matter whether you deliver the message in English or Spanish, as long as it appeals to the heart and mind of the Hispanic consumer,' says Ruiz.

Hispanics – who originate from 19 Spanish-speaking countries, plus Puerto Rico – naturally share common linguistic and cultural traits. But marketers nowadays favor highly-targeted campaigns. The whisky company which produces Chivas Regal uses salsa music in Florida to appeal to Cuban-Americans but switches to merengue to target Dominicans in New York. Beer companies like Heineken now often use regional accents and slang, depending on where their target audience both lives and comes from. 'It makes it come home to the consumer, who thinks, "These people are like me",' says Manuel Machado, President of the Association of Hispanic Advertising Agencies. 'Take Heineken's "Blackout" ad that aired in the northeastern United States some years back,' he goes on. 'In that ad, two Dominicans – speaking in distinct regional accents – stumble through their New York apartment during a power blackout trying to decide what to make room for in their cooler – milk or Heineken. The cervesa, of course! It was a great spot,' Machado concludes. 'Heineken reached their regional market.'

Such innovation will only become more commonplace as research exploring Hispanic consumer trends becomes more sophisticated. Hispanics now spend more time online per week than any other American group. Hispanic e-spending, which hit $8.1 billion last year, has prompted companies like AOL and Microsoft to invest more heavily in their Hispanic marketing initiatives. Car manufacturers are similarly fine-tuning their Spanish-language sales and customer-service sites. Steady increases in the number of viewers of Spanish-language television networks have also helped boost Hispanic TV advertising. 'We can no longer be ignored as just part of the melting pot,' says Machado. 'We are an important part of the American infrastructure. We are everyday people.' Corporate America obviously agrees.

729 words, adapted from *Newsweek*, 22 November 2004

4 Looking at the text

A The author says that US marketers have begun to see Hispanics in a different way. Copy these headings into your exercise book and make notes to explain the changes.

20th century

Attitude towards Hispanic market:

Reason:

Marketing strategy (in general):

21st century

Attitude towards Hispanic market:

Reason:

Marketing strategy (in general):

Example: 1

2

B Geben Sie den Inhalt der folgenden Sätze bzw. Ausdrücke auf Deutsch wieder. (Keine wortwörtliche Übersetzung.)

1 Hispanic marketing was little more than an afterthought to most major corporations in America. (lines 21/24)
2 In the 80s and 90s, Hispanic marketing consisted mainly of US ad agencies translating their mass market, English-language ads into Spanish. (lines 48/51)
3 … highly-targeted campaigns (line 73)
4 It makes it come home to the consumer. (lines 80/81)
5 Such innovation will become more commonplace as research exploring Hispanic consumer trends becomes more sophisticated. (lines 95/98)
6 Car manufacturers are similarly fine-tuning their Spanish-language sales and customer-service sites. (lines 103/105)

C A marketing consultant is relating the content of the article to a colleague. Complete this gapped summary with words from lines 48–61 and lines 95–113.

American companies now understand that they need innovative …[1] to reach certain Hispanic …[2]. In order to achieve this goal, they take …[3] that play a central role in Latino life and integrate them into their spots. The fact that Hispanics now buy so many products online has …[4] American firms to spend more money on presenting their products to Latino audiences. The increased number of people watching Spanish-language TV has also helped …[5] the number of commercials aimed at Hispanics. One Hispanic marketing expert even thinks that today's American …[6] is unthinkable without Latinos.

CROSS-CULTURAL SPOTLIGHT

British advertising compared to German advertising

In contrast to the frequently all-too-sober German ads which emphasize facts or appeal to trivial emotions in a very direct way, British adverts are subtle and full of black humour. There is a tendency to 'celebrate' the underdog and the loser and to make fun of the hero. On top of that, many UK advertisers like to caricature things that seem all too perfect. Advertisers naturally assume that the consumer is able to understand the irony and to interpret the message – which is sometimes only referred to indirectly – in the way intended by them. In international competitions, British ads regularly win the top awards.

5 Project – promoting your school

Doing projects p189

In groups, create an attractive advertisement promoting your school.

Here are some things you may wish to include in your advert:

- number and types of extra-curricular activities
- personal relationship to teachers
- academic standards
- school facilities
- school exchange programmes

Present your advert to the rest of the class. Which ad sells your school best? Why?

6 Listening

Listening skills p185

CD1/12 Advertising analyst Raymond Hunter is being interviewed on the latest trends in the field of advertising.

A Listen to the interview once. Which of these does Raymond Hunter talk about?

internet • TV • film • magazines • video games

B Work with a partner and match statements 1–5 with statements a–g.

1 Even before being officially released, the Lancer Evolution attracted a group of extremely dedicated fans.
2 Advertisers have been trying to find new sales pitches for some time.
3 Kraft Foods offers 80 different downloadable games.
4 Users of advertising games can't get their minds off them.
5 Advertisers using a digital platform get to know how intensively people visit their sites.

a This makes it easier for them to find customers who are really interested in purchasing their product.
b As a result, this type of advertising is especially attractive to companies.
c The reason was that it had been used in a popular video game.
d The booming global gaming market is now dominated by male teenagers.
e This is due to the fact that fewer and fewer people watch TV.
f Mitsubishi's American car dealers were hardly surprised by the car's success.
g The company is thus attracting millions of visitors to its website.

Now listen again and check.

7 Role play

In groups of 4, look back at any notes you took in exercise 6A and the statements in exercise 6B.

After that, give one of the following roles to each member of the group:

- Raymond Hunter;
- an online marketing manager from Mitsubishi;
- a teenager who plays advertising games;
- a parent who is unhappy about his/her child playing advertising games.

In your group discuss the advantages and disadvantages of digital advertising games.

After playing the game, people never forget our company.

The games attract new customers, but they also waste the customers' time!

These games keep kids away from their homework!

I'm not doing anything wrong. I'm only relaxing.

8 Language – gerund/infinitive

SPOT THE MISTAKES

Spot the mistakes and correct them. Say why they are wrong.

1 ~~He is used to make up funny ads.~~
2 ~~They would like capturing the Latino market.~~
3 ~~We expect meeting the new advertising executive tomorrow.~~
4 ~~I am looking forward to see the award-winning ads on TV tonight.~~
5 ~~Could you imagine to work in an advertising agency?~~
6 ~~Have you remembered programming the video to cut out the ads?~~
7 ~~It's not worth to place ads for beer in magazines aimed at young mothers.~~

The silliest ads around

An ad for fruit

They've finally succeeded in growing round bananas! There's only one problem – they taste like oranges.

An ad for Christmas presents

Dad: I've decided not to buy you a trumpet for Christmas, Ben.
Ben: Oh, please, Dad. I promise to play it only when you go to sleep.

Gerund

They've finally succeeded in growing round bananas!

Language check p201

Infinitive

I've decided not to buy you a trumpet ...
I promise to play it ...

Language check p201

1 Complete this letter of complaint to a commercial TV broadcaster using the gerund or the infinitive. Add prepositions if necessary.

Dear Sir or Madam

Once upon a time, I used ...[1] (enjoy) the live broadcasts of Formula One races on TV. I still remember ...[2] (be able to) see the entire race without one single commercial break. I was never afraid ...[3] (miss) the most exciting scenes.

While I don't mind you ...[4] (interrupt) comedy shows and documentaries, I do object to you doing that during Formula 1. Can't you avoid ...[5] (broadcast) your spots just when the race is drawing to its thrilling climax? I would like you ...[6] (change) your programming policy and expect you ...[7] (take) action in the near future. You should certainly stop ...[8] (present) major sport broadcasts in that way. I am sure many viewers share my opinion and, just like me, they will never get used ...[9] (be) confronted with such interruptions.

Finally, let me say that it's in your own interest to change things soon. I'm sure that if you don't, more and more viewers will be forced ...[10] (turn) to pay TV.

Yours faithfully
Andrew Galbraith

2 Re-write these sentences using the gerund or the infinitive. Add prepositions if necessary.

EXAMPLE Silvia said, 'Let's buy the pizza that was advertised on TV last night.'
Silvia suggested *buying the pizza that was advertised on TV last night.*

1 I don't want to pay a fortune for a watch just because it's advertised by a celebrity.
I object … .
2 He wanted to switch off the TV and go to bed early but he didn't.
He meant … .
3 They've managed to double their sales figures in the last six months.
They succeeded … .
4 Sally modelled once for an ad agency. She'll never forget it.
Sally will never forget … .

WATCH OUT!

while / during

They were lost in the dark ~~while~~ the power blackout.	➤ They were lost in the dark during the power blackout.
~~During~~ he was at the agency, he earned a very good salary.	➤ While he was at the agency, he earned a very good salary.

Translate the following sentences into English, using either *while* or *during*.

1 In den 90er Jahren war ein Ende des Werbebooms nicht abzusehen.
2 Während die Internetwerbung stark zunimmt, nehmen die Werbeeinnahmen beim Fernsehen eher ab.
3 Ich mag keine Werbung sehen, wenn ich einen Spielfilm anschaue.
4 Er dreht in den Werbepausen den Ton einfach ab.
5 Als sie die Seite im Internet suchte, erschien plötzlich eine fürchterliche Werbebotschaft auf dem Bildschirm.

Vocabulary review

A Without looking back at the texts, match words 1–6 with words a–f to make compound nouns to do with advertising. There may be more than one match.

1 online	a techniques
2 consumer	b agency
3 sales	c groups
4 advertising	d advertising
5 marketing	e power
6 spending	f pitches

B Look back at the texts to check. Find more compound nouns and other words to do with advertising and copy them into your vocabulary book.

5 Making a living

FOCUS

1 **In groups make lists of part-time jobs which you or other students do. What is good/bad about these jobs? Rank them, most attractive to least attractive.**

2 **Do this questionnaire to find out if you should do a part-time job.**

SHOULD YOU DO A PART-TIME JOB?

1 Why do you want to do a part-time job?

a Those new $150 Air Jordan basketball shoes are just the thing I need.

b My parents aren't cash machines and I'm tired of depending on them for money.

c I don't want my ability to pay for college to depend on winning the lottery.

2 How much homework do you have every night?

a Some nights, I'm up until midnight. Other nights, I switch on the TV at 8.

b Call me efficient! I'm done in less than 2 hours every night.

c Who keeps track? Sometimes I have homework, sometimes I don't. When I have homework, I just do it. Well – usually.

3 How involved are you in extra-curricular activities?

a I'm so busy, I'm thinking about getting myself cloned.

b Does watching TV count?

c I'm involved with some stuff, but there are times when nothing is going on.

4 How difficult are the subjects you're taking?

a There's always something challenging, but I'm organized and I get my work done on time.

b One word: English.

c One or two subjects are tough, but my school workload is pretty easy.

5 You're working at Big Burger and a kid drops a tray. The floor's a mess of milk-shake, burger, fries and ketchup. Your boss tells you to clean it up. What do you do?

a Ask someone else to do it. If the answer is no, then clean up the mess myself.

b Pretend I don't hear the boss, and start to do something else.

c Grab a mop and get to work.

6 How many hours do you see yourself working?

a Well, I'm at school and I have a social life, so no more than 20 hours a week.

b As many hours as I can get. More hours mean more cash.

c It depends on the job I take.

Check your score and personal part-time job profile on p162.

adapted from *Scholastic Choices*, New York, 1998

TEXT 1

Reading skills p170/171

CD1/13

Europe thinks about the meaning of life

SUNDAY, AUGUST 15 2004

IT'S AUGUST IN EUROPE, which means that if you're not a lifeguard, an Olympic athlete or a Florentine gelato vendor, you're probably on vacation. This year, though, the Germans and French may not find much peace as they kick back in their Tuscan villas and Majorcan beach houses. Their beloved European life-style, with its 35-hour workweek, frequent holidays and six-week vacations, is under threat as never before. The French government has weighed up repealing the country's mandatory 35-hour week, which would allow employers to demand longer hours. Recently, German industrial giants DaimlerChrysler and Siemens muscled their unions into signing contracts that lengthen work hours without increasing pay. Is Europe being forced to adopt the Protestant work ethic of the United States?

'It's not that we're becoming more Anglo-Saxon,' says the editor of the *Frankfurter Allgemeine Zeitung*. 'It's that we are having an encounter with reality.' But while Europeans have grown to recognize the economic forces that are driving the longer work hours – competition from low-wage countries in Eastern Europe and Asia, an aging population with fewer people in the labor force, the crushing financial burden of Europe's generous welfare benefits – this doesn't mean that they will accept the social costs, at least not without a fight.

For Europeans, a proper balance between work and play is more than a fringe benefit of prosperity. It is central to a way of life that most people here believe is superior to the American one: less harried, less materialistic, less dehumanizing. 'Americans define freedom as autonomy and mobility, which requires amassing wealth,' says Jeremy Rifkin, an American writer. 'Europeans define freedom in community – in belonging, not belongings. While Americans consider idleness to be almost a sin, Europeans place greater emphasis on leisure and even idleness.' This allows them to develop themselves and to cultivate their minds more than Americans do. An American living in Tuscany says, 'Italians who are not professionals often have more knowledge of the arts than Americans who are professionals! They'll spend a Sunday exploring a church with a fresco they've heard about.' With more free time, Europeans can also better nurture their families and contribute to their communities. Americans, caught in the frantic pursuit of success and the McMansions and the SUVs that come with it, don't have time for such a culturally and socially rich life.

It is tempting to dismiss the European model in favor of the American one, by pointing to the faster economic growth and superior productivity of the United States since the mid-1990s. But the fast pace of life takes a human toll that does not show up in economic statistics. For years, stressed-out Americans have fled to Europe for its gentler ways.

The question, of course, is whether the European society is sustainable. With a rapidly aging population, the competition of a global economy and new military burdens, young Europeans know they will have to work more than their parents did. Many older Europeans, however, will remember the last years of the 20th century as a kind of paradise.

504 words, adapted from *The New York Times*, 15 August 2004

1 Looking at the text

A Who might make these statements – Americans or Europeans? Who do you agree with? Why?

1 *Financial security is fine, but I'm just as interested in having enough time for my family and friends.*

2 *I don't need the government to take care of me. I'm willing to work hard and make enough money to look after myself.*

3 *I need at least one month of vacation. I need time to travel and to relax.*

4 *Leisure is necessary so that I can grow as a person and develop my interests.*

5 *Shorten the working week and create jobs for people who have trouble finding employment!*

6 *I don't mind having two or three jobs if that is what it takes to get rich.*

B Bearbeiten Sie die folgenden Aufgaben auf Deutsch.

1 Nennen Sie stichpunktartig die Gründe, die bei vielen Westeuropäern zu der Einsicht geführt haben, dass längere Arbeitszeiten vonnöten sind.

2 Erklären Sie die Aussage der folgenden Sätze. (Keine wortwörtliche Übersetzung!)

a Recently, German industrial giants muscled their unions into signing new contracts. (lines 22/25)

b Europeans have grown to recognize the economic forces that are driving the longer work hours. (lines 37/40)

c Europeans define freedom in community – in belonging, not belongings. (lines 64/66)

d The fast pace of life takes a human toll that does not show up in economic statistics. (lines 98/101)

CROSS-CULTURAL SPOTLIGHT

Vacation days and working hours in Germany, GB and the USA – a comparison

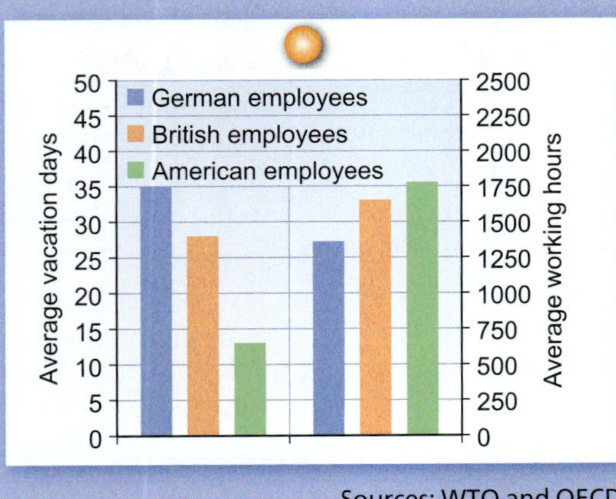

Sources: WTO and OECD

As many as 31% of working Americans report that they don't take all the days they are entitled to. They are afraid of endangering their job security.

Recent developments in Germany indicate that the labour market may be in for a fundamental change.

The competitive pressures related to globalization may soon force Germans to work longer hours.

2 Working with words

A Find the English equivalents of the following German words in the text.

lines 1–30
abschaffen/zurücknehmen
Arbeitsethos • fordern
unterschreiben • Urlaub
Vertrag

lines 31–50
Belastung • Gesamtzahl der Beschäftigten
großzügig • Sozialleistungen
vorantreiben /führen zu
Zwänge/Triebkräfte

lines 51–91
Menschen in akademischen Berufen
das Streben nach • überlegen (Adj.)
Wohlstand/Reichtum
Zugehörigkeitsgefühl

lines 92–116
nachhaltig/weiterhin finanzierbar
Schnelllebigkeit
total gestresst • Tribut fordern
Wettbewerb • verlockend

B Complete the following sentences with the correct form of the English verbs above.

1 The pressure of competition is … the trend toward automation.
2 Having to work 50 hours a week … on a person's health.
3 She was being paid less than her male colleagues, so she … equal pay.
4 Many Western European countries may soon have to … the 35-hour working week in order to be able to compete with the Chinese.
5 Harry is happy. He … the contract for his new job yesterday.

3 Writing

Text production p175/183

Choose <u>one</u> of the tasks.

1 Write a letter to the editor of *The New York Times*. Describe your attitude towards work and life. Write about 200 words.
2 Describe the cartoon. Write about 100 words.

"You don't have to be mad to work here – but it helps!"

TEXT 2

Reading skills p170/171

Trying to do it all

CD1/14

European men, these days, are embracing fatherhood with the round-the-clock involvement their partners have always dreamed of – changing diapers, coping with night feedings, packing lunches and bandaging knees. The time British dads spend with their kids has risen eightfold over the last 30 years. Today, 79% say they'd be happy to stay at home and 9 out of 10 say they're as confident as their partners in looking after the kids. 'These dads are going to be guides and mentors in a much more visible way than their own fathers were,' says Armin A. Brett, author of *Fathering your Toddler*.

That's good news for Europe, whose economic future depends on a rising birth rate. Studies show that women with involved partners are more inclined to have more than one child. To tempt moms back to work, governments are also putting in place more policies to help dads take time off. Britain, for instance, announced recently that fathers would be entitled to up to six months of paternity leave. In Germany, companies are required by law to give all employees up to three years parental leave and guarantee their jobs on return.

But all these devoted dads may have a harder time with the same issues women have faced for decades: namely, how to balance work and family. 'There's a constant feeling of guilt,' says Robin Mungrah, a 37-year-old London accountant with two children. 'No matter how early I leave work or how often I take the kids to the funpark at weekends, it never seems like enough.' Unlike women, many men find they're negotiating their new roles with little support or information. 'Men in my generation (25–40) have a fear of becoming dads because we have no role models,' says Jon Smith, author of *The Bloke's Guide to Pregnancy*. 'They often find themselves excluded from mothers' support networks, and are eyed warily at the playground.'

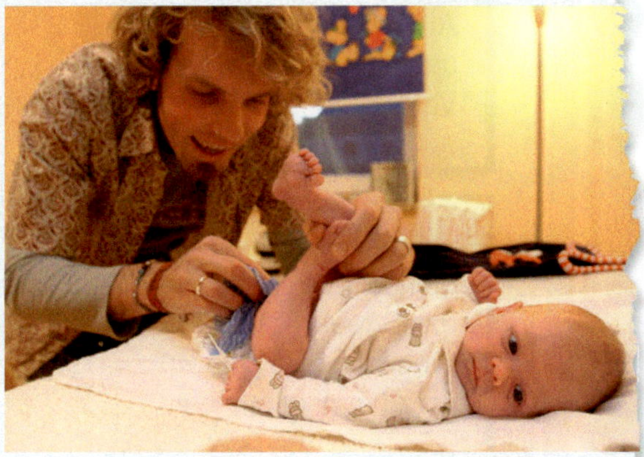

The challenge is particularly evident in the workplace. There, men are still expected to be breadwinners climbing the corporate ladder; tradition-minded bosses are often unsympathetic to family needs. In Denmark most new fathers only take two weeks of paternity leave – even though they are allowed 34. As much, if not more so than women, fathers struggle to be taken seriously when they request flexible arrangements. Though Wilfried-Fritz Maring, 54, a data-bank and internet specialist with a German firm, feels that the time he spends with his daughter outweighs any disadvantages, he admits, 'With my decision to work from home I dismissed any opportunity for promotion.'

Mindsets are changing gradually. When Maring became a father, the company equipped him with a home office and allowed him to choose a job that could be performed from there. A Danish telecom company initiated an internal campaign last year to encourage dads to take paternity leave; 97% now do. 'When an employee goes on paternity leave and is with his kids, he gets a new kind of training – in how to keep cool under stress,' says spokesperson Christine Eiberg Holm. For a new generation of dads, kids may come before the company – but it's a shift that benefits both.

520 words, adapted from *Newsweek*, 27 February 2006

4 Looking at the text

A Match the people (1–5) with five of the statements below (a–g). Two of the statements do not match.

1 Armin A. Brett
2 Robin Mungrah
3 Jon Smith
4 Wilfried-Fritz Maring
5 Christine Eiberg Holm

a These fathers will play a much more significant role in the lives of their kids than dads did 50 years ago.
b To be truthful, I made some sacrifices when I chose to take paternity leave but it's been worth it.
c Men can deal with the problem of how to balance work and family just as well as women can.
d My firm has come to realize that dads on paternity leave can gain experience that is useful to us when they return to their jobs.
e As far as I am concerned, paternity leave is superfluous. Small babies and toddlers don't need their fathers.
f My problem is, I'm always blaming myself for not finding enough time to spend with my kids.
g Mothers don't always offer help. In fact, I feel as if some of them are suspicious of dads who look after their kids.

B Geben Sie den Inhalt der folgenden Sätze auf Deutsch wieder. (Keine wortwörtliche Übersetzung.)

1 European men are embracing fatherhood. (lines 1/2)
2 Devoted dads may have a harder time. (lines 26/27)
3 They are negotiating their new roles. (lines 34/35)
4 They are eyed warily at the playground. (line 41)
5 Men are expected to be breadwinners climbing the corporate ladder. (lines 43/44)
6 Bosses are often unsympathetic to family needs. (lines 45/46)
7 The time he spends with his daughter outweighs any disadvantages. (lines 53/54)
8 It's a shift that benefits both. (lines 68/69)

C Answer the following questions on the text. Give short answers.

1 How has fatherhood changed over the last 30 years?
2 Why is an increase in the birth rate good for Europe?
3 According to the text, which laws have been made to help parents in Britain and Germany?
4 Describe the problems which fathers encounter in their new role.

D Could taking parental leave affect an employee in a negative way? If so, how?

E A student has read the text and is reporting to fellow students. Complete this gapped summary with words or short phrases from lines 1–46.

Like women, men nowadays also display an increasing amount of …[1] when it comes to assuming parental responsibility. In the last three decades, there has been an …[2] increase in the number of hours fathers devote to their children's upbringing. In fact, 90% of the dads claim they are no less …[3] than their partners with respect to their ability to effectively care for their young children. One real …[4] for today's fathers, however, lies in the fact that …[5] employers don't see any reason to offer additional support to young families. For that reason, most young fathers in Denmark hesitate to take the advantage of going on …[6] for as long as they would be entitled to.

5 Talking

Group discussions p186

A careers advisor is visiting your school. In preparation for the visit, discuss these job options.

Decide together which are the most promising with regard to the prospects they offer for your future.

6 Writing

Text production p175/184

Choose <u>one</u> of these tasks. Write about 200 words.

1 Fun Kids Camp, Traverse City, Michigan, is offering temporary employment to high school graduates who are talented in organizing recreational activities for young people. Write a letter of application.

2 Describe the development in the various sectors shown on the bar chart below and explain the trends by giving examples of jobs that have been affected.

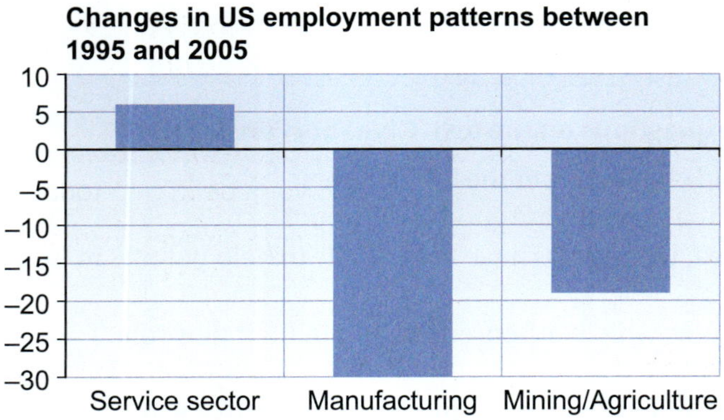

(Percentage figures correspond to the total workforce in the US in 1995 and 2005)
Sources: US Bureau of Labor Statistics Data, US Department of Agriculture (Economic Research Service)

7 Reading and listening

Listening skills p185

A **Read and listen to the song and complete the text.**

CD1/15

Allentown

Well we're living here in Allentown
And they're …[1] all the factories down
Out in Bethlehem they're killing time
… …[2] forms, standing in line

Well our fathers fought the Second World War
Spent their weekends on the Jersey Shore
Met our mothers in the USO
… …[3] to dance, danced with them slow
And we're living here in Allentown

But the …[4] was handed down
And it's getting very hard to stay

Well we're waiting here in Allentown
For the Pennsylvania we never found
For the …[5] our teachers gave
If we worked hard, if we …[6]

So the …[7] hang on the wall
But they never really helped us at all
No, they never told us what was real
…[8] and coke and chromium steel
And we're waiting here in Allentown

But they've taken all the …[9] from the ground
And the …[10] people crawled away

Every child had a pretty good shot
To get at least as far as their old man got
But something happened on the way to that place
They threw an American …[11] in our face

Well I'm living here in Allentown
And it's hard to keep a good man down
But I won't be … …[12] today
And it's getting very hard to stay
And we're living here in Allentown

Written by Billy Joel, from the album *The Nylon Curtain*, released by CBS, 1982

B **Erklären Sie auf Deutsch, wie die folgenden Redewendungen im Textzusammenhang zu verstehen sind.**

1 They're killing time. (line 3)
2 Every child had a pretty good shot to get at least as far their old man got. (lines 23/24)
3 It's hard to keep a good man down. (line 28)

C Work with the completed text and choose the most suitable answer.

1 The main theme of the song is
  a the decline of the unions.
  b automation.
  c the effects of unemployment.
  d the mining industry.

2 When the singer mentions people 'filling out forms, standing in line' (line 4), he implies that they are
  a applying for a new job.
  b opening a new bank account.
  c waiting to pick up food and clothes from a charity.
  d applying for unemployment benefits.

3 'The restlessness was handed down and it's getting very hard to stay' (lines 10/11) could best be interpreted as meaning that young people
  a want to leave town and find a quiet place to live in.
  b automatically have the same chances that their parents had.
  c would like to move away to have a better career than they have now.
  d are willing to move somewhere else, especially if they are unemployed.

4 The phrase 'they threw an American flag in our face' (line 26) means that people in Allentown were told to
  a be proud of America even if things weren't easy at that time.
  b be more rebellious.
  c give up on the American dream because it wasn't worth anything any more.
  d fly the 'Stars and Stripes'.

8 Writing

Text production p183

Describe and interpret the picture. Write about 100 words.

9 Language – mustn't/needn't

SPOT THE MISTAKES

Spot the mistakes and correct them. Explain why they are wrong.

1 ~~You mustn't babysit for us tonight because we won't be going out.~~
2 My boyfriend's parents are rich. ~~He mustn't do a part time job.~~
3 ~~Our careers advisor always tells us that we needn't give up before we've explored all the job options available.~~
4 ~~You mustn't ring up the boss. I've already arranged a job interview for you.~~

mustn't	**needn't**
We mustn't eat those mushrooms. They're poisonous.	We needn't eat them. We can sell them.

Language check p196

1 Translate the following sentences into English.

1 Wir dürfen das Angebot der Arbeitgeber nicht annehmen, weil wir dann die Mitglieder unserer Gewerkschaft im Stich lassen.
2 Das Projekt wurde aufgegeben. Jetzt muss er keine Überstunden mehr machen.
3 Wir dürfen auf keinen Fall vergessen, ihm zu seiner Beförderung zu gratulieren.
4 Du darfst dich niemals vom Fließband wegbegeben, solange es noch läuft.
5 In vielen Industriestaaten brauchen junge Menschen heute nicht mehr so viel zu arbeiten wie früher ihre Eltern.
6 Sally muss sich keine Sorgen machen, ihren Job zu verlieren, da sie eine feste Stelle bei Ford hat.

2 Complete the sentences using *mustn't* or *needn't* as required.

1 You … set the alarm clock for 6 a.m. Your shift doesn't start until noon.
2 Americans are convinced that they … give up the Protestant work ethic. In their opinion, doing so would lead to economic ruin.
3 Boss to worker: 'You … be late again. If you are, I will fire you.'
4 The employees … worry about job security because their jobs are guaranteed.
5 In view of the fact that the fast pace of life in the US takes a human toll, Americans … categorically dismiss the European model of employment.
6 I … buy private health insurance. I'm insured through the company.

WATCH OUT!

Connectors

~~Despite~~ employers like to train their employees themselves, they don't mind them having previous job experience. ➤ Although employers like to train their employees themselves, they don't mind them having previous job experience.

Complete this text, using the appropriate connectors.

When you go for an interview you should be neat and tidy …[1] (although/because/due to) the first impression you make on a potential employer is extremely important.
…[2] (Otherwise/In other words/For example), you might not get the job.
…[3] (Nevertheless/Moreover/In contrast), make sure you arrive on time.
…[4] (Despite/However/While), you needn't come too early; about ten minutes before the interview starts is fine.
You mustn't be arrogant …[5] (yet/while/as) most employers prefer employees who are modest. In addition, they like employees who are able to work in teams, …[6] (despite/even though/when) it might sometimes be easier for an employee to do the task on his/her own.
If you know a lot about a subject, don't start lecturing. …[7] (In other words/Nonetheless/On the contrary), don't use more than three or four sentences to make it clear that you know what you are talking about. Don't boast about all the wonderful job offers you've had, …[8] (what/which/that) would only indicate that you are not being honest.

Vocabulary review

Use these words from the two main texts to complete the text below.
Use a capital letter where necessary.

companies • economic • employees • hours • jobs • leisure time • productivity • work ethic

In general, most European workers enjoy having time off. Some Americans, however, think of …[1] as wasted time and believe that people should follow the traditional Protestant …[2] to ensure their own financial prosperity and security.

Compared with Europe, the United States has experienced faster growth and superior …[3] since the end of the last century. In today's global economy, young Europeans know they will have to work more than their parents did to ensure their …[4] future.

While almost everyone is complaining about having to work longer …[5] one group of …[6] in Britain and Germany is actually being encouraged to take time off work – new fathers. …[7] in these countries must allow fathers paternity leave. It goes without saying that their …[8] will be waiting for them when they go back to work.

6 In the public eye

FOCUS

1 In groups, talk about how often you use each of these media. What are their advantages/disadvantages? How reliable is the information they give?

2 Make two lists ranking the media above in order of a) importance and b) 'fun' factor. Explain to the class why you have decided on this order.

3 Match the headlines to quality papers or the popular press.

TEXT 1

Reading skills p170/171

CD2/2

Two newspaper articles

What drove Harry to lash out?

Prince Harry had to be held back by three minders after attacking a photographer and pinning him against a wall outside a top celebrity haunt early yesterday.

Harry snapped after complaining that the paparazzo had hit him in the face with a camera as he came out of a London nightclub.

The 20-year-old Prince, who spent three hours inside the exclusive Pangaea nightclub in Piccadilly drinking a £300 bottle of vodka and tequila slammers, was visibly shaken after giving the photographer a cut lip in the scuffle.

Harry left the scene in a chauffeur-driven car, burying his head in his knees, trying to contain his anger and frustration after a difficult few days in which he has been accused of cheating in his A-level art exams to help him gain a place as an Army officer cadet at Sandhurst.

But there was public sympathy for Harry after he snapped. Instant opinion polls suggested that at least two-thirds of the public thought it was acceptable for him to attack the paparazzo.

Provoked

Prince Charles's office at Clarence House confirmed there had been an altercation but insisted that the third in line to the throne had been provoked and was defending himself.

'Prince Harry was hit in the face by a camera as photographers crowded around him as he was getting into a car,' a spokesman said. 'He got a bump on the nose and reacted by pushing the camera back towards the photographer. We understand that the photographer's lip was cut.'

Pictures show that the Prince sprinted out of the nightclub and got into the car. He then re-emerged and ran over to one photographer, pushing him 20 ft across a pavement into a wall.

The Clarence House version of events was at odds with the account given by the photographer, Chris Uncle, 24, who reported the incident to police. He claimed that Harry had deliberately lashed out at him. Uncle is now deciding whether to make a formal complaint.

Mr Uncle said, 'Prince Harry was inside the car and we were all still taking pictures. He lashed out and then deliberately pushed my camera into my face. The camera struck me and cut my bottom lip. At the same time he was repeatedly saying, "Why are you doing this? Why don't you just leave me alone?"'

Harry's personal protection officer, Sergeant Leuan Jones, helped to restrain the prince, aided by another bodyguard and a nightclub bouncer.

Witnesses

Witnesses said they could not understand why Harry lost his temper. No one saw any sign of him being hit by Mr Uncle's camera. Some claimed that the prince had banged his head on the partially opened car door as he got in.

Freelance photographer Stephen Walters, 41, told how he watched in horror as the prince 'grunted loudly' before lunging at the paparazzo.

Walters said, 'When Harry came out of the club it looked as though he'd had a good night. He wasn't falling all over the place but he needed a bit of help. His two minders were escorting him to his chauffeur-driven car. The photographers were shouting at him to look their way. Harry was climbing into the back of the car and the next thing he was chasing one of the photographers and pushing him across the street. He must have pushed him around 20 ft. It took three of them to control him – there were his two minders plus the guy who works on the door. Harry didn't say anything audible to the photographers. He just sort of grunted and he was off. I think somebody had got quite close to him and he got upset. He was fuming. It was over very quickly. The whole thing lasted no more than 30 seconds.'

Scotland Yard said it had not received a formal complaint and did not expect to press charges against the prince.

Playboy Prince

The incident threw the spotlight on Harry's playboy image and his reputation as the Royal Family's rebel. It also follows a string of well-documented trips to other fashionable London nightspots. In the past few months Harry-spotters have seen him with a group of female friends in trendy Boujis, in South Kensington. He was also seen cavorting with topless model Lauren Pope, 20, at China White in Mayfair.

The controversy threatens to overshadow attempts to portray the prince as a sensitive, caring young man after his gap-year stay in Lesotho and his voluntary work coaching rugby to schoolchildren. In 2002 the Prince hit the headlines after he was seen drinking under age and smoking cannabis.

761 words, adapted from *The Daily Express*, 22 October 2004

The hounding of Harry as paparazzi smell money

As the night was coming to an end for the party set, the working day was just beginning for the paparazzi, whose income derives from catching celebrities falling out of nightclubs.

The dozen or so photographers who make their living from the London party scene were divided between several West End nightclubs hoping to spot a famous name.

Gradually, word got round that Prince Harry was inside Pangaea, an exclusive nightclub in Piccadilly which is a regular haunt for pop stars, footballers and socialites.

The photographers began to see pound signs: the right picture can make hundreds of thousands of pounds when sold to newspapers and celebrity magazines around the world. As one paparazzo put it, 'I thought Christmas had arrived early.' A spokesman for the photo agency, Exposure, said, 'Someone inside tipped us off that Harry had arrived there around 11 p.m. and was in there drinking tequilas.'

Steve Walters, a freelance photographer, said, 'I got there about 1.30 a.m. and there were six or seven photographers outside. By the time Harry eventually came out, there were about 20 of us.'

Moments before Harry left the club at 3.20 a.m., a limousine pulled up to wait on the opposite side of the street to the entrance of Pangaea, and doormen appeared to ready themselves for his departure. As there was still confusion as to which exit Harry would use, the paparazzi were spread around.

Mr Walters, 41, said, 'A few of us were at the front door as he came out and as soon as the others saw the flashbulbs, a whole gaggle of people came rushing towards the car that he was getting into. People from all sides were converging on the car, and some were far too close to him. Some of the less experienced photographers stayed in close for too long. It was all pretty hectic.'

Prince Harry and his minder crossed the road and walked round to the far side of the car to get into the back. Accounts conflict as to exactly what happened next.

According to the photographers, as the prince was half way into the car, he lunged at photographer Chris Uncle, 24, pushing his camera into his face and cutting his lip.

Clarence House's version of events is that Prince Harry reacted only after receiving a bump on the nose from a camera lens. Everyone agrees that the whole episode lasted less than 30 seconds.

Mr Walters said, 'Harry lost control. Chris Uncle is the most good-natured, mild-mannered photographer you will meet. He was pretty shaken up.'

Mr Uncle has been working as a paparazzo for just a few months. His mobile phone was later turned off and his agency, Big Pictures, is understood to have told him not to talk further to journalists.

Big Pictures was demanding £10,000 to use the photos Uncle took. Other photographers present were charging just a few hundred pounds. Many paparazzi earn little or no basic salary and rely on an occasional lucrative snatch to make their living.

Mr Walters said, 'There are amateurs who are angling for one big picture that will make them rich and famous. Those people can be unprofessional and take unnecessary risks. I prefer to play a long game where you take pictures that will be used again and again.'

An agreement between the Prince of Wales and newspaper editors that his sons would be allowed privacy while they were in full-time education ended for Prince Harry when he left Eton last year.

Since then, the prince has been seen by some as fair game and has become possibly the most photographed royal. He has begun to develop a reputation as a playboy, keen on drinking, smoking and keeping company with attractive girls. While still at school, he was caught smoking cannabis.

In the past year, the Clarence House public relations machine has worked hard to rid Prince Harry of his unwanted image. He spent two months in Lesotho, southern Africa, carrying out voluntary work and meeting HIV victims.

In his first extensive television interview last month, Harry spoke about his mother and his desire to follow her lead in charity work. 'I want to try to carry it on to make her proud,' he said.

Before taking up his place at the Royal Military Academy in Sandhurst last year, Prince Harry taught rugby to underprivileged children.

He has emerged into the spotlight after living with the knowledge that his mother, whom he lost at the age of 12, was often hounded by the press and died after being chased by paparazzi. It is not surprising that tensions emerged when he found himself in a situation that became so familiar to her.

781 words, adapted from *The Daily Telegraph*, 22 October 2004

1 Looking at the texts

A Match the statements (1–10) to *The Daily Express* or *The Daily Telegraph*.

1 Some photographers took unnecessary risks by standing too close to the Prince.
2 Prince Harry wants to do charity work like his mother did.
3 The Prince drank expensive alcoholic drinks.
4 Considering what happened to his mother, Harry's behaviour can be understood.
5 Prince Harry was in the nightclub for several hours.
6 Harry was drunk when he left the nightclub.
7 Three men had to hold the prince back after he had attacked the photographer.
8 Prince Harry chased a photographer and deliberately pushed him hard.
9 Somebody informed the paparazzi that Harry was visiting the nightclub.
10 Mr Uncle's agency wants a lot of money for the photos he took.

B The articles on pages 60 and 61 were accompanied by these photos. In groups, decide which photo belongs to which newspaper and discuss how they help prepare the reader for each story.

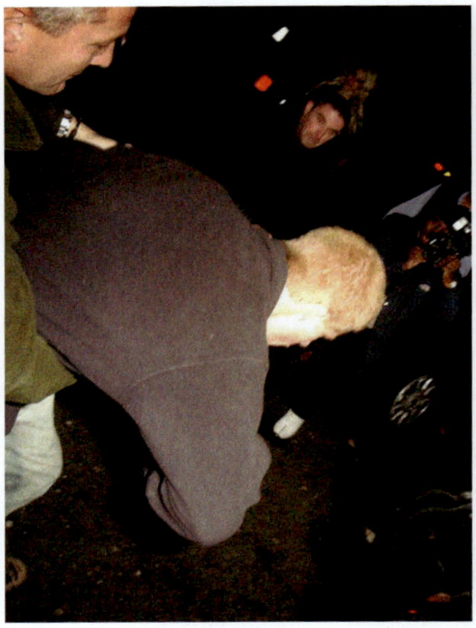

C In your group, analyze the articles. These points may help you:

Headlines

- Size, content, style
- How does each headline support the message of each article?

Language

- Style
- Is the news treated in a sensational or a factual way?
- In which different ways is Prince Harry referred to in each of the papers?

Content

- Is the information serious or superficial?

Sources

- Which newspaper says more about where it obtains its information?
- Why do you think it does this?

D Using your analysis, give a short statement on each paper and say why you would recommend it / not recommend it.

2 Writing

Text production p175

Choose one of these tasks and write about 250 words.

Write to the editor of one of the newspapers

1 voicing your opinion on their article about Prince Harry's clash with the photographer.
2 on the issue of freedom of the press versus respect for private life/religion.

3 Listening

Listening skills p185

CD2/3

A You are going to listen to five people talking about newspapers. Match the readers to the newspapers. There are two more newspapers than you need.

1 Robert Bruce
2 Julia Taylor
3 Erica Brown
4 John Ford
5 Sally Carter

a The Guardian
b The Daily Telegraph
c The Manchester Evening News
d Herald Tribune
e The Daily Mail
f The New York Times
g The Mirror

B Listen again and take notes. Why does each person like reading his/her particular newspaper?

CROSS-CULTURAL SPOTLIGHT

Newspaper-reading habits in the UK and the USA

Newspaper-reading habits in the UK are significantly different to those in the USA. More national newspapers are sold per head in Britain than in any other western country. British people often read more than one newspaper – a national quality or popular paper and a local or regional paper – and 'reading the papers' is part of the traditional British Sunday.

In the USA newspaper circulation has been in decline since 1990. Today only 54% of Americans read a newspaper during the week. There is also a vast difference in newspaper-reading habits between young and old in the USA. Put plainly, old people read newspapers and young people don't.

In the USA and the UK relatively few people read online editions of newspapers.

4 Project – presenting an English-language newspaper

Doing projects p189

Form groups and present a newspaper of your choice. Use the points for analyzing newspapers in exercises 1B and 1C.

TEXT 2

Reading skills p170/171

CD2/4

Reality TV: Should we watch?

Switch on the TV and they're everywhere – game shows, daytime talk shows, docusoaps and reality shows. Media around the world have discovered that so-called 'reality shows' are very profitable, so it's not surprising that some kind of reality show can be seen on most channels every day of the week.

Although not all of them are successful, many do achieve significant popularity and cultural prominence. As a young person, you are probably hooked on at least one reality TV series. Sometimes these shows can go pretty far. Reality shows like *Survivor* and *Big Brother* place strangers together in stressful, Darwinian battles of the fittest and reward the winners' competitive and cooperative skills with big cash prizes. The primary basis for most of these shows seems to be putting people in painful, embarrassing and humiliating situations so that the rest of us can laugh at them.

It's humiliation as entertainment. But why do these programmes appeal to viewers? Could it be that viewers are taking delight in the misfortunes of others simply because these things are not happening to them?

People's ability and willingness to take pleasure in such things could also stem from the fact that some of us feel increasingly isolated in today's society. The more distant we are from each other, the less we can empathize with others. At the same time, we cannot experience sympathy for people in difficult situations.

Some experts argue that one of the attractions of these kinds of shows is the supposed 'reality' of them – they are sold as unscripted, unplanned situations and reactions. These programmes are not as real as they pretend to be, however, as the situations are contrived and a large amount of footage is edited to make the best entertainment value for the viewers.

'Reality' shows are popular with producers because they are usually cheaper to make than other TV programmes. It is viewer ratings and not quality that matters most to network executives. It is also a fact that many reality TV producers fail to demonstrate much sympathy or concern with what the subjects of their shows experience, and injuries, humiliation and suffering merely seem to be the cost of doing business – the price you have to pay to achieve financial and commercial success.

Reality TV in all its glory is available to the viewing public seven days a week on TV and 24 hours a day on the internet.

If you find yourself enjoying the suffering and humiliation of others on a regular basis, you should begin to question your behaviour. Instead of passively accepting whatever the media companies try to feed you, take some time to reflect on why such programmes are made, and why you feel attracted to them. Perhaps you will find that your motives are not so good.

465 words, adapted from http://atheism.about.com/library/FAQs/phil/blphil_eth_realitytv.htm

5 Looking at the text

A Copy this flow chart into your exercise book. Complete it with information from the text.

Reality TV

Game shows | ...[1] | ...[2] | ...[3]

Concept: Participants are put in painful, ...[4] and ...[5] situations for viewers to laugh at.

They appeal to viewers because

people take delight in ...[6].
they feel increasingly ...[7].
they are attracted by ...[8].

They are popular among producers because

they are usually ...[9]
...[10] matter most.

Viewers should think about

why such programmes ...[11] and why people ...[12].

B Match the sentences (1–6) to six of the endings (a–h) to make statements which correspond with the information in the text. Two endings do not match.

1 Reality TV is very profitable
2 Even though reality TV shows as a genre are popular,
3 Most young people watch
4 Some viewers enjoy watching the candidates in stressful situations
5 The situations in reality shows are usually set up
6 If you enjoy reality TV shows,

a to ensure maximum entertainment for the viewers.
b because they themselves cannot feel for others.
c some of them don't attract many viewers.
d because they are interested in the celebrities who take part.
e you should think about why you find the suffering of others entertaining.
f and that is why you can see at least one reality show on TV every day.
g they are contrived and edited to make the shows interesting.
h at least one reality show.

6 Writing

Text production p183

Describe the cartoon. Write about 100 words.

Don't you understand? This is life. This is what's happening now. We can't just switch to another channel, you know.

7 Talking

Group discussions p186

Imagine you work in a TV production firm. Your team has to create a new show.

A Discuss these points in your group:

- who the target group is;
- the basic idea of the show;
- unique ideas which will make the show original and successful;
- the type of participants you would like to have on your show;
- the title of the show.

B Present your ideas to the class. Which show might be most successful? Why? Reach a consensus.

8 Language – adjectives and adverbs

SPOT THE MISTAKES

Spot the mistakes and correct them. Explain why they are wrong.

1 ~~Quality papers are often big than the popular papers.~~
2 ~~Paparazzi are as hungry than wolves when it comes to a good photo.~~
3 ~~TV producers try hardly to think up new types of shows.~~
4 ~~The new game show was accepted slow.~~
5 ~~The candidates are good prepared for the show.~~
6 ~~Reality shows are more cheap to make than other types of shows.~~

Tom is a slow worker. The paint he's using dries very quickly. Will he be voted out of the show soon?

Adjectives and adverbs

Tom is a slow worker.
The paint he's using dries very quickly.
Will he be voted out of the show soon?

Language check p203

Adjectives and adverbs

1 Work with a partner. Complete the text with the correct form of these words. Use each word only once.

adequate • difficult • happy • hard • high
ignorant • increasing • real • serious • successful

It comes as no ...[1] surprise that cheap TV productions are so ...[2] at the moment. Soap operas and reality shows gain ...[3] ratings while news programmes and other ...[4] programmes are ignored. In today's ...[5] times, many young viewers feel ...[6] when they can lose themselves in a dream world. Some sociologists are becoming ...[7] worried about this development. They predict a future in which ...[8] people glued to the TV will ...[9] be able to read and think for themselves. Other experts are concerned that young people growing up today will not be able to deal ...[10] with problems.

2 Make sentences using the correct form of the words in brackets. Add *as/than* where necessary.

EXAMPLE The circulation figures of popular papers are usually (high) that of the qualities.
The circulation figures of popular papers are usually *higher than* that of the qualities.

1 If you want reliable information, broadsheets are the (good) choice.
2 A subscription to an online edition is often (cheap) buying the print issue.
3 Popular papers don't inform readers (reliable) the quality papers.
4 Studies show that, of all types of papers, online papers attract (few) readers.
5 The amount of information available is growing (fast) ever before.
6 The internet is one of the (great) advances in communication.
7 The popular press often prints the (bad) news of the day.

3 Replace the adjectives in brackets with adverbs where necessary.

An article in the paper reports that people in Britain are becoming ...[1] (increasing) ignorant of how the rest of the world lives. The article quotes some ...[2] (new) research which has found out that ...[3] (hard) any programmes on the politics of developing countries are shown on British TV. The report also found out that the international documentary is ...[4] (virtual) dead and that reality TV and docusoaps ...[5] (total) dominate the media.
Programmes covering the lives, culture and politics of the rest of the world have been ... [6] (considerable) reduced. The number of programmes looking at society in developing countries has fallen ...[7] (dramatic). Even programmes made in developing countries themselves are ...[8] (large) failing to show the real world of the people who live there.

4 Make sentences. Add capitals where necessary.

Language check p203

1 popular / tabloids / in the uk / particularly / are
2 sex and crime stories / frequently / the popular press / carries
3 read / usually / a lot of newspapers / british people / on sunday mornings
4 has increased / the number of programmes available / on cable tv / enormously
5 enough quality shows / still / on tv / are there ?
6 you / did / the new soap opera / yesterday / watch ?

5 Work with a partner. Read the situations, then use a superlative + *ever* + the words in brackets in the correct form to give your opinion or ask your partner what he/she thinks.

EXAMPLE You've just watched a new reality show. It was very boring. Tell your partner:
(that / boring / show / see) *That was the most boring show I've ever seen.*

1 You've just read a really interesting article in the newspaper.
Tell your partner: (That / interesting / article / read)
2 You are talking about one of the *Big Brother* candidates. You think he is nice.
Tell your partner: (He / nice / person / appear on the show)
3 Your partner is a paparazzo.
Ask your partner: (Who / famous / person / take a photo of?)
4 You watch a daily soap opera. You like the soap opera a lot.
Ask your partner: (Which / good / soap opera / watch?)

WATCH OUT!

much/many/a lot of/little/few

How ~~many~~ money did the candidate win? ➤ How much money did the candidate win?

The winners often have ~~much~~ problems handling their fame. ➤ The winners often have a lot of problems handling their fame.

There weren't ~~much~~ people at the show. ➤ There weren't many people at the show.

The popular press has ~~little~~ problems with circulation figures. ➤ The popular press has few problems with circulation figures.

The paparazzi show ~~few~~ understanding for celebrities' feelings. ➤ The paparazzi show little understanding for celebrities' feelings.

Complete these sentences with *much, many, a lot of, little* or *few*.

1 The newspaper isn't very popular. It has very … readers.
2 Paul is very busy now that he is famous. He has … free time.
3 Did he take … good photos when he worked as a paparazzo?
4 It was clear that Haley wouldn't win the prize. She didn't have … of a chance.
5 We read … English newspapers when we were on holiday.
6 There was only … interest in the new docusoap.
7 … people believe that the situations are real.
8 I've never had … interest in celebrities.

Vocabulary review

A Complete this text with words from the three main texts. The first letter of each of the missing words is given.

British quality n…[1] have an excellent reputation throughout the world. Their e…[2] concentrate mainly on current affairs and their j…[3] are serious in their reporting. Popular papers and celebrity m…[4] attract their readers mainly with scandals and sensational stories. They often publish shocking or embarrassing photos of famous people which they buy from f…[5] photographers.

A lot of TV n…[6] executives are also interested in c…[7]. They know that presenting these people on their shows increases viewer r…[8].

All over the world, m…[9] of all types have realized that the lives of the rich and famous are certain to encourage people to buy their papers or watch their p…[10].

B Continue to add 'media' words to your vocabulary list.

7 Justice

FOCUS

1 Discuss these cartoons. Compare them.

2 Match four of these statements with the statistics below. One statement does <u>not</u> match.

1 There were more than twice as many adults as young people in prison in 2005.
2 By 2004, violent crime rates across the United States had dropped considerably compared to 20 years before.
3 Since 2002 there has been a sharp increase in arrests for violent crime.
4 In California, since 2001 violent crime rates have declined; crimes against property have increased.
5 While prison and parole rates have been rising slowly, probation rates among adults have risen rapidly over the last 30 years.

California

A

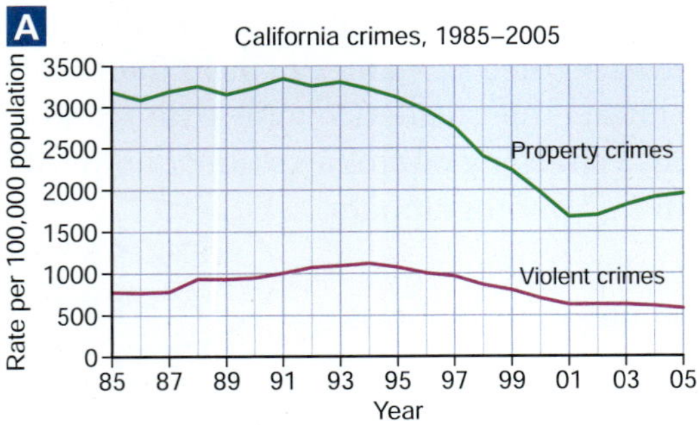

B

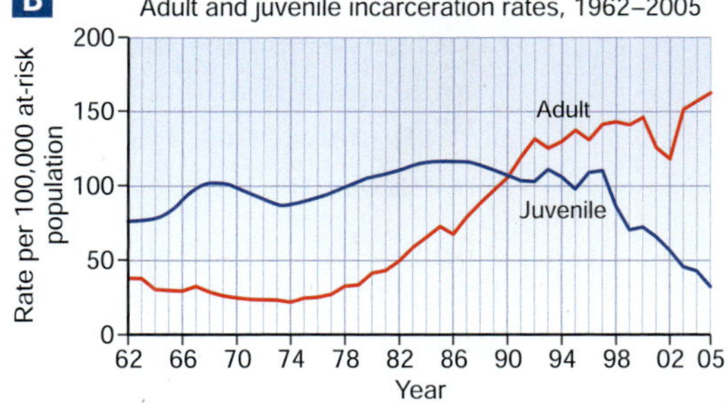

United States

C

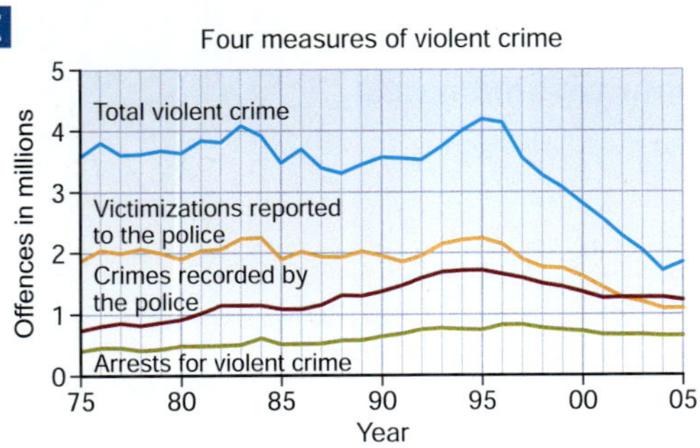

D

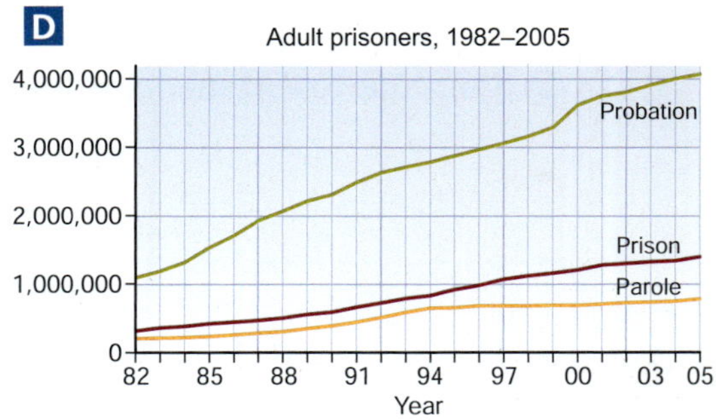

TEXT 1

Reading skills p170/171

CD2/5

Buried alive!

In the American game of baseball, a player who fails to strike (or hit) the ball three times in a row is declared 'out'. In the field of criminal justice, this baseball term, 'three strikes and you're out', refers to the practice of condemning criminals found guilty of having broken the law a third time to life imprisonment.

Brian Smith didn't know the two women who were shoplifting. They were caught on security cameras stealing sheets at the Los Cerritos mall in Los Angeles and received a two-year sentence.

But Smith was seen standing near the shoplifters as they committed their crime. Despite having no stolen goods, he was convicted of helping them to shoplift. Under California's 'three strikes' law. The 30-year-old received a 25-year-to-life sentence.

Smith's crime was to have two previous convictions, one 11 years earlier and the second six years before the shoplifting incident. Those convictions, for purse snatching in 1983 and burglary in 1988, earned him the dubious honour of being one of the first criminals to be sentenced by a Californian judge under the state's 'three strikes' law.

By September 2003, California, the US state with the highest prison population, was holding 7,234 prisoners under the 'three strikes' law.

Sitting in her Los Angeles home, Smith's aunt, Dorothy Erskine, a 70-year-old retired schoolteacher, recalls the family's reaction to his sentence. 'We were, like – is this really happening? Brian wasn't guilty so we thought he could get his sentence reduced on appeal. But he was advised not to appeal. And we were told that unless you have about $20,000 or $30,000 to pay for the right type of lawyer, your chances are very, very slim. I did not have $30,000.'

Three or four years after he went to prison, Smith suffered a stroke. 'They didn't notify anyone in the family that anything had happened to him,' said his aunt, 'I didn't find out until I went to visit him and they rolled him down in a wheelchair.'

Ms Erskine keeps a picture of her nephew in her living room. It shows a strong-featured young man in jeans and a blue shirt standing next to a Christmas tree. His hands behind his back, he smiles tentatively at the camera.

That picture was one of almost a hundred displayed on mock gravestones at a vigil held at Leipert Park, Los Angeles, last year for prisoners convicted under the 'three strikes' law. With the slogan 'Buried alive!'

above each name and case history, the gravestones show the types of crimes the prisoners had committed: Richard Morgan, 25 years for shoplifting a baseball glove; Herman Clifford Smith, 25 years for trying to cash a forged cheque for $193; Gilbert Musgrave, 25 years for possession of a stolen video recorder; George Anderson, 25 years for filing a false driving licence application; Johnny Quirino, 25 years for stealing razor blades.

Under the 'three strikes' law, 25 years means 25 years: prisoners have no chance of parole. The law was voted for in March 1994, under California's proposition system, in which the electorate votes directly for specific policy initiatives. But unlike the 'three strikes' laws operating in some other states, California's version does not restrict the law to violent crimes.

Sixty-five per cent of those imprisoned under the 'three strikes' law in California were convicted of non-violent crimes; 354 of them received 25-years-to-life sentences for petty theft of less than $250.

Opponents of this law point out that offenders sentenced under the law for drug possession outnumber the combined sum of prisoners serving sentences for murder, rape and assault with a deadly weapon. They also point to the cost of the sentencing policy, with the imprisonment of non-violent offenders under the 'three strikes' law estimated to cost the state nearly $1billion a year. With California's budget deficit increasing, they argue that this would be one easy way to save money.

Yet there is no indication that the law has led to a decrease in crime. Between 1993 and 2002 New York State, roughly comparable with California, but without a 'three strikes' law, saw its crime rate reduced by 27% more than California's.

In a referendum on 2nd November 2004, California voters had the possibility of reforming the 'three strikes' law and restricting it to serious, violent crimes. However, the majority of people (53.4%) supported their governor, Arnold Schwarzenegger, and voted to keep the 'three strikes' law as it was.

676 words adapted from *The Guardian*, 8 March 2004

1 Looking at the text

A Beantworten Sie stichpunktartig folgende Fragen auf Deutsch.

1 Was beinhaltet das in dem Text beschriebene Gesetz in Kalifornien?
2 Wann und wie wurde es verabschiedet?
3 Bei welcher Art von Straftaten wurde das Gesetz am häufigsten angewandt?
4 Wie hat sich das Gesetz auf die Kriminalitätsrate in Kalifornien ausgewirkt?

B Answer these questions in English. Give short answers.

1 Why did Brian Smith receive a much higher sentence than the two women who did the actual shoplifting?
2 Why did Smith's aunt decide not to appeal against her nephew's conviction?
3 What was the purpose of the vigil held at Leipert Park in Los Angeles?
4 Which three arguments are used by people who oppose California's 'three strikes' law?

C What does the slogan *Buried alive!* suggest?

2 Working with words

A Match the correct word or phrase (1–8) with eight of the definitions (a–j).

1 shoplifting (line 4)
2 crime (line 12)
3 commit (a crime) (line 12)
4 sentence (line 19)
5 parole (line 100)
6 petty theft (line 117)
7 offender (line 119)
8 imprisonment (line 127)

a an unlawful act
b do something wrong or illegal
c punishment handed out by a law court
d a rule which can be enforced by a court
e stealing something from a shop
f a person who has done something wrong or illegal
g decide in a law court that a person is guilty of a crime
h stealing something of little value from a person or place
i locking somebody up in a place from which they cannot escape
j permission given to a prisoner to leave prison earlier on condition that he/she behaves well

B Use words from the list above to complete this text. Change the form of the words if necessary.

A group called Families to Amend California's Three Strikes (FACTS) wants to restrict the use of the law to those who …[1] a violent crime. 'This law is cruel and absurd,' says Rosi Martinez, a member of FACTS. Her son is currently serving a 25-year …[2] for stealing CDs from a store. 'There are thousands of …[3] in prison who did minor things like selling marijuana or …[4] from a store. They are sent to prison for life without a chance of …[5]. The law should be used to …[6] murderers and other violent criminals who threaten public safety. What's the point of sending someone to prison for the rest of their life for …[7]? It does not decrease …[8] in our state and it costs the taxpayers millions of dollars.'

3 Writing

Text production p175

Write a letter to the governor of California explaining why the 'three strikes' law would be impossible in Germany. Write about 200 words.

Dear Governor

I have just read an article …

CROSS-CULTURAL SPOTLIGHT

Differences between British and American English

Which is more correct – British English or American English? Of course, both are equally correct. The most important rule of thumb is to be consistent in your usage of spelling, vocabulary and grammar.

Spelling: Use the spell check on your computer and choose which variety of English you would like.

Vocabulary: Your dictionary should say whether the term is used in British English (BE) or American English (AE).

Grammar: See Language check pages.

4 Listening

Listening skills p185

CD2/6 **You are going to hear a phone-in programme about teenagers and alcohol. Listen and match each statement with one of the people below.**

A

Catherine Cook, radio presenter

B

Peter, policeman

C

Sandra, psychologist

D

Scott, teacher

E

Marilyn, student

F

Colin, student

1 Alcohol consumption among teenagers is closely connected with crime.
2 It is probably the campaigns against drinking and driving that have reduced the number of teenagers killed in drunk-driving crashes in the US.
3 Underage drinking is a more serious problem in the UK than in most other parts of the world.
4 To tackle the problem of teenage drinking we need better education on the effects of drinking, not a new law.
5 Raising the drinking age to 21 would not only reduce the number of teenagers who drink irresponsibly, but also reduce crime.
6 Some of the problems could be solved if the police made sure that people had to show identification before they could buy alcohol – as in the US.

TEXT 2

Reading skills p170/171

CD2/7

Just along for the ride

I leaned back on the seat and watched the back of Dick's head as he steered. The '55 DeSoto rumbled along the rain-soaked street.

This evening's gonna be a total loss, I thought. Things have got pretty dull when all you've gotta do is drive around with a friend who just got his license. But it beats sitting at home. So there we were, the five of us, Dick and Phil were in front, Reid, Steve and I were in the back. We were all cold, damp and bored. Man, we needed something to do!

'This is real crummy. I think we ...'

I was cut off by Phil. 'Hey,' he said. 'Let's drive up to somebody – some kid – and flatten him.'

'What?' I said.

'We drive up slow, then swing open the door real fast, and knock the guy on his can.'

We all looked at him kinda funny.

'Well, it's something to do,' Phil said.

'Aw, why not? Okay, we'll do it.'

We began looking around for a victim.

'You guys are nuts,' I said. 'What if he calls the cops?'

'You worry too much. Whenever we wanna have some fun, you always chicken out.'

'There's one!'

It was raining hard, but we could see the blurred figure of some guy under a streetlight on the corner. Steve laughed.

'Oh wow! This is gonna be funny.'

A couple of us started laughing.

'Will you guys shut up?' said Dick. I guess it made him nervous.

The kid was about half a block away. The street wasn't too busy. Only a few cars were around. Dick started weaving across the road.

'Stop fooling around!' I said.

Steve got on the door, ready to open it. Then everything started happening too fast. The guy at the corner stepped out into the street. The car swerved. The door swung open, and Steve started falling out. He grabbed my arm, and we both fell back on the seat. Dick got scared and threw the car away from the kid. The headlights flashed on a frozen figure. I could see his face, eyes wide, mouth open. There was a squeal of tires on the slick street and a hollow thud as the figure was hurled, rolling across the roof. I got all mixed up.

'Ken Benjamin!' I said. 'I think it was Ken Benjamin!'

Dick slowed down. Then he suddenly started speeding down the street.

'Dick! Stop! I know that guy! Dick, will ya stop?' He didn't hear me. 'Stop the car! He's my friend!'

I hit him on the shoulder and grabbed his shirt. He turned around. Tears were blobbing up in his eyes.

'Shut up, you jerk! You want us to get nailed for manslaughter?' He hit my arm.

What a stupid thing to do! I got so scared that I started shivering like crazy. I just couldn't believe it. I felt sick.

'Hey!'

I looked up. It was Dick. He was looking in the rear-view mirror. There was a car behind us.

'Is he following us?' said Dick.

The car lunged forward as it picked up speed. I looked back. The headlights shone through the rain, about two or three hundred yards away. Dick hung a sharp right up a narrow street. Hardly anyone ever comes up this way, I thought. If he follows us up here, he's really following us. I looked back. The headlights were getting closer.

We turned into a winding road. I looked back and could see the brown Volvo as it cut through the street ponds. Yeah, I thought, a good guy would drive one of those Volvos. What if he catches us? Ken was my friend. *Hit and run, hit and run* kept going through my head. I kinda hoped that the guy in the Volvo would catch us.

We were out in the sticks by now. The road was winding a lot. The Volvo was making his move and he was closing fast. But as he rounded a curve, he turned too sharply and his car slid off the road. He couldn't have been hurt. Everyone was relieved. After that, Dick drove us all home.

It was 12.30 when I got home. Nobody was awake. I started pacing around the kitchen. I was so scared. I didn't know if we had killed him or not. I turned on the radio and listened to some music. But when the news came on, I turned it off.

You idiot, I thought. Ken was your friend. Go to his mom or something. Well, I didn't hit him! It's not my fault! Those other guys – it wasn't my idea – no! You were in the car. You're responsible, too. *Hit and run, hit and run*.

I got in my car and drove for a while. Then I started remembering things Ken used to say.

'I don't know what to do!' I was shouting as I drove. No answer. My mind burned. 'Go see Mrs Benjamin, you coward!'

But I couldn't. I just couldn't. When I got home, the lights were on. My mother was in her robe.

'Your friends are here,' she said. 'I don't think that two o'clock in the morning is the right time to ... '

I didn't listen. I just went into the front room. Dick walked up to me and said real low, 'I heard on the radio that he's not dead. He isn't even hurt bad.'

I didn't say anything. I just looked at him.

'No one knows,' he went on. 'So maybe we can get away with it.'

He could see I was getting mad. I could have killed him.

The others stood up and came over. I didn't say a thing. I just walked out the door, got in the car, and left.

It took me a while to find Ken's house. It was gray brick, and the lights were on. Maybe it wasn't gray. I don't know. Everything looked gray. I walked up and rang the doorbell.

1,000 words from Dennis Kurumada: *Just Along for the Ride*, US Information Agency, Washington DC 1972

5 Looking at the text

A Are the following statements true or false? Correct the false statements.

1 The narrator had just got his driving licence.
2 There were two friends in the car with him.
3 The teenagers in the car wanted to knock somebody over.
4 They approached a figure and then everything happened as they had planned.
5 The teenagers stopped the car to see if the person they'd hit was hurt.
6 After the accident they noticed that a police car was following them.
7 At home the narrator turned on the radio but he didn't listen to the news.
8 He went to the victim's house and sat outside in his car, thinking.

B Erläutern Sie die Bedeutung der folgenden Ausdrücke bzw. Sätze auf Deutsch. (Keine wortwörtliche Übersetzung.)

1 But it beats sitting at home. (line 4)
2 You always chicken out. (line 19)
3 The headlights flashed on a frozen figure. (line 32)
4 You want us to get nailed for manslaughter? (line 41)
5 We turned into a winding road. (line 51)
6 *Hit and run, hit and run* kept going through my head. (line 53)
7 Go see Mrs Benjamin, you coward. (lines 66/67)
8 So maybe we can get away with it. (line 75)

6 Working with words

Complete the text with the correct prepositions or adverbs. You can use some of the words more than once.

along • around • away • down • into • off • onto • round • through • up

The car roared …[1] the street. The five friends were driving …[2] aimlessly. When a figure stepped …[3] the street, they drove …[4] to him. Dick, the driver, threw the car …[5] from the figure, but it was too late. First Dick wanted to slow …[6] but then changed his mind and started speeding …[7] the street. When the youths noticed that a Volvo was following them, Dick accelerated and the car picked …[8] speed. Both cars started …[9] a winding road. In the rear-view mirror Dick could see the Volvo as it cut …[10] the puddles. Suddenly, when the Volvo was driving …[11] a bend, the driver turned too sharply and the car slid …[12] the road.

7 Talking

Group discussions p186

In groups, talk about the boys in the story. Discuss these points.

- Why did they decide to knock someone over?
- Should the narrator have tried harder to dissuade the others? Why / Why not?
- What do you think the narrator said when he went into Ken's house?
- How do you think the relationship between the narrator and the other boys will develop?
- What do you think Ken will do?

8 Language – conditionals 1, 2 and 3

SPOT THE MISTAKES

Spot the mistakes and correct them. Explain why they are wrong.

1 ~~If you would break the law three times in California, you would be in trouble.~~
2 ~~If I convince the jury that I'm not the hit and run driver, I walk out of the court free tomorrow.~~
3 ~~Young people in the US have to show their ID if they would buy alcohol.~~
4 ~~What did you do if you would be sent to prison?~~
5 ~~I'm not surprised when there is more teenage crime this year.~~
6 ~~If there weren't so many policemen at the football match last Saturday, the hooligans have not been caught.~~

Conditional 1

Two stupid bank robbers are driving to the bank. They have a box of dynamite on the back seat of the car. 'If you don't drive more carefully, the dynamite will explode,' says one of the robbers. 'Don't worry,' says the other robber. 'If it explodes, we can use the other box of dynamite in the boot.'

Conditional 2

Pete: If you found a $100 bill in the street, would you keep it?
Pat: Of course not. I'd spend it.

Conditional 3

A prisoner is telling another convict how he ended up in jail. 'I stole £936,897 and 72 pence from a bank. The police wouldn't have caught me if I hadn't stopped to count it all.'

Conditionals

Type 1: If you **don't drive** more carefully, the dynamite **will explode**.
If it **explodes**, we **can use** the other box of dynamite in the boot.

Type 2: If you **found** a $100 bill in the street, **would** you **keep** it?

Type 3: The police **wouldn't have caught** me if I **hadn't stopped** to count it all.'

Language check p201

1 Translate these sentences.

1 Der Unfall wäre nicht passiert, wenn er nicht so viel getrunken hätte.
2 Wenn meine Eltern nicht so weit weg vom Gefängnis wohnten, würden sie mich öfter besuchen.
3 Wenn Mike morgen nicht freigesprochen wird, wird er sehr enttäuscht sein.
4 An deiner Stelle würde ich das nicht klauen.
5 Was machst du, wenn wir morgen erwischt werden?
6 Wenn du mich nicht gewarnt hättest, hätte der Dieb mein Portemonnaie gestohlen.

2 Complete the sentences with the correct form of the verbs in brackets.

1 If we ... (want) to reduce juvenile delinquency, we ... (must) focus on teenage dropouts.
2 If people in the neighbourhood ... (report) all the crimes, even the trivial ones like spraying graffiti, the juvenile crime statistics ... (not/rise) considerably last year.
3 If Peter ... (not/be caught) spraying graffiti on the building last month, he ... (not/have to) pay £500 to have it cleaned up.
4 There ... (be) fewer accidents on Friday and Saturday nights if people ... (drink) sensibly.
5 If you ... (not/drink) so much last night, you ... (not/crash) the car.

WATCH OUT!

Language check p210

Problem words (2)

He didn't ~~rob~~ the books. ➤ He didn't steal the books.

Choose the correct words from the brackets to complete the sentences.

1 He was convicted of (robbing/stealing) a bank.
2 Some prisoners do nothing but (look/watch) videos all day long.
3 He was (happy/lucky) not to be caught by the police.
4 The criminal had to (get up/stand up) when the judge sentenced him.
5 Would you like me to (bring/take) you anything when I come to visit you in jail?

Vocabulary review

Complete this text with the correct words from the brackets.

Sixteen-year-old US high-school student Tony Mathews has a lot more to do after school than his homework. Tony acts as a volunteer ...[1] (judge/judgement) in a teenage court that decides on ...[2] (sentences/security) for young ...[3] (offenders/offensive) in Brooklyn, New York. The court deals with petty crimes such as truancy and vandalism, but does not handle major offences like ...[4] (possess/possession) of drugs, rape or ...[5] (murderer/murder).
The court uses peer pressure and ...[6] (penalties/punishments) to encourage young criminals to see the error of their ways. For example, graffiti-sprayers are sent to clean up their ...[7] (victims'/prison) properties. In doing this, the court hopes to turn juvenile offenders into ...[8] (responsible/responsibility) citizens.
The idea of using peer pressure to educate anti-social youths has been so successful in Brooklyn that other communities are thinking of copying this policy.

8 Preserving the planet

FOCUS

1 **Discuss this cartoon.**

2 **Talk in groups and decide where the words in the box should fit on the spider diagram below. Discuss the pros and cons of each source of energy.**

coal • gas • geothermal power • hydro-electric power • non-renewable
nuclear power • oil • solar power • tidal power • wave power
wind power • wood

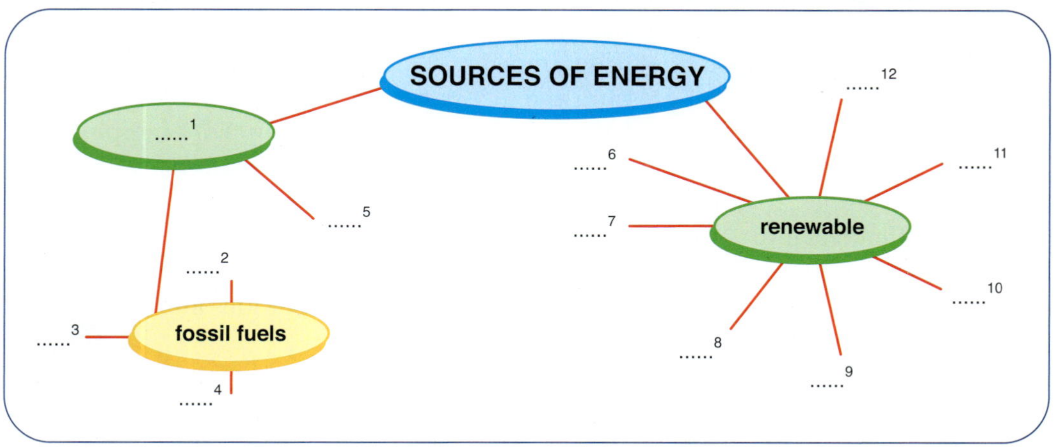

TEXT 1

Reading skills p170/171

CD2/8

The beauty of wind farms

OFF the coast of British Columbia, Canada, is an island called Quadra, where I have a cabin that is as close to my heart as you can imagine. From my porch on a good day you can see clear across the waters of The Georgia Strait to the snowy peaks of the rugged Coast Mountains. It is one of the most beautiful views I have seen. And I would gladly share it with a wind farm.

But sometimes it seems like I'm in the minority. All across Europe and North America, environmentalists, who supported wind energy in the beginning, are now locking horns with the wind industry over the location of wind farms. In Alberta, one group is opposing a planned wind farm near Cypress Hills Provincial Park, claiming it would destroy views of the park and disturb some of the last remaining native prairieland in the province. In the UK more than 100 national and local groups, led by some of the country's most prominent environmentalists, have argued that wind power is inefficient, destroys the ambience of the countryside, and makes little difference to carbon emissions. And in the US, the Cape Wind Project, which would site 130 wind turbines off the coast of affluent Cape Cod, Massachusetts, has come under fire from famous liberals, including Senator Edward Kennedy and Walter Cronkite.

It is time for some perspective. With the growing urgency of climate change, we cannot have it both ways. We cannot shout from the rooftops about the dangers of global warming and then turn around and shout even louder about the 'dangers' of windmills. Climate change is one of the greatest challenges humanity will face this century. It cannot be solved through good intentions. It will take a radical change in the way we produce and consume energy – another industrial revolution, this time for clean energy, conservation and efficiency.

We have undergone such transformations before and we can do it again. But first we must accept that all forms of energy have associated costs. Fossil fuels are limited in quantity and create vast amounts of pollution; large-scale hydroelectric power floods valleys and destroys animal habitat; nuclear power is incredibly expensive and creates radioactive waste.

Wind power also has its downsides. It is highly visible and can kill birds. The fact is, though, that any man-made structure can kill birds – houses, radio towers, skyscrapers. In Toronto alone, it is estimated that 10,000 birds collide with the city's tallest buildings every year. Compared with this, the risk to birds from well-sited wind farms is very low. Even at Altamont Pass in California, where 7,000 turbines were erected on a migratory route, only 0.2 birds per turbine per year have been killed. Indeed, the real risk to birds does not come from windmills but from a changing climate which threatens the very existence of bird species and their habitats. This is not to say that wind farms should be allowed to spring up anywhere. They should always be subject to environmental impact assessments. But a blanket 'not in my backyard' approach is hypocritical and counterproductive.

Pursuing wind power as part of our move towards clean energy makes sense. It is the fastest-growing source of energy in the world. Last year it was a $6 billion industry. The cost of wind-generated power has dropped dramatically over the past two decades because of larger windmills and greater knowledge of how to build, install and operate turbines more effectively. Prices are likely to decrease further as the technology improves.

Are windmills ugly? I remember when Mostafa Tolba, executive director of the United Nations Environment Programme from 1976 to 1992, told me how when he was growing up in Egypt, smokestacks belching out smoke were considered signs of progress. Even as an adult concerned about pollution, it took him a long time to get over the instinctive pride he felt when he saw a tower pouring out clouds of smoke.

We see beauty through filters shaped by our values and beliefs. Some people think wind turbines are ugly. I think smokestacks, smog, acid rain, coal-fired power plants and climate change are ugly. I think windmills are beautiful. They harness the power of the wind to supply us with heat and light and they provide local jobs. What they do not do is pollute our air or speed up climatic changes.

If one day I look out from my cabin porch and see a row of windmills spinning in the distance, I won't curse them. I will praise them. It will mean we are finally getting somewhere.

761 words, adapted from *The New Scientist*, 16 April 2005

1 Looking at the text

A Answer these questions. Give short answers.

1 UK environmentalists argue against using wind power. What do they say?
2 What problems does the author see in today's most common forms of energy?
3 The author mentions two disadvantages of wind power. What are they?
4 According to the author, why does it make sense to invest in wind power?
5 How will the author react when he sees windmills from his cabin porch? Why?

B Use words from the text to complete this gapped summary.

Even …[1] who were in favour of wind farms in the beginning object to them nowadays. They argue that windmills …[2] the countryside and are an …[3] source of energy because their energy output is relatively small.

We should not forget, however, that … …[4] will run out soon because resources are limited. In addition, these energy providers cause …[5] and lead to global warming. On top of this, nuclear power produces … …[6] which is difficult to dispose of.

Although some people believe that wind turbines are …[7], others are of the opinion that this also applies to smog and …[8] rain.

C Make a flow chart from the information in the text. Then use your flow chart to give a short talk on energy.

(See pages 28 and 65 for examples of flow charts.)

2 Working with words

A Match the words from the text (1–8) with eight of the definitions (a–j).

1 countryside (line 25)
2 wind turbines (line 28)
3 conservation (line 45)
4 hydroelectric (line 52)
5 habitat (line 53)
6 smokestacks (line 93)
7 belching out (line 94)
8 harness (line 104)

a the preservation of a valuable natural substance that exists in limited amount
b cause to experience something
c motors driven by wheels which themselves are driven by the wind
d the character and atmosphere of a place
e the tall chimneys of a factory
f control and use
g using the power of flowing water to produce electricity
h fields, woods, etc. outside town
i the natural environment of an animal or a plant
j emitting something with force

B Find a word from the text which fits all the expressions in each list.

EXAMPLE a wonderful … • a spectacular … • a breathtaking … • a room with a good …

The correct word is *view*.

1 a … opinion • a significant … • an ethnic … • belong to a …
2 … controls • a carbon dioxide … • a reduction of … • … of light
3 accept the … • meet a … • a serious … • a great …
4 nuclear … • radioactive … • … disposal • toxic …
5 air … • environmental … • noise … • … levels
6 ... an aim • … peace • … a policy of reform • … a career

Now choose one expression from each list. Use the expressions to write six sentences.

CROSS-CULTURAL SPOTLIGHT

Global attitudes towards energy

Culture tends to influence the way people consume energy. Behaviour, lifestyle and trust in technology determine a nation's attitude towards energy and the environment. In western Europe, where people are aware of global warming, governments try to reduce emissions by using nuclear power or by turning to alternative forms of energy. In the USA, where energy consumption is high, the government is optimistic that technical innovation will reduce greenhouse emissions.

Transport is one of the major culprits when it comes to environmental problems. In western Europe, public transport and petrol-saving automobiles are popular, whereas individual mobility is an important part of the American way of life. That said, there seems to be a downward trend in the buying of 'gas-guzzlers' (big cars which need a lot of petrol) in the USA at the moment.

3 Writing

▶ Text production p175

Choose one of these options. Write 150–200 words.

1 Write an email to a British friend telling him/her why you prefer to travel by car.
2 Write an email to a friend in the USA explaining how you save energy.

4 Project – helping your community save energy

▶ Doing projects p189

A In groups, discuss how people in your area might save energy.

B Discuss the various ideas in class. Use the best suggestions to develop a leaflet giving ten important tips on the issue.

TEXT 2

Reading skills p170/171

CD2/9

Save the planet – stay on the ground

A lot of people recycle newspapers and carrier bags, use buses and trains whenever possible and support the idea of switching to wind power. They care about the environment and are furious that we're destroying our planet. So why do they blow it by jumping on that cheap flight to Thailand, America or Majorca? Maybe they don't realize that the average jet pumps around a tonne of carbon dioxide into the atmosphere for every passenger it carries from London to New York. One return flight and they are responsible for more carbon dioxide production than a year's motoring.

With low-cost airlines mushrooming in the last few years, people who have never flown before have taken to the skies. As a consequence, aviation has the highest growth rate of all modes of transport worldwide. The number of passengers passing in and out of UK airports alone is forecast to double to 400 million a year by 2020.

Environmentalists warn, however, that unless demand is capped rigorously, growth in air travel will have alarming implications for the environment. Transport accounts for 20% of carbon dioxide emissions worldwide with aviation producing 13% of that 20%. Another 35% of CO_2 emissions is produced while generating electricity, 25% comes from households, trade and service industries, and 20% from heavy industry.

Jet engines do not only release carbon dioxide, their vapour trails of tiny ice particles at high altitudes also block the escape of infra-red radiation from the earth – and this heats up the atmosphere. Air travel is not only choking the world faster than any other form of transport, it is also the fastest-growing source of greenhouse emissions worldwide.

Why does the accumulation of carbon dioxide in the atmosphere pose such a threat? What is the problem with 'the greenhouse effect'? After all, the natural atmosphere of the Earth acts in a similar way to a greenhouse as naturally produced water vapour and methane trap heat in the lower atmosphere. It is, in fact, this natural greenhouse effect which creates the climate on Earth. Burning fossil fuels, however, produces a large amount of carbon dioxide, a gas which enhances this natural effect and gives rise to global warming by preventing the earth from reflecting solar heat back into space.

Scientists predict that if global carbon dioxide emissions aren't drastically lowered, worldwide temperatures will rise by up to 3.5 degrees Celsius this century, causing more hurricanes, floods and droughts. Sea levels will rise by up to 3 feet, swamping the Maldives, East Anglia and other regions.

Britain, according to some experts, might develop a climate similar to that in Provence, France. This means olive groves, orange trees and wild flamingos – but also the threat of malaria-carrying mosquitoes and very wet winters. On the other hand, some experts believe that the warm Gulf Stream could shift away from the UK, leading to a lowering of temperatures.

480 words, adapted from *The Observer*, 12 May 2002

5 Looking at the text

A Beantworten Sie stichpunktartig folgende Fragen auf Deutsch.

1 Welche Folgen hat das zunehmende Angebot von Billigflügen für die Umwelt?
2 Warum sind Düsentriebwerke für den Treibhauseffekt mitverantwortlich? Nennen Sie zwei Gründe.
3 Erklären Sie den vom Menschen verursachten Treibhauseffekt.

B Choose the most suitable option.

1 The title of the text could also be
   a Stop travelling to foreign countries.
   b Going by plane depletes the ozone layer.
   c Cheap flights are great for the aviation industry.
   d Flying is responsible for climatic change.

2 How can the author's attitude towards flying best be characterized? He/She
   a hates flying.
   b thinks flying is pure luxury.
   c believes the environment is more important than cheap holidays.
   d thinks flying will become more important this century.

3 Which of the following statements sums up the message of the first paragraph?
   a The author feels angry about global warming.
   b Alternative energy and caring about the environment are good things.
   c The tourist industry is mainly responsible for the greenhouse effect.
   d Even environmentally aware people sometimes behave thoughtlessly.

4 Which of the following could serve best as a heading for lines 14–21?
   a Low-cost airlines = high revenues
   b Cheap airlines conquer the skies
   c Unprecedented boom in air travel
   d Budget airlines fly to all destinations

5 The expression 'natural greenhouse effect' (line 47) refers to
   a plants which warm up the planet as they store heat.
   b heat trapped in the atmosphere by naturally produced gases.
   c fossil fuels which have not yet been burned.
   d the environment which encourages life on Earth.

6 What is the gist of lines 53–59?
   a Climatic changes caused by pollution will affect the earth in a very negative way.
   b The whole world will soon share the same type of climate.
   c The earth could become much colder quite soon.
   d Seas all over the globe will turn into swamps.

7 Lines 60–68 suggest that
   a the UK and France will experience the same climatic changes.
   b Britain will experience even more rain and more people will become ill due to changes in the climate.
   c the Gulf Stream will get colder.
   d even experts are not sure how the climate will change.

6 Working with words

A Find the words in the text that fit these definitions.

1 very angry
2 lines of white 'smoke' behind an aircraft as it flies
3 very small
4 danger
5 prevented from escaping
6 say in advance
7 periods of dry weather without enough water
8 a great amount of water

B Use these words to complete the letter to the editor below. Make sure you put the words into the correct grammatical form.

account for • destroy • effect • flood • melt • mushroom • reduce • stem from

Dear Sir/Madam

In your article, *Save the planet – stay on the ground* you report on the ...[1] the burning of fossil fuels has on the planet. Over the last few decades the number of cars, machines and devices which cause pollution has ...[2]. There is no doubt that a high amount of carbon dioxide ... ...[3] cars and planes. As the writer of the article clearly points out, if we don't ...[4] these emissions, the ice in polar regions will ...[5], leading to a rise in sea levels which will ...[6] coastal areas. Many scientists agree that the greenhouse effect already ... ...[7] a significant increase in the numbers of hurricanes and floods. If we don't want to see the planet ...[8] by the results of higher temperatures, we have to adopt an environmentally friendly lifestyle.

Yours faithfully
Susan Taylor

7 Listening

Listening skills p185

CD2/10 **Eric Ball is a research technologist with a leading car manufacturer. He is being interviewed by Car Magazine. Read 1–8 below then listen and decide if a or b is correct.**

1 How is the car industry trying to reduce emissions?
  a The industry is producing more and more electricity-powered vehicles.
  b Manufacturers are combining electric motors with conventional engines.

2 In towns, hybrids use
  a the electric motor.
  b a conventional gas engine.

3 The battery is charged by
  a the gas engine while the car is being driven.
  b plugging it into the mains at home.

4 How do hybrids help the environment?
  a They run more slowly than conventional cars.
  b They burn less fuel per mile.

5 Experts think the car of the future will be
  a a hybrid car.
  b a hydrogen fuel cell car.

6 Hydrogen fuel cell cars emit
  a no greenhouse gases.
  b water.

7 Car makers say that the future of fuel cell cars is
  a not very bright.
  b probably a bright one.

8 The major problem for fuel cell cars is the
  a problems obtaining the fuel.
  b high price.

8 Language – the passive

SPOT THE MISTAKES

Spot the mistakes and correct them. Explain why they are wrong.

1 ~~Our environment is endangered from man-made pollutants.~~
2 ~~Emissions from car engines reduce in the last decade.~~
3 ~~The greenhouse effect can trace back to burning fossil fuels.~~
4 ~~Are cars powered with fuel cells in future?~~

Thoughts about the environment by famous politicians

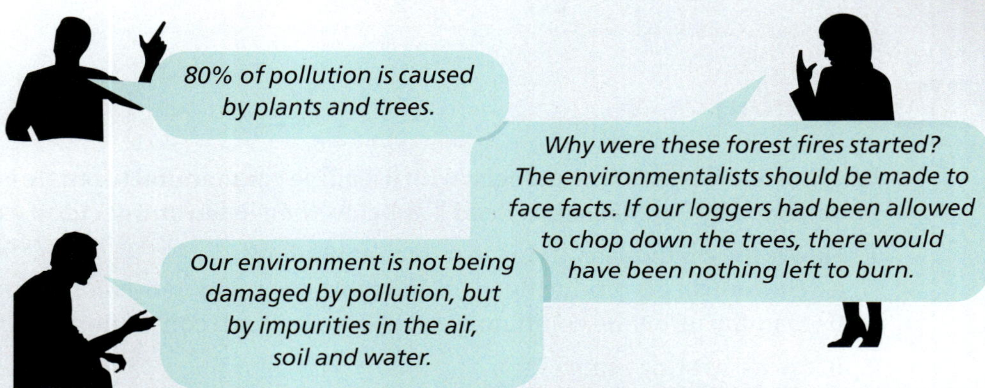

The passive

80% of pollution is caused by plants and trees.
Our environment is not being damaged by pollution.
Why were these forest fires started?

▶ Language check p199

1 Complete the text with the correct form of the verbs in brackets.

As protests against wind farms …[1] (hear) across Europe, solar cells …[2] (become) more and more important. Today all communication satellites …[3] (power) by photovoltaic cells. The technology …[4] (develop) many years ago, and since then many houses …[5] (equip) with solar cells. Environmentalists say more effort …[6] (should/make) in future to save energy. As environmental problems …[7] (continually/discuss), a lot of thought …[8] (go into) recycling methods. Up to now a significant amount of electronic scrap …[9] (reduce) by recycling. In future, appliances …[10] (design) with recycling in mind.

2 Translate these sentences.

1 Von den Industrieländern wird mehr Energie als je zuvor benötigt.
2 Das Leben auf unserem Planeten wird durch das Verbrennen fossiler Brennstoffe ernsthaft gefährdet.
3 Auf einem Umweltgipfel wurden Maßnahmen zur Verminderung von Treibhausgasen beschlossen.
4 Gute Fortschritte im Bereich Umwelt sind gemacht worden.
5 In einigen Industrieländern wurden Gesetze verabschiedet, die alternative Energien fördern sollen.
6 Gelder wurden bereitgestellt, um die Folgen der globalen Erwärmung genauer zu erforschen.
7 Man hofft, dass der Klimawandel gestoppt werden kann.
8 Eine Vielzahl von Pflanzen und Tieren könnte ausgelöscht werden, falls sich die Erde weiterhin erwärmt.

WATCH OUT!

False friends

Language check p210

~~Spare~~ the planet! ➤ Save the planet!

Choose the correct words from the brackets. Change the form if necessary.

Alternative energy is a very …[1] (current/actual) issue. Fuel Cells Innovative, a British energy company, are sure to …[2] (become/get) a prize for launching the most interesting earth-friendly product of the year. In the …[3] (meaning/opinion) of the jury, the new fuel cells are very innovative and a step in the right direction. Some people …[4] (think/mean) that we …[5] (mustn't/needn't) change from conventional to alternative energy forms but Martin Taylor, the …[6] (chef/boss) of Fuel Cells Innovative says that these people are wrong.

Vocabulary review

Complete the text below with these words. Use a capital letter when necessary.

acid rain • challenge • conservation • destroy
environmentalists • fossil fuels • hydro-electric
greenhouse effect • pollution • wind turbines

Since the 1960s, …[1] have been arguing that we must all pay more attention to the …[2] of our planet. If we don't make some radical changes to our modern industrialized lifestyle, they argue, we'll …[3] all the natural treasures of the earth, and there will be nothing left for future generations. … …[4] and the …[5] are just two signs that action is needed now to protect our environment from further damage. Will we be able to rise to the …[6]?

Using alternative sources of energy, such as …[7] power and … …[8] can also help to reduce our dependence on …[9], which cause enormous amounts of …[10].

9 High tech

FOCUS

1 **What roles do devices like these play in your life? Talk in groups.**

a

b

c

d

e

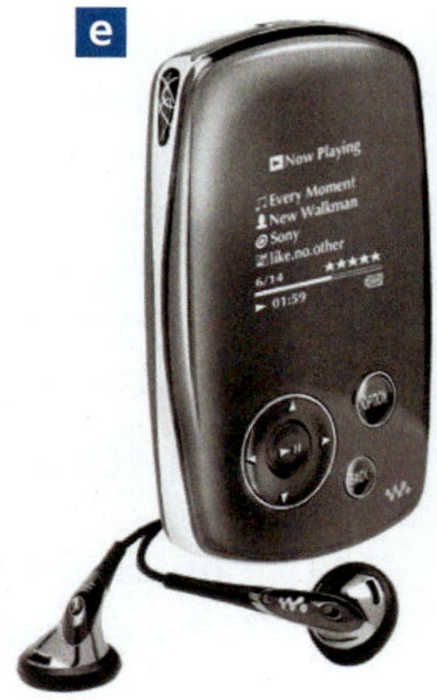

2 **Talk about the benefits and any drawbacks of these devices.**

3 **Do you feel that mobile phones make you too available to people who may want something from you? In your group, explain why or why not.**

I don't like it when …

You don't have to speak to … if you don't want to.

I don't mind getting calls at …

I hate getting calls from …

TEXT 1

Reading skills p170/171

Dances with robots

CD2/11

Dances with robots

Japan is working on a new generation of humanoid robots that may once and for all change the way we relate to machines.

Norihiro Hagita, a Japanese robotocist, recently put a three-year-old girl and her mother into a room with a robot and kept them there for two hours. At first, the girl and the robot chatted and played together. When the robot asked her to give him a hug, the girl happily complied. But after a time, the two of them ran out of new things to do, and the little girl plopped down on the floor for a nap. The robot waited to make sure the girl had truly lost interest, then approached her mother and struck up a conversation.

'Now here's the interesting part,' says Hagita, pointing to the girl on videotape. 'See how she sits up and watches? The robot is interacting with her mother and that's got her upset.' He can't help but grin. 'The robot has made her jealous.'

While engineers in most parts of the world try to make robots that perform specific and usually unpleasant tasks, from fighting wars to performing deep-sea salvage, Japanese engineers are obsessed with making the machines more human. Having put the country squarely in the lead in the industrial robot market for the past two decades, they're now working on a new generation of robots that will serve as playmates, pets and social workers. Hagita says, 'The goal is to build an intelligent environment for the symbiosis of robots and humans in everyday life. The real challenge is to come up with robots that can actually communicate with people.'

The key is to solve the enormous number of technical problems that stand in the way of making robots that are easy to live with – everything from understanding speech and gestures to making eye contact and having an awareness of a human's 'personal space'. Roboticists in Japan talk about a machine's 'social intelligence' or 'shared experience'.

The first members of the new humanoid generation are having a sort

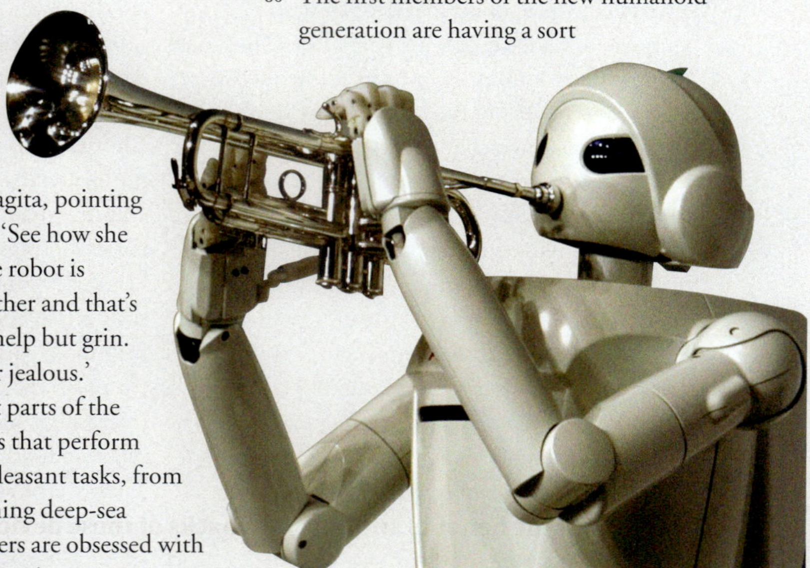

of coming-out party at the current World Expo in Aichi. Guests are welcomed by an android female receptionist who speaks 30,000 phrases in four languages and even knows how to defend herself against unwelcome advances from male homo sapiens. Toyota's so-called 'Partner' robots, which play musical instruments using artificial lips and lungs, have been drawing sell-out crowds at their concerts. Although these robots are a big improvement over the clunky devices of a few years ago, they're only a first draft. Scientists working in the laboratory are readying a new army of even more sensitive machines.

Giving robots a sense of touch is an important way of making them more human. At a research lab near Kyoto, Hagita and his colleagues are working on outfitting a prototype robot with authentic-looking skin fitted with thousands of tiny sensors. When you touch the robot on the back, it turns around and greets you.

Getting robots to understand real-life human speech may be the hardest job of all. Separating words from background noises and recognizing grammatical usage of words has proved to be a formidable problem. For this reason, scientists are trying to give robots means other than language to understand what people are telling them. One promising technology is intended to help robots figure out the relationships among the human partners they converse with. Hagita and his colleagues are programming the robots to note how long people spend with each other in a room and to take friendships among people into account when communicating with them. Understanding the variety of gestures and signs that people use to supplement language would help, too. Scientists thus hope that they will finally be able to program robots in a way that will help them understand that a smiling human is probably happy, while a frowning one usually isn't.

Wireless ID tags are another rich potential source of information. At a trade fair, a robotic receptionist could use ID tags to identify visitors and acquire information about them – what sort of work they do, where they're from and so on. Hagita's researchers have already used them during a trial in an elementary

school, where kids who had been equipped with the tags were surprised when the robots addressed them by name. Hagita joyfully recalls one sixth-grader who boasted to his friend that the robot 'likes me better' because the robot addressed him by name more often than the other boy. Other children told researchers that they felt sorry for the robot because no other children were playing with it. 'This is also a human relationship,' says Hagita. 'We've developed an agent. He's already a kind of human simulation.'

The tendency to regard life-like machines as unthreatening may have deeper roots in Japan's culture, where inanimate objects, ranging from teapots to Samurai swords, can have souls. The fact that Japanese researchers are now concentrating on future applications may also have to do with demographic developments: as the population ages, the Japanese are increasingly looking toward robots to help make up for the labor shortfall.

The government is promoting projects that have social applications, like nursing or child care. That may well give a push to the development of humanoids – for if robots are doing social work, they'll have to look and act considerably more like people than they do right now. And if Hagita and his colleagues have their way, that will happen sooner than you think.

910 words, adapted from *Newsweek*, 9 May 2005

1 Looking at the text

A Choose the most suitable answer.

1 The main intention of the author is to inform the reader about how
a things are developing in the field of industrial robots.
b new developments are making it easier for children to get on with robots.
c Japanese engineers are trying to design robots that have human traits.
d the Japanese are way ahead of engineers in other parts of the world.

2 According to the information in lines 26–41, Japanese engineers are no longer interested in developing robots that do unpleasant tasks because they
a know that other nations are now specializing in such fields.
b have recognized that such tasks are a thing of the past.
c consider themselves too good for such trivial tasks.
d are now pursuing a different concept.

3 Which of the following is **not** expressly mentioned in lines 42–65?
a The new generation of robots is more compact than former generations were.
b Making a robot comprehend human behaviour is still a difficult task.
c The concerts given by Toyota's 'Partner' robots are always full.
d The robotic receptionist at the World Expo is not able to deal with rude men.

4 When the author speaks of a 'coming-out party' (line 52), he is referring to
a a festivity at which the new robots reveal their secret inclinations.
b the fact that the new robots are presented to the public for the first time.
c a festivity held out-of-doors.
d a celebration at which roboticists discuss the latest advances in their field.

5 The author believes that ID tags (line 94) are a promising development because they
a simplify communication between robots and people.
b help engineers find out what projects their competitors are working on.
c make children less suspicious of robots.
d help robots learn from one another.

6 In lines 100–101 we learn that at an elementary school robots were put into service
a permanently.
b simultaneously.
c temporarily.
d unintentionally.

B Beantworten Sie die folgenden Fragen stichpunktartig auf Deutsch.

1 Welche unterschiedliche Zielsetzungen bei der Entwicklung neuer Roboter verfolgen die japanischen Ingenieure im Vergleich zu Ingenieuren in vielen anderen Industriestaaten?
2 Wie versuchen Wissenschaftler sicherzustellen, dass Roboter auf Menschen angemessen reagieren?
3 Wie lässt sich das Interesse der Japaner an Robotern und deren Weiterentwicklung erklären?

2 Working with words

A Match the following verbal phrases (1–6) with six of the appropriate explanations (a–i). There are three more explanations than you need.

1 to strike up (a conversation) (lines 17/18)
2 to come up with (lines 39/40)
3 to take (friendships) into account (lines 85/86)
4 to range from … to (lines 115/116)
5 to make up for (lines 121/122)
6 to have one's way (line 130)

a to make progress with
b to include a large variety of different things
c to start
d to produce
e to consider
f to be able to do what one wants to do
g to refuse to take part in
h to invent
i to compensate for

B You are telling a friend about *Dancing with robots.* Complete this gapped summary with words from lines 5–65 and lines 123–131.

The author claims that if children find that the robots they have made friends with are …[1] with other people, the children can actually become …[2] of these people. Now that the Japanese are the leading nation when it comes to the production of industrial robots, they are …[3] with developing robots that have … …[4] and which are …[5] to human feelings. Japanese roboticists are convinced that such robots will have many …[6] in fields in which there will soon be an acute shortage of manpower.

3 Writing

Text production p184

Describe the trends shown for the years 2002–2007. Write 80–100 words.

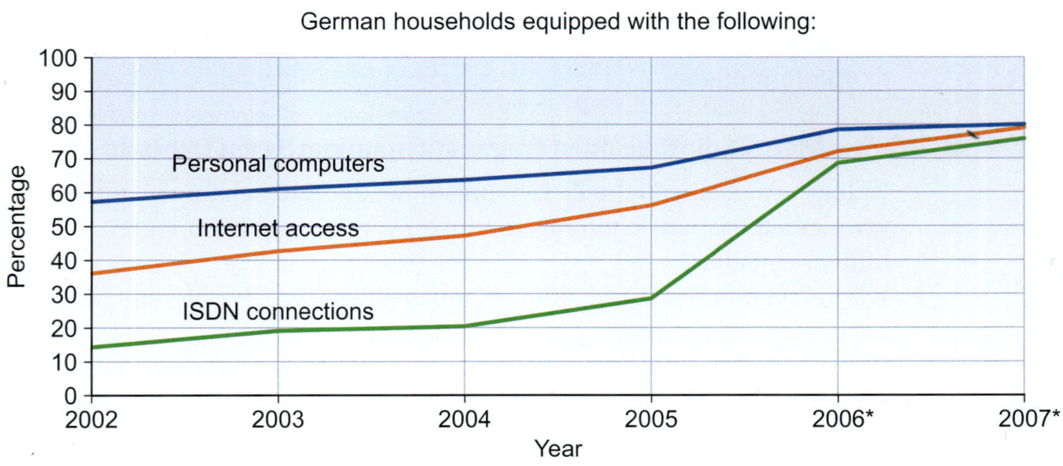

Source: http://www.destatis.de/print_e.php
* estimated figures

TEXT 2

Reading skills p170/171

CD2/12

Using global warming to create conditions for life on Mars

Injecting synthetic 'super' greenhouse gases into the Martian atmosphere could raise the planet's temperature enough to melt polar icecaps and create conditions suitable for sustaining biological life. In fact, a team of researchers suggests that introducing global warming on the Red Planet may be the best approach for warming the planet's frozen landscape and turning it into a habitable world in the future.

Scientists at the NASA Ames Research Center propose that the same types of atmospheric interactions that have led to recent surface temperature warming trends on Earth could be harnessed on Mars to create another biologically hospitable environment in the solar system. In a recent issue of Journal of Geophysical Research – Planets, published by the American Geophysical Union, the researchers report on the thermal energy absorption and the potential surface temperature effects which might occur if gases which are strong enough to melt carbon dioxide and ice are introduced on Mars.

'Bringing life to Mars and studying its growth would contribute to our understanding of evolution, and the ability of life to adapt and proliferate on other worlds,' Margarita Marinova, one of the NASA researchers said. 'Since warming Mars effectively reverts it to its past, more habitable state, this would give any possibly dormant life on Mars a chance to be revived and developed further.'

The researchers note that artificially created gases – which would be nearly 10,000 times more effective in generating a greenhouse effect than carbon dioxide – could be manufactured so that they only have minimal detrimental effects on living organisms and the ozone layer that would develop on the Red Planet if these gases were introduced. Damage would be low even if these artificially created gases retained an exceptionally long lifespan in the environment, which is what many scientists now assume. To back up their theory, the team of researchers created a computer model of the Martian atmosphere and analyzed four such gases, individually and in combination, that are considered the best candidates for the job.

Their study focused on fluorine-based gases, composed of elements readily available on the Martian surface, that are known to be effective at absorbing thermal infrared energy. The researchers anticipate that adding approximately 300 parts per million of the gas mixture to the current Martian atmosphere would spark an instantaneous, self-perpetuating greenhouse effect, creating an instability in the polar ice sheets that would slowly evaporate the frozen carbon dioxide on the planet's surface. They add that the release of increasing amounts of carbon dioxide would lead to further melting and global temperature increases that could then enhance atmospheric pressure and eventually restore a thicker atmosphere to the planet.

As the raw materials for the fluorine gases already exist on Mars, it is possible that astronauts could create those gases on a manned mission to the planet. It would otherwise be impossible to deliver extremely large quantities of these gases to Mars. The scientists conclude that introducing powerful greenhouse gases is the most feasible technique for raising the temperature and increasing the atmospheric pressure on Mars, particularly when compared to other alternatives like sprinkling sunlight-absorbing dust on the poles or placing large mirrors in the planet's orbit.

525 words, adapted from SpaceRef, www.spaceref.com/news/viewp.html?pid=16055

4 Looking at the text

A Complete these sentences, based on information from the text. Make any changes necessary so that your responses match the introductory statements.

The first sentence has been completed for you.

1 Mars could be turned into an environment suitable for human life by *introducing global warming*.
2 We might be able to understand how life developed over billions of years and how it could develop on other planets in the future if we managed to … and to … .
3 Restoring the original atmosphere on Mars would make it possible for organisms which are presently inactive to be … .
4 Although the artificially-produced gases might be around for a long time, they would only … .
5 The gases the researchers have in mind could be produced from … .
6 An introduction of newly-designed greenhouse gases on Mars would immediately cause … .
7 It's clear that astronauts would have to create the gases on Mars during a manned mission because it would otherwise … .
8 In comparison to other ideas that scientists are currently thinking of, bringing highly-effective gases to Mars is … .

B Find the English equivalents of these German words or phrases.

lines 1–24

aufrechterhalten
Forscher
Vorgehensweise
bewohnbar
(chemische) Reaktionen
nutzbar machen
lebensfördernd

lines 25–49

sich anpassen
sich vermehren
den ursprünglichen Zustand wiederherstellen
vorübergehend inaktiv
wiederbeleben
schädlich
annehmen (vermuten)

lines 50–80

selbsttragend zum Verdunsten bringen verstärken wiederherstellen
schlussfolgern praktikabel/machbar Umlaufbahn

5 Listening

Listening skills p185

CD2/13

Listen to this debate on the pros and cons of conducting space research and do the tasks below. The speakers are Dr Christian Konrad, who works for the European Space Agency, and Andrea Coulter, a British environmentalist.

A Decide if these statements are true or false. Correct the false statements.

1 Dr Konrad says that mankind is not naturally curious about the universe.
2 He is of the opinion that it took people on Earth a while to really appreciate the significance of manned space flights.
3 According to Ms Coulter, the space programme is a waste of time and effort and should not be continued, even if we do manage to overcome all our difficulties on Earth.
4 She claims that Dr Konrad's current space programme is simply intended to make NASA look good.
5 Dr Konrad says that most people would be willing to do without many of the practical applications that can be gained as a result of space flights.
6 Ms Coulter says that the satellites which orbit the Earth are of no benefit to Mankind. Long voyages into space are useful, though.

B Copy these headings into your exercise book. Then listen again and make lists.

Benefits arising from space exploration

Problems on earth which should be dealt with first

C In groups talk about other problems which should take priority over space exploration. Tell the class.

CROSS-CULTURAL SPOTLIGHT

Ambitions in space research all over the world

Did you know that it's not just America, Russia and Europe who launch missions into space? Canada, Brazil, Japan, China, India and even Nigeria also have their own space programmes.

In 2003, Nigeria launched NigeriaSat1, its first satellite, at an estimated cost of $13 million. Although this seems very little in comparison to NASA's annual budget of $15.3 billion, this is a vast amount of money for one of the poorest countries on earth. People may ask if this expenditure should be allowed in a country where 60% of the population live below the poverty line.

However, space research can be used to improve the quality of people's lives on earth, for example through improved telecommunications. Also, farmers can sometimes use satellite pictures to improve the efficiency of their farms – this is called *Precision Agriculture.*

6 Talking

Group discussions p186

Choose <u>one</u> of these tasks and talk in groups.

A In groups, rank the usefulness and desirability of these possible applications of wireless technology. Add more ideas. Report to the class.

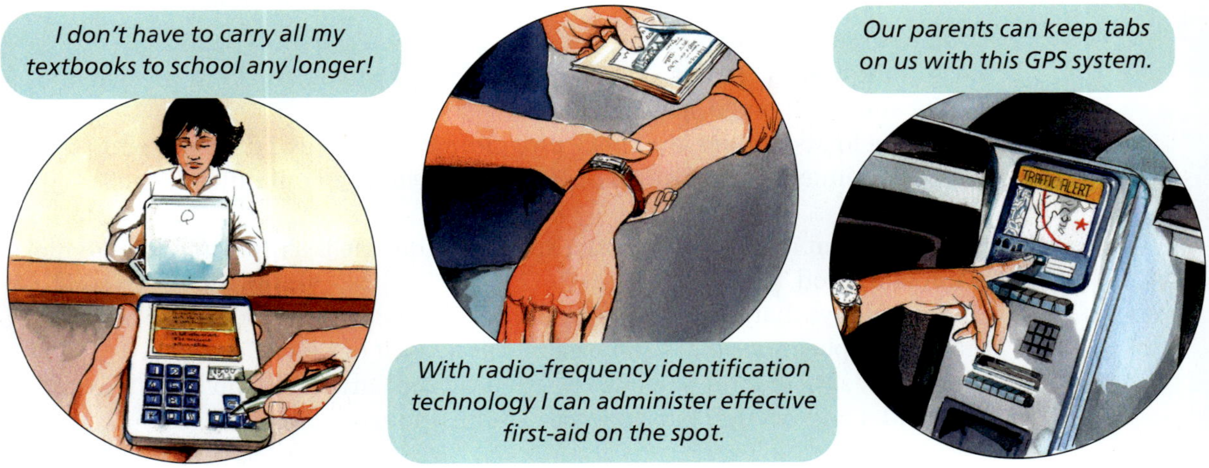

B Discuss these questions in groups. Report your ideas to the class.

- Is it right for certain governments to be spending billions on space exploration when we are confronted with enormous problems on our own planet? Why / Why not?
- Could you imagine living on a space station if given the opportunity? Why / Why not? What changes would you have to make to adapt to your new environment?

7 Writing

Text production p183

Describe and interpret this cartoon entitled *Robot looking for ice on Mars*. Write about 100 words.

8 Language – reported speech

SPOT THE MISTAKES

Spot the mistakes and correct them. Explain why they are wrong.

1 ~~The roboticist told the press that he has developed a new 'Partner' robot.~~
2 ~~The robot asked me if I will play with him.~~
3 ~~NASA reported one hour ago that the shuttle has landed.~~
4 ~~An African leader said that his country will turn to space exploration soon.~~
5 ~~Did the astronauts report that they are repairing the spacecraft~~?

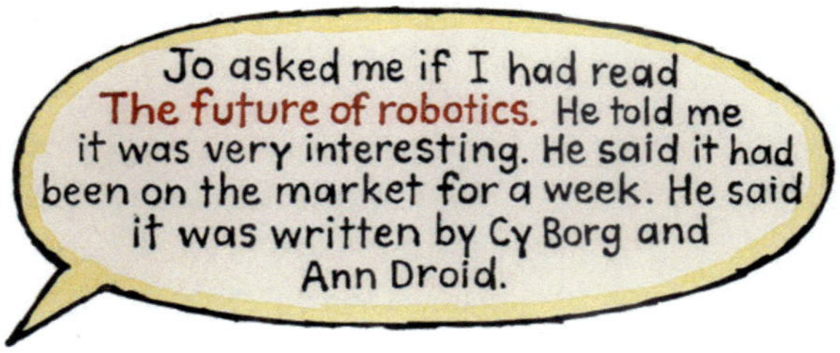

Reported speech

Jo asked me if I had read …
He told me it was very interesting.
He said it had been on the market for a week.
He said it was written …

Language check p197

1 Report the following things which you have read in the newspaper.

1 Every household in the UK will soon have its own 'Servant' robot.
→ *A robotics engineer told the press that …*
2 Manufacturing costs for robots were lower in June than in March.
→ *The company reported that …*
3 One of the top roboticists in Japan has decided to retire.
→ *A report in last month's Scientific American said that …*
4 Surveillance cameras have been used in Britain for a long time.
→ *The chief of security said that …*
5 The two astronauts are going into space again next month.
→ *The headline in yesterday's paper said that …*
6 NASA has landed an exploration crew on Saturn.
→ *An article in last Sunday's paper claimed that …*

2 Report these questions.

1 Paul: Did you watch *Voyager* yesterday?
Paul asked me …
2 Iris: Do you know where the robot exhibition is taking place?
Iris asked me …
3 Manuel: When are we going to get a homework robot, Mum?
On Saturday Manuel asked his mum …
4 Mary: Is Carol going to the Science Museum with you, Will?
Two weeks ago Mary asked Will …
5 Jamie: Can you help me with my computer, please, Angela?
Yesterday Jamie asked Angela …
6 Rose: Could I borrow your 2001 DVD next weekend, please?
On Monday Rose asked me …

WATCH OUT!

'wie' / 'als'

High-tech buyers are not spending as much money ~~than~~ in the past.	➤ High-tech buyers are not spending as much money as in the past.
Mr Hagita used to work ~~like~~ a computer scientist.	➤ Mr Hagita used to work as a computer scientist.
I think that other planets should be left ~~how~~ they are.	➤ I think that other planets should be left as they are.
For the producers of industrial robots, the situation is not ~~as~~ the one they were faced with some years ago.	➤ For the producers of industrial robots, the situation is not like the one they were faced with some years ago. (= … is not the same as …)
Dr Konrad, ESA's chief scientist, presented his arguments ~~like~~ an expert on space exploration.	➤ Dr Konrad presented his arguments as an expert on space exploration. (= He really was an expert.)
Ms Coulter presented her arguments ~~as~~ a long-time expert in this field.	➤ Ms Coulter presented her arguments like a long-time expert in this field. (= She wasn't an expert.)

Translate the following sentences into English.

1 RFID verspricht, das Leben wie keine andere Technologie zu verändern.
2 Bill Gates ist der Meinung, dass Unternehmer ebenso viel Grund hätten wie vor zehn Jahren, neue Computer zu kaufen.
3 Der Artikel des Autors klang so, als wäre er ein absoluter Befürworter der Raumfahrt.
4 Der Hobbyastronom hielt eine Rede wie ein renommierter Wissenschaftler.
5 Heute begeistert sich Herr Hagita für die Industrieroboter-Branche nicht mehr so wie vor Jahren.
6 Manche Skeptiker meinen, man solle die Atmosphäre des Mars so lassen, wie sie ist.
7 Margarita Marinova trat als Sprecherin der NASA auf.

Vocabulary review

Copy and complete the table without looking back at the two main texts.

verb	noun	adjective
***	absorption	***
–	scientist	***
***	interaction	***
adapt	***	***
***	simulation	***
–	***	technical
***	instability	***
***	application	***
analyze	***	***
***	sensor	***

10 The developing world

FOCUS

1 Discuss possible reasons for the situation described below.

If you reduced the world's population to a village of 100 inhabitants,

6 of the people in the village would own 59% of the village's resources,

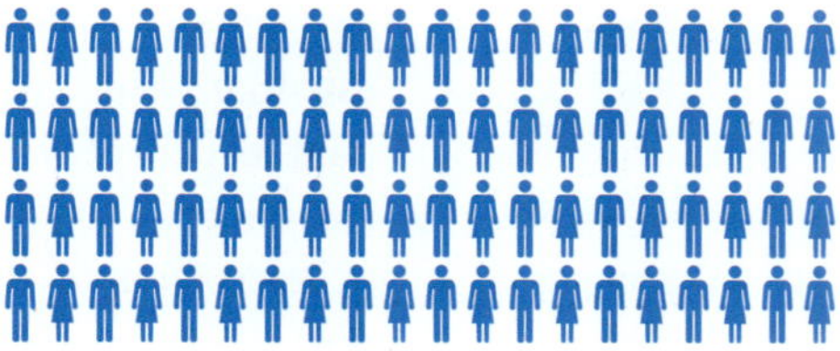

80 would be living in makeshift shelters without running water or proper sanitation,

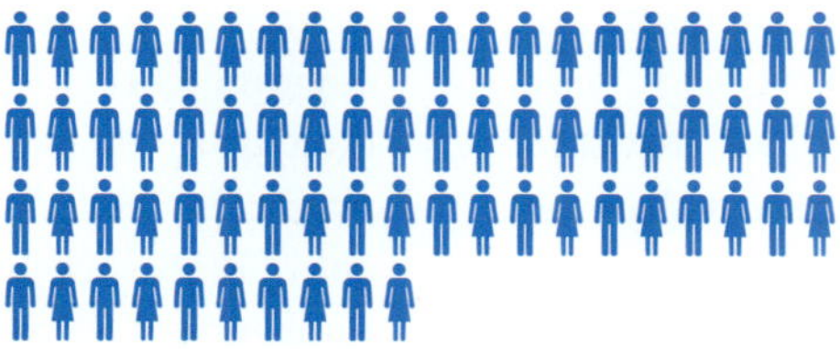

70 would be illiterate,

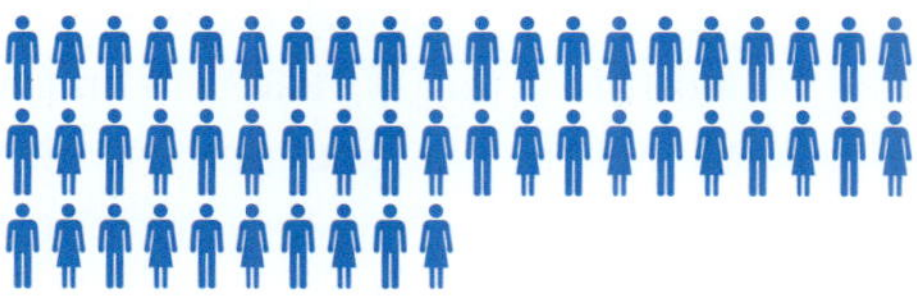

50 would be undernourished, if not actually starving.

2 Compare and contrast these photos.

TEXT 1

Reading skills p170/171

CD3/2

Three case studies

A Lagos, Nigeria

'Anything is possible in Lagos'

Lagos poet and musician 'AJ' Daga Tola lives in some of the worst urban conditions on earth. 'AJ' is an activist. The main road to his eight-foot-square shack in the Ajegunle slum is ankle-high in litter. The open drain down his alley overflows with black sewage. Fires smoulder below the nearby motorway bridge; permanently burned-out lorries and cars are dumped on either side of the road.

'Everyone here wakes up in anger,' says the man who has taken the initial letters of the slum as his first name. 'Day in, day out, poor people from all over Africa arrive in this place, still seeing Lagos as the land of opportunity. They are met at the bus stops by gangs of youths who demand payments. Only one in ten people have regular work.'

Roughly one million people live in Ajegunle – known in Lagos as 'Jungle City'. It is just one of many dozens of chaotic slum areas across the mega-city that now stretches over roughly 300 square kilometres. Some of the slums are built partly on water with families living an unhealthy existence in shacks balanced on stilts. All are dangerous, volatile and unhealthy.

There are few success stories; the main growth businesses in the ghetto, says AJ, are gangs and evangelical churches which promise a better life. 'The reality is that people must share rooms with 10 others,' says AJ. 'They have no rights as tenants. They have no ventilation, so they get ill. The drains do not work. It is abnormal to have electricity. The local, state and federal governments have all done nothing for us.'

Top priority for many communities is water and sanitation. 'Only 30% of the city has access to safe water,' says Olumuyiwa Coker, head of the newly privatized Lagos Water Corporation. He was staggered by what he found when he took office. 'More than 80% of the water was being stolen,' he says. Dr Tinubu, the state governor, has pledged to improve the water, fight corruption, clean up the waste and tackle the transport problem. Lagos, says the governor, has been abandoned by the world community. 'We are paying the price of corrupt leaders and businessmen. We have to convince people that Lagos is no longer run by corrupt people.' William Kingsmill, Britain's head of the Department for International Development in Nigeria, agrees. 'Nigeria has a track record of massive corruption. Debt relief is essential. The country has paid its debts twice over and still owes £35bn.'

Peter Ojumu, director of the local group Health Matters, says, 'The dreadful environment is linked directly to escalating health problems. Malaria, typhoid and TB, as well as sexually transmitted diseases, are all much more common now.'

Victor Omoshenin, a community worker, tries to see the situation from the bright side. 'A few years ago this community was even more dangerous,' he says. 'There was a high risk of stabbings, teenage pregnancies, fights, Aids. A lot of girls died after abortions done by the local chemist. But we started an education programme, set up a community clinic, listened to people and trained them to help themselves. In a few years it has improved a lot here. Anything is possible in Lagos.'

535 words, adapted from *The Guardian*, 5 March 2005

B Freetown, Sierra Leone

Desperation in Sierra Leone

In Brookfields, one of the many slums that climb the hills around Freetown in Sierra Leone, women and children with plastic containers of all shapes and sizes seek their daily water from a tiny trickle dripping from a crack in the rocks.

The air is filled with the smell of smoke and dust. Rather than attend school, groups of children work behind stalls, selling mangoes, bananas or cigarettes. Others play football or wander aimlessly between the shanties. Children make up almost half of the country's population. Many are malnourished with tell-tale swollen bellies.

Malaria, which results in death, is a major drag on the country's attempts to pull itself out of poverty. The disease, which can be prevented with a treated bed net costing less than £1, is endemic.

Most recent reports on life-expectancy give children born in Sierra Leone a 57.5% chance of not reaching 40 years of age. As for the country's schools, primary class sizes often exceed 100 and teachers often go unpaid for months.

When Sierra Leone won its independence in 1961, it was the second wealthiest nation in West Africa. After years of civil war, it is today the world's poorest, according to the UN.

197 words, adapted from *The Independent*, 18 January 2005

C Rumbek, Sudan

African schools become soup kitchens

School children are queuing in southern Sudan, near the war-ravaged town of Rumbek. The children are waiting in line, each child clutching a thin plastic cup. A teacher, who looks no more than a hungry child herself, carefully doles out a thin, grey maize-and-corn gruel that most parents in the West could never convince their children to eat. Each child gets one ladle of gruel, which they eat under the shade of the one tree in the dusty playground. It is the only meal they will get all day.

In the poorest parts of Africa, school teachers have learned that there is no point trying to educate children if their stomachs are empty. For this reason, schools have become soup kitchens, providing one meal a day for pupils who will not get anything to eat at home.

In villages where children are still seen as a source of cheap labour, schools that don't provide free meals take young workers away from the family farms while still leaving the parents with a hungry mouth to feed. Free school meals, however, keep pupils nourished; they thus encourage parents to send their children to school in the first place. Their children may not be working in the fields, but with a free school meal inside them, they are at least not going to take food out of the family pot.

228 words, adapted from *The Independent*, 18 January 2005

1 Looking at the texts

Text A

Match statements (a–h) with the corresponding speaker (1–6). Two statements do not match.

1 'AJ' Daga Tola
2 Olumuyiwa Coker
3 Dr Tinubu
4 William Kingsmill
5 Peter Ojumi
6 Victor Omoshenin

a What we've achieved shows that we should never give up hope.
b Global financial institutions are too greedy.
c Why do people come to Lagos? There is massive unemployment here.
d We will be able to pay back all of our loans within a few years.
e I'm worried about people drinking water that's unfit to drink.
f The living conditions of the inhabitants of Lagos are abominable; that's the root cause of all the diseases.
g If we want to receive outside aid, we have to prove that our government officials are honest.
h We are proud of the fact that we don't need help from abroad.

Text B

A volunteer worker summarizes the contents of Text B for a friend.
Complete the gapped summary with suitable words from the text.

The …[1] in the hills around Freetown are full of run-down houses. The children you see on the streets there during the day are obviously not …[2] school. You can easily tell that these kids are …[3] by looking at their bloated stomachs. If governments were to invest a very modest sum of money, many of the diseases that are so widespread would be …[4]. However, these illnesses are so …[5] that they, together with other factors, are to blame for the short …[6] of people in Sierra Leone. The country could be much richer if it hadn't squandered its resources in the years of the …[7] that started shortly after the country gained …[8].

Text C

Decide whether the following statements are true or false. Correct the false statements.

1 Teachers have to discipline the children who are queuing up for food.
2 The main challenge teachers in Sudan are confronted with is that they have to convince the school-children to eat.
3 The text describes in great detail the physical appearance of children who are undernourished.
4 Now that the children are offered free meals at school, their parents are more willing to let them attend school.
5 Many Sudanese teachers try to teach their students although they are fully aware that many of the children haven't yet had a meal on that school day.
6 The text says that free school meals are the prerequisite for children to be able to follow lessons at school.

2 Working with words

Find words or phrases in the three case studies that mean the same as the ones below.

'Anything is possible in Lagos'
a run-down area
b explosive
c no supply of fresh air
d dishonest

Desperation in Sierra Leone
e small stream of water
f underfed
g bloated
h the state of being poor

African schools become soup kitchens
i torn apart by fighting
j serving spoon
k inexpensive
l fed

CROSS-CULTURAL SPOTLIGHT

Women in industrialized and developing countries
In most industrialized nations, the law now states that men and women are born equal and should therefore have equal opportunities in education and employment. As a result, some (although not all) women have caught up with or even surpassed men in their academic and professional achievements. One result of women's liberation in the industrialized world has been a sharp decline in the birth rate. In contrast, the birth rate in developing countries is still very high. One of the reasons for this is the fact that most of the women have not gained equal rights with men. There is no equality of opportunity, they often lack basic education and few receive any formal professional training.

From a UN study, 2005
- *2005 – 6.5 billion people on earth*
- *2055 – 9.0 billion people on earth*
- *95% of this expected population growth will take place in developing countries*

UN demands for developing countries
- *primary school education (at least) for everybody*
- *sexual equality*
- *education and support in family planning*

3 Writing

Text production p175/180

Choose <u>one</u> of these tasks.
Write about 200 words.

1 Write an email to an American friend describing conditions in Lagos, Freetown or Rumbek. Use as many of the words from exercise 2 as possible.

2 Comment on this statement.

'When I give food to the poor, they call me a saint. When I ask why the poor have no food, they call me a communist.'
(Dom Hélder Camara, Brazilian priest)

Dom Hélder Camara

4 Project – looking at relief organizations

▶ Doing projects p189

In groups, investigate the work of one of the relief organizations listed below.

Here are some aspects you may want to look at:

- What parts of the world does the organization concentrate on?
- Who is it trying to help? How?
- How can volunteers get involved?
- What sort of tasks are they supposed to assume responsibility for?

The following websites may be useful.

Oxfam International: oxfam.org
International Federation of Red Cross and Red Crescent Societies: ifrc.org
CARE International: care.org
UNICEF (UN Children's Fund): unicef.org
WHO (World Health Organization): who.int
World Bank: worldbank.org
WFP (World Food Program): wfp.org
Peace Corps: peacecorps.org/
World Vision International: wvi.org
Catholic Relief Organization: catholicrelief.org
Australian Agency for International Development: ausaid.gov.au/

Present your findings to the class. Argue for your organization. Why is it the best / most important / most useful one?

5 Listening

▶ Listening skills p185

A **You are going to hear about some inventions that can make life in developing countries easier. Before you listen, decide with a partner what these things might be used for.**

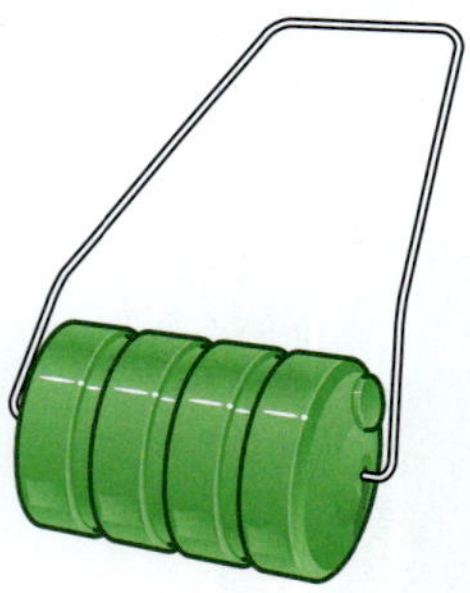

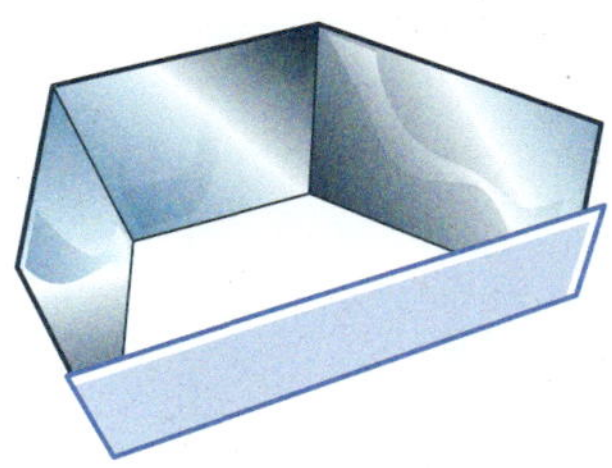

CD3/3

B **Now copy this table, listen, and complete the first two columns. Were your guesses correct?**

Name of invention	Description	Reason(s) for usefulness
***	***	***

C **Listen again and use the third column to write down why the inventions are useful.**

D **In groups, think up other inventions which might be of use in developing countries.**

TEXT 2

Reading skills p170/171

CD3/4

Fesito goes to market

Fesito, an African boy, is asked to take bananas to market because his father is ill. He sets off feeling very proud and self-confident, yet soon discovers that the task is more difficult than he anticipated. Things get worse when an old man, Musoke, asks him to put a load of pawpaws on the bike and take them to market as well. Fesito reluctantly agrees …

a Now the bike was even heavier, and Fesito's legs ached. He was disappointed. He had thought it would be very grand to go to market on his father's bicycle, but somehow it was very difficult. 'Still,' he thought, 'I am a man among men today. That is something.'

b The sun rose higher and soon there were many people on the road going to market. All along the sides of the road were women carrying water pots and children running behind them with hoops and sticks or small baskets of peanuts.

'Fesito, child! Wait a minute!'

He stopped. Who had called this time? Then he saw Kasiingi running up with three chickens hanging in a bunch, bound by the feet.

'Here, child, take my chickens to the market for me, please. It will save me much work. Be sure to bring me the right change – five shillings each. No, make the big one seven shillings.' Kasiingi held out the chickens.

'Do they think I'm a mule, to carry all their things?' thought Fesito. 'Would they do this to my father?'

c 'Kasiingi,' he said, 'where shall I carry three chickens with all these bananas and pawpaws?'

Kasiingi looked at the bundles. She screwed up her eyes and pointed to the top of the bananas. 'There child! There! Are you blind? There's room for ten chickens on top of your bananas!'

She took some banana-leaf twine and tied the three chickens on top of the bananas. Now the pile was so high Fesito could hardly reach the top with his hands.

'Mind you ride carefully! If my chickens arrive at the market dead, I shall tell your father!'

And he knew that Kasiingi never forgot to tell his father such things. He sighed and got onto the bicycle again.

'Weraba, Fesito! Don't forget my money!'

'Weraba, Kasiingi.'

d Now it was very hot. The sweat ran down his face and down his back under his shirt. His breath came in gasps. Would he get to market on time? It was farther than he'd thought. Every now and then he rode over a bump and the chickens clucked 'taaaaaak!' very crossly.

Presently he saw a small boy walking ahead of him. He was very thin and he walked slowly and not in a straight line. It was Kikyo. Kikyo had been very ill. Where was he going today?

'Eh, Kikyo!' he cried, riding up. 'Look at me! I'm taking the bananas to market. My father has the fever. Where are you going, Kikyo?'

'To the hospital, to get my medicine,' said Kikyo. 'Won't you let me ride with you, Fesito, please? My legs are tired already.'

'And where would you sit?' cried Fesito. All his crossness boiled up inside him. 'It is hard work for me with all these things. Old Musoke made me carry his pawpaws and Kasiingi made me carry her chickens. There is no room for mere children, Kikyo. Am I a pack mule to carry everyone to market? Use your own legs! Weraba!'

He rode on quickly, leaving Kikyo behind.

e But somehow Kikyo's face was still in front of him. Kikyo's eyes were big and his face was very sharp and thin. His ribs stuck out above his stomach and the joints of his legs were swollen, his arms and legs very thin. Should he not, after all, have taken Kikyo to the hospital? Kikyo had asked nicely. Kasiingo and old Musoke had not.

He sighed and stopped. He turned around and called, 'Kikyo! Come here quickly! Hurry! I'll take you to town if you sit very still and do not fall off. Hurry!'

Kikyo came shuffling up. 'Webali, Fesito. Thank you, my big friend.'

'Climb up and sit on the saddle,' said Fesito. 'And sit very still. If you wobble, the bicycle will topple over and everything will fall off.'

'Eh,' said Kikyo and climbed onto the saddle. He looked very pleased. 'Webali, my friend,' he said again. 'I shall sit as still as a mouse.'

f Fesito pushed and pushed. Only on the downhill could he ride. His legs and arms and back ached. It was as if the bicycle did not want to move at all. The road wavered like water in the heat and the screaming of the cicadas made his head swim. At last there was only one more hill to go.

Then Kikyo said, 'I'm hungry, Fesito. Can I take a banana?'

'No, they're to be sold at the market!' said Fesito. 'What will my father say if they're eaten on the way by children?'

'Eh,' said Kikyo. 'I see.'

But then Fesito thought of how thin Kikyo was. How small and hungry-looking. And he was only seven. He had suffered a lot for such a young one.

'Kikyo,' he said severely, 'you may take one banana. Only one! Take it very carefully and do not upset the pile.'

'Webali,' said Kikyo. He took a banana, peeled it, and began to eat. 'It is very good, Fesito. Webali.'

g And now they stood at the top of the hill that overlooked the town, lying red and brown between the yellow cassia trees. There were many people at the market under the mango trees. The men in their long robes stood talking and some were drinking beer. Women squatted by the stalls, their long bright dresses all the colors of the rainbow, like colorful birds resting in the shade.

'Eh, it is good to be going to market!' said Fesito. 'It is good to be a man among men, Kikyo.'

'Truly, Fesito, you are strong,' said Kikyo and took another bite of banana.

And Fesito's heart swelled out, big and full inside him, and he stood very straight as he looked down on the marketplace.

Just then there was loud laughter behind them. Fesito turned and saw Bosa, Kagwe, Waswa and Matabi run out from the bushes. He did not like Bosa and Bosa did not like him. He turned away from them and began to push the bicycle downhill.

1002 words, from Nelson Mandela's *Favourite African Folktales*, Tafelberg Publishers Ltd 2002

6 Looking at the text

A With a partner, match three of the following headings (1–5) with paragraphs (a–c). There are two more headings than you need.

1 Why do older people always know best?
2 They wouldn't treat my dad this way
3 Hop on board – there's plenty of room
4 Disappointment mixed with excitement
5 Don't count your chickens before they are hatched!

Now make up headings for paragraphs d–g. Tell the class. Which are the best / most suitable headings?

B Choose the correct explanation for these phrases from the text.

1 Make the big one seven shillings. (line 11)
 a Try to talk people at the market into paying seven shillings for the big chicken.
 b Charge seven shillings for the big chicken.
 c Try to make a profit of seven shillings on the big chicken.

2 She screwed up her eyes. (line 16)
 a Kasiingi squinted so that she could see the bananas more clearly.
 b She flashed Fesito a look of disappointment.
 c When she gazed up at the bananas, the glaring light hurt her eyes.

3 Presently he saw a small boy. (line 28)
 a Fesito watched a young boy.
 b Exactly at that moment, he saw a young boy.
 c After a short while he saw a young boy.

4 All his crossness boiled up inside him. (line 34)
 a Fesito was overcome by feelings of anger.
 b He was totally uncertain about which direction to take.
 c He was so confused that he felt hot.

5 Do not upset the pile. (lines 68/69)
 a Don't make the chickens nervous.
 b Make sure that nothing falls off.
 c Don't make the bicycle wobble.

6 Fesito's heart swelled out. (line 80)
 a Fesito was exhausted.
 b He was very scared.
 c Fesito was extremely proud of himself.

7 Talking

▶ Group discussions p186

In groups, make up an appropriate ending to *Fesito goes to market.* Make notes and tell the class. Which group has the most convincing ending?

8 Language – participle constructions

SPOT THE MISTAKES

Spot the mistakes and correct them. Explain why they are wrong.
(You may have to add a conjunction or preposition, e.g. *though*, *despite*, *with* or *while*.)

1 ~~Fetching water from a river for many years, some women in developing countries are now happy to be able to use the ©Hippo Rollers.~~
2 ~~Burdening with declining life expectancy, large parts of Africa are caught in a poverty trap.~~
3 ~~We teach them to cook, used the so-called 'boil-in-bag' technique.~~
4 ~~Faced with extreme destitution, many rural residents haven't given up hope.~~
5 ~~Life is becoming hard in the developing countries, many small farmers going out of business.~~
6 ~~Enjoying relatively high GNP growth rates, the USA is at present reluctant to lower its trade barriers.~~

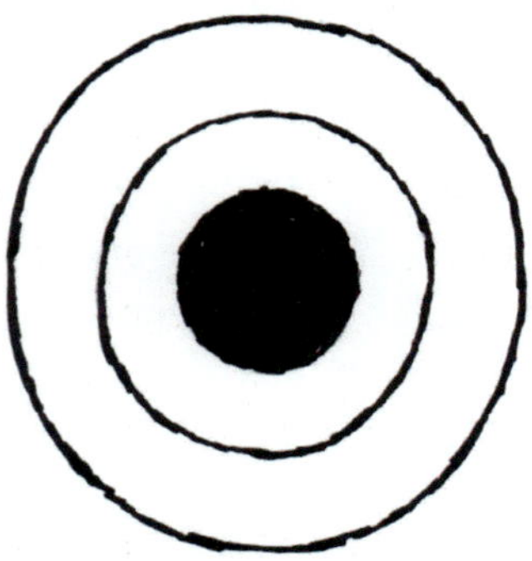

What is it?

A girl looking through a hole?
A fried egg lying on a plate?
A man wearing a hat, seen from above?

Participle constructions
A girl looking through a hole?
A fried egg lying on a plate?
A man wearing a hat, seen from above?

▶ Language check p204

1 Match the beginnings with the most appropriate endings.

EXAMPLE *1 + b Coordination of relief efforts is vital, with the United Nations assuming an important role.*

1 Coordination of relief efforts is vital,
2 Though convinced of the necessity of getting ahead,
3 If kept warm and fed from birth,
4 By fighting for free markets and fair trade,
5 New solar power stations have been introduced,

a many people are too weak to make the effort.
b with the United Nations assuming an important role.
c thus enabling independence from overland power grids.
d thus establishing lasting relationships with developing countries.
e we must make sure that they can sell their products for a fair price.

6 After showing the poor how to farm more effectively,
7 Although struggling hard to achieve fairer distribution of aid,
8 Local charities could adopt specific projects,

f many babies with low birth weight could be saved.
g Britain can pursue the goal of lifting people out of poverty.
h the British government is still far from reaching this goal.

2 Expand these sentences to replace the participles with relative clauses. (Sentence 4 requires two changes.)

1 The doctor leading the hygiene awareness campaign demands quick action.
2 Tetanus, virtually unseen in babies in the west, kills a million of them a year elsewhere.
3 The paper published today claims that high newborn mortality is due to a shortage of midwives.
4 He is holding a small bag containing the money collected in charity actions.
5 More than half the children born in Sierra Leone today will never reach the age of 40.
6 The high tariffs favoured by American farmers restrict export income in developing countries.

3 Show that you understand these sentences by expanding the *adverbial participle* clauses into a fuller statement.

EXAMPLE *Threatened by famine,* many children will do anything to get food.
As many children are threatened by famine, they will do anything to get food.

1 Groups of peasants work on the dusty fields, *weeding the rows of sparse corn.*
2 Small countries like Denmark have increased their development aid, *thus prompting others to follow their example.*
3 *Often securing lucrative deals through bribes,* western companies are as responsible for corruption as African governments.
4 *While watching the environment deteriorate in the Amazon basin,* enlightened Brazilians lose hope.
5 *With environmentalists concerned about sustainable growth in Latin America,* they call for a curb on logging.
6 *After learning that 80% of safe water in Lagos was being stolen,* the governor pledged to improve the situation.

4 Translate the following sentences into English, using participle constructions.

1 Obwohl der Westen offiziell die Idee der freien Marktwirtschaft befürwortet, hält er die Handelsschranken gegenüber Produkten der 3. Welt aufrecht.
2 Nachdem Experten ihre Hoffnung zuvor auf Hilfsprogramme setzten, sagen sie inzwischen mehr Wohlstand für Entwicklungsländer durch weitere Öffnung ihrer Märkte voraus.
3 Wenn den Entwicklungsländern faire Chancen auf dem Weltmarkt eingeräumt würden, könnten sie in wenigen Jahrzehnten der Armutsfalle entrinnen.
4 Da die amerikanische Regierung sich um die Interessen der Landwirte Sorgen macht, scheut sie vor diesem Schritt zurück.
5 Spenden sollten einen direkten Beitrag zur Selbstversorgung der Einwohner leisten und so dafür sorgen, dass die Gelder sinnvoll investiert werden.

WATCH OUT!

Language check p210

meaning / opinion

In my ~~meaning~~, the term 'development aid' is often misunderstood.	➤ In my opinion, the term 'development aid' is often misunderstood.
He is of the ~~meaning~~ that developing countries need more well-trained teachers.	➤ He is of the opinion that developing countries need more well-trained teachers.

Translate these sentences into English.

1 Ich bin der Meinung, dass es in unserem eigenen Interesse ist, den Entwicklungsländern zu helfen.
2 Manche Politiker scheinen die eigentliche Bedeutung des Begriffs „fairer Handel" nicht zu kennen.
3 Zu wenig Leute haben über die Art und Weise, wie Entwicklungshilfe am effektivsten geleistet werden kann, eine klare Meinung.
4 Sie wissen nicht, was es bedeutet, in Armut zu leben.

Vocabulary review

Complete the text using these words. Add capital letters where necessary.

difficult • disappointed • encouraging • expectancy • malnourished
medicine • preventable • relief • sanitation • suffer

…[1] children in developing countries with their swollen bellies are a sad sight to see. These children's families cannot afford to feed them and …[2] and other healthcare is also out of the question. Another reason why kids in developing countries …[3] is the prevalence of diseases such as malaria, which is in fact a …[4] illness. It is hardly surprising that the life …[5] of children born in the developing world is about half that of the average citizen living in an industrialized country. …[6] our government to offer help in the medical sector and to grant debt …[7] can only lead to an improvement in living conditions in developing countries if government corruption in these countries is also tackled.
Lack of educational opportunities and medical care in rural and war-ravaged areas cause many people to flee to urban areas. After arriving in the cities, they are often angry and …[8], finding themselves forced to live in extremely …[9] conditions in the slums. They are confronted with many new problems, e.g. poor …[10].

11

English spoken here

FOCUS

1 **Work in groups. You have two minutes to write down English words that are often used in German. Which group has the most words?**

2 **Stay in your group and do this quiz. Your teacher has the answers. How many answers did your group get right?**

Did you know?

Of the 100 words that experts recently listed as those that best reflect the 20th century in Germany, 15 are English words. Among them are words such as camping, jeans and stress.

Interested in finding out more facts and figures about the English language?

Have a guess!

1 The projected number of people around the world who will be reached by English within the coming decade is:

a 700,000,000 **b** 3,000,000,000 **c** 1,800,000,000

2 The percentage of books printed, of radio programmes broadcast and films released in English worldwide is:

a more than 25% **b** more than 35% **c** more than 50%

3 Match the following languages and the number of words they contain:

1 English	**a** 100,000
2 German	**b** 185,000
3 Spanish	**c** 616,500

4 The percentage of global computer text stored in English is:

a 47% **b** 62% **c** 80% **d** 99%

5 How many dialects does the English language have?

a 450 **b** 300 **c** 150 **d** 50

6 How many words does an English speaker need for an average conversation?

a 333 **b** 737 **c** 1,100 **d** 2,000

based on Richard Lederer, Doing a Number on English,
http://daphne.palomar.edu/jquintero/does/Doing/20a/20Number/20English.doc

TEXT 1

Reading skills p170/171

CD3/5

A talk given at the European Parliament

'Well, good evening, ladies and gentlemen. It's certainly a real pleasure to be with you tonight. The title of my talk is, "Europe's lingua franca?"
I have put this as a question because – like most things to do with Europe – it's not nearly as straightforward as you may think.

To begin with, the European Union is certainly democratic, at least when it comes to languages. All debates in the European Parliament and all documents – reports, laws, directives – have to be translated into twenty languages, including languages of at best "limited" use such as Latvian and Slovene. No wonder some of the Irish and the Catalans are now demanding that Irish Gaelic and Catalan become recognized EU languages.

In view of this, it won't surprise you to hear that the translation service is the most expensive of all the EU's activities after agriculture and regional development. We are in fact spending more money on translating and interpreting than on such desirable activities as environmental protection or aid to the developing world.

Still, most people at least agree on one thing: we can't go on like this. Something has to change. But what? And at whose cost? Well, one idea is that the EU should use just five so-called "European cultural languages", namely English, French, German, Italian and Spanish. Please note, by the way, the *alphabetical* order.

Now, this is fine if you happen to be a native speaker of one of these five languages, but it's pretty insulting if you're not. I'm sure, for example, that Scandinavians will be interested to hear that their greatest authors – Ibsen, Strindberg and Hans Christian Andersen – were not writing in "European cultural languages" at all, but, I suppose, in some strange Germanic dialects. And what about Portuguese, the language of the world's fourth largest country, Brazil, with its flourishing Nobel-Prize-winning literature? Is Portuguese not a "European cultural language"?

No, ladies and gentlemen, that's not going to work – and we *still* have a huge translation service. And that brings me to my main proposal tonight, and I do not apologize for it in any way. My proposal has, after all, a lot going for it: for one thing, it gets rid of the absurdly expensive and increasingly unworkable translation service; furthermore, it avoids the problem of dividing Europeans into two unequal classes by language; above all, it serves the needs of globalization.

My proposal is that English be officially recognized for what it indisputably is: the one and only truly pan-European language, as it is already recognized as the one and only truly world language.'

429 words, adapted from the transcript of a speech given in the European Parliament, November 2005

1 Looking at the text

A Answer the following questions. Give short answers.

1 Which two activities carried out by the EU are even more expensive than its translation service?
2 On which two activities mentioned by the speaker does the EU spend less money than on its translation service?
3 Why is Portuguese an important language even though it is not a 'European cultural language'?
4 What does the speaker propose at the end of the speech?
5 What does the proposal have going for it? Give three arguments.

B Geben Sie den Inhalt der folgenden Sätze auf Deutsch wieder. (Keine wortwörtliche Übersetzung.)

1 The title of my talk is … not nearly as straightforward as you may think. (lines 2/6)
2 This is fine if you happen to be a native speaker. (line 23)
3 My proposal has, after all, a lot going for it. (line 32)
4 It gets rid of the absurdly expensive and increasingly unworkable translation service. (lines 32/33)

C What is the point of the speaker mentioning Ibsen, Strindberg and Andersen? (line 25)

2 Working with words

Match the following words (1–6) with the corresponding German words (a–l) in the text. There are six more German words than you need.

1 interpret	3 note	5 insulting
2 desirable	4 pretty	6 indisputably

a hübsch	e unbestreitbar	i erstrebenswert
b notieren	f verwirrend	j indiskutabel
c übersetzen	g interpretieren	k beleidigend
d zur Kenntnis nehmen	h ziemlich	l hineinreden

▶ Group discussions p186

3 Talking

Talk in groups. What are the advantages / disadvantages of English as a world language? Tell the class your ideas, backing up your opinions with examples.

spelling

unite the world?

threat to other languages?

pop music

TEXT 2

Reading skills p170/171

CD3/6

Who owns English?

Non-native speakers transform the global language

a THE ENGLISH IMMERSION camp is built on a small island in the Yellow Sea. Subsidized by the provincial government, the camp comes complete with a Hollywood-style fake bank and airport, where students must conduct all transactions in English. 'Through the camp, we want to train capable global citizens, who can help Korea win international competitions in this age of globalization,' says the initiator of the program, Sohn Hak Kyu, Governor of the South Korean province where the camp is located.

WIN WITH ENGLISH

b Schools and institutions like the Korean camp are the front lines of a global revolution in which hundreds of millions of people are learning English, the planet's language for commerce, technology – and, increasingly, empowerment. From Caracas to Karachi, governments all over the world are pushing English, recognizing that along with computers, this language is the turbine engine of globalization. As one 12-year-old self-taught English speaker from China's southwestern Sichuan province says, 'If you can't speak English, it's like you're deaf and dumb.' To achieve fluency, non-native speakers are learning English at an ever-younger age. Last year primary schools in major Chinese cities began offering English in the third grade, rather than middle school. Some pregnant women even go as far as to speak English to their fetuses.

c For people all over the world, English has become the common linguistic denominator. Whether you're a Korean executive on business in Shanghai, a German Eurocrat hammering out laws in Brussels or a Brazilian biochemist at a conference in Sweden, you're probably speaking English. But despite – or perhaps because of – all the new variations of English which are emerging, it's the American and British versions (AE and BE) that still carry prestige. Given the fact that AE and BE are so popular, it is not surprising that more than 400 English-teaching companies are trying to break into China. On a recent visit to Bejing, the British Chancellor of the Exchequer Gordon Brown said the Chinese thirst to acquire English language skills was 'a huge opportunity for Britain,' which already boasts a £1.3 billion English-teaching industry. Linguist Jennifer Jenkins, an expert in world 'Englishes' at King's College London, says: 'Owning English is very big business.'

DOES YOUR ENGLISH EMBARRASS YOU?

d To see big business in action, one need only walk down London's busy Oxford Street, where ads promise instant access to the language of success. Above clothing stores, bustling English-language schools are packed with eager twenty-somethings from around the world. In one class that includes a South Korean business manager, a nurse from rural Japan and an Italian law student, the teacher asks: 'Do you want a lot of homework or a little?' The class is unequivocal: 'A lot!'

BUSINESS ENGLISH FOR BEGINNERS.

e

Why such enthusiasm? In a word, jobs. A generation ago, only the elite – diplomats, CEOs, etc. – needed English for work. That is changing quickly. 'Throughout organizations, more people need more English,' says David Graddol, author of the British Council report. In China, the Beijing organizing committee for the 2008 Olympics is pushing English among staff, guides, taxi drivers and ordinary citizens. For the lower-middle classes in India, English can mean a ticket to a prized call-center job. 'With call centers, speaking English is no longer *one* of the important skills needed to get a good job,' says Raghu Prakash, who runs an English-language school in Jaipur. 'It is *the* skill.' At the new Toyota-Peugeot plant in the Czech Republic, English is the working language of the Japanese, French and Czech staff. Jitka Prikrylova, director of a Prague English-language school, says: 'The world has opened up for us, and English is its language.'

f Technology also plays a huge role in the global triumph of English. Eighty percent of the electronically stored information in the world is in English and, according to the British Council, 66% of the world's scientists read in it. 'It's very important to learn English because (computer) books are only in English,' says Umberto Duirte, a Uruguayan IT student learning English in London. New technologies are helping people pick up the language, too: Chinese and Japanese students can get English-usage tips on their mobile phones. English-language teachers point to the rise of Microsoft English, where computer users are drafting letters, advised by the Window's spell check and pop-up style guides.

LEARN ENGLISH IN JUST 10 WEEKS!

g

All languages are 'works in progress'. But English's globalization, unprecedented in the history of languages, will revolutionize it in ways we can only begin to imagine. With native speakers a shrinking minority of the world's Anglophones, there's a growing sense that students should stop trying to emulate Brighton or Boston English, and embrace their own local versions. In a generation's time, teachers might no longer be correcting students for saying 'a book who' or 'a person which'. Jennifer Jenkins asks why some Asians, who have trouble pronouncing the 'th' sound, should spend hours trying to say 'thing' instead of 'sing' or 'ting'.

h

Not everyone is happy about English, or its advance. As the world adopts an international brand of English, it might be the native speakers who are losing out. Cambridge University professors who insist on speaking the Queen's English could be met with giggles – or blank stares. British or American business executives who jabber on in their own idiomatic English, without understanding how English is used by non-natives, might lose out on business deals. But it's not only the native speakers who are worried. The website of the Association for the Defense of the French Language displays a 'museum of horrors' – a series of digital pictures of English-language signs from Parisian streets. Others, however, say such defensiveness misses the point. 'This is not about English swamping and eroding local identities,' says David Graddol. 'It's about creating new identities – and about making everyone bilingual.'

955 words, adapted from *Newsweek*, 7 March 2005

4 Looking at the text

A Choose the most suitable answer.

1 The purpose of the article is to show
  a how learning English can make people happy.
  b the reasons for and effects of the internationalization of English.
  c that very soon, BE and AE will no longer have much influence.
  d which economic developments can influence a language.

2 The best headline for paragraph **a** is:
  a Korean island tries to lure tourists by creating Hollywood-like setting.
  b Korea subsidizes camp to train kids interested in government careers.
  c Young Koreans get familiar with global institutions.
  d English taught at camp imitating settings in which English is normally used.

3 Which of the following ideas concerning globalization is **not** expressly mentioned in paragraph **b**?
  a It is based on the spread of English.
  b It has led to changes in the field of education.
  c It has resulted in higher production figures for computers.
  d It makes people want to learn English at an ever earlier age.

4 The expression 'common linguistic denominator' in paragraph **c** means that
  a Britain can profit from the wish of millions to acquire English language skills.
  b the ways in which people do their jobs around the world are becoming increasingly similar.
  c all varieties of English spoken around the world are treated as equals.
  d many people around the world share the ability to speak English, no matter what they do professionally.

5 The best heading for paragraph **f** is:
  a Understanding English is a prerequisite for understanding technology.
  b New technologies help people to learn English.
  c New technologies and English language skills are interdependent.
  d Global triumph of English is reflected by impressive statistics.

6 The best heading for paragraph **g** is:
  a Languages are always changing.
  b The share of native speakers of English is decreasing.
  c Local versions of English are developing.
  d The coming changes in English usage may have to be accepted.

7 In paragraph **h**, the author says that in the future, company officials who speak traditional AE and BE may be the losers because
  a other English speakers will be disgusted by their antiquated way of speaking.
  b English speakers in other parts of the world will discriminate against them.
  c foreign business partners will find their way of speaking so old-fashioned that these foreigners will be terrified of doing business with them.
  d they won't really understand people who use English in new ways, thus missing out on new business opportunities.

B A German student is reporting on the contents of the text to her English teacher. Complete this summary with appropriate words from paragraphs c, d and e.

All over the world, English is …[1] in a variety of new forms. However, the fact that so many Chinese are yearning to …[2] language skills taught by British and American language schools shows that AE and BE still have a lot of …[3]. One …[4] whose job it is to evaluate the usage of English around the globe states that a lot of money can be made by teaching English to foreign students. Those who want to gain …[5] to the English language and not be …[6] by lack of skills, have the opportunity to attend one of many schools in London where classes are frequently …[7] with ambitious students. If we take a look at Asia, we find that working in a …[8] is something that many young people aspire to.

C Match the people mentioned in the text (1–6) with the appropriate statements (a–i). There are three more statements than you need.

1 David Graddol
2 Gordon Brown
3 Jennifer Jenkins
4 Raghu Prakash
5 Umberto Duirte
6 Sohn Hak Kyu

a Only if we prepare students well, will we be able to keep up with the progress being made in other countries.
b If I didn't have this skill, I could never keep up with the latest developments in the field of computer science.
c I admire these people for the dedication they devote to learning English as quickly as possible.
d I would see it as a chance for people around the world to experience life in a totally different way.
e This is the decisive prerequisite for employees to have a promising start in the labour market.
f Everyone I know speaks English. I would feel foolish if I didn't know how to.
g It's a waste of time for these people to concentrate on achieving perfection in a skill that won't really help them that much.
h In one or two decades, people in the Far East might be amused by the way I speak English.
i This huge demand opens up unprecedented opportunities for firms from our country and considering the office I hold, I am naturally gratified by this prospect.

5 Writing

Text production p175

Write a letter to the editor commenting on this view recently expressed in an article Write about 200 words.

'I hate the fact that more and more English words and expressions are creeping into the German language.'

6 Project – a foreign exchange programme

Doing projects p189

Your class would like to participate in a foreign exchange programme in an English-speaking country. In groups, brainstorm ideas which might help persuade the principal of your school to agree to the class participating.

Here are some points you may wish to think about:

- length of the programme
- costs involved
- free-time activities
- potential effect on school performance back in Germany.

Now produce a report presenting your ideas.
Which group has produced the most persuasive report?

7 Listening

Listening skills p185

You are going to hear a radio interview on the subject of English in rock and pop music. Before you listen, work with a partner and find the best match (a–f) for the following statements (1–6).

1 At the start of their career, ABBA decided to use English lyrics.
2 In the 1960s, the Beatles and the Rolling Stones were extremely popular.
3 Pop musicians are faced with lots of pressure.
4 On stage, artists sometimes perform one song in their audience's native language.
5 English is the lingua franca of pop.
6 Big international record companies are only interested in sales figures.

a They set an example that was followed by many others.
b They are reluctant to award contracts to bands that sing in their native language.
c This is proven by the fact that so many international pop artists perform their songs in English.
d That doesn't usually go down very well with their listeners.
e They continue to earn huge royalties.
f They have to meet the demands of both their fans and record companies.

CD3/7

Now listen and check.

8 Role-play

'German-language pop and rock songs played on German radio should be guaranteed a quota of at least 35% so that English-language songs don't dominate the airwaves.'

Discuss in groups of five. Each member of the group should choose one of these roles.

German pop singer
presenter of a pop music programme
spokesperson for a German record company
listener who favours English-language pop and rock music
journalist who thinks the rules of supply and demand should apply

Report your ideas to the class. If you have not come to an agreement in your group, give reasons why you were unable to reach a consensus.

9 Language

WATCH OUT!

Language check p210

current(ly) / actual(ly)

If you want to find out about ~~actual~~ events in the EU, go to the official EU website. ➤ If you want to find out about current events in the EU, go to the official EU website.

Translate these sentences into English.

1 Die aktuellen Ausgaben für den Übersetzungsdienst der EU sind viel zu hoch.
2 Derzeit versuchen die Koreaner durch die Förderung des Englischunterrichts die Grundlage für weiteren wirtschaftlichen Fortschritt zu erzielen.
3 Einige Bands schaffen es nie wirklich, in die internationalen Charts zu kommen.
4 Sollte die aktuelle Quote für deutschsprachige Songs im Radio erhöht werden?

Vocabulary review

Use these words to complete the text.

command • empowerment • fluency • linguistic • native • pronunciation • Queen's • rules • skills • spelling • universal • variations

Today English is the common ...[1] denominator – the language that unites the peoples of the world. It is well on its way towards becoming a ...[2] language. However, the spread of English is taking its toll on the language and is worrying purists who fear that the proper ...[3] and ...[4] might be lost. While the ...[5] English, the most prestigious form of English, is now used by a shrinking number of speakers, many regional ...[6] of the language are developing across the world.

Recognizing the growing importance of English, Asians, in particular, are keen on acquiring more and more language ...[7] and ultimately hope to achieve ...[8]. They are well aware of the fact that with English, they can accomplish ...[9] through which they can control their own destinies.

Many Asian governments are subsidizing language courses, knowing that their citizens will only be able to improve their standard of living if they have sufficient ...[10] of the English language. They are thus trying to recruit ...[11] speakers from England or the USA so that Asian students of the language can become more familiar with the ...[12] applying to pronunciation and grammar.

12 Settling down in other cultures

FOCUS

1 **Work with a partner. List these qualities/characteristics for the ideal marriage partner in order of importance: 1 = most important; 12 = least important. Tell the class and agree on one ranking for the whole class.**

Our survey on your ideas for the ideal marriage partner – here are the things you said were important:

- having the same religious beliefs
- earning potential
- being able to communicate feelings
- not much difference in age
- appearance
- ability to be a good parent
- same social background/class
- sharing similar set of values
- coming from the same ethnic background
- responsible/reliable
- being soulmates
- sharing same hobbies

2 **What is unimportant when you choose a marriage partner? Make a list on the board.**

TEXT 1

Reading skills p170/171

CD3/8

The story of Niraij and Shweta

When Niraij Kapur went to India on holiday, he had little idea what his parents had in store for him. But several years and a near-divorce later, he's finally getting the hang of his arranged marriage ...

At the tender age of 25, I had an arranged marriage. I didn't mean to. I went on holiday to India, and returned one week later with a chunky gold wedding ring, a medallion-man Om symbol of God strapped around my neck, and an 18-year-old wife I didn't know, had little in common with, and was terrified of spending the rest of my life with.

I grew up in Northern Ireland, surrounded and influenced by non-Asians. The Asian community in Ulster was predictably close-knit and determined to keep Indian values alive: no smoking, no drinking, no dating or sex before marriage and study, study, study. I was therefore required to pursue my interests – specifically, my relationships with non-Asian Irish girls – in secret. Aged 18, I moved to London, where I continued going out with white girls. And then, seven years on, I went to India on holiday with my parents, in the hope that the trip might help me recover from a particularly severe case of heartbreak.

Within 10 minutes of arriving in New Delhi, I was whisked away to my aunt's house. My parents had arranged for me to meet friends of the family, whose beautiful 18-year-old daughter wanted to marry. I didn't pick up the words 'arranged' and 'get married', all I heard was 'beautiful 18-year-old'. And so I happily changed into a suit and tie and borrowed some aftershave from my father, who sat me down for a chat. You know you're in trouble when your father gives you dating advice and chooses your tie.

Her name was Shweta and she had long dark hair, warm brown eyes, a delicious milk-chocolate complexion and she welcomed me with a warm hello. I thought, but didn't say: 'Oh, you could do so much better than me.' We talked. She asked me things like: 'What do you want in your career?' and 'How many kids would you like?' I countered with dumb questions like: 'Titanic won 12 Oscars, but Top Gun was a better film – why didn't it win more?'

After 20 minutes, my parents asked me if I'd like to marry Shweta. And then, something strange happened. My recent heartbreak, combined with a burgeoning fear of ending up alone, was compounded by the heady, unreal qualities of being so far from home. I did the unthinkable. I said yes.

Four days later, I endured an 18-hour, Bhangra-dancing, curry-eating, flash-photography extravaganza in New Delhi. My wedding. Directly afterwards, Shweta and I flew back to my two-bedroom terraced dump in freezing South Harrow, with its small fridge replete with frozen TV dinners for one. Every time I asked Shweta if she was OK, she would cry. I thought, if I was married to someone as unattractive as me, I'd cry too. Yet I did little to help her. I even resented her. Having spent years living alone, I was an independent male who, in the tradition of Indian men, had been brought up to do nothing around the home. Now, I had to not only share my life, but be told by Shweta that I was a slob.

Shweta left her friends, family, further education, everything to be with a man she didn't know, because that was expected of her. Unlike in India, neighbours in South Harrow do not welcome you with open arms; they don't even say 'Hello'. I worked 12-hour days and commuted for a further two hours; we spent little time together and she became more and more isolated. When Shweta met my colleagues, she had nothing in common with the chain-smoking, heavy-drinking one-night-standers, and they couldn't care less about a foreign girl who didn't indulge in Westernized habits. Gradually, I began to believe that I had ruined a woman's life because I couldn't deal with my own loneliness. And now I couldn't deal with hers.

It was like this for two years, after which most couples consider divorce. Indians believe, rightly or wrongly, that British people get divorced too easily, and should fight tooth and nail to keep their marriage alive. However, after two years of unhappiness, I was prepared to be as British as you like. Shweta and I agreed to separate, but we were too scared to tell our parents. We dared each other to make the call. Neither one of us could. We were too chicken. And it was this, in the midst of such a miserable scenario that prompted us to do something we had not done in a long time: we laughed.

Magically, after that, we were able to talk openly. Shweta explained why she was so unhappy, described all the sacrifices she had made to be with me. Quite why this hadn't occurred to me before is beyond me. I understood, finally, that I had to become much more modern to make this old-fashioned, traditional ideal work.

So I changed. We both changed. I learned Hindi. Shweta began voraciously reading English newspapers and magazines. Every week, I sat through three-hour Bollywood movies; in exchange, Shweta watched East Enders with me, throwing in the occasional comment of the 'Why are they all so miserable?' variety. I learned to cook pasta, do the dishes, iron.

I took out a bank loan so that Shweta could begin a college course. We started enjoying our time together. I learned to share my life and Shweta grew to love England for all its greatness and flaws. In between, we had a beautiful baby girl. Shreya has not only helped us appreciate how beautiful life is, she has given us another common bond. And I've discovered that, just as I suspected before I met Shweta, arranged marriages are not whirlwind, roller-coaster, lust-filled journeys. However, I now know that what they can be is safe and secure and there for the long term. Mine is. It may not be a perfect love, but, all things considered, it's really not bad at all.

983 words, adapted from *The Observer*, 22 February 2004

1 Looking at the text

A Work together with a partner and find a definition for 'arranged marriage' based on the text. Then compare your definition with the rest of the class.

B Decide whether the following statements are true, false or not mentioned in the text. Correct any false statements.

1 Niraij used to be one of the lads but now he is taking steps to mend his ways.
2 Shweta was a very rebellious daughter who never complied with her parents' wishes.
3 One problem in their relationship was Niraij's upbringing which left him unprepared for marriage.
4 He agreed to his parents' suggestion because he felt desolate and like a fish out of water.
5 Shweta found it easy to make the transition to life in Britain and she had lots of help.
6 By and large, arranged marriages are far more successful than love matches.

2 Working with words

Complete this email with words or short phrases from the text.

Send Chat Attach Address Fonts Colors Save As Draft

To: alice-c@gm.uk

Cc:

Subject: Hi Alice

Dear Alice

So now you are considering …[1] to Pedro! I have to say that your letter took me by surprise. But, please, promise that you will do me one favour: find out about his culture before you marry it! I say 'it' because you are not only marrying him, but also his parents, his siblings – probably a very … - …[2] family who think that their Pedro … … … … …[3] than choose you!! And you have so little … …[4] with each other!

Let me put it bluntly: are you afraid of ending up alone? Is that the reason behind your decision?

You see, Niraij and I come from the same background, but when I think back to our beginnings I still shudder. I had such a difficult time adjusting to the British culture and …[5]. This was, obviously, … …[6] the fact that he was never there for me.

I had made so many …[7] – had left my family, my friends – for what? I …[8] his colleagues who spent more time with him than I did, and who … …[9] drinking and (to me) senseless conversation. After two years, we both considered …[10], but we were both … …[11] to phone our parents and tell them that it was over. Thank God we didn't – and today I would … … … …[12] to keep our marriage going.

But what did I have to endure! And we belong to the same ethnic group, which very clearly is a … …[13].

Now you, leaving England for Brazil, not even able to speak a word of Portuguese. Are you really sure you want to …[14] your …[15] in a foreign country with someone you hardly know?

Love

Shweta

3 Writing

Text production p180

In some cultures people marry partners chosen for them by their families. According to some surveys, these 'arranged marriages' are more likely to be successful than love matches.

Comment on this statement from your own personal perspective. Write about 250 words.

4 Talking

Should Ayesha, 24, and Franco, 39, get married? They are very much in love and believe they are soul mates. However, they have a number of problems.

Our families disapprove of the marriage. We are from different countries.

Our families follow different religions. We are from completely different social backgrounds.

I am 15 years older than Ayesha. She is going to law school; I'm a car salesman.

I can't speak Spanish and Franco can't speak Turkish – we speak to each other in English. He is from Spain; I'm from Turkey.

Make two teams, one 'for', one 'against'. In your team, work together to prepare your arguments and then discuss the topic with the opposing team.

5 Project – discrimination in the UK

Doing projects p189

Your class will be divided into six groups. Each group should research a different issue that has received attention because of discrimination. In the end, each group should present its findings to the rest of the class, focusing on the current biases and legal struggles surrounding this issue.

The following websites are provided as a starting point for you to begin your research.

Sexual orientation (homosexuality):
https://www4.indymedia.org.uk/en/2005/03/307946.html
http://www.lawyers.com/legal_topics
http://www.natfhe.org.uk/down/legariwo.pdf

Race/Ethnicity:
www.blink.org.uk
www.cre.gov.uk

Women:
http://www.womenandequalityunit.gov.uk/research/
http://www.eoc.org.uk/

Religion (Arab/Islam):
http://www.homeoffice.gov.uk/rds/pdfs/hors220.pdf

The elderly:
http://news.bbc.co.uk/1/hi/health/4575641.stm

People with disabilities:
http://www.disability.gov.uk/

TEXT 2

Reading skills p170/171

My son the fanatic

CD3/9

Parvez

The story is set in an industrial town in northern England. The author, Hanif Kureishi, is a successful British writer and the son of a Pakistani immigrant.

Surreptitiously the father began going into his son's bedroom. He would sit there for hours, rousing himself only to seek clues. What bewildered him was that Ali was getting tidier. Instead of the usual tangle of clothes, books, cricket bats, video tapes, the room was becoming neat and ordered; spaces began appearing where before there had been only mess.

Initially Parvez had been pleased: his son was outgrowing his teenage habits. But one day, beside the dustbin, Parvez found a torn bag which contained not only old toys, but computer discs, video tapes, new books and fashionable clothes the boy had bought just a few months before.

Also, without explanation, Ali had parted from the English girlfriend who used to come often to the house. His old friends had stopped ringing.

For reasons he didn't himself understand, Parvez wasn't able to bring up the subject of Ali's unusual behaviour.

a	

One remark Parvez did make, 'You don't play your guitar any more,' elicited the mysterious but conclusive reply, 'There are more important things to be done.'
Yet Parvez felt his son's eccentricity as an injustice. He had always been aware of the pitfalls which other men's sons had fallen into in England.

And so, for Ali, he had worked long hours and spent a lot of money paying for his education as an accountant.

He had bought him good suits, all the books he required and a computer. And now the boy was throwing his possessions out!

The TV, video and sound system followed the guitar.

b	

Even the unhappy walls bore marks where Ali's pictures had been removed.
Parvez couldn't sleep; he went more to the whisky bottle, even when he was at work.
He realized that it was imperative to discuss the matter with someone sympathetic.

Parvez had been a taxi driver for twenty years. Half that time he'd worked for the same firm.

c	

They preferred to work at night, the roads were clearer and the money better.

They slept during the day, avoiding their wives. Together they led almost a boy's life in the cabbies' office, playing cards and practical jokes, exchanging lewd stories, eating together and discussing politics and their problems.

But Parvez had been unable to bring this subject up with his friends.

d	

And he was afraid, too, that they would blame him for the wrong turning his boy had taken, just as he had blamed other fathers whose sons had taken to running around with bad girls, truanting from school and joining gangs.

For years Parvez had boasted to the other men about how Ali excelled at cricket, swimming and football, and how attentive a scholar he was, getting straight 'A's in most subjects.

Was it asking too much for Ali to get a good job now, marry the right girl and start a family?

e	

His dreams of doing well in England would have come true. Where had he gone wrong?

But one night, sitting in the taxi office on busted chairs with his two closest friends watching a Sylvester Stallone film, he broke his silence.

'I can't understand,' he burst out. 'Everything is going from his room. And I can't talk to him any more. We were not father and son – we were brothers! Where has he gone? Why is he torturing me?'

And Parvez put his head in his hands.

Even as he poured out his account the men shook their heads and gave one another knowing glances. From their grave looks Parvez realized they understood the situation.

'Tell me what is happening!' he demanded.

f	

Now it was clear. Ali was taking drugs and selling his possessions to pay for them. That was why his bedroom was emptying.

'What must I do then?'

Parvez's friends instructed him to watch Ali scrupulously, and then be severe with him, before the boy went mad, overdosed or murdered someone.

Parvez staggered out into the early morning air, terrified they were right.

His boy – the drug addict killer!

756 words, from Hanif Kureishi: *Love in a Blue Time*, Faber and Faber, 1997

6 Looking at the text

Choose the sentences (1–8) which fit into the gaps (a–f). There are two extra sentences which do not fit any of the gaps.

1 Like him, most of the drivers were Punjabis.
2 To him, family was all that mattered.
3 The reply was almost triumphant.
4 Soon the room was practically bare.
5 Maybe his supervisor?
6 Once this happened, Parvez would be happy.
7 He was too ashamed.
8 He was aware that he had become slightly afraid of his son, who, alongside his silences, was developing a sharp tongue.

7 Talking and writing

Text production p180

1 In groups, discuss possible endings for the story. Choose the best idea.

2 Write your ending and read it to the class. (Write about 120 words.) Which ending is most convincing? Why?

8 Listening

Listening skills p185

A CD3/10

You are going to listen to members of Britain's different ethnic minority groups talking about racism, their identity and so on.

Copy this grid into your exercise book. While listening to the recording for the first time, complete the grid.

Speaker	Country of origin	Profession
1		
2		
3		
4		
5		
6		

B Now copy this grid into your exercise book.

	Thoughts on				
	Identity	Inequality	Racism	Politics	Solutions
Speaker					
Speaker					
Speaker					

Make two groups, A and B, and listen to the recording again. This time make notes on the speakers' thoughts and complete the grid with details for your group.

Group A: Listen and make notes on speakers 1, 3, 5.
Group B: Listen and make notes on speakers 2, 4, 6.

9 Writing

Text production p185

Sie verbringen Ihre nächsten Ferien in Großbritannien bei Bekannten, und man hat Sie gebeten, in einem Youth Club ein Referat über die Situation von Minderheiten in Deutschland zu halten.

Lesen Sie den Text auf Seite 130 und fassen Sie die wichtigsten Punkte bezüglich der Situation an der Adolf-Reichwein-Schule und der Situation türkischer und ausländischer Kinder im Allgemeinen zusammen.

Orientieren Sie sich an den hervorgehobenen Textstellen und vervollständigen Sie die Zusammenfassung (100–150 Wörter).

The Adolf-Reichwein school is situated in the Frankfurt district of Zeilsheim ...

Eine Frankfurter Schule, an der die Deutschen die Minderheit sind von Canan Topçu

„Liegt heute was Besonderes an?" Barbara Frank-Hummel schaut in die Runde. Die Klassenlehrerin hat das mit ihren Schülern so ausgemacht: Wenn einer Kummer hat, wird vor dem Unterricht darüber gesprochen. Heute meldet sich ein Kind. „OK", sagt die Pädagogin, „dann klären wir das erst einmal."

Murat ist dran. Der dunkelhaarige Junge hat Sorgen. Aufgeregt erzählt der türkische Schüler, dass einer aus der Klasse Scheuerpulver in die Blumenerde gekippt habe. „Das Zeug ist zum Reinigen der Tische gedacht und kein Düngemittel", erklärt Barbara Frank-Hummel.

Sie ist Lehrerin der Klasse 5a an der Adolf-Reichwein-Schule im Frankfurter Stadtteil Zeilsheim. Von den 17 Schülern sind 13 Kinder von Einwanderern, davon haben sieben türkische Eltern. Natürlich gibt es immer wieder Probleme. Aber einen Zusammenhang mit der Nationalität ihrer Schüler stellt die Lehrerin selten fest. „Das sind eher vorpubertäre Hänseleien."

Ihrer Herkunft sind sich die Jungen und Mädchen wohl bewusst, das aber spielt offensichtlich keine Rolle. Auf die Frage, ob sie gehänselt werden, weil sie ausländischer Herkunft seien, reagieren sie mit Kopfschütteln. An der Adolf-Reichweinschule ist es „normal", Ausländer zu sein. Schließlich sind mehr als die Hälfte der Jungen und Mädchen, die die Schule besuchen, Kinder von Einwanderern. Geprägt von der ehemaligen Hoechst AG, leben in Zeilsheim viele Arbeiter, ein großer Teil davon Ausländer. Die Probleme der Schüler hätten deshalb eher soziale als ethnische Ursachen.

„Außergewöhnlich" seien die Sprachprobleme der bikulturell aufwachsenden Kinder nicht, sagt Frank Hummel. Die ausländischen Schüler ihrer Klasse unterschieden sich in den Schulleistungen „nicht wesentlich" von denen ihrer deutschen Klassenkameraden. Sie widerspricht der vorherrschenden Meinung, dass ausländische, insbesondere türkische Kinder, obwohl hier zur Welt gekommen und aufgewachsen, Schwierigkeiten mit der deutschen

Sprache hätten: „Selbst wenn sie nicht besonders gut sprechen, muss das ja nicht so bleiben." Die Sprachkompetenz sei ja nicht statisch, sondern entwickle sich weiter, wenn sie gefördert werde.

„Das Sprachniveau der Schüler ist insgesamt niedriger", stellt Schulleiter Joachim Knab fest, bei deutschen wie nicht deutschen Kindern. Und das hänge wohl mit dem Einzugsgebiet der Adolf-Reichwein-Schule zusammen. Zeilsheim habe eben eine „problematische Sozialstruktur". Die elfjährige Pinar ist Tochter einer Migrantenfamilie. Ihre Mutter Songül kam als Siebenjährige mit ihren Eltern nach Deutschland. Die Türkin ging hier auf die Hauptschule und hat keine Berufsausbildung. Mit 17 Jahren heiratete sie einen Landsmann, schon ein Jahr darauf bekam sie ihr erstes Kind. Heute leidet die 33-Jährige darunter, dass sie keine „Qualifikationen" hat. Ihre Eltern konnten sie damals nicht unterstützen, „weil sie sich nicht auskannten". Sie will es besser machen. Wie die meisten hier aufgewachsenen türkischen Eltern wünscht Songül ihrem Sohn und ihrer Tochter Pinar den sozialen Aufstieg. Und so manches Kind schafft den Sprung auch, wie die Statistiken belegen. Während Anfang der 80er Jahre bundesweit nur rund 8000 türkische Studenten die Universität besuchten, sind es jetzt dreimal so viele.

Pinars Mutter legt Wert auf zweisprachige Erziehung. „Zu Hause wird Türkisch gesprochen", sagt Songül. Denn sie hat sich sagen lassen, dass die Kinder sich mit der zweiten Sprache leichter tun, wenn sie die Muttersprache beherrschen. Deutsch könne ihre Tochter mit ihren Freunden sprechen. Dass Pinar Kontakt zu deutschen Kindern hat, ist für die türkische Mutter selbstverständlich.

„Engstirnige Familien, traditionelle türkische Väter, die ihre Kinder abschotten, gibt es natürlich auch", sagt Barbara Frank-Hummel. Aber die Lehrerin hat etwas gegen „Verallgemeinerungen". Aus Einzelbeispielen sollten keine falschen Schlüsse gezogen werden. Sie erfahre immer wieder, dass sich türkische Eltern sehr viel Gedanken um die Zukunft ihrer Kinder machten. Manche hätten sogar zu hohe Leistungserwartungen und überschätzten deren Fähigkeiten. Grundsätzlich seien türkische Väter und Mütter offen für Gespräche.

„In der öffentlichen Diskussion wird das Sprach- und Integrationsproblem zu wenig differenziert", meint auch Schulleiter Knab. Dass ausländische und deutsche Kinder jeweils unter sich bleiben und sich immer mehr isolieren – an seiner Schule sieht er dieses Problem jedenfalls nicht. Natürlich gibt es in Frankfurt auch Schulen mit hohem Ausländeranteil, wo es nicht so rosig aussieht. Doch die gehen angesichts der gegenwärtigen Diskussion um die Integration von Ausländern lieber in Deckung.

Dabei liefert eine aktuelle Studie Grund zu Optimismus: „Ausländische Kinder sind nicht nur in der Schule, sondern auch in der Freizeit integriert", heißt es in der jüngst abgeschlossenen Untersuchung des Deutschen Jugendinstituts in München. Die Studie „Multikulturelles Kinderleben", für die rund 1200 nicht-deutsche Jungen und Mädchen in Frankfurt, München und Köln befragt wurden, widerlegt die gängige Meinung, es gebe Ausgrenzungen. Für die befragten Fünf- bis 13-Jährigen spiele bei der Wahl von Freunden die Abstammung keine Rolle, heißt es darin. Pinar verhält sich ganz typisch: „Nach der Schule treffe ich mich mit meinen Freundinnen", sagt sie, „mal mit türkischen, mal mit deutschen". Wer eben gerade Zeit zum Spielen hat. Wenn sie sich abgrenzt, dann in eine ganz andere Richtung: Von Jungens will die Elfjährige im Moment nämlich noch nichts wissen, egal, ob türkische oder deutsche.

von Canan Topçu *Frankfurter Rundschau*, 16 February 2000

10 Language

WATCH OUT!

want

My parents ~~want that I marry~~ Niraij. ➤ My parents want me to marry Niraij.

Shweta's brother ~~wants not that she lives~~ in England. ➤ Shweta's brother doesn't want her to live in England.

Translate these sentences into English.

1 Meine Verwandten erwarteten nicht unbedingt, dass ich als Inder aufwachsen sollte.
2 Ich möchte nicht, dass du mit ihm ausgehst.
3 Möchtest du, dass ich dich heute Abend anrufe?
4 Warum wollten deine Freunde nicht, dass Shweta mit uns kommt?
5 Aber Niraij erwartet, dass du kommst.
6 Die meisten europäischen Eltern wollen, dass ihre Kinder aus Liebe heiraten.
7 Warum willst du, dass ich die „East Enders" anschaue?
8 Will er nicht endlich aufhören, ständig mit seinen Freunden rumzuhängen, statt seine Zeit mit dir zu verbringen?

Vocabulary review

A With a partner use the clues to unscramble these words from the two main texts.

yietbrdaplc – knowing in advance that something will happen
tjueciins – something that is unfair or morally wrong
ulipryctalra – especially
nlpnataixeo – a statement that tries to make clear why something happened
nuisappsneh – the state of being miserable and sad
tnae – tidy, in order
liflpyeaicsc – precisely
hnyuck – thick and heavy
veeers – strict
nhssaaebflio – in fashion
faliynl – lastly, at last
oinsseossp – a belonging, something that someone owns

B Put the words into three categories, nouns, adjectives and adverbs, and use them to produce a word families table in your vocabulary book. In some cases you may not be able to complete all the fields.

noun	adjective	adverb
***	***	***

13 Going global

FOCUS

1 **Talk in groups. How does globalization affect you personally? Does it affect your area in any way? How? Make a list.**

2 **What does this picture tell us about globalization?**

3 **Look at this list.**

a employee in charge of moving containers around the Hamburg port of entry
b truck driver from the Czech Republic
c automobile worker at a General Motors plant in the USA
d college graduate who is fluent in several languages
e factory worker employed by an export-oriented firm in China
f farmer with a small patch of land in Mali
g textile worker in a factory in Germany

Who are the winners and who are the losers when it comes to globalization? Explain why.

TEXT 1

Reading skills p170/171

Four case studies

CD4/2

A Gong Zheng, China

Mr Dou Shu Chen lives near Gong Zheng, in the most northern province of China. He has been a supplier of milk to a multinational food company for ten years, i.e. shortly after it invested the money necessary to build a factory in his remote region.

Once he started delivering milk to the company on a regular basis, his life changed. Originally he had one cow; today he owns six cows and three heifers. Thanks to a higher and more regular income, he was able to build a new house. But more importantly, income from dairy farming has allowed him to finance things that are quite uncommon in rural China: Mr Chen is sending his son to high school and his daughter to university.

Multiplying the positive impact of a global firm in a local market also requires the right incentives. A premium paid for better milk quality is one of the typical win-win situations that motivated Mr Chen. Since the price paid for milk delivered to the factory is based on bacteriological quality, he needed drastic changes in dairy farm management. He succeeded and today he thinks that one of the major advantages of working with the company is that it differentiates between various levels of milk quality. The better the quality, the higher the price they pay.

218 words, adapted from http://humanglobalization.org/cases/caseDouShuChen.htm

B San Antonio, Texas

When the 819 employees at the Levi Strauss production facility in San Antonio were informed that the company was going to close down its San Antonio plant – along with all its other North American plants – as part of a restructuring program, they were shocked.

Clara Flores, 54, a hem sewer in San Antonio who worked for the company for 24 years, says that Levi is providing retraining and other benefits to ease the pain. But she adds that it will be hard to find a comparable job: $18 an hour, four weeks annual paid vacation and family health and dental insurance for just $24 a week. She wonders whether it will ever again be possible to find an employer willing to offer fringe benefits like those.

Levi Strauss is just one example of the many American companies that are outsourcing jobs to countries where labor and other costs are lower than in the US. Within the last couple of years, the US has lost nearly 3 million factory jobs.

Marivel Gutierez, 43, who also had 24 years of service with Levi, admits that workers elsewhere would benefit from outsourcing. 'There still probably is an American dream for them,' she says. 'But what about us? What happens to *our* American dream?'

210 words, adapted from *The New York Times Up Front*, Scholastic Inc., 26 April 2004

C Bass Strait off Tasmania, Australia

Islands in the remote Bass Strait off Tasmania once served local markets in southern Australia with rock lobsters. Although not a large market, demand and prices were reliable and steady, and did not lead to over-fishing.

In the last decade, with transportation improvements and increased international demand, local fisheries have been devastated due to the increasing desire for rock lobsters in the emerging global cities of Hong Kong and Shanghai. Literally, lobsters caught in the Bass Strait on Monday are on dinner plates in China on Tuesday.

Among the outcomes of these changes: rock lobsters, once a local staple food, are now too expensive for most residents to eat; fishing licenses have been bought up by outside investors.

This leaves many fishermen, who once owned their own boats or licenses, either as day-workers, working on the boats of outside investors, or unemployed.

A sustainable resource that once provided a good living for local people in Tasmania is being destroyed due to global processes beyond their control, changing a long established way of life.

Finally, although a few of the locals have profited handsomely from private ventures with outside investors, much of the community is suffering, a situation that will only worsen as fishing grounds become depleted.

205 words, adapted from http://geoc.uconn.edu/ViasCourse.htm

D Youngstown, Ohio

SARA SAMSON

Sara Samson, a 37-year-old single mom busy raising two kids, is pleased with the effects globalization has had on her life. She says, 'Given what I earn – just above the minimum wage – I like the lower prices and sometimes better quality of goods that come from global trade. As a cashier at Wal-Mart, I earn about $13,800 a year before tax. According to a government study on poverty in America, that means that I'm one of those 31 million Americans who worry about getting enough food for the family every month. The prices of toys, TV sets, clothes, energy and food all reflect the fact that more things are coming from overseas, where workers often get paid less – sometimes a lot less. My TV came from Korea, I buy clothes made in a Caribbean country and shoes made in Indonesia. My little old Ford has a Japanese Mazda motor and was built in Mexico. Globalization is OK with me because the lower prices help me and my family survive.

168 words, adapted from http://www.earthwindow.com/grc2/SaraSamson/

1 Looking at the texts

A Match the following phrases (1–6) with six of the explanations (a–h). There are two more explanations than you need.

1 to require the right incentives (Text A, lines 10/11)
2 to differentiate between the levels of quality (Text A, lines 15/16)
3 to ease the pain (Text B, line 11)
4 to offer fringe benefits (Text B, line 17)
5 to deplete fishing grounds (Text C, lines 18/19)
6 the minimum wage (Text D, lines 3/4)

a to pay a price that reflects the standard of the product being sold
b to supply extras on top of an employee's salary
c the lowest pay possible
d to underestimate the problems caused by a job
e to need appropriate forms of motivation
f to exhaust the supply of a staple food
g to make job loss less traumatic
h to restock the live resources in a particular part of the ocean

B Choose the correct answer.

1 In Text A, it is said that offering the right incentives helps
a farmers to better distinguish between levels of quality.
b multinational companies to become more competitive.
c farmers only if they get a premium at the same time.
d multinational companies to do more good for communities.

2 The employees at the Levi plant in Texas who were given notice said that they
a would soon be relocated to another Levi plant elsewhere in the world.
b still firmly believed in the 'American dream'.
c thought it would be difficult to find an employer who would offer the benefits they had grown used to.
d realized that family health and dental insurance plans were becoming more expensive all the time.

3 Rock lobsters are expensive and hard to come by because
a local fishermen are now out of work.
b wealthy Australians have bought up the rights to fish for lobster, thereby jacking up the price.
c the inhabitants of big Asian cities have developed a healthy appetite for lobster, thus causing the depletion of supplies in Australian waters.
d local Australians have become so prosperous that their demand for lobster outstrips supply.

4 Which of the following would make the best headline for Text C?
a Worldwide demand leads to depletion of fishing grounds
b Globalization benefits emerging global cities
c Globalization to blame for destruction of local markets and resources
d Not all locals suffer as a result of globalization

5 Another way of expressing the word 'literally' in Text C, line 8 is
  a more often than not.
  b as a result.
  c according to newspaper reports.
  d as a matter of fact.

6 Which of the following would make the best headline for Text D?
  a Single mom happy to finally be able to feed her family
  b Low prices on imported products a result of low wages overseas
  c Low income bracket mom profits from the new global economy
  d Single mom glad to be able to buy goods where they are cheapest

2 Writing

Text production p184

Interpret the table shown below saying how it relates to globalization. Write 100–120 words. Then say what figures you would project for the year 2012 and explain why.

Telephone lines per 1,000 people	East Asia and the Pacific	Developed countries (OECD)	Average (worldwide)
1990	17	392	99
2000	104	524	163
*2005	263	680	190

Source: UNDP Human Development Report 2002
* estimated figures

3 Listening

Listening skills p185

CD4/3

A Listen to a discussion on social issues and decide which basic positions Jim Smith and Nancy Broughton hold.

B Listen again, take notes and complete the sentences below.

1 Nancy and Jim disagree on the reasons for job loss. Nancy blames it on ... while Jim makes ... responsible for it.
2 According to Jim, globalization creates lots of jobs in the service sector because ... .
3 Nancy is unhappy about the new types of jobs which are being offered in today's economy because they involve ... .
4 Jim defends globalization by pointing out that it leads to ... .
5 Nancy mentions some disturbing effects of job loss. She says it is associated with ..., ... and ... .
6 She thinks that the government should demand ... from firms that outsource jobs. The money should be used to ... .
7 Nancy criticizes globalization's effects on workers in developing countries, citing ... .
8 Jim says that the workers prefer to work for multinational companies instead of ... .

4 Role play

In groups of 6, look at pages 134/135 and the notes you made for exercise 3 on page 137. Give one of these roles to each member of the group:

- Mr Dou Shu Chen;
- Clara Flores;
- an unemployed fisherman from Tasmania;
- Sara Samson;
- Jim Smith;
- Nancy Broughton.

Note down arguments for/against globalization from the point of view of your character. Then discuss in your group whether globalization is a positive or a negative development.

Globalization has given me a better life.

My local community suffers, while rich private investors benefit.

Globalization exploits cheap labour.

How can we encourage entrepreneurs to stay where they are?

Without globalization, I would have to struggle to feed my family.

Could globalization help increase tax revenues?

5 Writing

Text production p175/183

Choose <u>one</u> of these tasks.

1 A friend has just been transferred to an office in China. Write to your friend saying why you would/would not be willing to work there, too. Write about 250 words.

2 Explain in about 250 words why this scene is remarkable by German standards.

Ho Chi Minh City, Vietnam: 1,000 workers making shoes for a multinational company

TEXT 2

Reading skills p170/171

Out of India

CD4/4

http://www.cbsnews.com/page1

Getting Started Latest Headlines Google Apple Amazon eBay Yahoo! News

Out of India

For decades, American manufacturers of everything from jeans to semiconductors have searched the world for the cheapest labor they could find. It may have cost hundreds of thousands of American jobs, but it has made US products more affordable. Now, some of the most well-known companies are moving a whole new class of jobs overseas. They call it outsourcing. Not the old economy assembly line jobs, but jobs in the new economy – anything that involves a computer or a telephone. Today, the person at the other end of the line is more likely to be in India than in Indiana.

To many American employers, India is Nirvana. It has a stable democracy, an enormous English-speaking population and a solid education system that each year churns out more than a million college graduates, all happy to work for a fraction of the salary of their American counterparts. India epitomizes the new global economy. It's a country with a background of grinding poverty that often looks as if it's on the edge of collapse. And yet, whether you know it or not, when you call Delta Airlines, American Express, IBM or Hewlett Packard's technical support number, chances are you'll be talking to an Indian in India.

'We do our customer servicing there,' says Raman Roy, chairman of a leading outsourcing company. He helped start the Indian call center boom in the 1990s when he came up with a business plan for American companies to direct their calls to India. His company had to build its own generators and its own satellite phone systems. The call centers are cool, self-sufficient islands in an uncertain sea of chaotic Indian street life. Inside, round-the-clock, they keep America on the line. 'We service the globe. We service all parts of the world, irrespective of what time it is here or there,' says Roy.

New Delhi is nearly 11 hours ahead of New York, so manning the phones of the call center is largely night work. By day, the agents – as they're called – are dutiful Indian sons and daughters. By night, they take on phone names such as Sean, Nancy and Celine so they can sound like the girl or boy next door. 'My real name is Sangita. And my pseudo name is Julia,' says one agent. 'Julia Roberts is my favorite actress.' American movies are part of an agent's training in how to sound all-American.

Lavanya Prabhu is a call center trainer who guides young Indians through the labyrinth of American English. She instructs her students in the typical American phrases and idioms and tries to de-Indianize them.

It's difficult for job-seekers to get in. In fact, Prabhu says they accept approximately five out of 100 applicants. On any given day in New Delhi, Bombay and Bangalore, the call goes out for new call center recruits as

Done

http://www.cbsnews.com/page

Getting Started Latest Headlines Google Apple Amazon eBay Yahoo! News

Raman Roy

more and more American companies come calling. The call center employees earn $3,000 to $5,000 a year, in a nation where the per-capita income is less than $500. Sangita enthusiastically mentions the fringe benefits offered by her employer which include free private transport to and from work plus the sheer heaven of an air-conditioned workplace.

There are few aspects of your telephone life that do not sooner or later end up in India – from someone talking you into a new credit card, to your attempt to return your mother-in-law's wonderful gift, to making sure you've paid that bill. Another area where Indians play an important role is debt collection. Actors are employed as they can play both the part of a sweet talker who gently reminds the debtor that he or she is behind in making payments as well as that of a tough talker who becomes more aggressive.

Partha Iyengar, an analyst working for an American research company in India, comments on recent developments regarding globalization: 'We've had globalization in the manufacturing sector with the auto industry, and Japan really emerging as a major auto power. We've had globalization in the low-end manufacturing industry with China emerging as a global power. But this is the first time in the knowledge industry that we have globalization impacting two countries on such a large scale – India and the US. The reason the companies are coming here is to really be more competitive – and that can't be bad for the Indian economy.' Iyengar believes that the effect of outsourcing on the Indian economy has been quite dramatic. 'There are some estimates that say that the whole outsourcing revolution, if we can call it that, will really be one of the key factors in moving India towards developed economy status.' At which time, India would probably outsource to China, for the same three reasons the US outsources to India – money, money and money.

How much can an American company save by outsourcing jobs? 'You save anywhere between 30 to 50%,' says Raman Roy. This is enough to dazzle the most patriotic CEO, and so one of the biggest American banks, JP Morgan-Chase, prefers to hire Indian stock analysts instead of American ones. Then there is the field of taxes. Last year, only a thousand US tax returns were prepared in India. The estimates for next year are that about 200,000 tax returns will be prepared there. 'Geography is history. Distances don't matter any more,' adds Roy. Beyond the success and the money that is being made in the call center business, there's a terrific sense of national pride that India is making its mark in this very sophisticated way. Says Roy: 'We want to show that as a workforce, as a labor pool, we are equivalent to, if not better than, anybody else. Anywhere in the world.'

Done

957 words, adapted from http://www.cbsnews.com, 60 Minutes, 1 August 2004

6 Looking at the text

A Match the statements (a–h) with the corresponding speaker (1–4). Two statements do not match.

1 Sangita 2 Lavanya Prabhu 3 Raman Roy (2×) 4 Partha Iyengar (2×)

a The fact that so many US companies are coming to India, looking for ways to reduce costs, will definitely help my country to catch up with the industrialized world.
b I consider myself extremely lucky to be employed here. Most of my fellow-citizens are faced with almost unbearable heat and humidity when at work.
c The way things are going, India will profit from globalization even more than the US when it comes to the growth rate of its Gross Domestic Product.
d The customers don't want to hear English being spoken with a thick Indian accent. That's why I'm working hard with my pupils to get a grip on that problem.
e I hope we'll soon be superior to the rest of the world as far as our employees are concerned.
f Our pronunciation is far from perfect. But at the moment, that doesn't really matter.
g It was rough when we started about 15 years ago. Lots of things weren't functioning, so we had to improvise most of the time.
h The present wave of globalization is different.

B Bearbeiten Sie die folgenden Aufgaben auf Deutsch.

1 Geben Sie den Sinn der folgenden Ausdrücke bzw. Sätze wieder.
   a She tries to de-Indianize them. (line 37)
   b It's difficult for job-seekers to get in. (line 38)
   c … talk someone into a new credit card (line 48)
   d … tough talker (line 53)
   e … low-end manufacturing industry (line 59)
   f Geography is history. (line 78)
   g India is making its mark. (line 81)

2 Beantworten Sie stichpunktartig die folgenden Fragen.
   a Erklären Sie kurz, wie ein ‚call center' funktioniert.
   b Warum ist Indien für amerikanische Investoren so attraktiv?
   c Welche Vorzüge genießen Inder, die in einem ‚call center' arbeiten?
   d In welchen Schüben hat sich die Globalisierung in Asien bis heute vollzogen, und wie unterscheidet sich dabei die momentane Globalisierungswelle von den früheren?

7 Talking

A local, mid-sized company has announced that it is planning to outsource jobs to the Czech Republic. In groups, discuss suggestions that could be made to dissuade the firm from outsourcing jobs. Report back to the class.

Here are some points you may wish to think about:
- language barrier
- short and long-term effects on workers who lose their jobs
- responsibilities of employers
- effects of unemployment on local community
- ways to reach a compromise

8 Language

WATCH OUT!

'bei'

Mr Chen lived ~~by~~ his parents because he couldn't afford to have a flat of his own. ➤ Mr Chen lived with his parents because he couldn't afford to have a flat of his own.

Translate the following sentences into English.

1 Sara Samson arbeitet als Kassiererin bei der Firma Wal-Mart.
2 Wenn die Firma sie entlässt, muss sie bei ihren Eltern leben.
3 Bei der augenblicklich hohen Arbeitslosigkeit in Deutschland sollten es die Unternehmen vermeiden, Arbeitsplätze ins Ausland zu verlagern.
4 Bei der Abfahrt des Zuges mit der IBM-Delegation versammelte sich eine riesige Menschenmenge am Bahnhof in Shanghai.
5 Den Angestellten, die bei der Firma Levis in Texas arbeiteten, wurde gekündigt.
6 Bei der enormen Geschwindigkeit der Globalisierung dürfen wir nicht überrascht sein, dass Jobs in den Industriestaaten schnell verloren gehen.

Vocabulary review

Complete the text with these words.

access • emerging • exploit • invest • liberalization • low-wage • multinational • outsourcing • per capita • sufficient • sweatshops • ventures

Many …[1] firms are keen on gaining …[2] to new markets these days. They trust that governments around the world will push for trade …[3] and thereby make it easier for big corporations to …[4] capital outside the countries where they have their corporate headquarters. Many of these firms are interested in establishing joint …[5], especially in …[6] countries where …[7] income is relatively modest. By …[8] jobs away from the industrialized nations, the firms sometimes go as far as to knowingly …[9] employees in the developing countries, forcing them to work under terrible conditions in …[10]. However, some people are more optimistic about the long-term consequences of globalization. They say that eventually, it will allow the poorer countries to reach developed economy status and thus become more self-…[11], i.e. less dependent on aid from the industrialized nations. Others see globalization as a way for the underprivileged in those countries which have …[12] markets to catch up with the richest countries on their own.

14 Dealing with terrorism

FOCUS

1 **Talk in groups about the photos. Where was it? What happened? Why?**

2 **Continue in your groups and discuss these questions.**

- Which acts of terrorism have been in the news recently?
- Can any acts of terrorism be justified? Why / Why not?

TEXT 1

Reading skills p170/171

CD4/5

World of terror

a **As the new century began, an epidemic of terrorism spread panic around the globe. In world capitals, leaders fortified their security and restricted their public appearances. Ordinary citizens felt unsafe walking the streets of major cities, while the terrorists themselves were like phantoms – everywhere and nowhere at the same time, seemingly able to strike at will. The horrific September terrorist attack in the United States sent the stock market reeling and sparked anti-immigrant sentiment. Another attack, in Madrid, plunged Spanish politics into turmoil over issues of war and peace. Politicians in the US soon took to describing the war on terror as a struggle of good versus evil.**

The year was 1901.

As frightening as modern terrorism is, the bitter fear it generates would have been familiar to those alive at the turn of the 20th century. A few decades before, Russian revolutionaries had killed Tsar Alexander II with a bomb in St. Petersburg. In 1897 the Spanish prime minister was assassinated just as Cuba's drive for independence was boiling over; within a year, Spain was at war with the United States. In 1901 William McKinley, 25th President of the US, was assassinated by a 28-year-old anarchist. Thirteen years later, a Serbian terrorist shot and killed Archduke Ferdinand, heir to the throne of Austria, and triggered World War I.

b Obviously, terrorism – defined as the systematic use of murder, injury and destruction, aimed at achieving political ends by blackmailing political leaders and individual citizens – has the power to alter the course of history. The 9/11 attacks in New York and Washington, the train bombings in Madrid, the blood-curdling headlines from Israel and Iraq are proof of that. And, with the additional threat posed by weapons of mass destruction, it does seem that humanity has crossed into a dangerous new era, in which a new breed of terrorists, armed with fearsome new weapons, has acquired the means to challenge even the most powerful nations on Earth. How did the world come to this point?

c Terrorism is as old as the story of mankind. It appears in the history of ancient Greece and Rome – the assassination of Julius Caesar (44 BC) was an act of terror – and terrorism has appeared in practically every century since then, and in every part of the world. But much has changed in just the past century, starting with the choice of targets. In the past, the typical victim of terrorism was an emperor or a king, a president, a general, or at least a government official. Terrorists would actually call off an attack in order to spare innocent lives, because indiscriminate killing was considered immoral and politically unwise. Many of today's terrorists have no such inhibitions.

Motives and goals have also changed. A century ago, terrorism was mainly used by groups and individuals who wanted either to incite revolution or, in the case of Ireland and the Balkans, to achieve nationhood. A look at the geography of terror around 1970 shows the same basic trends – left-wing terrorism in Germany, Italy and Latin America and nationalist or separatist terrorism in Northern Ireland,

Spain's Basque region and the Middle East. Today, however, extreme Islamist groups such as al Qaeda have moved to the vanguard of global terrorism and are operating in 68 countries worldwide. According to Osama Bin Laden and other leaders, al Qaeda is motivated by the Islamic tradition of jihad, or holy war, to defend the faith against non-believers. They see themselves as engaged in a global struggle against a corrupt and an oppressive enemy, the West.

d Terrorists have very little in common ideologically. What they share, however, is a willingness to use the same brutal tactics to achieve their goals. They are not, despite a popular misconception, driven to terrorism by personal poverty. The leaders and many of the foot soldiers in the Islamic movements come from solidly middle-class backgrounds, and some, like Bin Laden, from very wealthy families. That's not to say that social factors like poverty and despair don't radicalize populations. But hunger by itself does not necessarily lead to political violence; many of the world's poorest nations report little or no terrorism. Nor is it true that terrorism occurs in the most oppressive regimes. There was little terrorism in Stalinist Russia or Saddam Hussein's Iraq. In contrast to the 'state-terror' which was used by the Nazis against anyone who dared voice their opposition, Germans who were opponents of the Third Reich hardly ever resorted to acts of terrorism to achieve their ends. Terrorism needs a certain amount of freedom to mobilize its supporters and to get organized, and it needs charismatic leaders capable of inspiring recruits to face danger or death. It suffocates in a dictatorship, which itself practises a form of terrorism.

e What can be done to counter, or at least to defuse, the danger of terrorism in the future? Some movements are open to political solutions, especially those demanding greater political autonomy, such as the Kurds in Turkey. But the more radical groups like al Qaeda are not interested in compromises; they demand total victory.

f In the long term, such white-hot fanaticism may burn out and even disappear. But in the meantime, we are faced with one of the most dangerous passages in human history. For the first time ever, terrorists have a potential for harm that defies imagination, should weapons of mass destruction fall into their hands. Civilization will prevail – it always has – but there can be no final victory in the 'war on terror', which, in one form or another, will continue as long as there are conflicts on Earth.

917 words, adapted from *National Geographic*, November 2004

1 Looking at the text

A Answer the following questions on the text. Give short answers.

1 Why is modern-day terrorism potentially a more serious problem than terrorism of the past?
2 Compare the motives and goals of terrorists in the late 19th and 20th centuries and those of terrorists at the moment. What are the differences?
3 In what way are many people mistaken about modern-day terrorists?
4 Under what circumstances does terrorism flourish, and what factor inhibits it?
5 Which types of terrorist groups might be open to discussion about their demands?
6 Which types of terrorist groups are probably not interested in discussion? Why?

B Geben Sie den Sinn der folgenden Sätze auf Deutsch wieder. (Keine wortwörtliche Übersetzung.)

1 Politicians took to describing the war on terror as a struggle of good versus evil. (lines 8/9)
2 It seems that humanity has crossed into a dangerous new era. (lines 35/37)
3 Extreme Islamist groups have moved to the vanguard of global terrorism. (lines 70/72)
4 Terrorists' potential for harm defies imagination. (lines 136/138)

C Match the following headlines (1–8) with the appropriate paragraph (a–f). Two of the headlines don't match.

1 Modern-day terrorists have changed their tactics
2 Roots of today's terror movements often misunderstood
3 Regional solutions can be found
4 Terrorism: a temporary problem
5 Parallels to the more recent past
6 Terrorists could soon have the means to shape our political future
7 In one way or another, the challenge posed by terror will continue
8 Experts question civilization's ability to overcome the threat

2 Working with words

A Match the following expressions (1–6) from the text with their German equivalents (a–i). Three of the German expressions don't match.

1 to send reeling (line 6)
2 to plunge into turmoil (lines 7/8)
3 to call off (line 54)
4 to have inhibitions (line 58)
5 to defuse (line 124)
6 to burn out (line 133)

a auf Talfahrt schicken
b entschärfen
c abblasen
d versagen
e verkünden
f in ein Chaos stürzen
g gehemmt sein
h in sich zusammenbrechen
i schwindelig werden lassen

B A student has summarized the text for a short report on terrorism. Complete the gapped summary with the appropriate words or phrases from lines 26–57 and lines 81–122 in the text.

Terrorism is not a new phenomenon but has appeared in various forms over the centuries. The main goal of terrorists is to …[1] governments into fulfilling their demands, however unacceptable they may be. What is particularly frightening about the situation today is that terrorists might even be prepared to use …[2] if they could ever gain possession of them. What's more, today's terrorists are indifferent to their …[3]. They don't care if innocent citizens become their …[4] because they are not concerned about a person's right to life. …[5] acts of brutality are no longer seen as immoral deeds. In view of the extremely harsh living conditions that many people in the world are subjected to, and in view of …[6] governments that don't respect their basic human rights, it is relatively easy for terrorist leaders to …[7] quite a few dissatisfied citizens in these regions. For this reason, the terrorists are able to find a sufficient number of …[8] who are willing to help them achieve their evil goals.

3 Talking

Group discussions p186

Choose one of the tasks below. Talk in groups. Tell the class your ideas.

1 Make up a list of things and values which make life worth living.

2 Terrorists go to extremes to achieve their goals; some become suicide bombers. Discuss possible motives. What could be done to discourage acts of terrorism?

4 Writing

Text production p175

Choose one of these tasks and write about 250 words.

1 You have read this statement in an article in an English-language newspaper. Write a letter to the editor giving your views on the subject.

> People should be prepared to give up civil liberties in order to enable the government to protect the country from terrorism more effectively.

2 A friend from Northern Ireland, where acts of terrorism have been taking place for many years, has expressed this opinion in an email. Write a reply, stating whether you agree or disagree and why.

> **We should never give in to the demands of terrorists. Not under any circumstances!**

TEXT 2

Reading skills p170/171

CD4/6

Extremely loud and incredibly close

Nine-year-old Oskar Schell is talking to a man he happens to meet about an event which has been weighing on his mind. The dialogue begins with the man talking.

He said, 'What is it?'

'Nothing.'

'Are you all right?'

I wanted to keep the tears in, but I couldn't.

He said, 'I'm so, so sorry.'

'Can I tell you something that I've never told anyone else?'

'Of course.'

'On that day, they let us out of school basically as soon as we got there. They didn't really tell us why, just that something bad had happened. We didn't get it, I guess. Or we didn't get that something bad could happen to us. A lot of parents came to pick up their kids, but since school is only five blocks from my apartment, I walked home. My friend told me he was going to call, so I went to the answering machine and the light was beeping. There were five messages. They were all from him.'

'Your friend?'

'My dad.'

He covered his mouth with his hand.

'He just kept saying that he was OK, and that everything would be fine, and that we shouldn't worry.'

A tear went down his cheek and rested on his finger.

'But this is the thing that I've never told anyone. After I listened to the messages, the phone rang. It was 10:22. I looked at the caller ID and saw that it was his cell phone.'

'Oh, God.'

'Could you please put your hand on me so I can finish the rest?'

'Of course,' he said, and he scooted his chair around his desk and next to me.

'I couldn't pick up the phone. I just couldn't do it. It rang and rang, and I couldn't move. I wanted to pick it up, but I couldn't. The answering machine went on and I heard my own voice.'

Hi, you've reached the Schell residence. Here is today's fact of the day: It's so cold in Yukatia, which is in Siberia, that breath instantly freezes with a crackling noise that they call the whispering of the stars. On extremely cold days, the towns are covered in a fog caused by the breath of humans and animals. Please leave a message.

'There was a beep. Then I heard Dad's voice.'

Are you there? Are you there? Are you there?

'He needed me, and I couldn't pick up. I just couldn't pick up. I just couldn't. *Are you there?* He asked eleven times. I know, because I've counted. It's one more than I can count on my fingers. Why did he keep asking? Was he waiting for someone to come home? And why didn't he say "anyone"? *Is anyone there?* "You" is just one person. Sometimes I think he knew I was there. Maybe he kept saying it to give me time to get brave enough to pick up. Also, there was so much space between the times he asked. There are fifteen seconds between the third and the fourth, which is the longest space. You can hear people in the background screaming and crying. And you can hear glass breaking, which is part of what makes me wonder if people were jumping.

Are you there? Are you there? Are you there? Are you there? Are you there? Are you there? Are you there? Are you there? Are you there? Are you there? Are you

'And then it cut off. I've timed the message, and it's one minute and twenty-seven seconds. Which means it ended at 10:24. Which was when the building came down. So maybe that's how he died.'

'I'm so sorry,' he said.

'I've never told that to anyone.'

He squeezed me, almost like a hug, and I could feel him shaking his head. I asked him, 'Do you forgive me?'

'Do I forgive you?'

'Yeah.'

'For not being able to pick up?'

'For not being able to tell anyone.'

He said, 'I do.'

630 words, from Jonathan Safran Foer: *Extremely Loud and Incredibly Close*, Houghton Mifflin Compan, 2005

5 Looking at the text

Answer the following questions.

1 What is the event behind the story? Find clues in the text and make a list.
2 Which passages in the text reveal that Oskar is having a hard time coping with the situation emotionally? Explain.
3 Which passages in the text show that the man is also emotionally upset by what he hears? Explain.
4 Why does Oskar feel sure that his father wanted to talk to him and not to somebody else?

6 Talking

Discuss these questions in groups. Then report back to the class.

1 In your opinion why was Oskar unable to pick up the phone when his father called?
2 Why does he tell a total stranger what happened?

7 Writing

Text production p185

Ein Austauschschüler aus London hat den Text auf der nächste Seite gelesen, aber nicht ganz verstanden. Er hat Sie gebeten, Informationen über mögliche Gründe, warum es auch in Deutschland zu gewaltsamen Ausschreitungen kommen könnte, zu nennen.

Vermitteln Sie mögliche Vorkehrungen, die eine Stadt oder ein Bundesland erprobt hat, und die Erfahrungen, die dabei gemacht wurden.

Orientieren Sie sich an den markierten Textstellen und erstellen Sie eine Zusammenfassung des Berichtes. (100–150 Wörter)

Der Gewalt zuvorkommen
Die Polizei versucht, mit Moscheevereinen zu kooperieren

von Mirja Kuckuk

Kann das, was gegenwärtig in Frankreich passiert, sich in ähnlicher Form auch in Deutschland ereignen? Auch wenn die Situation in den Nachbarländern sehr unterschiedlich ist, fürchten manche, dass auch in der Bundesrepublik hohe Arbeitslosigkeit, mangelnde Bildungschancen und alltägliche Ausgrenzung zu einer „Explosion" führen könnten. Umso notwendiger ist die Intensivierung des Dialogs, wie dies der Vorsitzende des Zentralrats der Muslime in Deutschland, Nadeem Elyas, fordert. Der Bundesvorsitzende der Türkischen Gemeinde in Deutschland, Kenan Kolat, ruft nach einem interkulturellen Ansatz bei der vorschulischen und schulischen Bildung.

Das Bemühen um bessere Kontakte war auch das wichtigste Stichwort bei einer Fachkonferenz über die Kooperation von Polizei und Muslimen in Stuttgart. Die deutschen Polizeibehörden wollen die Moscheevereine verstärkt als Partner für die Vorbeugung und Bekämpfung von Verbrechen gewinnen. „Die Folgen fehlgeschlagener Integration werden uns gerade in den Vororten von Paris vor Augen geführt", mahnte der baden-württembergische Landespolizeipräsident Erwin Hetger. Aus Stuttgart, Essen und Berlin liegen bereits Ergebnisse über Kooperationen mit den Moscheevereinen vor. Zusammen mit der Landeszentrale für politische Bildung und mit Ditib, dem – vom türkischen Religionsministerium gelenkten – größten Moscheeverein, erprobten die Beamten der Krimimalprävention 18 Monate ein Modellprojekt. Das Ziel: Vorbehalte gegenüber den Staatsdienern abbauen, Vertrauen gewinnen und Gewalt vorbeugen. (...)

Ihre bisherigen Erfahrungen haben die Städte in einem Leitfaden zusammengefasst, der (...) an die Polizeien der Länder und des Bundes verteilt werden soll. Darin wird dazu ermuntert, vergleichbare Projekte zu starten. (...) Der Leitfaden vermittelt freilich nicht nur positive Erfahrungen. Freimütig wird auch die Befürchtung geäußert, dass bei unzureichender Prüfung der Ansprechpartner die Polizei für verfassungsfeindliche Bestrebungen instrumentalisiert werden könnte. Ohnehin, so der Stuttgarter Landespolizeichef Hetger, sei die Initiative kein Mittel zur Bekämpfung des fundamentalistischen Terrors. Er hoffe aber, dass „Hass-Situationen wie derzeit in Frankreich" durch die Dialogbereitschaft vermieden werden können.

Dass Integrationspolitik Früchte tragen kann, zeigt das Beispiel von Stuttgart. Die Stadt gilt bei rund einem Drittel Ausländeranteil als sicherste Metropole der Republik. Oberbürgermeister Wolfgang Schuster (CDU) führt dies auf das Zusammenwirken von Stadtverwaltung, Polizei und bürgerlichem Engagement zurück. Landesweit steht die Polizei mit 180 Moscheevereinen im Dialog. Verstärkt ausländischstämmige Polizisten einzusetzen, lehnt Hetger aber ab: „Wenn Dolmetscher gefragt sind, setzen wir natürlich bilinguale Beamte ein. Aber unsere Sprache ist und bleibt Deutsch." 1993 hat Baden-Württemberg den Vollzugsdienst für Beamte mit Migrationshintergrund geöffnet. Von den 24600 Polizisten kommen 128 aus dem Ausland.

Obwohl nur etwa 15 Prozent der 45000 Muslime in Baden-Württemberg in den Moscheevereinen organisiert sind, ist der Ditib-Vorsitzende Bekir Alboga von der Effizienz der neuen Kooperationsinitiative überzeugt: Auch wenn nicht alle Muslime in die Gotteshäuser gingen, dürfe man die Strahlkraft der Moscheen nicht unterschätzen.

slightly abbreviated, from the *Süddeutsche Zeitung*, 14 November 2005

8 Listening

Listening skills p185

CD4/7

A historian is speaking about the background to the conflicts in Northern Ireland. Listen, take notes and decide whether these statements are true or false. Correct the false statements.

1 A large number of Protestants moved to Northern Ireland in the early 17th century.
2 The fact that Ireland is divided into two parts plays a bigger role in the conflict than religion.
3 Casualties of the conflict were limited to those fighting with the various paramilitary groups.
4 The victims of the clash on 'Bloody Sunday' were people demonstrating for more liberties on the Catholic side.
5 The acts of violence which took place in the last three decades of the 20th century were opposed by most Catholics and Protestants living in Northern Ireland.
6 The peace process in Northern Ireland is, by now, irreversible.
7 Today, the Protestants are willing to give in to the demands of the Catholics.

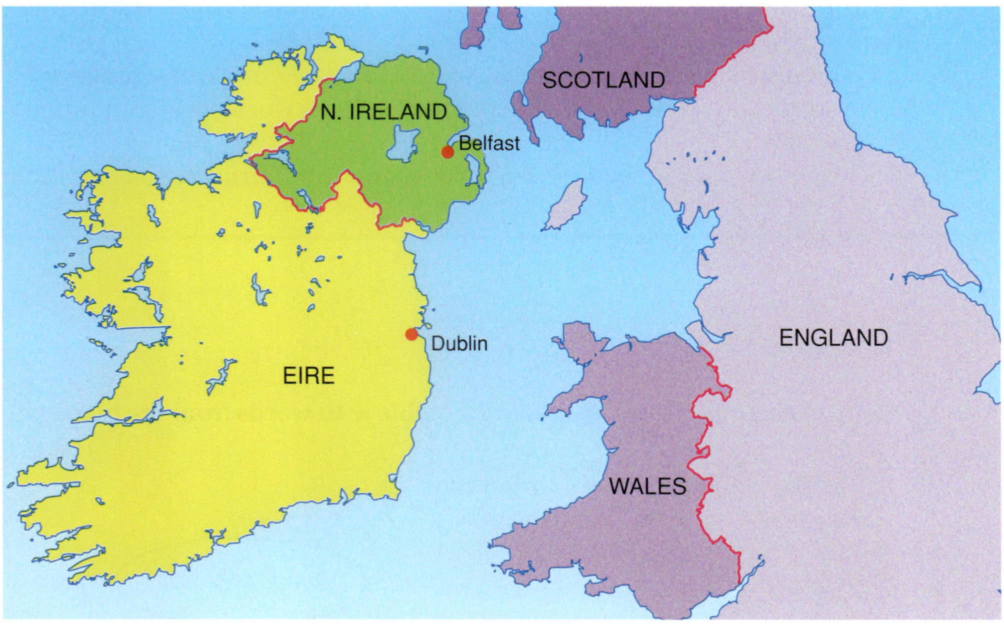

9 Project – following developments in Northern Ireland

Collect information on Northern Ireland from newspapers, the internet and other media. Make a wall chart display and update the material whenever new developments take place.

Doing projects p189

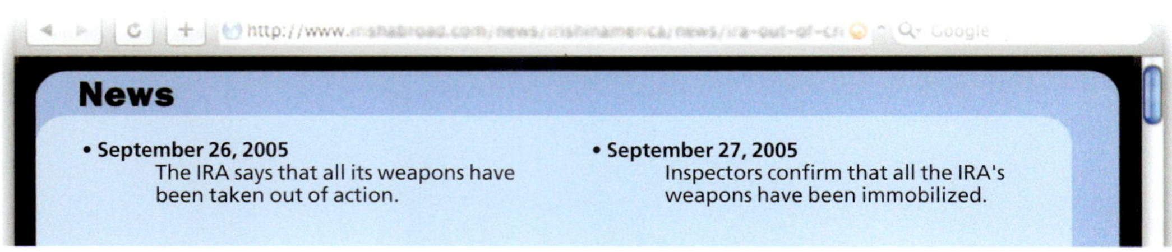

10 Language

WATCH OUT!

Problem words (3)

Language check p210

Levels of political violence may well ~~raise~~ if the problem of poverty is not solved. ➤ Levels of political violence may well rise if the problem of poverty is not solved.

Choose the correct word or phrase from the brackets to complete each sentence.

1 The windows of the President's car are made (out from / in / of / out) bullet-proof glass.
2 The bomb went off right (next / nearly / besides / beside) a busy street café.
3 When we refer to something as *aktuell* in German we mean that it is (actual / actually / current / currently).
4 The terrorists escaped and are being (looked after / looked for / searched after) by the police.
5 The negotiators hope to reach a settlement (in the next day / in the next time / in the next future / in the near future).
6 Officials found it necessary to (check / control / proof / prove) the packages.
7 Rescue agencies (stood / stayed / kept / further kept) working until they freed all the survivors.
8 The (last / least / latest / newest) evidence seems to confirm the suspect's alibi.

Vocabulary review

Copy and complete the word families table with words from the two texts.

verb	noun	adjective
radicalize	***	***
***	despair	***
***	***	corrupt
defy	***	***
***	danger	***
***	***	oppressive
murder	***	***
***	***	horrific
threaten	***	***
***	security	***
***	***	separatist

15 Into the future

FOCUS

1 **Match the photos (1–5) with the headlines (a–g). There are two more headlines than you need.**

a Cloning

b Producing fertilizer

c Growing human body parts

d Reproducing extinct species

e BREEDING NEW PETS

f Improving food crops

g Eradicating genetic diseases

2 **How much do you know about genetic engineering? Talk in groups and make notes about the possible benefits and drawbacks.**

Now take turns with other groups at the board to collect your ideas. Rank the ideas from 'best-case scenario' to 'worst-case scenario'.

TEXT 1

Reading skills p170/171

CD4/8

The brave new world of genetic engineering

Getting Started Latest Headlines Google Apple Amazon eBay Yahoo! News

Dolly – born 1997 died 2003 Did she die young because she was a clone?

The birth of a cuddly lamb named Dolly, an exact genetic duplicate of a six-year-old ewe, will forever be regarded as a watershed in man's attempts to redesign nature. Coming in 1997, the announcement that a team of British scientists had successfully cloned an adult sheep caused a sensation worldwide. It also sparked off and fuelled a heated debate about the ethical implications of such a feat. Sceptics voiced concern that genetic engineering would prove to be a slippery slope towards a dangerous new world in which the manipulation of human genes might bring about a nightmare scenario of selective genetic breeding. This dilemma has yet to be resolved.

However, with animal cloning experiments already successfully turning out rows and rows of genetically identical sheep, calves, mice, pigs and rats, it now seems only a matter of time before Dolly will find her macabre reference point in her first 100% human counterpart. Indeed, a number of secretive researchers have already conferred upon themselves the dubious honour of having produced such a being, but their claims have remained unverified. Eerily, science fiction's portrayals of the return to life of history's geniuses or the extension of some mad dictator's demagogy through the totalitarianism imposed by his own clone suddenly appear far less of a fanciful notion.

Yet in today's world of science 'fact', experts already foresee DNA chips capable of scanning a newborn's genetic profile and determining 'risk' factors stemming from undesirable physical or psychological attributes – a future set-up that is bound to be a source of cheer to employers and insurance providers alike. From there on it is but a short step to the elimination of 'design faults' through corresponding diagnosis and subsequent manipulatory procedures being conducted on newly fertilized embryos.

Cloning is hailed by many scientists as being a major breakthrough for research in medicine and human ageing and, within these fields, biotechnology is regarded as providing the most likely means of unlocking cures for Parkinson's disease and a variety of cancers. Similarly, inherited diseases such as multiple sclerosis and arthritis may soon be eradicated, while stem cells from discarded human foetuses lend themselves to being grown and manipulated for 'therapeutic cloning' purposes to create, for

Done

instance, skin for burn victim transplants.

Additionally, scientists are engaged in trials to 'grow' a whole gamut of human organs and tissue based on an array of genetic material – part human and part animal – by allowing human-type hearts to beat and develop in pigs or by injecting human neural cells into the brains of foetal chimpanzees. Scientists involved in producing such chimera, as these part-human/part-beast hybrids are called, justify their experimental research by pointing out the dearth of human donor organs.

While science continues to forge ahead in this manner, ethicists increasingly call for an international ban on all forms of human cloning, their argument being that, despite the possibility of some miraculous Eureka-type findings, unbridled experimentation undeniably threatens to do immeasurable and irreparable harm to mankind. There will be, the ethicists maintain, nobody on hand to reverse the effects of the terrifying dramas that will certainly unfold after overly ambitious experiments fail.

In the light of these prospects and the rapidity of biotechnological advances, the extent to which man should be redesigning nature is an issue whose resolution will allow no further delay. Opponents of genetic engineering acknowledge this and regard as paramount the immediate implementation of internationally enforceable measures to restrict research in the field of human cloning.

580 words, compiled from HYPERLINK "http://www.bbc.co.uk" http://www.bbc.co.uk and other websites

1 Looking at the text

Choose the best answer.

1 With the words 'brave new world' in the headline the author wants to express the idea that genetic engineering represents a
   a great chance for mankind.
   b potential danger.
   c better world.
   d scientific breakthrough.

2 In the text, Dolly is a symbol for
   a a sheep.
   b scientific progress.
   c a turning point in genetic engineering.
   d the limitations of genetic engineering.

3 Sceptics are afraid that genetic engineering will eventually lead to
   a over-population.
   b nostalgia for dictatorships.
   c attempts to produce 'perfect' beings, both animal and human.
   d documentation of genetic profiles leading to an invasion of privacy.

4 When he refers to 'design faults' (line 30), the author means
   a problems with computer programs used for genetic analysis.
   b the drawbacks of computer diagnosis.
   c genes which make people age rapidly.
   d 'undesirable' genetic characteristics.

5 Supporters of genetic engineering argue that, among other things, it helps
   a produce better human beings.
   b advance medical research.
   c pharmaceutical companies.
   d develop exciting new types of animals.

6 Ethicists argue that cloning should be
   a banned worldwide.
   b legally controlled.
   c restricted to certain countries.
   d limited to the plant world.

2 Working with words

A Find a word or phrase from the text which fits the expressions in each list.

EXAMPLE the doctor's ... • ... of a fault • the wrong ...
to be skilled in ... • ... of a fatal illness • an initial ...

The correct word is *diagnosis.*

1 the subject under ... • a political ... • a lively ... • an open ... • a lengthy ... a heated ...
2 ... discussions • ... questions • ... views • ... implications • ... standards ... problems
3 suggest a ... • consider the ... • an exciting ... • exhaust every ... there is a strong ... that • rule out the ...
4 dangerous ... • inherited ... • contagious ... • blood ... • characteristic ... symptoms of ...
5 a complicated ... • conduct an ... • a large scale ... • the result of an ... a laboratory ... • an ... on animals
6 a controversial ... • a political ... • the point at ... • avoid the ... • a vital ... debate an ...

Now write six sentences using one expression from each list.

B Complete the gapped summary with words from the text.

The cloning of a sheep in 1997 started a debate on the ...[1] consequences of genetic engineering. Opponents of this kind of research fear selective genetic ...[2] of living species in the future. They are afraid that soon man may even ...[3] a cloned human being. People's genes could be scanned and information on undesirable ...[4] could be passed on to insurance companies. Scientists could start to 'repair' genetic faults by manipulating ...[5]. Though this research may help to ...[6] diseases and to grow human organs as replacement parts to solve the shortage of donor organs, there is a moral ...[7] between what is technologically possible and ethically acceptable. Thus the introduction of new international ...[8] to control genetic engineering is a matter of urgency.

3 Writing

Describe this cartoon using about 100 words.

Text production p183

4 Listening

Listening skills p185

CD4/9

Chris Gibb, CEO of a biotech company, is being interviewed about the possibility of solving the world's food problem by producing GM crops.

Before you listen, copy the flow chart into your exercise book. Then listen and complete.

GM crops

1st type: …[1] 2nd type: …[2]

Disadvantages
- create unnatural organisms
- …[3]
- …[4]

Advantages
- healthier food
- …[5]
- …[6]

Producers of GM crops

- How many farmers grow GM crops?
  …[7]
- In how many countries?
  …[8], including …[9] and …[10].

Of the companies producing GM crops,
- Monsanto produces more than …%[11]
- another …[12] companies produce the remainder.

The problem sceptics see with these companies is that they will
- …[13] • …[14] • …[15]

5 Project – finding out how near we are to human cloning

In groups find out as much as possible about recent developments. Present your findings to the class in the form of a poster.

Doing projects p189

6 Writing

Text production p185

Sie haben Bekannte in den USA und berichten ihnen in einer E-Mail auf Englisch über die Haltung eines Teils der deutschen Intellektuellen zur Gentechnik.

Orientieren Sie sich an den hervorgehobenen Textpassagen und fassen Sie den Text in 100–150 Wörtern zusammen.

Interview: „Menschenzucht ist nicht machbar".

Die Biologin Christiane Nüsslein-Volhard wendet sich gegen die Verbreitung von Horrorvisionen im Zusammenhang mit der Gentechnik. Sie unterhält sich mit einem Journalisten des „Tagesspiegel".

Tagesspiegel: *Deutsche Intellektuelle streiten sich seit Jahren um das Thema Gentechnik und Menschenzüchtung. In der Diskussion fällt auf: Der Biotechnik wird fast durchweg eine negative Rolle zugewiesen. Beispiele: Der Journalist Thomas Assheuer schrieb, dass die Gentechnik „absolute Freiheit" und „namenlosen Schrecken" bedeute; der Philosoph Rüdiger Safranski entwarf eine Zukunftsvision, nach der „Genbanken patentierte Eigenschaften" verkaufen, „Vernichtung unwerten Lebens" an der Tagesordnung sein werde und die „Entfesselung der gentechnischen Zivilisation" bevorstehe. Machen Sie als Genforscherin solche Attacken betroffen?*

Nüsslein-Volhard: Eher ärgerlich. Es ist erstaunlich, dass Leute so viel Platz in den Zeitungen eingeräumt bekommen, um über etwas zu diskutieren, von dem sie so wenig Ahnung haben. Die geistige Elite scheint weder zu wissen, was denkbar, noch, was möglich ist. Bevor ein Philosoph Gentechnik in seine Theorien einbaut, sollte er sich erst mal gründlich informieren über das, was eigentlich machbar ist, statt alles durcheinander zu werfen und Horrorvisionen zu verbreiten. Die ganze Debatte ist völlig überzogen – viel Lärm um Nichts. Alles, was da erörtert wird, ist so wahnsinnig weit weg vom Machbaren. Aber die Bevölkerung wird verschreckt. Mich irritiert, dass die Philosophen sich offenbar mit keinem Biologen beraten haben, bevor sie mit einem solchen Streit an die Öffentlichkeit gingen. Die wissenschaftlichen Zusammenhänge sind sehr kompliziert und nicht leicht zu durchschauen, auch nicht für Biologen selbst.

Tagesspiegel: *Der Gedanke, dass der Mensch einen Körper hat und ein von biologischen Lebensvorgängen bestimmtes Wesen ist, scheint vielen Vertretern des deutschen Geisteslebens eine unangenehme und eher fremde Vorstellung zu sein. Müssen Sie da noch Aufklärungsarbeit leisten?*

Nüsslein-Volhard: Ich glaube schon. Aber das ist traditionsgemäß in Deutschland so. Hierzulande bekommt man etwas auf die Finger, wenn man den Menschen in eine Reihe mit den Tieren stellt. Doch das ist für einen Biologen nun einmal eine spannende und reizvolle Sache, man kann durch den Vergleich so viel lernen. Man erfährt, wie verwandt wir mit anderen Lebewesen sind, man denke nur an unsere Instinkte und manches mehr. Wir sind ähnlich, aber nicht gleich. Es ist sehr spannend, herauszufinden, was die Unterschiede ausmacht. Gibt es doch, bei sehr großer Verwandtschaft, kaum ein identisches Gen bei Affe und Mensch. Wir haben natürlich eine Sonderstellung. Aber der Vergleich ist trotzdem spannend.

Tagesspiegel: *Sind die Visionen von der drohenden gentechnischen Zivilisation für Sie ein Ausdruck von Wissenschaftsfeindlichkeit?*

Nüsslein-Volhard: Was ich abschreckend finde, ist dieses Pochen auf Ignoranz, was die Naturwissenschaft angeht, dieser Hochmut. Man ist stolz auf seine Lateinkenntnisse, und auf eine Fünf in Mathe. Da gibt es eigentlich keine gemeinsame Basis, es fehlen Diskussion und Dialog zwischen Natur- und Geisteswissenschaftlern. Ich fände es wünschenswert, wenn Geistes- und Naturwissenschaften sich näher kommen würden, um gemeinsam eine moderne Anthropologie zu entwickeln. Wir sollten aufeinander zugehen. Aber wir haben keine gemeinsame Sprache. Ein Beispiel: Beim Wort „Selektion" denkt ein Geisteswissenschaftler zuerst an Auschwitz, ein Naturwissenschaftler aber an Darwins Buch über die natürliche Selektion, die Auslese bei der Entstehung der Arten. Wir müssen diese gemeinsame Sprache wieder finden, damit wir in Zukunft über solche gesellschaftlich wichtigen Fragen vernünftig und fundiert miteinander reden können.

505 words, from Der *Tagesspiegel*, 27 September 1999

TEXT 2

Reading skills p170/171

CD4/10

Exploring the future of home technology

a With airships poised in the stratosphere to beam back 120 Mbps broadband services, what might our networked home of 2025 be like? Coming home, we gain entry biometrically by pressing palm and fingers against a panel at the front door. A light indicates recognition and the door unlocks. In the hall, a control panel carries out a spoken command to close the curtains.

b Music, video and games await activation on a centralized media server whose A/V streams are sent by wireless tablets or remote controls to any room with the equipment to handle them. So that things run smoothly, the tablets and remote controls will 'talk' with one another using internet protocols, each one a node on a domestic intranet.

c At a mega-plasma display in the family room, we select music or films by scrolling through images of albums and covers, using subscription service software or by deciding to purchase full digital rights. This involves embedded technology which automatically connects devices – part computer, part consumer electronics – by TCP/IP.

d In the bedrooms, sensors recognize ID tags embedded in clothes removed from drawers or the wardrobe; a mirror display lights up to suggest clothes to match – reminding us in the process that a dry-cleaned angora sweater is due for collection. We're given wash-care instructions when sorting through the laundry basket, but our home-care robot knows it'd be unwise to hang out washing when the colour of the pegs warns us of a change in the weather; otherwise, there's always the plastic sheet automatically pulled over the washing when the rain finally starts.

e Sensors in Granny's bed monitor her state of health, triggering messages to mobiles if there's some suspected complication. If Dad habitually gets up during the night, the toilet seat is warmed in advance and the way to the bathroom lit. The toilet flushes automatically and everything returns to normal when he gets back into bed.

f Cooking while commuting sounds strange, but we'll be able to tell our oven to start cooking dinner using remote control. No problem with dangerous bugs in our food because, even though it's been in there from 8 in the morning till 6 in the evening before roasting, the meat won't spoil as the oven acts as a refrigerator till the heat kicks in.

g If we don't feel like cooking, we might put a delivery service magnet on the kitchen bulletin board on our return and have it check out today's specials. Alternatively, we pop a frozen meal into the microwave, the bar code on the inner container telling the oven exactly how to cook it. We're also unlikely to have run out of beer to drink along with it as the fridge will have ordered fresh supplies from the shop when we got down to the last three cans.

h Apart from the dubious entertainment value derived from talking to the fireplace to light it, there are serious practical benefits to be had from such technology. If our cellar threatens to flood while we're away on holiday, we could be sent a warning by text message. We could then take immediate action to avert the disaster and prevent ourselves having to wade through the water on our return to rescue the stranded cat.

533 words adapted from HYPERLINK "http://www.bbc.co.uk" http://www.technology.com/future-home/file

7 Looking at the text

Complete the sentences by matching the beginnings (1–6) with six of the endings (a–h). There are two more endings than you need.

1 Your home-care assistant will refuse to hang up washing
2 If you're late getting away from the office,
3 Apart from allowing entry to the front door,
4 An elderly family member's rapid breathing
5 The downloading of copyright material
6 If a water tank develops signs of a leakage,

a will be taken care of by my subscription software.
b will be detected by his/her mattress.
c via the business advertising magnet on the bulletin board.
d if the clothes pegs have changed colour.
e the oven's cooking cycle can be adjusted remotely so that your meal doesn't overcook.
f we'll be alerted so we can avert further disaster.
g will dominate the networked home.
h biometrics might well enable computer logins.

8 Working with words

A With a partner, match these definitions (1–5) with words in the text.

1 a small board for controlling the operation of electrical or other apparatus (paragraph a)
2 the very large screen on modern TV sets (paragraph c)
3 identifying labels (paragraph d)
4 a thing which works a device from a distance (paragraph f)
5 an arrangement of thick and thin parallel lines which can be read by a computer (paragraph g)

B Complete the gapped summary with words from the text.

A broadband …[1] throughout the home will provide a host of …[2] benefits for us by … [3] our daily chores; From hanging out …[4] or automatically ordering groceries when …[5] run low, our appliances will be capable of being re-set by …[6] to adapt to changes in schedule. The immense pleasure …[7] from the sheer volume of entertainment available to us through our media …[8] service will also be a huge plus – not to mention the reaction time gain on home security and personal …[9] issues when warning messages are …[10] by suspicious circumstances.

9 Talking

Group discussions p186

Decide in groups which of the innovations mentioned in the text might have a realistic chance of being introduced. Decide, too, if they are really necessary.

10 Language

WATCH OUT!

Language check p210

(not) sensible / (in)sensitive

Some people are highly ~~sensible~~ about research on discarded human foetuses. ➤ Some people are highly sensitive about research on discarded human foetuses.

Decide whether to use *sensible/sensitive*, or their negative forms *not sensible / insensitive*.

1 It is … to pile up dishes in a sink with an automatic tap!
2 DNA chip implantation at birth may prove too … an issue for many voters.
3 Scientists often appear … to the feelings of the general public.
4 … arguments, put forward logically, may partially reduce GM hysteria.

Vocabulary review

A Work with a partner and unscramble these words from the texts. Put them into two lists – genetic engineering / home technology. The first letters have been given.

aaobbddnr b …
eeodknrtw n …
eonrsss s …
aeobcdr b …
eeicgnt eeibdgnr g … b …
auhmn eegns h … g …
aeeechrrrss r …
eeomrt ooclntrs r … c …
aeichmr c …
eiooobcghlnty b …
eeebdddm eoocghlnty e … t …
eocln c …

B With your partner, find six other thematically-related words from the texts. Jumble the letters of the words and pass them to another pair. How quickly can they unscramble the words?

Unit 5 Making a living

FOCUS 2 p48

SCORING CARD

Should you do a part-time job?

Check your answers and add up your points.

Question	Your answer	Points
1	a	2
	b	4
	c	6
2	a	4
	b	6
	c	2
3	a	2
	b	6
	c	4
4	a	6
	b	2
	c	4
5	a	4
	b	2
	c	6
6	a	6
	b	2
	c	4

So, what's your job profile?

If your final score is …

12 to 20 points
Don't work, at least not yet. School should be your top priority. Furthermore, you don't yet seem to have a responsible attitude towards the money you would earn.

21 to 28 points
You're ready to try working part-time, but ease yourself into it by working as few hours as possible and then slowly increasing the number. As you're still at school, 15 to 20 hours a week is a full workload.

29 to 36 points
Start searching the job ads! You're organized with your schoolwork and your extra-curricular activities. You've got the time to devote to part-time work – and your goal is more than just earning money to buy material goods. The world of work is waiting for you! Go for it!

Reference section

LANGUAGE STUDY SKILLS

I How to deal with unknown words

II Reading skills

III Text comprehension

IV Text production

V Listening skills

VI Group discussions

VII Presentation skills

I How to deal with unknown words

In the *Oberstufe* you will meet quite a lot of new words, particularly towards the end of the course when texts become longer and more demanding. For this reason, knowing how to deal with new words is a **key skill** that you can't do without.

1 Word recognition

Don't use a dictionary, use your head!

When you come across a new word, don't use your dictionary until you have tried quicker and easier ways of finding out what the word means.
Ask yourself these **three key questions**:

1 Is the word given in an annotation?

2 Do I really need to know what this word means, or can I understand the sentence without it?

3 Can I work out what the word means by thinking about
   a international words ➤ I.1.a
   b similarities between English and German ➤ I.1.b
   c what I know about word formation ➤ I.1.c
   d the context ➤ I.1.d
   Also look out for synonyms used elsewhere in the text.

a International words

A large number of words – for example *computer, jeans* and *steak* – are international words that are the same in many languages. Other examples of such words are:

airbag	hi-fi	microchip	software
astronaut	laser	modem	talk show
biker	leggings	off-road	terrorist
container	manager	printer	trainer
fast food	marketing		

b Similarities between English and German

In addition to these international words, there are two other big groups of words that are very similar in English and German.

The first and biggest group contains words such as *to bring, to come, friend, garden, house, mother, street, winter,* and so on, that come from an old form of German. It is, of course, usually easy for German speakers to recognize the meanings of such words. Watch out for 'false friends', though! ➤ p210

The second group of very similar words is made up of vocabulary based on words from other languages, usually Latin or Greek (German, 'Fremdwörter').

aggressive	democracy	paragraph	risk
biology	depressive	poetic	socialism
combined	formality	politics	traditional
conflict	hurricane		

c Word formation

Ever since you started learning English, you have come across words which you could easily understand at once. This is because they are words formed with vocabulary you already know or can easily recognize.

Here is a review of what you probably know about word formation so far:

- We use prefixes to change the meaning of words:

prefixes	meanings	examples
dis-	'not' / 'opposite'	agree ➤ disagree
in-		correct ➤ incorrect
im-		possible ➤ impossible
ir-		responsible ➤ irresponsible
un-		friendly ➤ unfriendly
mis-	'not correctly'	understand ➤ misunderstand
re-	'again'	discover ➤ rediscover

- We also use prefixes to build on the meaning of the basic word, for example:

prefixes	meanings	examples
anti-	'against'	clockwise ➤ anticlockwise
co-	'together'	educational ➤ co-educational
inter-	'between' / 'from one to another' / 'together'	national ➤ international
micro-	'very small'	chip ➤ microchip
sub-	'under' / 'below' / 'lower in level'	zero ➤ subzero
super-	'above' / 'more than' / 'over' / 'very efficient'	power ➤ superpower
tele-	'far' / 'over a long distance'	communications ➤ telecommunications
trans-	'across' / 'beyond' / 'into another state or place'	form ➤ transform

- We use suffixes to change the form of words. If you know one form, the suffix will help you understand other forms of the same word. Here are some examples.

Changing **verbs** into **nouns**

verb	suffix	noun
organize prepare	-ation	organization preparation
express pollute	-ion	expression pollution
bake open	-er	baker opener
begin feel	-ing	beginning feeling
argue move	-ment	argument movement

Changing **verbs** into **adjectives**

verb	suffix	adjective
advise change move	-able	advisable changeable movable
care love	-ing	caring loving

Changing **nouns** into **adjectives**

noun	suffix	adjective
continent industry	-al	continental industrial
beauty help	-ful	beautiful helpful
day life	-ly	daily lively
hunger	-y	hungry

Changing **adjectives** into **nouns**

adjective	suffix	noun
stupid criminal	-ity	stupidity criminality
happy ill	-ness	happiness illness

Changing **adjectives** into **adverbs**

adjective	suffix	adverb
awful strange environmental	-ly	awfully strangely environmentally
democratic	-ally	democratically

d Looking at the context

You can often guess the probable or approximate meaning of a word by looking at its context, i.e. by thinking about the topic and the meaning of the sentence it appears in.

Learning by doing 1

Working out words from the context

Can you work out what the words in italics could mean in German?

1 Your *ordinary* Joe can't afford a house here any longer. The workers' houses have all been bought by rich people and been *gentrified.*
2 Business is bad at the moment and we don't expect it to *rally* for at least a year. All the signals are very *inauspicious*, I'm afraid.
3 Ellie has had a *terrific* idea. We needn't *amend* the book after all. She says we can just *alter* the title to fit the contents.
4 The police *grilled* Fred for hours but they had to let him go. They know he was *implicated* in the robbery but they can't prove it. It looks as if Fred's *got away with it.*

2 Using a dictionary

You are allowed to use an English–English or monolingual dictionary both in class and in exams. If you can't work out the meaning of a word by other means, dictionaries are an essential tool. Like any other tool, however, you have to learn how to use a dictionary effectively and efficiently. What follows is a guide, but only *you* can get familiar with your dictionary and only *you* can do the necessary practice.

To get started, make sure you look at the key to your dictionary's entries. The key gives you an overview of what your dictionary has to offer.

Key to dictionary entries

headword, with end-of-line hyphenation point, and pronunciation (*see inside back cover*)

fend·er /ˈfendə(r)/ *n* **1** a low metal frame placed around a fireplace to prevent burning coal from falling out. **2** a soft solid object such as a mass of rope or a rubber tyre, hung over the side of a boat to prevent damage when it comes next to another boat or to land. **3** (*US*) **(a)** a MUDGUARD over the wheel of a bicycle. **(b)** = WING 4.

meanings separated by numbers or, when closely related, by letters

headwords with same spelling separated by different numbers

fer·ment[1] /fəˈment(r)/ *v* to change or make sth change by means of a chemical reaction involving esp YEAST or bacteria: [V] *Fruit juices ferment if they are kept a long time.* ◦ *(fig) His anger fermented inside him.* [Vn] *Yeast is used in fermenting sugar to produce alcohol.* ▸ **fer-men-ta-tion** /ˌfɜːmenˈteɪʃn/ *n* [U]: *Sugar is converted into alcohol through (the process of) fermentation.*

fer·ment[2] /ˈfɜːment/ *n* [U]: political or social excitement or uncertainty: *The country was in (a state of) ferment.*

Fer·ris wheel /ˈferɪs wiːl/ *n* [U]: (also **big wheel**) *n* (at a FAIR[3](1), etc) a large upright revolving wheel with seats hanging from its edge for people to ride in.

synonym of headword

fer·rule /ˈferuːl;/ *US* ˈferəl/ *n* a metal ring or cap placed on the end of a stick, an UMBRELLA, etc to stop it becoming damaged.

American pronunciation (*see inside back cover*)

word not in defining vocabulary (*see Appendix 10*)

part of speech (see inside front cover for abbreviations)

ferry /ˈferi/ *n* (a) a boat (**a**) a boat that carries people and goods across a stretch of water: *catch/take the ferry* ◦ *the cross-channel ferry service.* (**b**) the place where such a service operates: *We waited at the ferry for two hours.* ▶ **ferry** *v* (*pt, pp* **fer·ried**) to transport people or goods by boat, aircraft, etc for a short distance, sometimes regularly over a period of time: [Vnp] *Can you ferry us across?* [Vnpr] *ferry goods to the mainland* ◦ *ferry the children to and from school* [Vn, Vnpr] *planes ferrying food (to the refugees).*

verb codes before examples that illustrate them (see Study pages **B4–8***)*

fer·til·ize, -ise /ˈfɜːtəlaɪz/ *v* [Vn] **1** to introduce POLLEN into a plant so that it develops seed, or SPERM into an egg or a female animal so that a young animal, etc develops inside: *a fertilized egg/cell* ◦ *Flowers are often fertilized by bees as they gather nectar.* **2** to make soil, etc more FERTILE(1) by adding a substance such as MANURE to it: *fertilize the garden.*
▶ **fer·til·iza·tion, -isation** /ˌfɜːtəlaɪˈzeɪʃn;/ *US* -ləˈz-/ *n* [U]: *successful fertilization by the male.*
fer·til·izer, -iser *n* [C, U] a natural or artificial substance added to soil to make it more FERTILE(1): *chemical fertilizers* ◦ *a bag of fertilizer* ◦ *Get some more fertilizer for the garden.* Compare MANURE.

derivatives section with special symbol ▶

cross-reference to contrasted word

a What dictionaries tell you

As well as telling you the meaning of the **headword** in various contexts (often in sample sentences) all monolingual dictionaries approved for use in the *Oberstufe* also give you information on:

- **spelling** and **splitting** (hyphenating) rules
- the **word class** or **part of speech** (adjective, verb, noun, etc.)
- **pronunciation** and **stress**
- **forms** and **derivatives** (plurals, formation of past tense, related words and expressions)
- **register** (colloquial, formal, etc.)
- differences between **British English (BE)** and **American English (AE)**, and perhaps notes on other forms of English, such as Australian, as well.

In addition to the above, dictionaries also provide you with valuable information on such things as whether a verb takes an object or whether a noun is countable or uncountable. Please don't ignore this information. It will help you avoid mistakes.

b How to use a dictionary efficiently

- Only use them when you must.
- Read through the **list of abbreviations** used in your dictionary and make sure you understand what they mean.
- **Note all the words** you want to look up before turning to your dictionary. Look up the words in alphabetical or reverse alphabetical order.
- You may find **unknown words** in the definitions or context sentences given in the dictionary. If you do, don't panic or give up. Use your word recognition skills before looking further in the dictionary.
- Note the **part of speech** of the word you want to look up – e.g. noun – and ignore all the other entries for that word.
- When you have found the meaning, **write it down immediately**. If you don't, you may have to look it up again.

If you get into these good dictionary habits now, you won't waste any time in exams!

Learning by doing 2

Working with your dictionary

Read the text then use your dictionary to do the exercises below.

The world's last mammoth rain forest

The green tangle that is the Amazon rainforest is among the most complex environments in the world. But the threat to this massive expanse is as simple as a mathematical equation. The Amazon forest holds about one-third of the world's remaining tropical woods, but Brazil accounts for only four per cent of the tropical timber market. So, as expected, Brazilian and international timber companies have set their sights on where most of the tropical wood remains – the Amazon.

1 Which part of speech is **mammoth** (headline)? Replace it with another word without changing the meaning.
2 Which part of speech is **tangle** (line 1)? Which meaning of 'tangle' applies here? Give the dictionary entry (number / letter) and a possible German translation.
3 Which part of speech is **expanse** (line 3)? Which dictionary entry applies here (number / letter)? Name two adjectives that are often used with this word.
4 Which part of speech is **holds** (line 4)? Give the dictionary entry (number / letter) and a possible German translation. Give an English expression for *ich vertrete die Ansicht / bin der Ansicht, dass …* using the word 'hold'.
5 What kind of expression is **(have) set their sights on** (line 7)? Give a possible German translation.

3 Collocations and compounds

a Collocations

A **collocation** is a combination of words that make up a generally accepted fixed expression.

For example, the **noun** *team* collates with **another noun**, *captain* to make the expression *team captain*. It does not, however, collate with *leader* – as in German – or with other possible alternatives like *boss, head, chief* or *commander*.

Similarly, *head* collates with *teacher* to make *head teacher*, but it doesn't collate with, say, *executive*. If you were to say, 'Jane Brown is the *head executive* of our firm', you would be understood. The correct collocation, however, is *chief executive*.

In the same way, the **noun** *photo* collates with the **verbs** *take* and *shoot* to form the collocations *to take a photo* and *to shoot a photo*. It does not collate with *make*, though, as it does in German.

▶ For this reason, it is essential to learn collocations as complete units. In other words, don't learn just *love*, learn *to fall in love*.

b Compounds

Some words go together so often that they become a **compound**. They may be with or without a hyphen, or they may become one word:

daughter-in-law • car park • airport

The more frequently words are used together, the closer they become. For example, in the last 50 years, we have seen *air port* change to *air-port* and then to *airport*. Because of changes like these, you may see compounds written in different ways. If in doubt, check them in a good, up-to-date dictionary such as the Oxford Advanced Learner's Dictionary.

II Reading skills

1 Close reading for detail

All the units in this book contain two long English texts with detailed work on content and vocabulary. In the first ten units, these texts are also used to illustrate a grammar point. Close reading for detail is an essential skill that you cannot do without.

Follow these steps.

Step 1 Read the **title** and ask yourself what the text is probably about. If there is an **introduction** to the text, read this, too. It is generally in simpler language and is intended to help you. You might also want to look at any **photos** or **illustrations** accompanying the text to get a better idea of the contents.

Step 2 Read the text through to get the **general sense**. Concentrate on the key words (nouns and verbs, sometimes qualified by adjectives and adverbs).

Step 3 Look at the **content questions**. These will give you an idea of what the examiner thinks is important and what to look for.

Step 4 Now read the text **in detail**, sentence by sentence. If you have borrowed your coursebook from your school, don't mark texts. Make a list of words in an exercise book. Otherwise mark any words you don't understand with a highlighter or by underlining them. If there is a sentence that you can't understand at all, don't panic. Ignore it for the moment and return to it later. If there are a lot of unknown words, don't panic, either. You will certainly be able to work out the meaning of some of them, and you might not need to know their meaning at all. ➤ I.1

Use your **dictionary** to find out the meaning of those words that you can't understand by other means. Only look up words that you really need to know. ➤ I.2

When you have dealt with the unknown words, read through the text a third time as a continuous piece of prose. Then answer the questions.

2 Skimming for gist

Skimming for gist is reading a text quickly for its general sense without worrying about every word. This is what we do when we read a newspaper article in our mother tongue.

In practice, however, skimming is not as easy as it sounds. The problem is that some people don't have the self-confidence to dive in and hope for the best. They worry too much. They may start skimming, but soon panic and reach for their dictionary.

Follow these steps.

Step 1 Read the **title** and, if there is one, the **introduction** to the text to find out what the topic is.

Step 2 Study the **exercises** carefully before you begin reading and learn to **recognize skimming exercises**, e.g. *Read the text and say what the writer's opinion on career women is.*

Step 3 Concentrate on the **key words**. These are sense-transmitters like nouns, verbs and maybe adjectives/adverbs that qualify them. Use word recognition skills wherever possible. ➤ 1.1

Step 4 If you can't understand an important key word, **read on**. Many such words become clear from the context or are even explained by a synonym just a few lines further on.

Step 5 As a rule, texts used for skimming have a **clear structure**. Arguments and evidence are presented logically and the most important points are often repeated for emphasis or in the conclusion.

3 Working with key words and expressions

As you know, words fall into a number of groups or 'classes' according to what function they have. Some words are 'structural', such as 'am' in the sentence, *I **am** writing this now* and 'have been' in *You **have been** warned!* Similarly, prepositions and many adverbs express time, place and relationship between people and things. Articles and connectors (*and, but, because*, etc.), pronouns and devices such as question tags (..., *have you?* ..., *isn't it?*) are also 'structural' words and phrases.

▶ Structural words and phrases do not have much to do with the basic or 'core' sense of a text.

Core sense is expressed by nouns, verbs and verb groups (*can come, ought not to go*) and sometimes by qualifiers (adjectives and adverbs). These word classes are often called 'sense transmitters'.

Learning by doing 3

Recognizing sense transmitters

Look at this sentence from a letter to the editor. The letter is about an article dealing with single parents. Copy out the 'sense transmitters'.

I'd like to object most strongly to the one-sided articles on lone parents that have appeared in your paper in recent months. Just because a man or woman is bringing up children alone, this does not mean that he or she is a bad parent. Most single parents are as conscientious as two-parent families.

You will find that **focusing on key words and expressions** will not only help you to work faster and more effectively, it will also make reading less wearisome and more enjoyable.

III Text comprehension

1 Multiple choice

The multiple choice section is made up of a number of questions or incomplete statements followed by four answers or options for answering the question or completing the statement. **Only one** answer or option **is correct**.

▶ Three of the answers or options for finishing the statement are so-called 'distracters' which seem to be correct at first glance but which, on closer inspection, prove to be wrong. **Never** mark more than one answer/option on your exam paper. If you do, you will lose points.

Multiple choice tasks are designed to test both overall and detailed comprehension of an authentic English-language text.

You may be asked to answer questions regarding

- the general theme of the text,
- specific information in a certain paragraph,
- the author's personal attitude,
- the meaning of idiomatic phrases.

You may also be required to specify what information is not mentioned in the text.

Follow these steps.

Step 1 Skim the text, **reading for gist**. ➤ II.2

Step 2 Read the questions and deal with any pertaining to gist (often the first or the last question). Do this by looking at the options given and eliminating those that seem particularly improbable or illogical.

Step 3 Find the line(s) in which **specific information** is referred to. Take a closer look at this/these particular passage(s) and choose the correct option.

If asked to identify **information not provided in the text**, read all of the options and eliminate the ones which relate to information which is mentioned in the text. One option should be left over. This is the answer.

If asked to **identify the author's attitude or intention**, look for passages that reveal the author's opinions and/or emotions.

2 Multiple matching

In this type of exercise, you are asked to make correlations between ideas which are related to one another in some way. The aim of the exercise is for the student to demonstrate that he/she has understood specific information contained in either a longer text or several short paragraphs. The items are offered in two separate lists.

You may be asked to match

- questions and answers,
- headings and paragraphs,
- headings and summaries,
- speakers and statements,
- beginnings and endings of sentences.

Each of these multiple matching tasks needs to be dealt with individually.

Matching **questions and answers**
Read the answers for gist, then make the appropriate matches.

Matching **headings and paragraphs**
Read the relevant paragraphs for gist, then make the appropriate matches.

Matching **headings and summaries**
Read the introduction to each paragraph very carefully; often it contains the information crucial for understanding the content of that particular paragraph.
If that doesn't help you, continue reading the rest of the paragraph.

Matching **speakers and statements**
Find each speaker in the text and read carefully what he/she says. Choose a statement which expresses similar or identical ideas. You may find that details such as age, profession, ethnic background, etc. help you match speaker and statement.

Matching **beginnings and endings of sentences**
Look closely at the text to find the appropriate references to either the beginning or the ending of the sentence with regard to content. Make sure you understand what is said in the appropriate passage and then look for a logical match.

3 Gapped summary

In this type of exercise, you are presented with the summary of either a short text or individual paragraphs of a longer text. This summary contains gaps which you are to complete with appropriate words contained in the original text or paragraphs. The aim of the exercise is to test text comprehension rather than knowledge of vocabulary.

Follow these steps.

Step 1	Find the passage in the original text which corresponds to the gapped sentence in the summarized text.
Step 2	Find a word in the original text which completes the gapped sentence in a way that reflects the meaning of the original text. Looking for the appropriate form of the missing word (noun, verb, adjective, adverb) will prove helpful.

4 Short answer questions / Sentence completion

This type of exercise consists of either

- **questions** that have to be answered using appropriate statements provided in the text or
- **incomplete sentences** that have to be completed with information contained in the text.

Follow these steps.

Step 1	Read the question/incomplete sentence carefully.
Step 2	Look for **key words** or **phrases** in the text that also appear in the question/incomplete sentence or which are very similar to them. As soon as you have found one aspect, look for others in the same paragraph. In most cases, they are grouped together.

▶ You will normally be informed about the number of aspects needed to answer the question. Make sure you provide the required number of aspects. **Do not give more aspects than asked for** as examiners will deduct points if you do.

5 Mediation – English to German

In this type of exercise, you are expected to

- **relate information** or
- **explain the meaning** of a difficult sentence or idiomatic phrase from an English-language text in German.

In doing so, you **must not translate literally**. The aim of the exercise is to prove that you have understood the meaning of the relevant text passage(s), sentence(s) or phrase(s).

Follows these steps.

Step 1	The question will be in German. Read it carefully.
Step 2	Look for **key words** or **phrases** in the text which are the same as, or similar to, words and phrases in the question.
Step 3	Check your dictionary to see if the phrase to be mediated is explained.

▶ Make sure you use the explanation in the **context** used in the text.

Step 4 Make notes.

Step 5 As soon as you have found one aspect, look for others in the same paragraph. In most cases, they are grouped together.

Step 6 Relate in German what you have found out.

▶ Make sure you provide the number of aspects asked for.

IV Text production

1 Letters and emails

You may be asked to write three different types of letters: a personal letter (e.g. a letter or an email to a pen-friend), a letter to the editor of a newspaper or magazine or a letter of application.

Personal letters are generally informal in style – you just write down what you would say to the person in a face-to-face conversation. For this reason, personal letters make use of colloquial language and conversational devices such as short forms (*I'm, we're,* etc.) and question tags (…, *don't you?, aren't we?,* etc.).

Nonetheless, the normal style conventions apply to a personal letter, too. You would certainly use more formal language when writing to an older person you don't know very well than you would when writing to a member of your family or to a close friend of your own age.

In a **letter to the editor** you comment – positively or negatively – on the content of a specific article you have just read in a newspaper or magazine. A letter to the editor should be rather formal in style in order to be convincing and to stand a chance of being printed in the paper or magazine.

A **letter of application**, in which the writer applies for a job or vacant position, is more formal than a personal letter. The most important thing to remember when writing a letter of application is to be clear and concise. Use separate parts for each point.

Structure

All letters consist of an **introduction**, the **main arguments** (backed up with examples or explanations) and a **conclusion**.

Opening and closing letters

Dear Sir/Madam	Yours faithfully (BE) Yours truly (AE)	impersonal, formal
Dear Ms Evans Dear Sally	Yours sincerely (BE) Sincerely yours (AE)	personal, formal
Dear Harry	Yours Best wishes Best regards	personal, informal

a A personal letter

- Write today's date at the top right-hand corner of the page.

Introduction

- Begin your first sentence with a capital leter.
- Start off by thanking the addressee for his or her last letter.
- If appropriate, apologize for not having written earlier and state why.
- Briefly refer to the most important point made in the addressee's last letter.

April 21 20.. *(American English)*
21 April 20.. *(British English)*

Dear Emily

Thanks very much for your letter which I received last week. I must apologize for not writing sooner but I've been busy preparing for my final exams which I will be taking in June. I'm glad to hear that you and your family are well. It was certainly interesting to hear about ... (*your plans for the summer, the concert which you attended, etc.*)

Main part

- After writing your introduction, proceed by mentioning your reason for writing your letter.
- If appropriate, present your arguments together with examples or explanations.

In your letter, you asked me to explain why ... (*I'm planning to work during my entire vacation / I want to have my own flat as soon as possible / I don't intend to study at university, etc.*). For one thing, ... (continue by presenting your first argument)

Conclusion

- State that you have to close now (and possibly why).
- Don't forget to inquire about how the addressee (and, perhaps, the rest of the family) is.
- Ask the addressee to give your regards to family members or friends you have in common.
- Let the addressee know that you hope to hear from him/her again soon.

Well, that's it for today. I'm in a bit of a hurry because ... (*my Mom wants me to help her do the shopping / my little brother needs some help with his homework, etc.*). Please give my regards to your sister. Hope to hear from you very soon.

Love (Best regards/Kind regards/Best wishes)

Alexander

b A letter to the editor

- Write your address and the date at the top right-hand corner of the page.

▶ Remember – you do **not** write your name at the top of an English letter.

Introduction

- Refer to an article you have recently read in the newspaper or magazine you are writing to.
- Say that you were particularly shocked/pleased to read the opinions of the author.
- Say that you would like to make some critical/positive remarks about it.

> Kirchstrasse 34
> 86489 Deisenhausen
> Germany
>
> March 20 20 ..
>
> Dear Sir/Madam
>
> I was shocked/disturbed/pleased/gratified to read the article about ... which appeared in the March 18, 20.. issue of your paper and which outlined a rather controversial point of view. Having gained several years of experience in this regard, I feel obliged to protest vigorously/I must say I agree whole-heartedly.

Main part

- Refer to the aspects of the article which particularly shocked or pleased you.
- State the reasons for your feelings, i.e. explain why you agree or disagree with the author of the article.

Conclusion

- Encourage the paper to either stick to their point of view or to change it.
- Make suggestions as to how the paper or magazine should deal with the particular problem in future issues.

Expressing approval

> In conclusion, I hope you will continue to report on this issue in the way you have so far, so that the general public will become more aware of the problem at hand.
> I look forward to reading further articles on this topic.

Expressing disapproval

> In view of the critical remarks I have made above, I certainly hope you will reconsider your editorial policy and explore the issue from a different angle in the future. Doing so would certainly contribute to an enlightened perspective on the part of your readers.

c A letter of application

- Write your address and today's date at the top right-hand corner of the page
- Write the potential employer's name and address at the top left-hand corner of the page, just above the formal greeting.

Introduction

- Refer to a specific job that has been advertised and mention where you saw the ad.
- Say that you would like to apply for the job.

Schlossallee 15
86381 Krumbach
Germany

12 April 20..

LonTours Ltd.
47 Palace Road
London SW6 7HJ
England

Ref: Tourist Office Assistant

Dear Ms Adams

I read your advertisement in today's issue of *The Times* in which you state that you are looking for a motivated assistant to work in your office. I would like to apply for the position.

Main part

- Briefly introduce yourself and say why you are interested in doing the job.
- Explain why you feel you are qualified for the job.
- Provide information about your educational background.
- State what previous experience you have in this field.

I am 22 years old. I was born and brought up in Bonn but moved to Bavaria last year for personal reasons. This summer I will complete my course of studies at the Berufsoberschule, Munich, where my main focus is on business adminstration. Before starting this course, I successfully completed three years at vocational school where, among other things, I studied English and French. I very much enjoyed putting my language skills to good use in my vacation job at the Munich Tourist Information Office last year.
I would welcome the chance to expand my knowledge of the tourist industry and would especially like to do this in London.

Conclusion

- Say when you will be available for an interview and when you could start work.
- Mention anything you are enclosing with your letter.
- Say that you hope to get the job.

I will be available for an interview at any time that is convenient for you and I can start work in August. I am enclosing my CV and a copy of my school-leaving certificate. As I am very enthusiastic about getting the job, I hope to receive a positive reply from you in the near future.

Yours sincerely

Susanne Müller

Encl.

Susanne Müller's CV

Susanne Müller

Personal details

Name	Susanne Müller
Address	Schlossallee 15, 86381 Krumbach, Germany
Date and place of birth	28 May 19.., Bonn
Nationality	German
Daytime phone number	+49-8282-1897
Email address	su-mue@web.de

Education

08/20..–present	Berufsoberschule, Munich (Further Education College); 3-year course in Business Administration
09/20..–05/20..	Ludwig-Erhard-Berufskolleg, Bonn (vocational school); Abitur (equivalent of A-levels), average grade: 2.6
07/19..–07/20..	Carl-Schurz-Realschule, Bonn (selective secondary school); school-leaving certificate (equivalent of GCSE); average grade: 2.1 on a 6-point scale from 1 (very good) to 6 (very unsatisfactory)

Work experience

Summer 20..	vacation job, Andrea Michaelis, lawyer, Bonn (administrative work)
Summer 20..	vacation job, Tourist Information Office, Munich

Interest and skills

Languages	German, native speaker; English, advanced (including business English); French, intermediate
IT skills	MS Office (Word, Excel, PowerPoint)
Other	driving licence, EU class C
References	references can be supplied on request

d emails

The difference between letters and emails is not limited to the way in which they get from A to B. There are also important differences in form or layout and in style. Unlike business letters, emails often make use of spoken language, i.e. short forms (*it's, hasn't, we'd*) and informal style, e.g. *Please let us know* ... rather than *We would be grateful if you could advise us* .... .

- There is no need to write your address or the date in an email.
- You can start with

Dear (name)	(quite formal),
Good morning / afternoon (name)	(standard),
Hello / Hi (name)	(informal).

Introduction

- Say clearly what the email is about.
- If you are answering an email, say something like *Thank you / Thanks for your email about* ...

Main part

- Get your message across as clearly as possible in as few words as possible.

▶ Emails are meant to be read and dealt with quickly so don't irritate the recipient by writing long paragraphs. KISS! (Keep it short and simple.)

Conclusion

- Thank the other person for his/her trouble/help or say that you hope the arrangements you have made are satisfactory.
- Always ask the other person to get in touch if necessary.
- Sign off with *Best regards/wishes, All the best* or simply *Yours.*

2 Compositions

There are basically two ways of approaching this writing task, depending on the topic itself. You may decide that it is appropriate to approach the topic from a *dialectic* point of view, i.e. by dealing with both the positive and negative sides of the problem and then coming to a solution. In many cases, this is advisable – particularly when no simple and clear-cut solutions seem to be at hand. On the other hand, you may feel compelled to argue either for or against a certain course of action because you have strong opinions on the matter.

If you are asked to present reasons for acting in a particular way or to explore the background of a problem, it is necessary to provide a logical sequence of arguments that build upon one another. Always build up to a climax, with your most convincing argument appearing last.

Structure

As in the case of letters, a composition consists of an **introduction**, the **main part** and a **conclusion**. Remember that your arguments must always be illustrated by appropriate examples or explanations. You are usually expected to provide three arguments.

Introduction

In your opening paragraph, the reader needs to be led up to the topic you plan to write about. This can be done in various ways, depending on the topic and your own personal preferences. You may, for example, make a reference to

a a historical development and how things are different now,
b a current topic of debate that needs to be dealt with at the moment,
c some shocking event that requires immediate attention,
d stagnation in society, meaning that change is desperately needed now,
e a quotation from a well-known figure in public life,
f the latest statistics/figures published by a well-known source.

Your next step is to directly pose a question regarding how to deal with the state of affairs you have just described.

Avoid expressing your own personal opinion in the introduction; reserve this for the conclusion.

Learning by doing 4

Introducing a topic

Match the references listed above (a–f) with these examples of how to introduce the topic of dealing with ways to overcome the high unemployment rate among German juveniles (1–6).

1 Germany has been confronted with the problem of massive unemployment for decades now. This problem is particularly serious for school leavers who find they have been let down by politicians. How can this problem finally be solved?
2 Last week a group of German skinheads attacked a student from Africa studying at a German university. A sociologist who has studied such attacks in detail says that they result from the frustration of young people not being able to find employment in today's job market. Many people thus believe it is high time for politicians to finally address this problem. But what measures could they adopt?
3 At the moment, one of the heated debates taking place in German society is that of how to deal with youth unemployment in an increasingly globalized economy. What options do we have to deal with this potentially threatening situation?
4 The latest employment statistics published yesterday in the 'Tagesspiegel' reveal that up to 20% of school leavers are unable to find a suitable apprenticeship. What can be done to make sure these people don't find themselves permanently unemployed?
5 In the past, it was relatively easy for German school leavers to find suitable jobs but nowadays, young people who graduate are faced with the prospect of long-term unemployment right away. That raises the question of what can be done to solve this potentially explosive situation as soon as possible.
6 The other day, a leading German politician stated: 'The only way to get Germany back on track again is to force young school leavers to accept any apprenticeship offered to them.' Is this really the right way to overcome unemployment among young people in Germany?

Main part

In the main part you have to develop three arguments pertaining to one and the same topic. It is sufficient to provide either an explanation or an example to back up your argument.

Learning by doing 5

Developing arguments

A Put the following arguments in the correct order (a–c). Once again, the topic involves the question of how to deal with high unemployment rates among young people in Germany.

Another way to improve the situation is for the government to invest more heavily in education.

Similarly, it can be argued that the unemployment rate among juveniles will only drop if growth in *all* sectors of the economy is stimulated by the government.

No one can seriously doubt that companies need to be given more incentives to offer high-quality job training programmes.

B Decide which of the following are explanations and which are examples. Match them to arguments (a–c) above.

1 One such incentive could consist of a tax break for companies that offer such programmes to school leavers.
2 If the rules regulating hiring and firing were relaxed, companies would be less reluctant to hire new workers.
3 Providing the financial means to employ more teachers would surely enable schools to improve the performance of weak students who haven't been making the grade. The Scandinavian countries have demonstrated that by improving their school systems, the unemployment rate among young people can be kept very low.
4 This is necessary due to the fact that the more recent PISA studies have shown that German schools are no longer among the best in the world. German school-leavers thus have a slim chance of competing successfully in the job market.
5 Such programmes would enable young people to acquire the skills necessary to survive in today's economic climate, which, because of globalization, is intensely competitive.
6 It is easy to see that companies will simply not be willing to hire juveniles unless there is enough overall demand for the company's products and the prospect of being able to make a reasonable return on their investment.

Conclusion

The concluding paragraph of your composition should contain a very brief summary of the most important arguments and/or your personal opinion. In the ideal case, you should try to expand on the topic, i.e. try to put it in a larger context. However, you should avoid presenting and developing a new argument here. Remember that arguments should clearly be reserved for the main part of your composition.

Learning by doing 6

The conclusion

Here are two conclusions to the composition you have been working on above. Choose the better one. Say why you have chosen it.

a In conclusion, I would like to say that it is primarily up to the government to change the current state of affairs. Leaving things as they are not only involves the danger of young people falling victim to radical political ideas presented by right or left-wing demagogues, it is also unethical to rob young people of the chance of getting ahead in life.

b To conclude, we should remember that leaving things as they are might encourage young people to fall victim to radical political ideas. For example, many extreme factions are using unemployment as an argument to encourage young people to join their parties. They are setting up youth clubs and organizing rallies. The government has to do something about this problem before it gets out of hand.

3 Describing/interpreting cartoons and pictures

After briefly describing what you see and relating what any captions or speech bubbles say, your task is to interpret the message the cartoonist or photographer is trying to convey. You should neither interpret the cartoon or picture superficially nor over-interpret it.

Step 1	Describe what you see. Take a good look at the people and the objects and consider their size. Also look carefully at facial features that may reveal emotions and/or character.
Step 2	Interpret the message. Take the details and their relevance into account. Consider whether the 'message' of the cartoon/picture is serious or trivial, humorous or sad. If the cartoonist or photographer is referring to current events or political controversies, mention them.

4 Describing statistics and graphs

When dealing with **statistics** and **graphs**, you are required to interpret numbers.

Graphs, **charts** and **tables** show how two or more sets of information are related.
A **graph** has a vertical and horizontal axis and **describes trends**.
A **bar chart** is divided into columns and is often used to **compare information**.
A **pie chart** is a circle divided into segments and is usually used to show percentages.
A **table** is a set of facts and figures arranged in columns and rows. It is used to **describe trends** and **compare information**.

Verbs and **nouns** help you to **describe growth and decline** in a diagram.

Direction	**Verb**	**Noun**
up	climb	climb
	increase	increase
	rise	rise
	go up	
	soar	
	reach a peak	
	flatten off	
	recover	
	decline	decline
	decrease	decrease
	dip	dip
	drop	drop
	fall	fall
	slide	slide
down	bottom out	
level	remain constant	
	not change	no change
	stabilize	stabilization
fluctuation	fluctuate	fluctuation

Adjectives and **adverbs** can be used to express the **quality** or **rate** of changes in a graph.

Adjective	Adverb
slight	slightly
gradual	gradually
steady	steadily
steep	steeply
sharp	sharply
sudden	suddenly
slow	slowly
dramatic	dramatically
fast	fast

EXAMPLES

Sales of CDs increased steadily.
There was a sharp fall in the sales of cassettes.
Sales of MP 3 players remained constant.

- In your interpretation of the graph, only include information which is needed to explain the overall trend or to compare and contrast information.

- Don't forget that there is a limited number of words available for this task.

5 Mediation – German to English

In grade 13, you will be asked to mediate information from a long, German text. The information to be mediated is highlighted. **Only mediate the highlighted passages.** In doing so, you must **not translate literally**.

Follow these steps.

Step 1	The question will be in German. Read it carefully.
Step 2	Skim the whole text for gist.
Step 3	Now turn your attention to the highlighted passages. Make notes **in German** of the points you need to use to answer the question.
Step 4	Read through your German notes, making sure that you have covered all the points.
Step 5	Complete the task by writing the required text in **English**.

- This is **not a translation exercise**. The aim of the exercise is to prove that the student has understood the meaning of the relevant text passages. If you have covered **Steps 1–4 carefully**, you will be able to do this.

V Listening skills

1 Preparing to listen

Before listening, activate what you already know about the topic you are going to hear. Look at any photos, illustrations or statistics. Most important, read the listening comprehension question thoroughly. Doing all of this will help you **predict** what you will probably hear. Always **take notes** while you are listening.

2 Listening for gist

When listening for gist, try to understand the important ideas of the text and, especially, the ideas you need to fulfil the task.

- Don't concentrate on single words or specific text passages. Try to understand the main 'message(s)' in the text.

3 Listening for detail

In spoken language, people often repeat themselves, so listen for repetitions and signal words,

e.g. *In other words …* (i.e. something will be explained more carefully),
I'm afraid that … (something negative will follow),
Why don't you … ? (a piece of advice will be given).

Pay attention to easy to understand words, e.g. names of people and places, numbers, words and expressions which are similar to German words and expressions.

▶ Do not try to translate specific words.

If you don't understand something, let it pass. After the listening exercise is over, try to guess the bits you did not understand completely. Above all, don't panic!

VI Group discussions

Whether you take part in a group discussion structured as a role-play or as a consensus-finding activity, keeping the following points in mind can help you to perform well.

- The criteria teachers use to assess your performance are as follows:
  language competence,
  contribution to task achievement,
  strategic competence.

1 Preparing for a discussion

- Learn and use the *Language for discussion* phrases from the flap on the inside back cover of the book.
- Think carefully about your ideas on the topic when preparing for the discussion. Make a mental note of the most important items and try to bring them in during the discussion. Make sure your arguments are based on facts.

2 During the discussion

- During the discussion, structure your arguments logically.
- Anticipate what other participants may say and be prepared to react appropriately.
- Speak clearly, distinctly and not too fast. Try to remain confident and calm. Some deep breaths right before the discussion may help you.
- Keep eye contact with the other participants.
- Keep in mind that a group discussion is a team performance. It is essential that all participants get an equal chance to speak, so neither monopolize the discussion nor be too quiet. Try to involve quiet and shy participants by asking them what they think.
- One member of the group should give a summary of the whole discussion at the end.

VII Presentation skills

1 Giving a presentation or a talk

a Preparation

Step 1 Collect ideas and information on the topic by brainstorming, looking in books, checking the internet, etc. Select the ideas which are most useful in supporting your topic.

Step 2 Group these ideas into logical units.

Step 3 Put these units into a sequence which makes up a clear thread.

Step 4 When giving talks on **non-controversial subjects**, e.g. global warming, measures against unemployment, divide your talk into three sections:

1 **Introduction** statement of topic and your opinion/ideas (about 15% of the whole talk or presentation)
2 **Development** evidence to support your opinion/ideas (about 75%)
3 **Conclusion** repetition of your opinion/ideas and a very brief summary of most important reasons (about 10%).

If you are talking about **controversial topics** such as euthanasia or the legalization of drugs, then you can divide your talk up like this:

1 **Introduction** proposal on the solution to a controversial problem, e.g. 'Hash should be legalized'. Do not give your own opinion yet. (about 10% of the whole talk or presentation)
2 **Development I** arguments against the proposal ('cons') (about 40%)
3 **Development II** arguments for the proposal ('pros') (about 40%)
4 **Conclusion** your own opinion with brief summary of reasons. (about 10%)

Step 5 Read through your presentation or talk several times and prepare postcard-sized prompt cards with brief notes and key words which will help you to remember important aspects during your presentation or talk.

Step 6 Find out about the venue, and order and test any equipment you are going to use. If you are using visual aids for your presentation or talk, it is always important to practise using them in this preparation phase.

b Visual aids

1 Use visual aids to show how things look, work or relate to each other.

2 Choose a visual aid which is suited to your material and the situation.

3 Use a flip chart or the board for recording audience feedback or for collecting ideas.

c Giving the presentation or talk

Before you start, lay out your materials (script, prompt cards, etc.) and set up your equipment.

Begin by greeting the audience and thanking them for coming. Then move on quickly to an attention-grabber to establish positive contact with the audience, e.g. a quotation, a provocative statement or an interesting question. 'Visuals', e.g. a photo or an object connected with the topic, are also good attention-catchers.

▶ Avoid jokes. These can fall flat, particularly in a foreign language, and then your talk will start with an embarrassed silence.

During the talk or presentation, use **signalling language** (first, to sum up, etc.) to help the audience understand more easily what you are talking about.

Encourage **questions** to involve the audience. If you don't want your audience to ask spontaneous questions during your presentation or talk, however, say that there will be time for questions at the end.

Use **language** which your audience will understand easily. Try not to use a lot of technical words if your audience might not be too familiar with them.

Stick to the **KISS** (keep it short and simple) rule to give an effective presentation or talk.

In the conclusion, summarize the main points you made in the body of the presentation. Finish with a short, memorable sentence.

d Question phase

Try to anticipate questions you might be asked and prepare answers.
Never say 'I don't know', but offer to find the answer.
Never start a debate with one person.
Thank the audience for their attention when all the questions have been answered.

- Smiling can break the ice and can help to win the audience.
- Use short, concise sentences of not more than nine or ten words. KISS!
- Don't try to be funny and never treat a serious subject flippantly.
- Try not to read word for word from your notes or papers. Use your prompt cards. (Look at what TV chat show hosts do.)
- Look at your listeners, but not always at the same person. Good speakers scan the room from side to side and back to front as they talk.
- Stand up straight. This will improve your voice and make you look and feel confident. Don't walk around. Be relaxed and confident – imagine that you're talking to a friend.
- Speak clearly and emphasize important points strongly. Vary the volume of your voice in accordance with the points you want to get across. Mark important points by speaking more loudly and slowly, but don't shout. Again, imagine you are talking to a friend.
- Support important points with gestures, but don't overdo it by acting.

Useful phrases and expressions for presentations and talks

Good morning/afternoon/evening. My name is …
The topic of my presentation/talk is …
I'm going to talk about …
First, I'll talk about … Second, …
If you have any questions, please feel free to interrupt me. / I'd prefer to take them at the end.
To begin, I'd like to look at …
I'd like to focus on …
Let me give you an example.
OK. Now I'd like to show you …
As you can see, this graph/column/picture shows …
Can everybody see that?
Before I finish, I'd like to summarize the key points.
So, if there are any questions, I'd be happy to answer them.
Are there any more / any final questions?

2 Doing projects

A project is a longer piece of individual or pair work that is produced largely outside the classroom and generally without the direct help of a teacher – though he or she will, of course, advise you. You will usually work on your project in a group.

Projects fall into four stages, which you should work through systematically:

a Planning the project
b Collecting information
c Compiling information
d Presenting the finished project

a Planning

One hour invested in planning your project can save hours of unnecessary work later on. Good planning will also help you to produce a more interesting and understandable project file.

Divide your topic into logical sub-sections. Make a mind map or notes about anything and everything that has to do with the topic. Then organize this material into a manageable form.

Learning by doing 7

Organizing material

These words have to do with environmental protection in the home. Make a mind map or list them under the headings below.

pest control • waste avoidance • unnecessary use of cars, motorbikes • disposing of toxic substances (paint, oil, etc.) controlling consumption • cleaning agents • temperature regulation • insulation against heat loss • recycling • weed control • stand-by switches • unnecessary electric gadgets

Energy **Toxic substances**

Waste

When you have a clear and practicable list of topics and sub-topics, go on to the next stage. Don't forget, though, that the project plan can be revised in accordance with the information you collect.

b Collecting information

According to topic, you can get information from some or all of these sources:

- your family, friends and neighbours; other pupils; teachers of other subjects
- encyclopaedias; yearbooks; reference books (school and public library)
- the press, particularly weekly news magazines and specialist magazines
- TV, particularly the third programmes and the English-language channels CNN, NBC and BBC World
- radio, particularly Voice of America, BBC World Service, *Deutschlandfunk*
- local banks: firms and utilities working in your topic area
- local charities; pressure groups, e.g. Greenpeace
- information services of government departments; chambers of commerce (*Industrie- und Handelskammer*)
- information agencies such as the British Council, America House, *das Deutsch-Amerikanische Institut*, United States Information Service (USIS)
- the internet

▶ When collecting material, try to select an English-language source whenever possible. If you have to use German sources, don't try to translate this material into English. It is much better to make brief English notes from the German information and then compose your own English text.

c Compiling information

Here are some useful tips. They sound obvious but are frequently ignored.

- Organize your project file with dividers between each section and sub-section. Keep your file tidy!
- Keep a detailed and an up-to-date list of contents and materials.
- Always note the source of information, with date, as soon as you find it. When you use oral information from family, friends and so on, give the source, e.g. Anecdotal, Ebersbach, 23.08.06.
- Don't make piles of material for filing later. File material as soon as you find it.
- Use a separate paragraph for each point with generous spacing between paragraphs.
- Use sub-titles or paragraph headings whenever possible. This will help you to organize your material logically and to give a clear presentation.
- Collect illustrations and graphics – line graphs, pie charts, column and bar charts – to support texts. Visual material will make your presentation much more interesting and understandable. Use colour when you can.

d Presenting your project

You may be asked to present your project to the rest of the class or even at an open day or parents' evening. See the tips on Giving a presentation or a talk. ➤ VII 1

Grammar section

I Language check

Die folgende Übersicht zeigt Ihnen auf einen Blick die in *Focus on Success – Erweiterte Ausgabe* behandelte Grammatik und bietet Ihnen einen schnellen Zugriff auf alle Grammatikerläuterungen.

1 The simple present

1 I **go** to the disco once a week.
2 We **live** in Bavaria.
3 Mr Brown **teaches** us English every day.
4 **I don't like** chocolate.
5 **Does** he **like** chocolate?

- Wir gebrauchen das **simple present** für sich ständig wiederholende Ereignisse (1, 3) oder Handlungen und für permanente Zustände oder Situationen (2).
- Mit Ausnahme der 3. Person Singular (*he, she, it*) hat das **simple present** dieselbe Form wie der Infinitiv (1). Die **3. Person Singular** endet auf *-s*/ *-es* (2).
- Ist **kein Hilfsverb** im Satz vorhanden, bilden wir die **Verneinung** und **Fragen** mit der entsprechenden Form von *to do* (3).

Das **simple present** wird häufig mit den folgenden **Zeitangaben** benutzt:

- *always, never, often, rarely, seldom, sometimes*
- *generally, mostly, normally, regularly, usually*
- *every day/week/month/…, every morning/afternoon/…*
- *on Mondays/Tuesdays/…, on weekdays*
- *in (the) summer/winter/…*
- *at Christmas/Easter, at weekends*

2 The present progressive

1 **I'm calling** (at the moment) to say that Ben's ill.
2 He**'s staying** in bed today.
3 The computer **isn't working**.
4 **Are** you **sleeping**?

- Wir benutzen das **present progressive** (auch **present continuous** genannt) für Vorgänge, die im Moment des Sprechens oder Schreibens tatsächlich passieren (1).
- Wir gebrauchen es auch für vorübergehende bzw. außergewöhnliche Situationen (2).
- Das **present progressive** bilden wir mit dem Präsens von *be* und der -ing-Form des Vollverbs (1–4).
- Da beim **present progressive** immer ein Hilfsverb vorhanden ist, bilden wir die **Verneinung** mit not/n't (3).
- **Fragen** bilden wir durch Umstellung (4).

Das **present progressive** wird oft mit den folgenden **Zeitangaben** benutzt:

- *at the moment, at present, now, this week/month*

▶ Beachten Sie, dass einige Verben normalerweise **keine progressive**-Form haben. (Siehe Liste gegenüber.)

3 The simple past

1 We **wanted** to go to the USA last year.
2 She **went** on a school trip to London.
3 Jasmin **did not enjoy** her holiday in Rimini last summer.
4 Where **did** you **go** last year?

- Wir benutzen das **simple past**, um völlig abgeschlossene Handlungen bzw. Situationen in der Vergangenheit zu schildern (1).
- Bei **regelmäßigen** Verben bilden wir das **simple past** durch das Anhängen von *-ed* an den Infinitiv (1).
- Die unregelmäßigen Verben haben eine Sonderform (2, 3), die man sich einfach merken – auswendig lernen! – muss. (Siehe S. 208)
- Ist **kein Hilfsverb** im Satz vorhanden, bilden wir die **Verneinung** und **Fragen** mit *did* (3, 4).

Das **simple past** wird mit den folgenden **Zeitangaben** häufig benutzt:

– *yesterday, the day before yesterday, the week/month/... before last*
– *last night/week/month/summer/December/Easter/...*
– *two/three/ ... hours/days/years/... ago*
– *in 2005 / in the 20th century...*
– *at that time, in those days*

4 The past progressive

1 The teacher **was talking** to Heather **during the break**.
2 The tourist **was taking** a photo when a lion (suddenly) **sprang** towards him.
3 I **wasn't doing** anything particular when he **came** around.
4 **Were** you **having** breakfast when I **phoned**?

- Möchten wir ausdrücken, dass eine Handlung zu einem bestimmten Zeitpunkt oder während eines bestimmten Zeitraumes in der Vergangenheit **im Gange** war, benutzen wir das **past progressive** (auch **past continuous** genannt)(1).
- Wir benutzen das **past progressive** auch, um zu verdeutlichen, dass eine Handlung im Gange war, als ein neues Ereignis (plötzlich) eintrat (2, 3, 4).
- Wir bilden das **past progressive** mit *was/were* und der *-ing*-Form des Vollverbs (1).
- Da beim **past progressive** immer ein Hilfsverb vorhanden ist, bilden wir die **Verneinung** mit *not/n't* (3).
- **Fragen** bilden wir durch Umstellung (4).

▶ Beachten Sie, dass diese Verben normalerweise **keine progressive**-Form haben:

be, believe, doubt, feel [meinen], *hate, hear, imagine, know, like/dislike, love, mean, notice, prefer, realize, recognize, remember, see* [begreifen], *seem, suppose, think* [meinen], *understand, want, wish*

5 The present perfect

1 I**'ve bought** a new car.
2 I **haven't seen** the new film yet.
3 How long **have** you **had** it?
4 We**'ve had** snow **for** two weeks.
5 She**'s had** a cold **since** December.

- Wenn wir ausdrücken wollen, dass irgendetwas geschehen ist, ohne dass der genaue Zeitpunkt des Ereignisses wichtig ist, benutzen wir das **present perfect** (1).
- Das **present perfect** bilden wir mit *have/has* und der 3. Form des Vollverbs (1).
- Die **Verneinung** wird durch das Einfügen von *not/n't* unmittelbar nach *have/has* gebildet (2).
- **Fragen** bilden wir durch Umstellung (3).
- Die Form wird sehr oft mit *for* bzw. *since* verwendet (4, 5). (Im Deutschen steht dafür „seit" plus Gegenwart.)
- Häufig benutzen wir das **present perfect** auch mit folgenden **Zeitangaben**:

– *already, still (not), (not) yet*
– *(not) ever, just, lately, never, recently*
– *so far this week/month/…, till/until now*

6 The present perfect progressive

1 I**'ve been learning** English since I was 10.
2 They**'ve not been speaking** to each other lately.
3 **Has** he **been singing** in the choir for long?

- Wir benutzen das **present perfect progressive (present perfect continuous)** für länger andauernde, zeitlich ausgedehnte Handlungen und Situationen, die in der Vergangenheit begonnen haben und zum Zeitpunkt des Sprechens bzw. Schreibens noch nicht beendet sind (1).
- Das **present perfect progressive** bilden wir mit *have/has been* und der *-ing*-Form des Vollverbs (1).
- Die **Verneinung** wird durch das Einfügen von *not/n't* unmittelbar nach *have/has* gebildet (2).
- **Fragen** bilden wir durch Umstellung (3).

▶ Beachten Sie, dass einige Verben normalerweise **keine progressive**-Form haben. (Siehe Liste unter **past progressive**, S. 193.)

7 The future

A will

1 In the future people **will use** public transport more often.
2 We can only hope that everyone **will accept** this shift in attitudes.
3 You've forgotten your purse? Don't worry. I**'ll lend** you some money.
4 Ms Smith **will not be** at the meeting this afternoon.

5 I **won't come** either.
6 **Will** he **get** the job?

- Das **will-Futur** benutzen wir für zukünftige Situationen bzw. Ereignisse, die mit (praktischer) Sicherheit eintreten werden (1); Erwartungen, Vermutungen und Hoffnungen (2); spontane, „unüberlegte" Entscheidungen (3).
- Das **will-Futur** bilden wir mit *will* + Infinitiv des Vollverbs. Es hat für alle Personen die gleiche Form (1, 2, 3).
- Die **Verneinung** bilden wir durch das Einfügen von *not* unmittelbar nach *will*. Im gesprochenen Englisch sagt man häufig *won't* (4, 5).
- **Fragen** werden durch Umstellung gebildet (6).

Das **will-Futur** kommt mit den folgenden einleitenden Verben und Ausdrücken oft vor:

– *believe, expect, forecast, hope, imagine, suppose, think*
– *It's clear/obvious that …, There's no doubt that …*

B going to

1 Look at these clouds. It'**s going to rain** soon.
2 This time **I'm going to get** good marks in the class test.
3 Tom **isn't going to work** at the club any more.
4 When **are** you **going to sit** your driving test?

- Das **going to-Futur** benutzen wir für Ereignisse und Situationen, die nach Meinung des Sprechers bald eintreten werden (1); zukünftige Pläne und Absichten (2).
- Das **going to-Futur** bilden wir mit *am/ is/ are* + *going to* + Infinitiv (1, 2).
- Die **Verneinung** bilden wir durch das Einfügen von *not/n't* unmittelbar nach *am/is/are* (3).
- **Fragen** werden durch Umstellung gebildet (4).

C The present progressive / the simple present

1 We'**re leaving** the house at 10.30.
2 The bus **goes** at 11 o'clock.

- Wir können auch das **present progressive mit einem Adverb der zukünftigen Zeit** für bereits feststehende Pläne und Verabredungen verwenden (1).
- Genau wie im Deutschen benutzen wir auch im Englischen das **simple present mit einem Adverb der zukünftigen Zeit**, um fest terminierte Vorgänge (Fahrpläne, Stundenpläne, Programme usw.) anzugeben (2).

▶ Beachten Sie, dass der **Gebrauch des Futurs** in gewissem Maße von der Absicht oder Sichtweise des Sprechers abhängt. Dies gilt insbesondere für das **going to-Futur** für zukünftige Ereignisse. Daher ist es im Zweifelsfall ratsam, das neutralere **will-Futur** zu benutzen.

8 Modal auxiliary verbs

1 He **can speak** several languages.
2 You **must accept** your new situation.
3 We **needn't go** to work today.
4 **May** I **interrupt** you?

- Möchten wir sagen, was geschehen kann, muss, darf, soll usw., benutzen wir ein modales Hilfsverb in Verbindung mit einem Vollverb (1–4).

▶ Beachten Sie, dass im Englischen – anders als im Deutschen – ein Hilfsverb nie ohne Vollverb steht.

Vergleichen Sie:
– Lena kann Spanisch. → *Lena can speak Spanish.* NICHT: ~~can Spanish~~

- Modale Hilfsverben – nicht jedoch die Ersatzverben (siehe unten) – haben bei allen Personen immer die gleiche Form, einschließlich der 3. Person Singular (keine -*s*-Endung) (1, 2).
- Wir bilden die **Verneinung** durch das Einfügen von *not* unmittelbar nach dem Hilfsverb (3).
- **Fragen** werden durch Umstellung gebildet (4).
- Abgesehen von *could* in der Bedeutung „Fähigkeit", können wir modale Hilfsverben nur im Präsens und – mit einer geeigneten Zeitangabe – mit zukünftiger Bedeutung benutzen, zum Beispiel:

– You **can go** home now.	(Präsens)
You **can go** home an hour early tomorrow.	(Futur)
– **I must write** these letters now.	(Präsens)
I must write a long report next week.	(Futur)

▶ Möchten wir ein modales Hilfsverb z.B. in der Vergangenheit verwenden, müssen wir ein geeignetes Ersatzverb gebrauchen:

must	The provider **had to block** access to the internet last December.	
can	I **couldn't start** the car yesterday.	(Fähigkeit)
	We **weren't allowed to go** home early last Friday.	(Erlaubnis)

Übersicht der modalen Hilfsverben nach Funktion

Funktion	**Modale(s) Hilfsverb(en)**
Fähigkeit	*He **can** speak several languages.* *The first satellites **could** only transmit sound.*
Möglichkeit	*With your qualifications you **could** work abroad.* *The boss **may** come in at any moment.* *He **might** ask you what you are doing.*

Bitte	***Can** I have a word with Ms Sims, please?*	(neutral)
	***Could** I speak to Ms Sims, please?*	(höflich)
	***May** I interrupt you?*	(betont höflich)
	***Might** I ask you a personal question?*	(äußerst höflich)
Erlaubnis	*You **can** go in now.*	(neutral)
	*The boss is free. You **may** go in now.*	(gefällig)
Verbot	*We **mustn't** be late for work tomorrow.*	
Pflicht	*You **must** wear a hard hat in the factory.*	
Wahl	*Most shop workers **needn't** work on Sundays.*	
Empfehlung	*You **should** get better qualifications.*	(neutral)
	*You **ought to** get better qualifications.*	(etwas betont)
	*You **must** get better qualifications.*	(streng)

9 Reported speech

A Aussagesätze

1 Some people **claim** that 'servant' robots **are putting** people out of work.
2 The speaker **reminded** his audience that there **were** some jobs robots **couldn't do**.

- Wenn wir einem Dritten berichten möchten, was während eines Gespräches gesagt wurde, benutzen wir die **indirekte Rede** (1, 2).
- Wir benutzen bei Verwendung der indirekten Rede ein einleitendes Verb wie *claim, say, remind, answer, think, mention* usw., um zu verdeutlichen, dass wir berichten.
- Steht das einleitende Verb in der Vergangenheit – also *said, answered, mentioned* usw. –, dann verschieben sich die Zeiten wie folgt:

direkte Rede	indirekte Rede
simple present *she works hard*	**simple past** *she worked hard*
present progressive *she is working hard*	**past progressive** *she was working hard*
simple past *she worked hard*	**past perfect** *she had worked hard*
past progressive *she was working hard*	**past perfect progressive** *she had been working hard*
present perfect *she has worked hard*	**past perfect** *she had worked hard*
present perfect progressive *she has been working hard*	**past perfect progressive** *she had been working hard*

CONTINUED ON PAGE 198

CONTINUED FROM PAGE 197

past perfect	**(keine Verschiebung)**
she had worked hard	–
past perfect progressive	**progressive (keine Verschiebung)**
she had been working hard	–
will	**would**
she will work hard	*she would work hard*
am/is/are going to	**was/were going to**
she is going to work hard	*she was going to work hard*
would/might, etc.	**(keine Verschiebung)**
she would work hard	–
would have/might have, etc.	**(keine Verschiebung)**
she had been working hard	–

▶ Beachten Sie, wie wir die modalen Hilfsverben verschieben:

Modalverb	Bedeutung	indirekte Rede
can	Fähigkeit	*could, was/were able to*
can	Erlaubnis	*was/were allowed to*
may	Möglichkeit	*might*
may	Erlaubnis	*was/were allowed to*
must	Pflicht	*had to*
mustn't	Verbot	*was/were not allowed to*
needn't	freie Wahl	*did not/didn't have to*

- Außer wenn wir über ein Gespräch, das am selben Tag stattgefunden hat, berichten, müssen fast alle **Zeit-** und einige **Ortsangaben** entsprechend der folgenden Tabelle geändert werden. (Angaben, die nicht aufgeführt sind, bleiben unverändert.)

direkte Rede	indirekte Rede
today	*on that day*
tomorrow	*the next day*
yesterday	*the day before*
the day after tomorrow	*two days later*
the day before yesterday	*two days before*
next day/Friday/week/Christmas/…	*the following day/Friday/week/Christmas/…*
last Friday/week/summer/…	*the Friday/week/summer/… before*
two years/months/weeks/… ago	*two years/months/weeks/… before*
now, at present	*then*
at the moment	*at that moment*
at this time	*at that time*

here *in this place*	*there* *at that place*
this *these*	*that* *those*

B Fragesätze

1 A member of the audience **asked what had led** to the widespread use of robots in factories.
2 She **wanted to know if/whether** her job **was endangered**.

- Bei indirekten **Fragen** unterscheiden wir zwischen Fragen mit Fragewort (1) und Fragen ohne Fragewort (2).
- Bei Fragen **mit Fragewort** wird das Fragewort übernommen (1).
- Bei Fragen **ohne Fragewort** benutzen *if* bzw. *whether* (= ob), um zu verdeutlichen, dass es sich um eine Frage handelt (2).
- Alle anderen Änderungen erfolgen wie bei den Aussagesätzen (siehe **Aussagesätze** oben).

C Bitten, Aufforderungen und Befehle

1 Lucy **asked the roboticist to show her** the robot.
2 He **told her not to go** too close to it.

- **Bitten** werden meist durch *asked* (= bitten) (1), **Aufforderungen** und **Befehle** durch *told* (= sagen) (2) eingeleitet.
- Bei **positiven Sätzen** erscheint das Verb als *to* + Infinitiv (1).
- Bei **negativen Sätzen** setzen wir *not* unmittelbar vor *to* (2).

▶ Beachten Sie, dass diese beiden Verben immer mit einem Objekt stehen, das die angesprochene Person erwähnt (1, 2). Ist dies vom Kontext her nicht erkennbar, dann müssen wir einfach einen passenden Begriff einsetzen.

Vergleichen Sie:

- Jack said, 'Ann, can you tell Carol to give me a ring, please?'
- Jack asked Ann to tell Carol to give him a ring.
- Ben said, 'Don't enter the studio when the red light is on.'
- Ben told everybody not to enter the studio when the red light was on.

10 The passive

1 Measures **are being introduced** to reduce traffic pollution.
2 Pollution **is caused by** some thoughtless people.

- Ist der Verursacher einer Handlung unbekannt oder zweitrangig, benutzen wir das Passiv. In erster Linie steht also das Ergebnis des Vorganges im Vordergrund (1).
- Möchten wir den Verursacher doch angeben, benutzen wir einen *by-agent* (2).

▶ Beachten Sie, dass der Agent mit *by* – auf keinen Fall *from*! – eingeleitet wird.

- Das Passiv bilden wir mit einer Zeitform von *be* und der 3. Form des Vollverbs:

Zeit	Zeitform von *be*	3. Form
simple present	*am/is/are*	*caused*
present progressive	*am/is/are being*	*introduced*
simple past	*was/were*	*buried*
past progressive	*was/were being*	*built*
present perfect	*has/have been*	*installed*
present perfect progressive	*has/have been being*	*negotiated*
***will*-Futur**	*will be*	*blocked*
***going to*-Futur**	*am/is/are going to be*	*sacked*

- Beim Gebrauch von modalen Hilfsverben verfahren wir nach folgendem Muster:

bei Aussagen	(Hilfsverb + *be* + 3. Form)	*must be displayed*
bei Fragen	(Hilfsverb + Subjekt + *be* + 3. Form)	*can … be persuaded*

▶ Beachten Sie, dass das Verb *be* immer unverändert im Infinitiv bleibt.

11 The impersonal passive

1 **It is said that** petrol should cost more.
2 Freiburg **is thought** to be a town full of ecologists.

- Wir benutzen das **impersonal passive** vor allem dann, wenn wir uns objektiv bzw. unbeteiligt ausdrücken möchten. Daher kommt diese Struktur oft in Polizeiberichten, seriösen Zeitungsartikeln usw. vor.
- Bei Verben des Berichtens, Denkens usw. benutzen wir häufig das Satzmuster:
  – *It is/was/…* + 3. Form des einleitenden Verbs + *that*-Fügung (1).

  Hier sind weitere Beispiele dieses Musters:

Aktiv	Some **say** that companies which cause pollution should be heavily fined.
Passiv	**It is said that** companies which cause pollution should be heavily fined.
Aktiv	Experts **recommended** that more be spent on public transport.
Passiv	**It was recommended** that more be spent on public transport.

- Möchten wir das Subjekt der *that*-Fügung betonen, können wir folgendes Muster benutzen:
  – Subjekt + *is/was/…* + 3. Form + *to be* + andere Satzteile (2).

  Vergleichen Sie:

Aktiv	Many **believe** that the minister is thinking of raising fuel taxes.
Passiv	The minister **is believed to be** thinking of raising fuel taxes.

▶ Beachten Sie, wie wir den *by-agent* in solchen Passivsätzen gebrauchen:

Aktiv	The speaker felt that the idea was too radical.
Passiv	The idea was felt to be too radical **by** the speaker.

12 Conditionals

1 If we **invest** in new technology, a lot of people **will lose** their jobs.
2 If they **take part** in re-training schemes, people **won't have to worry** about finding new employment.
3 We **won't have** political censorship if we **don't start** to censor the internet.
4 **Will** we soon **have** political censorship if we **start** to censor the internet?

- Ein **Konditionalsatz** besteht aus zwei Teilen: dem ***if*-Teil** und dem **Hauptteil**. Der ***if*-Teil** drückt eine **Bedingung** aus, der Hauptteil eine **Folge** (1).

- Bei **Konditionalsätzen** kommen folgende **Zeitmuster** am häufigsten vor:

Typ I	*If + simple present*	+	*will*-Futur
Typ II	*If + simple past*	+	*would* + Infinitiv
Typ III	*If + past perfect*	+	*would have* + 3. Form des Verbs

- Je nach Sinn können wir den *if*-Teil, den Hauptteil oder beide Teile des Satzes **verneinen** (2, 3).

- Bei **Fragen** dagegen können wir nur den **Hauptteil** zu einer Frage bilden. Dann steht dieser Teil **an erster Stelle** (4).

- Wir setzen *if*-Sätze gemäß der **Wahrscheinlichkeit** der zu erwartenden Folge ein:

Typ I: Folge (fast) sicher

*If we **invest in** new technology, a lot of people **will lose** their jobs.*
d.h. Viele Leute werden (vermutlich) ihre Stellen verlieren, da wir (sehr wahrscheinlich) in die neue Technologie investieren werden.

Typ II: Folge theoretisch möglich, aber kaum wahrscheinlich.

*If we **invested in** new technology, a lot of people **would lose** their jobs.*
d.h. Es ist kaum zu erwarten, dass viele Leute ihre Stellen verlieren werden, da wir (wahrscheinlich) in die neue Technologie nicht investieren werden.

Typ III: Folge unmöglich, da die Zeit, in der die Voraussetzung dafür hätte geschaffen werden können, schon abgelaufen ist.

*If we **had invested in** new technology, a lot of people **would have lost** their jobs.*
d.h. Der Sprecher weiß schon, dass keiner den Job verloren hat, da wir in die neue Technologie nicht investiert haben.

13 Gerund/Infinitive

1 Max **enjoys playing** football.
2 Can you **afford to buy** that DVD collection?
3 Cem and Julie **continued to meet** even though they had spilt up.
4 Cem and Julie **continued meeting** even though they had split up.
5 Alison **normally likes going** to parties, but **today** she would **prefer to stay** at home.

- Nach einigen Verben folgt immer die *-ing*-Form (**gerund**) (1).

Am wichtigsten sind:

admit, avoid, consider, deny, enjoy, finish, imagine, mention, mind (etwas dagegen haben)*, miss, practise, risk, suggest*

- **Nach einigen Verben** folgt immer der Infinitiv (**infinitive**) (2).

  Die **wichtigsten** Verben dieser Gruppe sind:

  afford, choose, decide, expect, hope, mean, promise, refuse, want

  ▶ Nach den Verben *begin, continue, intend* und *start* können der **Infinitiv** oder die *-ing*-**Form beliebig benutzt werden** (3, 4).

- Einige Verben werden **je nach Bedeutung** entweder mit dem **Infinitiv** oder mit der **-ing-Form** benutzt. Die **wichtigsten** Verben dieser Gruppe sind:

  like, dislike, love, hate, prefer

- Wenn von einer **allgemeingültigen Situation** die Rede ist, folgt auf diese Verben die **-ing-Form**. Handelt es sich aber um eine **Ausnahmesituation**, dann verwenden wir den **Infinitiv** (5).

advise, allow, encourage, forbid, permit, recommend

Handelt es sich um einen **konkreten Einzelfall**, verwenden wir mit diesen Verben ein **Objekt + den Infinitiv**.

*I strongly **advise you to be** more polite to people.*

Wenn es sich aber um eine **allgemeine Situation** handelt, dann steht das nachfolgende Verb in der **-ing-Form**.

*Most firms don't **allow smoking** in their offices.*

forget/remember

Die Struktur ***forget/remember*** **+ *-ing*-Form** bezieht sich auf die Vergangenheit. Sie drückt etwa die Idee „Ich werde nie vergessen ..." aus. Beachten Sie, dass „die Vergangenheit" sich nicht auf *forget/remember* bezieht, sondern auf das nachfolgende Verb.

*I still **remember getting** my first bicycle.*
*I'll never **forget going** to the Rock against Hunger concert last year.*

Die Struktur ***forget/remember*** **+ Infinitiv** dagegen bezieht sich auf die Zukunft. Sie drückt etwa die Idee aus „Ich darf nicht vergessen, etwas zu tun" bzw. „ich habe noch etwas zu tun, weil ich es bis jetzt vergessen habe".

*Dad, please **remember/don't forget to pick me up** from the station.*
*Oh dear. I **forgot/didn't remember to pick Sally up** from the station.*

regret

Die Struktur ***regret*** **+ *-ing*-Form** drückt Bedauern über eine vergangene Situation bzw. einen vergangenen Vorfall aus. Häufig handelt es sich um verpasste Chancen.

*I really **regret leaving** school without qualifications.*
*I know they will **regret buying** such a big, expensive car.*

Die Struktur ***regret* + Infinitiv** – fast immer mit einem Verb des Mitteilens wie *inform, say, tell* kombiniert – drückt eine schlechte Nachricht aus.

*I **regret to say** that I can't attend the meeting tomorrow.*
*We **regret to inform** you that the vacancy has now been filled.*

stop

Bedeutet stop „aufhören, etwas zu tun", steht das nachfolgende Verb in der **-*ing*-Form**. Bedeutet aber stop „kurz anhalten, um etwas anderes zu tun", folgt ein Verb im **Infinitiv**.

*For heaven's sake **stop shouting** at me.*
*I'm a little late because I **stopped to give** somebody a lift.*

try

Bedeutet *try* „irgendetwas ausprobieren", steht das nachfolgende Verb in der **-*ing*-Form**. Bedeutet aber *try* „sich anstrengen, etwas zu tun", folgt ein Verb im **Infinitiv**.

*I **tried phoning** Ellie, but she wasn't at home.*
*We**'ll try to repair** your computer by the weekend.*

14 Adjectives and adverbs

1 John has a **new** DVD player.
2 He always buys **expensive** equipment.
3 My computer has become **very slow**.
4 That CD sounds **terrible**.
5 We can make printouts **quickly** and **cheaply**.

- Möchten wir **Personen** oder **Sachen** näher beschreiben, benutzen wir **Adjektive** (1, 2).
- Adjektive stehen **unmittelbar vor** Substantiven oder **unmittelbar nach** einer Form von *be* bzw. *become* oder *seem*, die *be* ersetzen können (3).
- Wir benutzen **Adjektive** auch mit Verben wie *feel, look* [aussehen], *sound, smell* und *taste*, die eine **sinnliche Wahrnehmung** ausdrücken (4).
- Möchten wir ein **Tätigkeitsverb** näher beschreiben, setzen wir ein Adverb **unmittelbar nach** dem Verb bzw. Verb + Objekt (5).

  ▶ Beachten Sie, dass im Englischen – anders als im Deutschen – ein Verb und sein Objekt nicht durch ein Adverb getrennt werden können.

- Wir benutzen Adverbien auch, um **Adjektive**, **andere Adverbien** und **ganze Sätze** näher zu bestimmen:

*iPods have become **surprisingly cheap**.*	(Adverb + Adjektiv)
*My fax machine prints out **terribly slowly**.*	(Adverb + Adverb)
***Luckily** Gerd left a message on my mailbox.*	(Satzadverb)

15 Comparison of adjectives and adverbs

1 A hundred years ago life was **slower** and people may have been **happier**.
2 Which technological innovation is the **most/least important**?
3 Today you can copy data **more easily than** ever before.

- **Einsilbige Adjektive** und **zweisilbige Adjektive**, die auf -y enden – zum Beispiel easy, *happy* und *lucky* –, werden mit *-(i)er/-(i)est* gesteigert (1).
- Mehrsilbige Adjektive und **Adverbien**, die auf *-ly* enden, werden mit *more/most* gesteigert (2, 3).

  ▶ Beachten Sie, dass eine kleine Anzahl von Adverbien, die dieselbe Form wie das entsprechende Adjektiv haben, mit *-er/-est* gesteigert werden. Die wichtigsten aus dieser Gruppe sind *early, fast, hard* und *long*.

- Möchten wir Personen oder Sachen im Satz miteinander vergleichen, haben wir folgende Möglichkeiten:

– Kein Unterschied	***as** good **as***	genau so gut wie
– Unterschied	***not as** good **as***	nicht so gut wie
– Unterschied	*better **than***	besser als

16 Word order – positions of adverbs of time, place and frequency

1 She goes shopping **every week**.
2 They play in a club **in Doherty Street**.
3 **Last year** we went to India for our holidays.
4 Paul and Emily went to **the USA last year**.
5 She **always finishes** school early on Fridays.
6 He **is never** at home when I call.
7 I like to stay at home **now and then**.

- Zeitangaben (Wann?) und Ortsangaben (Wo?, Wohin?) stehen in der Regel am Satzende (1, 2).
- Möchten wir jedoch die Zeit eines bestimmten Ereignisses hervorheben, können wir die Zeitangabe an die erste Stelle setzen (3).
- Stehen eine Zeitangabe und eine Ortsangabe zusammen am Satzende, dann gilt die Reihenfolge Ort vor Zeit (alphabetisch merken: O vor Z!) (4).
- Besteht eine Häufigkeitsangabe aus einem Wort, z.B. *always, often, sometimes*, steht sie unmittelbar vor dem Vollverb (5).
- Eine **Ausnahme** bildet das Vollverb *be*, in welchem Fall das Adverb **direkt dahinter** steht (6).
- Besteht die Häufigkeitsangabe aus mehreren Wörtern, z.B. *every day, now and then*, steht sie wie eine Zeitangabe am Satzende (7).

17 Participle constructions

1 Malaria, preventable with a treated bed net **costing** less than one pound, is endemic.
2 Many men believe that any work **involved** with cooking is a woman's chore.
3 **Losing** more and more people to AIDS, Africa now needs effective help more urgently than ever before.
4 **Burdened** with declining life-expectancy, large parts of Africa are caught in a poverty trap.

5 **Having fetched** water from a river for many years, some women in developing countries are now happy to be able to use the ©Hippo Roller.
6 **Despite facing** extreme destitution, many rural residents haven't given up hope.
7 Donors should invest in projects that help local inhabitants become self-supporting, **thereby making** sure that the money isn't wasted.
8 Poor infrastructure is a key barrier to economic growth in Nepal, **thus causing** huge additional costs to the transport of commercial goods.
9 Life is becoming hard in the developing countries, **with** many small farmers **going** out of business.
10 AIDS represents a major challenge to sub-Saharan Africa, currently **killing** more than two million people every year.

Die englische Sprache ist geprägt durch häufige Verwendung von Partizipialkonstruktionen.

Diese ermöglichen einen eleganteren Sprachfluss. Partizipialkonstruktionen verkürzen

- nicht notwendige Relativsätze; dabei kann entweder das *present participle* (1) oder das *past participle* (2) verwendet werden.
- adverbiale Nebensätze; in diesen Fällen unterscheidet man zwischen Partizipialkonstruktionen ohne Konjunktion (3–5) und solchen mit Konjunktion (6–9). In Sätzen ohne Konjunktion ist der Inhalt des Satzes auch ohne eine solche klar. Dagegen sind Konjunktionen nötig, um zu verhindern, dass der logische Zusammenhang des Satzes verloren geht. Zum Beispiel wird der Inhalt von Satz 6 unklar, wenn die Konjunktion *despite* ausgelassen wird. Wie bei der Verkürzung von Relativsätzen kommen auch bei der Verkürzung von adverbialen Nebensätzen das *present participle* (3, 6–9) und das *past participle* (4) zur Anwendung. Darüber hinaus wird hier auch noch das *perfect participle* verwendet (5), und zwar um die Vorzeitigkeit der Handlung im Nebensatz auszudrücken. *(Nachdem sie jahrelang Wasser aus dem Fluss geholt hatten, …)*
- Schließlich verknüpft man mit einer Partizipialkonstruktion zwei Hauptsätze zu einem einzigen Satz, und zwar ausnahmslos mittels *present participle* (10).

18 Relative clauses and contact clauses

1 Car manufacturers are designing cars **which/that** can use hydrogen fuel cells.
2 Wildernesses are being spoiled by tourists **who/that** want to go to 'unspoiled' places.
3 Tony filled in a Dateline questionnaire **(which/that)** he found on the internet.
4 Fred Foley is a paparazzo **whose** photos sell for huge sums of money.
5 Call centre employees, most of **whom** come from India, work long hours.
6 Some non-GM crops are attacked by pests **against which** they have no resistance.

- Wir benutzen Relativsätze, um den Hauptsatz durch zusätzliche Informationen genauer zu bestimmen.
- Für **Sachen** benutzen wir das Relativpronomen *which* bzw. *that* und für **Personen** *who* bzw. *that* (1, 2).
- Steht das Relativpronomen für das **Objekt des Hauptsatzes**, dann können wir es weglassen (3). Wir nennen solche Relativsätze **contact clauses**.
- Um **Besitz** bzw. **Zugehörigkeit** anzuzeigen, gebrauchen wir *whose* unmittelbar **vor** dem **Substantiv** bei Personen und Sachen (4).

- Steht eine **Präposition** vor dem **Relativpronomen**, benutzen wir *whom* für Personen und *which* für Sachen (5, 6). In solchen Fällen ist der Gebrauch von *that* nicht möglich.

19 Defining and non-defining relative clauses

1 The first Europeans **who** settled in Australia came from Britain.
2 Sydney, **which** is famous for its unusually designed opera house, is situated on the south-eastern coast of Australia.

- Sehen Sie zunächst den **ersten Beispielsatz** an. Ohne den Relativsatz *who settled in Australia* ist der Sinn des Hauptsatzes *The first Europeans came from Britain* offensichtlich falsch bzw. unvollständig. Relativsätze dieser Art – die wesentlich für das Verständnis des gesamten Satzes sind – nennen wir **defining relative clauses** (notwendige Relativsätze).

- Sehen Sie jetzt den **zweiten Beispielsatz** an. In diesem Fall ist die Aussage des Hauptsatzes *Sydney is situated on the the south-eastern coast of Australia* ohne den Relativsatz völlig verständlich, weil der Relativsatz *which is famous for its unusually designed opera house* eine zusätzliche, also nebensächliche, Information enhält. Daher nennen wir solche Relativsätze **non-defining relative clauses** (nicht-notwendige Relativsätze).

▶ Beachten Sie, dass notwendige Relativsätze immer **ohne** trennende **Kommas** benutzt werden. Dies signalisiert, dass sie fester Bestandteil der Hauptaussage sind.

20 Group nouns

1 Our **school** is quite big. **It's got** nearly 1,500 pupils.
2 My **family**, **which** is spread all over the world, **likes** to get together at Christmas.
3 **The Netherlands is** one of the smallest countries in the EU.
4 The **clergy – who are** often confused by modern morality – **have accepted** that they must move with the times.

- Im modernen Englisch werden **group nouns**, wie *school* und *family*, mit der **3. Person Singular** und ggf. mit dem Relativpronomen *which* verwendet (1, 2). Dies gilt auch für die Pluralnamen von Staaten und Staatengemeinschaften, z.B. *the Netherlands, the USA* (3).

- **Andere group nouns** dieser Art sind:

– *band, bank, choir, class, club, college, company, court, firm, government, group, jury* [Geschworene], *orchestra, parliament, party, public, ministry, society, staff* [Mitarbeiterschaft], *university*

– *the Azores, the Bahamas, the Dutch Antilles, the Gulf States, the Philippines, the Seychelles, the United Nations ...*

▶ Beachten Sie, dass die group nouns clergy, *military* und *police* **immer** mit der 3. Person Plural und ggf. mit dem Relativpronomen *who* verwendet werden (4).

21 Countables and uncountables

1 Visit our website for more **information** on our firm. NICHT ~~informations~~
2 Have you read the paper today? The political **news is** interesting. NICHT ~~news are~~
3 Where can I get **some advice**? NICHT ~~an advice~~

- Einige wichtige **Substantive** sind **zählbar im Deutschen**, **nicht jedoch im Englischen** (1, 2).

Diese Substantive können also nicht ohne weiteres mit dem unbestimmten Artikel *a/an* oder mit einem Zahlwort benutzt werden.

Hier ist eine Liste solcher Wörter, die Sie auswendig lernen sollten:

advice, baggage, damage, data, equipment, evidence, furniture, garbage [Abfall], *information, knowledge, luck, luggage, machinery, news, progress, research, rubbish, work (housework, homework)*

- Möchten wir diese Substantive im Plural verwenden, dann müssen wir *some, a bit of* bzw. *a piece of* hinzufügen (3).

22 The definite article

1 **Sociologists** say that **violence** is increasing among young people.
2 Is **the current trend** partly caused by **the violent films** they watch?
3 **Most sentences** are not tough enough.
4 Nearly **half the prisoners** in **British prisons** are under 25.
5 **Spring** is my favourite season but **the spring** we're having this year is more like **winter**.
6 We had **breakfast** late this morning so we came to school **by car** instead of **by bus**.
7 They are thinking of legalizing soft drugs in **the Netherlands**.

- Hat ein Substantiv eine allgemeine, uneingeschränkte Bedeutung – also „alle ohne Ausnahme" – dann steht es ohne Artikel (1, 5).

- Ist die Bedeutung eines Substantives auf bestimmte Fälle eingeschränkt, benutzen wir den Artikel (2, 5).

- Ferner wird der Artikel in den folgenden Fällen und Wendungen im Englischen – anders übrigens als im Deutschen – nicht gebraucht:
  - bei *most* in der Bedeutung „die meisten" (3)
  - bei öffentlichen Gebäuden im allgemeinen Sinn (4)
  - bei Mahlzeiten (6)
  - bei Verkehrsmitteln (6)
  - bei Straßennamen
  - bei Tageszeiten, Wochentagen, Monaten und Jahreszeiten im allgemeinen Sinn (5)

- Der Artikel wird verwendet nach *all* und *half* (4) und mit den Pluralnamen von Staaten (6).

▶ Beachten Sie, dass der bestimmte Artikel im Englischen (viel) seltener als im Deutschen benutzt wird. Daher: *When in doubt, leave it out!*

IRREGULAR VERBS

Infinitive	Past Tense	Past Participle	
arise	arose	arisen	*entstehen*
be	was/were	been	*sein*
beat	beat	beaten	*schlagen*
become	became	become	*werden*
begin	began	begun	*starten, anfangen*
bind	bound	bound	*fesseln, binden*
break	broke	broken	*brechen, kaputtmachen*
bring	brought	brought	*bringen*
broadcast	broadcast	broadcast	*senden, ausstrahlen*
build	built	built	*bauen*
burn	burnt (burned)	burnt (burned)	*brennen*
buy	bought	bought	*kaufen*
catch	caught	caught	*fangen*
choose	chose	chosen	*wählen*
come	came	come	*kommen*
cost	cost	cost	*kosten*
cut	cut	cut	*schneiden*
deal	dealt	dealt	*handeln, sich beschäftigen mit*
dig	dug	dug	*graben, bohren*
do	did	done	*tun, machen*
draw	drew	drawn	*zeichnen*
dream	dreamt (dreamed)	dreamt (dreamed)	*träumen*
drink	drank	drunk	*trinken*
drive	drove	driven	*fahren*
eat	ate	eaten	*essen*
fall	fell	fallen	*fallen*
feel	felt	felt	*fühlen*
fight	fought	fought	*(be)kämpfen*
find	found	found	*finden*
fly	flew	flown	*fliegen*
forget	forgot	forgotten	*vergessen*
freeze	froze	frozen	*frieren*
get	got	got	*bekommen*
give	gave	given	*geben*
go	went	gone	*gehen*
grow	grew	grown	*wachsen*
have	had	had	*haben*
hear	heard	heard	*hören*
hide	hid	hidden	*(sich) verstecken*
hit	hit	hit	*schlagen*
hold	held	held	*halten*
hurt	hurt	hurt	*weh tun*
input	input (inputted)	input (inputted)	*eingeben*

keep	kept	kept	*behalten*
know	knew	known	*wissen, kennen*
lay	laid	laid	*legen*
lead	led	led	*führen*
learn	learnt (learned)	learnt (learned)	*lernen*
leave	left	left	*(weg)gehen, (ver)lassen*
let	let	let	*lassen, erlauben*
light	lit (lighted)	lit (lighted)	*erleuchten, entzünden*
lose	lost	lost	*verlieren*
make	made	made	*machen, tun*
mean	meant	meant	*bedeuten*
meet	met	met	*treffen*
pay	paid	paid	*bezahlen*
put	put	put	*legen, stellen*
read	read	read	*lesen*
ride	rode	ridden	*fahren, reiten*
rise	rose	risen	*steigen, sich erheben*
ring	rang	rung	*klingeln*
run	ran	run	*laufen, verwalten*
say	said	said	*sagen*
see	saw	seen	*sehen*
seek	sought	sought	*suchen*
sell	sold	sold	*verkaufen*
send	sent	sent	*senden*
set	set	set	*setzen, stellen, legen*
shake	shook	shaken	*schütteln*
show	showed	shown (showed)	*zeigen*
shut	shut	shut	*schließen*
sing	sang	sung	*singen*
sink	sank	sunk	*(ver)senken*
sit	sat	sat	*sitzen*
sleep	slept	slept	*schlafen*
smell	smelt (smelled)	smelt (smelled)	*riechen*
speak	spoke	spoken	*sprechen*
speed	sped	sped (speeded)	*rasen*
spell	spelt (spelled)	spelt (spelled)	*buchstabieren*
spend	spent	spent	*ausgeben*
stand	stood	stood	*stehen*
steal	stole	stolen	*stehlen*
swim	swam	swum	*schwimmen*
take	took	taken	*nehmen*
teach	taught	taught	*unterrichten*
tear	tore	torn	*zerreißen*
tell	told	told	*erzählen*
think	thought	thought	*denken*
throw	threw	thrown	*werfen*
understand	understood	understood	*verstehen*
wake	woke	woken	*wecken*
wear	wore	worn	*tragen*
win	won	won	*gewinnen*
write	wrote	written	*schreiben*

PROBLEM WORDS AND FALSE FRIENDS

Fremdsprachenlernen ist faszinierend. Man stolpert immer wieder über erstaunliche Dinge. So gibt es im Englischen etwa eine Reihe von Wörtern, die mehrere Bedeutungen haben können (ähnlich wie im Deutschen). Solche Wörter kann man als Problemwörter sehen. Es gibt auch deutsche und englische Wörter, die zwar gleich oder ähnlich aussehen, gleich oder ähnlich klingen, die jedoch ganz verschiedene Bedeutungen haben. Solche Wörter nennt man False Friends – man kann sich auf sie nicht verlassen.

Hier ist eine kleine Auswahl von Problemwörtern und falschen Freunden. Machen Sie sich eine Notiz, wenn Sie derartigen Wörtern begegnen, und ergänzen Sie die Liste. Dann werden Sie diese Wörter gut beherrschen.

NOUNS

brochure	Prospekt, Faltblatt
prospect	(Zukunfts-)Aussicht
chef	(Chef-)Koch
boss	Chef / Chefin (einer Firma)
look	Blick, Aussehen
to watch (v)	ansehen
meaning	Bedeutung
opinion	Meinung
mobile phone (BE) / cell phone (AE)	Handy
handy (adj.)	praktisch, nützlich, geschickt

ADJECTIVES

actual	eigentlich, tatsächlich
current	aktuell
the latest	die neueste
the last	der/die/das Letzte
last	letzte(r,s), am Ende
at last	endlich, schließlich
sensible	vernünftig
sensitive	sensibel

ADVERBS

actually	eigentlich
currently	zurzeit, momentan
for (two days)	seit (zwei Tagen)
(two days) ago	vor (zwei Tagen)

least	am wenigsten
at least	wenigstens, zumindest
possibly	möglicherweise, vielleicht
eventually	schließlich, endlich

PREPOSITIONS

beside	neben
besides (adv.)	außerdem
next	nächste(r,s)
nearly (adv.)	fast, beinahe

VERBS AND VERB PHRASES

to be lucky	Glück haben (to ~~have luck~~)
to be happy	glücklich sein
to become	werden
to get	bekommen
to blame sb for	jdm die Schuld geben an, für
to disgrace sb, oneself	jdn/sich blamieren
to borrow	borgen, ausleihen
to lend	verleihen
to bring sb/sth	jdn/etwas mitbringen
to take sb/sth	jdn/etwas irgendwohin bringen
to discuss sth	etwas besprechen (to discuss ~~about~~)
to get up	aufstehen
to stand up	sich erheben
keep (working)	(an der Arbeit) bleiben
stay (working)	dranbleiben
to look	aussehen
to look after sb/sth	sich um jdn/etwas kümmern
to look for sb/sth	nach jdn/etwas suchen
to look into sth	etwas untersuchen
to lose	verlieren
to loosen	locker machen, lösen
loose (adj)	locker, nicht fest
to make sth	etwas machen, herstellen
to make sth of ~	etwas herstellen aus ~
to make out	etwas ausschreiben, entwickeln, entziffern
to mean	bedeuten
to think, to believe	meinen, glauben
to prove	beweisen, sich erweisen als
to check (on)	überprüfen, nachprüfen, kontrollieren
to raise	heben
to rise	hochgehen, aufgehen
to rob	(aus)rauben
to steal	stehlen, entwenden
to start off	etw. anfangen
to take off	starten, abheben
to wonder (if...)	sich fragen (ob...) wundern
to be surprised	überrascht sein, sich

CHRONOLOGISCHES WÖRTERVERZEICHNIS

Dieses Wörterverzeichnis enthält alle wichtigen Wörter der Units 1 – 15 in chronologischer Reihenfolge.

Abkürzungen:

adj	adjective	*abbr*	abbreviation	*eg*	for example
adv	adverb	*infl*	informal	*ie*	in other words
conj	conjunction	*lit*	literal	*sb*	somebody
n	noun	*GB*	chiefly British English	*sth*	something
phr	phrase or idiom	*AE*	chiefly American English	*usu*	usually
pl	plural				
pp	past participle			⇔	opposite of
prep	preposition				
v	verb				

UNIT 1 HAPPINESS IS ...

8 **express** *v* [ɪk'spres] to show a feeling or an opinion by words or actions

9 **make the world go round** *phr* [meɪk ðə ˌwɜːld gəʊ 'raʊnd] to be very important for sth

reveal *v* [rɪ'viːl] to make sth known that was unknown before

average *adj* ['ævərɪdʒ] normal, standard

increasingly *adv* [ɪn'kriːsɪŋli] more and more

boost *v* [buːst] to increase sth in number, value or strength

splash the cash *phr* [splæʃ ðə 'kæʃ] to spend a lot of money on sth

night out on the town *phr* [naɪt aʊt əv 'taʊn] an evening that you spend in town enjoying yourself

quick fix *phr* [kwɪk 'fɪks] quick solution to a problem

long-term *adj* [ˌlɒŋ'tɜːm] for a long period of time

rest with/on *v* ['rest wɪð, ɒn] to depend on, be based on

take for granted *phr* [ˌteɪk fə 'grɑːntɪd] to not be grateful enough to a person or thing

have a laugh *phr* [həv ə 'lɑːf] to have fun

be aware that *v* [bi ə'weə ðət] to realize

route *n* [ruːt] a way of achieving sth

adept *adj* [ə'dept] very good or skilful at sth

short-term *adj* [ˌʃɔːt'tɜːm] for a short period of time

pick-up *n* ['pɪkʌp] sth that makes you feel better/happier

mood *n* [muːd] the way that you feel at a particular time

enhancer *n* [ɪn'hɑːnsə] sth that improves sth else, makes sth better

get used to *v* [get 'juːst tə] to become familiar with (*sich an etw gewöhnen*)

source *n* [sɔːs] a place, person or thing where sth comes or starts from

improvement *n* [ɪm'pruːvmənt] *Verbesserung*

well-being *n* ['welbiːɪŋ] the state of being healthy and happy

continually *adv* [kən'tɪnjuəli] happening again and again

iː	ɪ	e	æ	ɑː	ɒ	ɔː	ʊ	uː	ʌ	ɜː	ə
see	sit	ten	bad	arm	got	saw	put	too	cut	bird	about

wear off *v* [ˌweər ˈɒf] to become less strong or to disappear completely
spokesperson *n* [ˈspəʊkspɜːsn] a person who is chosen to speak for a group or organization
heritage *n* [ˈherɪtɪdʒ] traditions that have existed for a long time
matter *v* [ˈmætə] to be important
fancy *v* [ˈfænsi] to like, to desire
do sb the world of good *phr, infl* [du ðə ˌwɜːld əv ˈgʊd] to really benefit/help sb

10 **summarize** *v* [ˈsʌməraɪz] to give a short description of sth, including the most important points
according to *prep* [əˈkɔːdɪŋ tə] as shown/said by
satisfy *v* [ˈsætɪsfaɪ] to make sb pleased by doing sth he/she wants
additional *adj* [əˈdɪʃənl] added, extra
explanation *n* [ˌekspləˈneɪʃn] a statement that makes a situation clear or understandable
in the long run *phr* [ɪn ðə lɒŋ ˈrʌn] after a long time, in the end
occasional *adj* [əˈkeɪʒənl] done or happening from time to time but not very often
treat *n* [triːt] sth that is very special or enjoyable, that one saves for special occasions
pleasure *n* [ˈpleʒə] an event or activity that makes you happy
lift sb's mood *phr* [lɪft ˈmuːd] to make sb feel better
be surrounded by *v* [bi səˈraʊndɪd baɪ] to have sth/sb all around you

11 **lend sth to sb** *v* [lend tə] *jdm etw ausleihen*
borrow sth from sb *v* [ˈbɒrəʊ frəm] *sich von jdm etw ausleihen*
be rolling in *phr* [bɪ ˈrəʊlɪŋ ɪn] to have a lot of sth (especially money)
coincidence *n* [kəʊˈɪnsɪdəns] the surprising fact of two or more things happening at the same time by chance
put sb in a good mood *phr* [ˌpʊt ɪn ə gʊd ˈmuːd] to make sb feel good
agree *v* [əˈgriː] to be of the same opinion as sb
disagree *v* [ˌdɪsəˈgriː] to be of a different opinion (⇔ agree)

12 **take responsibility** *v* [teɪk rɪˌspɒnsəˈbɪləti] *Verantwortung tragen*
set aside *v* [set əˈsaɪd] to put sth to one side (here: to plan, to reserve)
time-slot *n* [ˈtaɪm slɒt] a period of time
appendix *n* [əˈpendɪks] a section at the end of a book that gives further information
learning type *n* [ˈlɜːnɪŋ taɪp] *Lerntyp*
adapt (to sth) *v* [əˈdæpt tə] to change your behaviour because the situation you are in has changed
vary *v* [ˈveəri] to become different, to change
personal success *n* [ˌpɜːsənl səkˈses] achieving what you want in life, doing well
self-expression *n* [ˌself ɪkˈspreʃn] the act of saying or doing what one believes in
family values *n* [ˈfæməli væljuːz] a set of beliefs about how you should behave in a family
come tops *phr* [kʌm ˈtɒps] to be the most important, to be the best, to win
value *v* [ˈvæljuː] to think sb/sth is very important
do sb a good turn *phr* [du ə gʊd ˈtɜːn] to do sb a favour, to do sth nice/kind for sb
have faith *v* [həv ˈfeɪθ] to have a strong belief (in sb/sth), to trust
looks *n* [lʊks] one's appearance (*Aussehen*)
genius *n* [ˈdʒiːniəs] sb with a very great and unusual talent
exam preparation *n* [ɪgˌzæm ˌprepəˈreɪʃn] the process of getting ready for an exam
put into practice *v* [ˌpʊt ɪntə ˈpræktɪs] to make sth happen, to implement sth
take notes *v* [teɪk ˈnəʊts] to write sth down so that you remember it
pursue *v* [pəˈsjuː] to continue with sth, to find out more about sth
particular *adj* [pəˈtɪkjələ] here: individual

13 **kettle** *n* [ˈketl] *Wasserkocher*
receiver *n* [rɪˈsiːvə] the part of the telephone that is used for listening and speaking

tʃ	dʒ	ʃ	ʒ	θ	ð	ŋ	s	z	v	w
chips	jet	ship	garage	thing	the	ring	ice	as	very	wet

get in touch *phr* [get ɪn 'tʌtʃ] to contact sb
be on the road *phr* [bi ɒn ðə 'rəʊd] to travel
be in *phr* [bi 'ɪn] to be at home
tough *adj* [tʌf] difficult
truth *n* [tru:θ] sth that is true
leave a message *phr* [li:v ə 'mesɪdʒ] *eine Nachricht hinterlassen* (here: *auf dem Anrufbeantworter*)
in vain *phr* [ɪn 'veɪn] without success
ashtray *n* ['æʃtreɪ] a small dish for cigarette ash
end up (as sth) *v* [ˌend 'ʌp əz] to find yourself in a position that you did not intend or expect
hearth *n* [hɑ:θ] the floor of a fireplace and the area in front of it
prompt *v* [prɒmpt] to help sb continue speaking, to give them an idea
pass *v* [pɑ:s] to reach the necessary standard in an exam
do well *v* [ˌdu: 'wel] to get good marks in an exam
whisper *v* ['wɪspə] to speak very quietly
disappointment *n* [ˌdɪsə'pɔɪntmənt] *Enttäuschung*

14 **to not matter a damn** *phr* [nɒt ˌmætər ə 'dæm] to make absolutely no difference
decent *adj* ['di:snt] satisfactory, of an acceptable standard
yobbo (GB) *n, infl* ['jɒbəʊ] boy or young man who behaves badly in public
dole (GB) *n, infl* [dəʊl] money that the state gives every week to people who are unemployed
try and make a go of it *v, infl* [ˌtraɪ ən ˌmeɪk ə 'gəʊ əv ɪt] to try sth
bloke (GB) *n, infl* [bləʊk] man
get trampled on *v* [get 'træmpld ɒn] to be treated unfairly
plenty *adv* ['plenti] a lot of
peak *v* [pi:k] to reach the highest level, value or rate
degree *n* [dɪ'gri:] a qualification gained by successfully completing a course at university or college
rehearse *v* [rɪ'hɜ:s] to practise
pretty *adv, infl* ['prɪti] quite, rather
cigarette butt *n* [ˌsɪgə'ret bʌt] cigarette filter that you throw away
scatter *v* ['skætə] to drop or throw things in different directions over a wide area
spark *n* [spɑ:k] a small bright piece of burning material
turn into *v* ['tɜ:n ɪntə] to become, to change into
argument *n* ['ɑ:gjumənt] an angry discussion between two or more people who do not agree with each other
pay sb a visit *v* [peɪ ə 'vɪzɪt] to go and see sb
go spare *phr, infl* [gəʊ 'speə] to become very angry
serves you right *phr* [sɜ:v ju 'raɪt] *geschieht dir recht*
whistle *v* ['wɪsl] *pfeifen*
hard-edged *adj* [ˌhɑ:d 'edʒd] *kalt, bitter*
bitterness *n* ['bɪtənəs] anger and unhappiness as a result of sth bad happening
depend on sb *v* [dɪ'pend ɒn] to be sure that sb will help you, to rely on sb
see to sth *v* ['si: tə] to do what is necessary

15 **appropriate** *adj* [ə'prəʊpriət] suitable or right
ending *n* ['endɪŋ] the end of a story, film, etc.
fail *v* [feɪl] to be unsuccessful in sth
achieve *v* [ə'tʃi:v] to gain sth, to get sth done
drop out of sth *v* [ˌdrɒp 'aʊt əv] to leave or stop doing sth before you have finished it
waste time *v* ['weɪst taɪm] *Zeit verschwenden*
suitable for sb/sth *adj* ['su:təbl fə] appropriate or convenient for sb/sth
shortly *adv* ['ʃɔ:tli] soon, in a short time
hang up *v* [ˌhæŋ 'ʌp] *auflegen*

16 **spot** *v* [spɒt] to find
written excuse *n* [ˌrɪtn ɪk'skju:s] *schriftliche Entschuldigung*
habit *n* ['hæbɪt] sth that sb does very often
swap *v* [swɒp] to exchange, to give sth for sth else
gig *n* [gɪg] concert

17 **brackets** *n* ['brækɪts] *Klammern*
unscramble *v* [ˌʌn'skræmbl] to put in the correct order

i:	ɪ	e	æ	ɑ:	ɒ	ɔ:	ʊ	u:	ʌ	ɜ:	ə
see	sit	ten	bad	arm	got	saw	put	too	cut	bird	about

UNIT 2 GOING PLACES

18 **make up** *v* [ˌmeɪk ˈʌp] to invent
caption *n* [ˈkæpʃn] words that are written above or below a picture
19 **spire** *n* [ˈspaɪə] a tall pointed tower often seen on a church
brim with *v* [ˈbrɪm wɪð] to be full of sth
treasure *n* [ˈtreʒə] a collection of very valuable objects, sth that is very valuable
sparkling *adj* [ˈspɑːklɪŋ] *glitzernd, funkelnd*
wonder *n* [ˈwʌndə] sth that causes you to feel surprise or admiration
delight *n* [dɪˈlaɪt] great pleasure
Lake District [ˈleɪk dɪstrɪkt] beautiful holiday destination in the Northwest of England
guarantee *v* [ˌgærənˈtiː] to promise
make the most of [meɪk ðə ˈməʊst əv] *das Beste aus etwas machen*
cookery *n* [ˈkʊkəri] the skill or methods of cooking (preparing food to eat)
stunning *adj* [ˈstʌnɪŋ] very attractive, impressive
varied *adj* [ˈveərid] different from each other, changing
tranquil *adj* [ˈtræŋkwɪl] calm and quiet
surroundings *n* [səˈraʊndɪŋz] everything that is near or around you
cottage *n* [ˈkɒtɪdʒ] a small and (usually) old house
refreshed *adj* [rɪˈfreʃt] to feel fresh and full of energy again
invigorated adj [ɪnˈvɪgəreɪtɪd] to feel fresher and more energetic
lonely *adj* [ˈləʊnli] to feel alone
vulnerable *adj* [ˈvʌlnərəbl] to be easy to attack, hurt, or defeat
common ground *n* [ˌkɒmən ˈgraʊnd] land open to everyone (*gemeinsames Land*)
threatened *adj* [ˈθretnd] to be in danger of being hurt
participate *v* [pɑːˈtɪsɪpeɪt] to take part in sth
care for *v* [ˈkeə fə] to look after
captive *adj* [ˈkæptɪv] not free
on-site *adv* [ˌɒn ˈsaɪt] *vor Ort*
conservation *n* [ˌkɒnsəˈveɪʃn] the protection of the natural world
20 **hike** *v* [haɪk] to go for a long walk in the countryside, often up and down hills
faraway *adj* [ˈfɑːrəweɪ] distant
unfortunately *adv* [ʌnˈfɔːtʃənətli] unluckily
scenery *n* [ˈsiːnəri] *Landschaft*
out in the open *adv* [ˌaʊt ɪn ði ˈəʊpən] *im Freien*
afford *v* [əˈfɔːd] to have enough money or time to be able to do sth
explore *v* [ɪkˈsplɔː] to travel around a place and find out more about it
21 **spider** *n* [ˈspaɪdə] *Spinne*
abroad *adv* [əˈbrɔːd] in or to another country or countries
motorbike *n* [ˈməʊtəbaɪk] *Motorrad*
behaviour *n* [bɪˈheɪvjə] the way that you act
avoid *v* [əˈvɔɪd] here: to try not to do sth
uncomfortable *adj* [ʌnˈkʌmftəbl] here: unhappy, embarrassed, anxious
22 **fieldwork assistant** *n* [ˌfiːldwɜːk əˈsɪstənt] sb who helps with outdoor research
exploraholic *n* [ˌɪksplɔːrəˈhɒlɪk] (not a real word) sb who loves exploring
term *n* [tɜːm] word
pure *adj* [pjʊə] here: only
secretive *adj* [ˈsiːkrətɪv] not telling people about sth you are doing or want to do
admit *v* [ədˈmɪt] to agree, often without wanting to, that sth is true
environment *n* [ɪnˈvaɪrənmənt] *Umwelt*
local *adj* [ˈləʊkl] nearby
consider *v* [kənˈsɪdə] to think about sth
package holiday *n* [ˈpækɪdʒ hɒlədeɪ] *Pauschalreise*
the masses *n* [ðə ˈmæsɪz] *die große Masse* (*der Bevölkerung*)
fastest-growing *adj* [ˌfɑːstɪst ˈgrəʊɪŋ] expanding quickly
forecast *v* [ˈfɔːkɑːst] to say what will probably happen in the future
convince *v* [kənˈvɪns] to succeed in making sb believe in sth
harmful *adj* [ˈhɑːmfl] causing harm, not good for you
welfare *n* [ˈwelfeə] here: health
selfish *adj* [ˈselfɪʃ] always thinking of yourself first

tʃ	dʒ	ʃ	ʒ	θ	ð	ŋ	s	z	v	w
chips	jet	ship	garage	thing	the	ring	ice	as	very	wet

irresponsible *adj* [ˌɪrɪ'spɒnsəbl] not thinking about the consequences of one's actions, not responsible
evil *adj* ['iːvl] (very) bad
cause harm *v* [kɔːz 'hɑːm] *schädlich sein, einen Schaden anrichten*
subtle *adj* ['sʌtl] not very strong
re-brand *v* [ˌriː'brænd] here: re-name
charity *n* ['tʃærəti] an organization that collects money to help people in need
volunteer *n* [ˌvɒlən'tɪə] sb who offers to help/work without being paid
assure *v* [ə'ʃʊə] to make sth sure or certain
offer *v* ['ɒfə] to give or provide sth (here: *anbieten*)
opportunity *n* [ˌɒpə'tjuːnəti] a chance to do sth
benefit *n* ['benɪfɪt] sth that has a good or useful effect

23 **exclude** *v* [ɪk'skluːd] to leave out, to not include
ecological *adj* [ˌiːkə'lɒdʒɪkl] *ökologisch*
issue *n* ['ɪʃuː] a problem or subject for discussion
superior *adj* [suː'pɪəriə] better than normal, better than sth/sb else
apply to *v* [ə'plaɪ tə] to concern (*betreffen*)
Developing World *n* [dɪ'veləpɪŋ wɜːld] *Entwicklungsländer*
tribe *n* [traɪb] *Stamm*
check out *v* [ˌtʃek 'aʊt] to have a look at
be responsible towards *v* [bi rɪ'spɒnsəbl təwɔːdz] *verantwortlich umgehen mit*
division *n* [dɪ'vɪʒn] here: a difference
privileged *adj* ['prɪvəlɪdʒd] having an advantage (over sb else)
speak out against *v* [ˌspiːk 'aʊt əgenst] *sich gegen etwas aussprechen*
border *n* ['bɔːdə] the line that separates two countries (*Grenze*)
invent *v* [ɪn'vent] to make up
emphasize *v* ['emfəsaɪz] to make clear, to highlight
exaggerate *v* [ɪg'zædʒəreɪt] to make sth seem larger, smaller, better, worse, etc. than it is
damage *v* ['dæmɪdʒ] to do harm, to break (*beschädigen*)
focus on sth *v* ['fəʊkəs ɒn] to give all your attention to sth
concern *v* [kən'sɜːn] to be of importance to sb
attack *v* [ə'tæk] to try to hurt sb or sth

24 **opposite** *adj* ['ɒpəzɪt] here: *gegenüberliegend*
receipt *n* [rɪ'siːt] *Quittung*
amount *n* [ə'maʊnt] quantity, number (*Menge*)

25 **one fifth** *n* [wʌn 'fɪfθ] *ein Fünftel*
tour operator *n* ['tʊər ɒpəreɪtə] a company that organizes holidays
guess *v* [ges] to suggest an answer without being sure of all the facts
anthropology *n* [ˌænθrə'pɒlədʒi] the study of human beings
employee *n* [ɪm'plɔɪiː] a person who works for sb else
extensive *adj* [ɪk'stensɪv] here: a lot of
travel experience *n* [ˌtrævl ɪk'spɪəriəns] the travelling sb has done
vacant *adj* ['veɪkənt] not filled
apply for *v* [ə'plaɪ fə] *sich bewerben*
charming *adj* ['tʃɑːmɪŋ] very pleasing or attractive

26 **intend** *v* [ɪn'tend] to plan or want to do sth
gap year *n* ['gæp jɪə] time between school and university when many young British people work or go travelling

27 **go without saying** *phr* [ˌgəʊ wɪðaʊt 'seɪɪŋ] to be clear

UNIT 3 KEEPING FIT

28 **range** *n* [reɪndʒ] different things that belong to the same group
flow chart *n* ['fləʊ tʃɑːt] *Flussdiagramm*
suit *v* [suːt] to be right for sb
demand *v* [dɪ'mɑːnd] to need (here: *benötigen, verlangen*)
rowing *v* ['rəʊɪŋ] *Rudern*
rock climbing *n* ['rɒk klaɪmɪŋ] *Klettern*
cycling *n* ['saɪklɪŋ] *Radfahren*
whitewater rafting *n* [ˌwaɪtwɔːtə 'rɑːftɪŋ] *Wildwasserfahren*
hang-gliding *n* ['hæŋ glaɪdɪŋ] *Drachenfliegen*
parachuting *n* ['pærəʃuːtɪŋ] *Fallschirmspringen*
cliff diving *n* ['klɪf glaɪdɪŋ] *Klippen-Kunstspringen*

iː	ɪ	e	æ	ɑː	ɒ	ɔː	ʊ	uː	ʌ	ɜː	ə
see	sit	ten	bad	arm	got	saw	put	too	cut	bird	about

enthusiastic *adj* [ɪnˌθjuːziˈæstɪk] very interested, excited
keen *adj* [kiːn] very interested in sth, wanting to do sth
29 **target market** *n* [ˈtɑːgɪt mɑːkɪt] *Zielgruppe*
educated *adj* [ˈedʒukeɪtɪd] having learnt a lot of things to a high standard
vigorous *adj* [ˈvɪgərəs] strong, full of energy
downtown (AE) *adv* [ˈdaʊntaʊn] in the centre of town
till *prep* [tɪl] until, up to the time or event mentioned
dawn *n* [dɔːn] very early in the morning, when the sun comes up
advertising lines *n* [ˈædvətaɪzɪŋ laɪnz] *Werbesprüche*
ad *abbr* [æd] advertisement
proclaim *v* [prəˈkleɪm] to make sth known officially or publicly
promise *v* [ˈprɒmɪs] to say that you will or will not do sth
wing *n* [wɪŋ] *Flügel*
collapse *v* [kəˈlæps] here: to sit down because you are exhausted
take refuge *v* [teɪk ˈrefjuːdʒ] here: *sich eine Auszeit gönnen*
booze *n, infl* [buːz] alcohol
earth-shaking *adj* [ˈɜːθ ʃeɪkɪŋ] so loud that the floor is vibrating
vigorously *adv* [ˈvɪgərəsli] with a lot of energy
strut your stuff *phr, infl* [ˌstrʌt jɔː ˈstʌf] to dance
trembling *adj* [ˈtremblɪŋ] shaking
revival *n* [rɪˈvaɪvl] the act of becoming strong again
rush *n* [rʌʃ] a time when many people try to get sth (*Andrang*)
right around the clock *phr* [ˌraɪt əraʊnd ðə ˈklɒk] until the morning
system *n* [ˈsɪstəm] here: body
fast-forward *adj* [ˌfɑːst ˈfɔːwəd] here: hyper, nervous
din *n, infl* [dɪn] noise
glide *v* [glaɪd] to slide
slender *adj* [ˈslendə] thin, narrow
can *n* [kän] *Dose*
blotto *adj, infl* [ˈblɒtəʊ] drunk
pint *n* [paɪnt] a measure of liquid (568ml)
not to mention *phr* [nɒt tə ˈmenʃn] (used for emphasis) and also; as well as
legion *n* [ˈliːdʒən] a large group
college crammer *n, infl* [ˈkɒlɪdʒ kræmə] student who is working very hard (usually just before an exam)
brainpower *n* [ˈbreɪnpaʊə] here: concentration, ability to think and work late
cover *v* [ˈkʌvə] here: to drive
turn in *v* [ˌtɜːn ˈɪn] to finish work for the day and go to bed
concoction *n* [kənˈkɒkʃn] mixture of different ingredients or things
fizzy *adj* [ˈfɪzi] full of bubbles
manifestation *n* [ˌmænɪfeˈsteɪʃn] a sign of sth existing or happening
mankind *n* [mænˈkaɪnd] all the people in the world
stimulant *n* [ˈstɪmjulənt] sth that makes the body or mind more active
caffeine *n* [ˈkæfiːn] *Koffein*
ingredient *n* [ɪnˈgriːdiənt] *Zutat*
hugely *adv* [ˈhjuːdʒli] very
Austrian *adj* [ˈɒstriən] *österreichisch*
solid *adj* [ˈsɒlɪd] hard and firm; here: large, big
jolt *n, infl* [dʒəʊlt] here: amount, portion
stuff *n* [stʌf] *Zeug*
blend *v* [blend] to mix
ounce *n* [aʊns] measure of weight (28g)
counter *v* [ˈkaʊntə] to fight
physical *adj* [ˈfɪzɪkl] bodily
fatigue *n* [fəˈtiːg] tiredness
increase *v* [ɪnˈkriːs] *steigern*
alertness *n* [əˈlɜːtnəs] *Aufmerksamkeit*
rank *v* [ræŋk] to have or to give a place in an order of importance
mood-altering *adj* [ˈmuːd ɔːltərɪŋ] changing how sb feels
eclipse *v* [ɪˈklɪps] to make sth else seem less interesting or important
the likes of *phr* [ðə ˈlaɪks əv] things like ..., people like ...
pervasiveness *n* [pəˈveɪsɪvnəs] here: available everywhere
concern *n* [kənˈsɜːn] worry
scientist *n* [ˈsaɪəntɪst] *Wissenschaftler/in*
advocate *n* [ˈædvəkeɪt] a person who supports a particular plan or action

tʃ	dʒ	ʃ	ʒ	θ	ð	ŋ	s	z	v	w
chips	jet	ship	garage	thing	the	ring	ice	as	very	wet

dampen *v* ['dæmpən] here: to weaken
copycat *n, infl* ['kɒpikæt] *Nachmacher,* here: *nachgeahmtes Produkt*
30 **consume** *v* [kən'sjuːm] here: to drink
mention *v* ['menʃn] to talk about sb/sth
wide awake *adj* [waɪd ə'weɪk] *hellwach*
exhausted *adj* [ɪg'zɔːstɪd] very tired
frightened by *adj* ['fraɪtnd baɪ] scared of sth/sb
fuss *n* [fʌs] unnecessary nervous excitement or activity
to be in favour of *phr* [bi ɪn 'feɪvər əv] *befürworten*
organism *n* ['ɔːgənɪzəm] *Organismus*
availability *n* [əˌveɪlə'bɪləti] *Erhältlichkeit, Vorhandensein*
shelter *n* ['ʃeltə] sth that provides protection
utmost *adj* ['ʌtməʊst] greatest
32 **intoxicated** *adj* [ɪn'tɒksɪkeɪtɪd] very excited
thrill *n* [θrɪl] a strong feeling of excitement
exertion *n* [ɪg'zɜːʃn] *körperliche Anstrengung, Bewegung*
vast *adj* [vɑːst] huge, extremely big
capability *n* [ˌkeɪpə'bɪləti] *Fähigkeit*
hobble around *v, infl* ['hɒbl əraʊnd] *herumhumpeln*
sore *adj* [sɔː] painful
decrease *v* [dɪ'kriːs] *abnehmen*
hooked *adj* [hʊkt] addicted to sth (*von etwas abhängig sein*)
approach *n* [ə'prəʊtʃ] *Ansatz*
overcome *v* [ˌəʊvə'kʌm] to succeed in defeating sth (*überwinden*)
make a pact *phr* [meɪk ə 'pækt] *einen Pakt schließen*
drag sb out *v, infl* [ˌdræg 'aʊt] to persuade sb to come out with you
vice versa *phr* [ˌvaɪs 'vɜːsə] *und umgekehrt*
progress *n* ['prəʊgres] improvement
security *n* [sɪ'kjʊərəti] confidence
muscle tone *n* ['mʌsl təʊn] *Muskeltonus*
circulate *v* ['sɜːkjəleɪt] to move around continuously
oxygen *n* ['ɒksɪdʒən] *Sauerstoff*
satisfying *adj* ['sætɪsfaɪɪŋ] when sth makes you feel good, content, happy
glow *n* [gləʊ] a warm light; here: a warm feeling inside
reward *n* [rɪ'wɔːd] *Belohnung*
effort *n* ['efət] *Anstrengung*
guilty *adj* ['gɪlti] being responsible for doing sth wrong
major *adj* ['meɪdʒə] here: big, important
in contrast to *phr* [ɪn 'kɒntrɑːst tə] *im Gegensatz zu*
attend *v* [ə'tend] here: *antreten*
competitively *adv* [kəm'petətɪvli] to do sth with the goal of winning
a sense of *n* [ə 'sens əv] a feeling of
competitor *n* [kəm'petɪtə] sb taking part in a competition, e.g. a race
goal *n* [gəʊl] aim, purpose
innocently *adv* ['ɪnəsntli] without realizing the consequences
compulsive *adj* [kəm'pʌlsɪv] forced, uncontrollable
drive *n* [draɪv] energy or motivation to do sth
at the expense of *phr* [ət ði ɪk'spens əv] *auf Kosten von*
worth *n* [wɜːθ] value
spell racing doom *v* [spel 'reɪsɪŋ duːm] here: to mean the end of a racing career
deposit *v* [dɪ'pɒzɪt] here: to store
erase *v* [ɪ'reɪz] to eliminate
ticking back on the clock *phr* [ˌtɪkɪŋ ˌbæk ɒn ðə 'klɒk] here: the racing time is getting worse
clock up *v* [ˌklɒk 'ʌp] *zurücklegen, erreichen, schaffen*
to match *v* [mætʃ] to equal
competitive spirit *n* [kəmˌpetətɪv 'spɪrɪt] *Wettkampfgeist*
take over *v* [ˌteɪk 'əʊvə] to take control
lose sight of *phr* [ˌluːz 'saɪt əv] *aus den Augen verlieren*
limitation *n* [ˌlɪmɪ'teɪʃn] barrier, limit
rest *n* [rest] *Erholung*
special *adj* ['speʃl] *besonders*
case *n* [keɪs] *Fall*
recovery time *n* [rɪ'kʌvəri taɪm] time that it takes before you are fit again
mortal *adj* ['mɔːtl] *sterblich*
irritable *adj* ['ɪrɪtəbl] easily annoyed, angry
in retrospect *phr* [ɪn 'retrəspekt] looking back
discomfort *n* [dɪs'kʌmfət] not feeling comfortable or happy
rewarding *adj* [rɪ'wɔːdɪŋ] sth that fills you with a feeling of satisfaction

iː	ɪ	e	æ	ɑː	ɒ	ɔː	ʊ	uː	ʌ	ɜː	ə
see	sit	ten	bad	arm	got	saw	put	too	cut	bird	about

challenge *v* ['tʃælɪndʒ] *herausfordern*
bring forth *v* [brɪŋ 'fɔ:θ] to bring out in sb, to activate
height *n* [haɪt] here: achievements (*Höhe*)
33 **over the span of a year** *phr* [ˌəʊvə ðə 'spæn əv ə jɪə] *im Verlauf eines Jahres*
announce *v* [ə'naʊns] to make sth known publicly
get sb out on the roads *v* [ˌget 'aʊt ɒn ðə rəʊdz] to motivate sb to join you outside
necessary *adj* ['nesəsəri] needed (*nötig*)
corresponding *adj* [ˌkɒrɪ'spɒndɪŋ] related, similar
challenge *n* ['tʃælɪndʒ] *Herausforderung*
pose *v* [pəʊz] to cause or create
overexert *v* [ˌəʊvərɪg'zɜ:t] to do too much sport
force *v* [fɔ:s] to make sb do sth when they do not want to
compete *v* [kəm'pi:t] to try to win or achieve sth
stiff *adj* [stɪf] *Muskelkater haben*
addicted *adj* [ə'dɪktɪd] not being able to stop doing sth
cope with sb/sth *v* ['kəʊp wɪð] deal successfully with a difficult situation
gradually *adv* ['grædʒuəli] slowly, step by step
intense *adj* [ɪn'tens] very great, strong or serious
kick *n, infl* [kɪk] here: excitement, satisfaction
push yourself very hard *v* [pʊʃ ˌveri 'hɑ:d] to make yourself work very hard
eliminate *v* [ɪ'lɪmɪneɪt] to remove
unintentionally *adv* [ˌʌnɪn'tenʃnəli] not on purpose, without realizing
obligatory *adj* [ə'blɪgətri] sth that you must do
agitated *adj* ['ædʒɪteɪtɪd] worried or excited
hindsight *n* ['haɪndsaɪt] *im Nachhinein*
ordinary *adj* ['ɔ:dnri] normal, not special or different from others
34 **reach an agreement** *v* [ri:tʃ ən ə'gri:mənt] to agree on sth
deal with *v* ['di:l wɪð] here: to be about
inexperienced *adj* [ˌɪnɪk'spɪəriənst] *unerfahren*
tighten *adj* ['taɪtn] here: to make sth stricter
safety rules *n* ['seɪfti ru:lz] *Sicherheitsvorschriften*
reduce *v* [rɪ'dju:s] to make less
be banned *v* [bi 'bænd] to not be allowed to do sth
supervision *n* [ˌsu:pə'vɪʒn] *Betreuung*
safety measures *n* ['seɪfti meʒəz] *Sicherheitsvorkehrungen*
treat *v* [tri:t] to look after
injured *adj* ['ɪndʒəd] hurt
35 **entitle** *v* [ɪn'taɪtl] to allow
36 **gym** *n* [dʒɪm] *Fitnessstudio*
equipment *n* [ɪ'kwɪpmənt] *Geräte (im Fitnessstudio)*
length *n* [leŋθ] *eine Länge (im Schwimmbad)*
37 **take off** *v* [ˌteɪk 'ɒf] to get started, to become successful
column *n* ['kɒləm] *Kolumne*

UNIT 4 POINT OF SALE

38 **appealing** *adj* [ə'pi:lɪŋ] attractive or interesting
annoying *adj* [ə'nɔɪɪŋ] making you feel angry and/or frustrated
emission *n* [i'mɪʃn] *Abgas*
run out of sth *v* [ˌrʌn 'aʊt əv] to finish your supply of sth, to not have anything left
conscious *adj* ['kɒnʃəs] *bewusst*
subconscious *adj* [ˌsʌb'kɒnʃəs] *unterbewusst*
desire *n* [dɪ'zaɪə] the feeling of wanting sth strongly
unspoiled *adj* [!ʌn'spɔɪld] not polluted or harmed
yearn (for sb/sth) *v* ['jɜ:n fə] to want sb/sth very much
eternal *adj* [ɪ'tɜ:nl] without beginning or end, sth that lasts forever
mobility *n* [məʊ'b'ləti] *Beweglichkeit, Mobilität*
ambiguous *adj* [æm'bɪgjuəs] sth that can mean more than one thing
exaggerated *adj* [ɪg'zædʒəreɪtɪd] seeming better, worse, greater, larger, etc. than it is

tʃ	dʒ	ʃ	ʒ	θ	ð	ŋ	s	z	v	w
chips	jet	ship	garage	thing	the	ring	ice	as	very	wet

39 **forecast** *n* ['fɔ:kɑ:st] prediction (*Vorhersage, Prognose*)
caution *n* ['kɔ:ʃn] great care, the act of being careful
breed *v* [bri:d, bred] to (re)produce; here: bred = *hervorgerufen durch*
modest *adj* ['mɒdɪst] here: small
increase *n* ['ɪŋkri:s] *Anstieg*
expenditure *n* [ɪk'spendɪtʃə] amount of money spent
surge *v* [sɜ:dʒ] to move forwards with great strength
come of age *phr* [kʌm əv 'eɪdʒ] *erwachsen werden*
marketer *n* ['mɑ:kɪtə] company that sells products
concerned *adj* [kən'sɜ:nd] worried
sales pitches *n* ['seɪlz pɪtʃɪz] *Verkaufstechnik*
spread *n* [spred] *Ausbreitung*
fuel *v* ['fju:əl] *anregen, anheizen*
engaging *adj* [ɪn'geɪdʒɪŋ] interesting, fascinating
aim at *v* ['eɪm ət] to point/target at; here: *ausgerichtet auf*
measure *v* ['meʒə] *messen*
in terms of *phr* [ɪn 'tɜ:mz əv] *in Bezug auf*
insignificant *adj* [ˌɪnsɪg'nɪfɪkənt] not important
rival *v* ['raɪvl] to be at least as good as sth else, to compete with sth
including *prep* [ɪn'klu:dɪŋ] *einschließlich*
respond *v* [rɪ'spɒnd] to react or answer
observe *v* [əb'zɜ:v] to watch
complaint *n* [kəm'pleɪnt] the act of saying that you are dissatisfied with sth (*Klage*)
particularly *adv* [pə'tɪkjələli] especially
skip *v* [skɪp] *überspringen*

40 **cause** *v* [kɔ:z] to make sth happen
seek sth *v* [si:k] to look for sth
gain *v* [geɪn] to get or win sth
on their way out *phr, infl* [ɒn ðeə ˌweɪ 'aʊt] becoming unpopular
permit *v* [pə'mɪt] to allow
sophisticated *adj* [sə'fɪstɪkeɪtɪd] advanced and/or complicated
lack of *n* ['læk əv] *Mangel an, Fehlen von*
comparable *adj* ['kɒmpərəbl] *vergleichbar*
shape *n* [ʃeɪp] *Form*
come to terms with *phr* [kʌm tə 'tɜmz wɪð] to deal with sth, to accept sth difficult
intent *n* [ɪn'tent] plan or purpose
globe *n* [gləʊb] world
justified *adj* ['dʒʌstɪfaɪd] right in doing sth, having a good reason for sth
minor *adj* ['maɪnə] very small
make sense of sth *phr* [meɪk 'sens əv] to be possible to understand sth
expressly *adv* [ɪk'spresli] clearly (*ausdrücklich*)
dislike *v* [dɪs'laɪk] to not like
hamper *v* ['hæmpə] to make sth difficult, to disturb
be prejudiced against sb/sth *adj* [bi 'predʒudɪst əgenst] *Vorurteile haben gegen jdn/etw*

41 **obvious** *adj* ['ɒbviəs] very clear
virtually *adv* ['vɜ:tʃuəli] almost completely
block out *v* [ˌblɒk 'aʊt] to stop
be reckoned with *v* [bi 'rekənd wɪð] to be expected
select *adj* [sɪ'lekt] carefully chosen
entertaining *adj* [ˌentə'teɪnɪŋ] interesting and amusing

42 **praise sth/sb** *v* [preɪz] to say that sth/sb is good
circle *n* ['sɜ:kl] a group of people who have the same interest or profession (*Kreis*)
appeal to sb *v* [ə'pi:l tə] to be attractive or interesting to sb
afterthought *n* ['ɑ:ftəθɔ:t] sth that you think of or add to sth afterwards
promising *adj* ['prɒmɪsɪŋ] *vielversprechend*
spending power *n* ['spendɪŋ paʊə] ability to buy things or spend money
sheer *adj* [ʃɪə] complete, absolute
undeniable adj [ˌʌndɪ'naɪəbl] *nicht zu übersehen, unbestreitbar*
top *v* [tɒp] to be better than sth/sb
be faced with *v* [bi 'feɪst wɪð] to be confronted with
astounding *adj* [ə'staʊndɪŋ] amazing, surprising
win over *v* [ˌwɪn 'əʊvə] to persuade sb to agree with you or support you
unprecedented *adj* [ʌn'presɪdentɪd] never having happened or done before, unusual

i:	ɪ	e	æ	ɑ:	ɒ	ɔ:	ʊ	u:	ʌ	ɜ:	ə
see	sit	ten	bad	arm	got	saw	put	too	cut	bird	about

consist of sth *v* [kən'sɪst əv] *aus etw bestehen*
turn to *v* ['tɜːn tə] *sich wenden an*
employ *v* [ɪm'plɔɪ] here: to use
values *n* ['væljuː] *Werte*
connect with *v* [kə'nekt wɪð] here: *ansprechen*
ironically *adv* [aɪ'rɒnɪkli] strange or amusing because sth is unexpected
poll *n* [pəʊl] *Umfrage*
43 **originate from** *v* [ə'rɪdʒɪneɪt frəm] to come from
common *adj* ['kɒmən] widespread, usual, shared by many people
trait *n* [treɪt] quality, a part of sb's character
favour *v* ['feɪvə] to prefer
highly-targeted *adj* [ˌhaɪli 'tɑːgɪtɪd] *genau auf eine Zielgruppe zugeschnitten*
switch to *v* ['swɪtʃ tə] *wechseln zu*
target *v* ['tɑːgɪt] to aim at
air *v* [eə] to play on the radio or show on TV
stumble *v* ['stʌmbl] *stolpern*
power blackout *n* [ˌpaʊə 'blækaʊt] a period of time when the electricity is not working
cooler (AE) *n* ['kuːlə] box/bag for keeping food and drink cool, e.g. on a picnic
spot *n, infl* [spɒt] advertisement
commonplace *adj* ['kɒmənpleɪs] normal
research *n* [rɪ'sɜːtʃ] a detailed and careful study
fine-tune *v* [ˌfaɪn 'tjuːn] to adjust, to improve
steady *adj* ['stedi] developing or happening at a constant rate
viewer *n* ['vjuːə] person that watches sth, e.g. TV
obviously *adv* ['ɒbviəsli] clearly
44 **relate sth to sb** *v* [rɪ'leɪt tə] to tell sb about sth
gapped *adj* [gæpt] with words missing
innovative *adj* ['ɪnəveɪtɪv] new
resort to *v* [rɪ'zɔːt tə] here: to use
audience *n* ['ɔːdiəns] a group of people who are watching or listening to sth, e.g. the TV or a play
commercial *n* [kə'mɜːʃl] advertisement
frequently *adv* ['friːkwəntli] often
all-too-sober *adj* [ˌɔːl tuː 'səʊbə] very serious about life, not enjoying jokes
underdog *n* ['ʌndədɒg] a person who is in a weak position
caricature *v* ['kærɪkətʃʊə] describe sb/sth in an exaggerated way to make them/it seem funny
assume *v* [ə'sjuːm] to expect sth to be true
refer to *v* [rɪ'fɜː tə] to mention or talk about sb/sth
intended *adj* [ɪn'tendɪd] *gewollt*
promote *v* [prə'məʊt] to advertise sth
facility *n* [fə'sɪləti] *Einrichtung*
appearance *n* [ə'pɪərəns] the way that sth/sb looks
45 **release** *v* [rɪ'liːs] here: to put a product on the market for people to buy
dedicated *adj* ['dedɪkeɪtɪd] giving a lot of your time, energy to sth; committed, enthusiastic
appear *v* [ə'pɪə] to seem
outdated *adj* [!aʊt'deɪtɪd] old-fashioned, not up to date
get their minds off sth *phr* [ˌget ðeə maɪndz 'ɒf] to be distracted, stop thinking about or doing sth
pick *v* [pɪk] to choose
purchase *v* ['pɜːtʃəs] to buy
thus *adv* [ðʌs] like this, in this way
in view of sth *phr* [ɪn 'vjuː əv] because of sth, as a result of sth
devise *v* [dɪ'vaɪz] to invent, to design
46 **succeed** *v* [sək'siːd] to be successful in doing sth
entire *adj* [ɪn'taɪə] whole
interrupt *v* [ˌɪntə'rʌpt] to stop sth or make a break in it
draw to *v* ['drɔː tə] to come to
thrilling *adj* ['θrɪlɪŋ] very exciting
climax *n* ['klaɪmæks] *Höhepunkt*
take action *v* [teɪk 'ækʃn] to do sth quickly (often to solve a problem)
47 **pay a fortune** v [peɪ ə 'fɔːtʃuːn] to pay a lot of money
celebrity *n* [sə'lebrəti] a famous person
be hooked on *v* [bi 'hʊkt ɒn] to be addicted to
earn *v* [ɜːn] *verdienen*
salary *n* ['sæləri] money that you get for working, wages

tʃ	dʒ	ʃ	ʒ	θ	ð	ŋ	s	z	v	w
chips	jet	ship	garage	thing	the	ring	ice	as	very	wet

UNIT 5 MAKING A LIVING

48 **make a living** *v* [meɪk ə 'lɪvɪŋ] to earn money to be able to buy the things you need
cash machine *n* ['kæʃ məʃi:n] *Geldautomat*
keep track *v* [ki:p 'træk] to make a note of sth, to check (*die Übersicht behalten*)
extra-curricular *adj* [ˌekstrə kə'rɪkjulə] not part of the normal school subjects
workload *n* ['wɜ:kləʊd] amount of work that you are given
drop *v* [drɒp] *fallen lassen*
tray *n* [treɪ] *Tablett*
mess *n* [mes] sth that is untidy and/or dirty
fries *n* [fraɪz] chips (*Pommes*)
pretend *v* [prɪ'tend] *so tun als ob*
grab *v* [græb] to take sth suddenly or quickly
mop *n* [mɒp] *Wischmopp*
mean *v* [mi:n] *bedeuten*
score *n* [skɔ:] the number of points you get in a game
job profile *n* ['dʒɒb prəʊfaɪl] description of a job

49 **lifeguard** *n* ['laɪfgɑ:d] a person at a beach or pool who saves people's lives
vendor *n* ['vendə] a person who sells things
vacation *n* [və'keɪʃn] holiday
kick back *v* [ˌkɪk 'bæk] to relax
beloved *adj* [bɪ'lʌvd] liked a lot, favourite
frequent *adj* ['fri:kwənt] often
threat *n* [θret] a person or thing that may hurt or damage sb/sth
weigh up *v* [ˌweɪ 'ʌp] to consider sth carefully (*abwägen*)
repeal *v* [rɪ'pi:l] *widerrufen, aufheben*
mandatory *adj* ['mændətəri] having to do sth, compulsory (*obligatorisch*)
giant *n* ['dʒaɪənt] *Riese*
muscle *v* ['mʌsl] to use strong persuasion
(trade) union *n* ['ju:niən] *Gewerkschaft*
lengthen *v* ['leŋθən] to make longer
editor *n* ['edɪtə] a person whose job it is to prepare a book, newspaper, TV show etc
encounter *n* [ɪn'kaʊntə] an unexpected meeting
recognize *v* ['rekəgnaɪz] to accept or admit that sth is true
low-wage countries *n* [ˌləʊ 'weɪdʒ kʌn-triz] *Niedriglohnländer*
age *v* [eɪdʒ] to become older
labor force (AE) *n* ['leɪbə fɔ:s] the workers (*Arbeiterschaft*)
crushing *adj* ['krʌʃɪŋ] here: enormous, extremely heavy
burden *n* ['bɜ:dn] a responsibility or task that causes a lot of worry
welfare benefits *n* [ˌwelfeə 'benɪfɪts] money the state gives to the unemployed, single parents, disabled people and the elderly
proper *adj* ['prɒpə] right
fringe benefit *n* ['frɪndʒ benɪfɪt] an extra advantage that is given to you
harried *adj* ['hærid] here: stressful
amass *v* [ə'mæs] to collect
wealth *n* [welθ] a large amount of money, property, etc.
community *n* [kə'mju:nəti] *Gemeinde*
belongings *n* [bɪ'lɒŋɪŋz] the things that you own (*Hab und Gut*)
idleness *n* ['aɪdlnəs] laziness
sin *n* [sɪn] *Sünde*
emphasis *n* ['emfəsɪs] importance; *Betonung*, here: *Wert*
leisure *n* ['leʒə] free-time
Tuscany ['tʌskəni] *Toskana*
fresco *n* ['freskəʊ] *Freske*
nurture *v* ['nɜ:tʃə] to look after
contribute *v* [kən'trɪbju:t] to give a part of the total, together with others
frantic *adj* ['fræntɪk] hectic, very busy; worried and frightened
pursuit *n* [pə'sju:t] the act of doing or organizing sth, wanting to achieve sth (*das Streben*)
tempting *adj* ['temptɪŋ] attractive
dismiss *v* [dɪs'mɪs] to say or think that sth is not important
pace *n* [peɪs] the speed at which you do sth or at which sth happens
toll *n* [təʊl] the amount of damage done
gentle *adj* ['dʒentl] calm, soft

i:	ɪ	e	æ	ɑ:	ɒ	ɔ:	ʊ	u:	ʌ	ɜ:	ə
see	sit	ten	bad	arm	got	saw	put	too	cut	bird	about

sustainable *adj* [sə'steɪnəbl] able to continue in a certain way for a long time (*aufrechtzuerhalten*)

50 **be entitled to** *v* [bi ɪn'taɪtld tə] to have the right to do sth

endanger *v* [ɪn'deɪndʒə] to cause danger to sb/sth

indicate *v* ['ɪndɪkeɪt] to show sth

pressure *n* ['preʃə] *Druck*

51 **equal** *adj* ['i:kwəl] the same in value, size, number, etc.

pay *n* [peɪ] the money you get for doing a job

52 **embrace** *v* [ɪm'breɪs] *hier:(bereitwillig) übernehmen*

fatherhood *n* ['fɑ:ðəhʊd] the experience of being a father

involvement *n* [ɪn'vɒlvmənt] the act of being a part of sth

diaper (AE) *n* ['daɪpə r] *Windel*

bandage *v* ['bændɪdʒ] *etw verbinden, bandagieren*

eightfold *adv* ['eɪtfəʊld] *achtfach*

confident *adj* ['kɒnfɪdənt] not worried about doing sth

guide *n* [gaɪd] sb who shows you (how to do) sth

mentor *n* ['mentɔ:] sb who is always there to give advice when you are learning sth

fathering *v* ['fɑ:ðərɪŋ] *bevatern, Vater sein für*

toddler *n* ['tɒdlə] a child aged approximately between two and four years old

involve *v* [ɪn'vɒlv] *engagieren*

inclined *v* [ɪn'klaɪnd] likely

tempt *v* [tempt] to encourage sb to do sth by offering them sth good

place, put in *v* [pleɪs, pʊt ɪn] *beschließen*

time, take ~ off *phr* [taɪm, teɪk ɒf] *sich frei nehmen*

paternity leave *n* [pə'tɜ:nəti li:v] time a father takes off work to look after his child(ren)

devoted *adj* [dɪ'vəʊtɪd] *hingebungsvoll*

decade *n* ['dekeɪd] = ten years

balance *v* ['bæləns] *in Übereinklang bringen*

guilt *n* [gɪlt] here: the bad feeling you have when you have done sth wrong

accountant *n* [ə'kaʊntənt] *Buchhalter/in*

funpark *n* ['fʌnpɑ:k] a park with lots of fun activities for children

negotiate *v* [nɪ'gəʊʃieɪt] here: to find a way of dealing with sth

role model *n* [rəʊl 'mɒdl] sb who you like and respect and therefore try to copy

support network *n* [sə'pɔ:t 'netwɜ:k] here: people who help you if you are having problems

eye sb/sth warily *phr* [aɪ 'weərɪli] *jdn misstrauisch beobachten*

breadwinner *n* ['bredwɪnə] person who earns money to support his/her family

climb *v* [klaɪm] to go up

corporate ladder *n* ['kɔ:pərət 'lædə] *Unternehmensleiter*

unsympathetic *adj* [ˌʌnˌsɪmpə'θetɪk] not interested in sb else's problems or needs

request sth *v* [rɪ'kwest] to ask for sth

outweigh *v* [ˌaʊt'weɪ] *überwiegen, wettmachen*

disadvantage *n* [ˌdɪsəd'vɑ:ntɪdʒ] ⇔ advantage

promotion *n* [prə'məʊʃn] getting a new, more important job, often with better pay

mindset *n* ['maɪndset] *Denkart, Mentalität*

initiate *v* [ɪ'nɪʃieɪt] to start sth

shift *n* [ʃɪft] development, change

53 **be truthful** *v* [bi 'tru:θfl] *die Wahrheit sagen*

make a sacrifice *v* [meɪk 'sækrɪfaɪs] *etw opfern*

superfluous *adj* [su:'pɜ:fluəs] not necessary; too much

encounter *v* [ɪn'kaʊntə] to meet, experience

54 **assume** *v* [ə'sju:m] to take on, accept (*übernehmen)*

with respect to *phr* [wɪð rɪ'spekt tə] *hinsichtlich*

effectively *adv* [ɪ'fektɪvli] here: successfully

hesitate *v* ['hezɪteɪt] not being sure whether to do sth or not

recreational activities *n* [ˌrekriˌeɪʃənl æk'tɪvətiz] activities to help you relax

affect *v* [ə'fekt] to influence

55 **coke** *n* [kəʊk] *Steinkohlenkoks*

crawl *v* [krɔ:l] to move around on your hands and knees

to have a pretty good shot *phr* [həv ə ˌprɪti gʊd 'ʃɒt] to have a chance

tʃ	dʒ	ʃ	ʒ	θ	ð	ŋ	s	z	v	w
chips	jet	ship	garage	thing	the	ring	ice	as	very	wet

it's hard to keep a good man down *phr* [ɪts ˌhɑːd tə ˌkiːp ə gʊd mæn 'daʊn] it is difficult to stop sb who is good

56 **decline** *n* [dɪ'klaɪn] a process or period of becoming weaker

imply *v* [ɪm'plaɪ] to say sth indirectly

restlessness *n* ['restləsnəs] feeling of being unable to relax or be still

hand down *v* [ˌhænd 'daʊn] to pass sth on (often to the next generation)

57 **poisonous** *adj* ['pɔɪzənəs] *giftig*

private health insurance *n* [ˌpraɪvət 'helθ ɪnʃʊərəns] *private Krankenversicherung*

insured *adj* [ɪn'ʃʊəd] *versichert*

58 **previous** *adj* ['priːviəs] happening before or earlier

neat *adj* [niːt] arranged or done carefully (*ordentlich*)

tidy *adj* ['taɪdi] well arranged, in order (*aufgeräumt*)

first impression *n* [fɜːst ɪm'preʃn] *erster Eindruck*

scruffy *adj* ['skrʌfi] untidy and dirty

on time *adv* [ɒn 'taɪm] punctual; not late or early

modest *adj* ['mɒdɪst] here: ⇔ arrogant

lecture *v* ['lektʃə] to tell other people how to do things

boast *v* [bəʊst] to talk with too much pride

prosperity *n* [prɒ'sperəti] the state of being successful, wealth

be concerned about *v* [bi kən'sɜːnd əbaʊt] to be worried about

counterpart *n* ['kaʊntəpɑːt] *Gegenstück*

severe *adj* [sɪ'vɪə] very bad, very serious

UNIT 6 IN THE PUBLIC EYE

59 **popular press** *n* ['pɒpjələr pres] *Boulevardpresse*

60 **lash out at sb/sth** *v* [ˌlæʃ 'aʊt ət, əgenst] to suddenly attack sb/sth

minder *n* ['maɪndə] a person whose job is to look after or protect sb/sth

pin sb against sth *v* [ˌpɪn ə'genst] to keep sb/sth in one position so that it is impossible for them to move

haunt *n* [hɔːnt] a place that sb visits regularly

snap *v* [snæp] to lose one's patience

slammer *n* ['slæmə] type of cocktail

scuffle *n* ['skʌfl] fight

bury *v* ['beri] here: to hide

contain *v* [kən'teɪn] here: to control, to try and keep inside you

accuse *v* [ə'kjuːz] to say that sb has done sth wrong

cheat *v* [tʃiːt] to act in an unfair or dishonest way to get an advantage for yourself

Sandhurst ['sændhɜːst] famous military college in Great Britain

altercation *n* [ˌɔːltə'keɪʃn] a disagreement, a fight

bump *n* [bʌmp] *Beule*

re-emerge *v* [ˌriː ɪ'mɜːdʒ] to come (back) out of somewhere

ft; feet *n* [fiːt] a measure of length (1 ft = 30.48cm)

pavement *n* ['peɪvmənt] the path at the side of the road for people to walk on

be at odds *phr* [bi ət 'ɒdz] to disagree with

account *n* [ə'kaʊnt] a report or description of sth that has happened

deliberately *adv* [dɪ'lɪbərətli] on purpose

personal protection officer *n* [ˌpɜːsənl prə'tekʃn ɒfɪsə] bodyguard

restrain *v* [rɪ'streɪn] to hold back

aid *v* [eɪd] to help

bouncer *n* ['baʊnsə] *Türsteher*

temper *n* ['tempə] mood

bang *v* [bæŋ] to hit sth hard

freelance *adj* ['friːlɑːns] a person who works independently, often for many different employers

grunt *v* [grʌnt] to make a noise like a pig

lunge at *v* ['lʌndʒ ət] to suddenly move forwards, especially when trying to attack sb

chase *v* [tʃeɪs] to run after

audible *adj* ['ɔːdəbl] sth that is loud enough to be heard

upset *adj* [ˌʌp'set] unhappy

fuming *adj* ['fjuːmɪŋ] very angry

press charges *v* ['pres tʃɑːdʒɪz] *anzeigen*

string *n* [strɪŋ] a series of, many

fashionable *adj* ['fæʃnəbl] modern, up to date, good-looking (especially clothing)

cavort *v* [kə'vɔːt] *sich tummeln*

iː	ɪ	e	æ	ɑː	ɒ	ɔː	ʊ	uː	ʌ	ɜː	ə
see	sit	ten	bad	arm	got	saw	put	too	cut	bird	about

overshadow *v* [ˌəʊvəˈʃædəʊ] to cause sth/sb to seem less important or successful
portray *v* [pɔːˈtreɪ] to describe sb/sth (*darstellen*)
sensitive *adj* [ˈsensətɪv] *sensibel*
caring *adj* [ˈkeərɪŋ] worried about or interested in how other people feel
61 **hounding** *n* [ˈhaʊndɪŋ] the act of following and disturbing sb
party set *n* [ˈpɑːti set] group of people that have been to a party
derive *v* [dɪˈraɪv] to come from
tip sb off *v* [ˌtɪp ˈɒf] to give sb a tip, to give sb secret information
pull up *v* [ˌpʊl ˈʌp] to stop (a car)
appear to do sth *v* [əˈpɪə] to look as if you are doing sth
ready yourself *v* [ˈredi jɔːself] to get ready to do sth, to prepare yourself for sth
gaggle *n* [ˈgægl] a group
converge *v* [kənˈvɜːdʒ] to move towards
experienced *adj* [ɪkˈspɪəriənst] *erfahren*
far side *n* [fɑː ˈsaɪd] the side that is furthest away from you
conflict *v* [ˈkɒnflɪkt] to disagree or be different (from each other)
shaken up *adj* [ˌʃeɪkən ˈʌp] shocked
charge v [tʃɑːdʒ] to ask sb to pay a certain amount of money
rely on *v* [rɪˈlaɪ ɒn] *sich verlassen auf*
snatch *n, infl* [snætʃ] here: opportunity
privacy *n* [ˈprɪvəsi] *Privatsphäre*
fair game *phr* [feə ˈgeɪm] here: OK to be photographed
rid sb of sth *v* [ˈrɪd əv] to make sb free of sth
underprivileged *adj* [ˌʌndəˈprɪvəlɪdʒd] having less money, rights, opportunities, etc. than other people in society
emerge *v* [ɪˈmɜːdʒ] to come out, to step into
tension *n* [ˈtenʃn] here: conflict
familiar *adj* [fəˈmɪliə] well-known
62 **considering** *conj* [kənˈsɪdərɪŋ] *bedenkt man*
drunk *adj* [drʌŋk] *betrunken*
accompanied *adj* [əˈkʌmpənid] here: printed with sth else
sensational *adj* [senˈseɪʃənl] trying to cause a feeling of great excitement or interest in people

factual *adj* [ˈfæktʃuəl] neutral, full of facts, not sensational
recommend *v* [ˌrekəˈmend] *empfehlen*
63 **voice your opinion** *v* [vɔɪs jɔːr əˈpɪniən] to express your view
clash *n* [klæʃ] a fight or serious disagreement
plainly *adv* [ˈpleɪnli] clearly
64 **docusoap** *n* [ˈdɒkjusəʊp] documentary soap
surprising *adj* [səˈpraɪzɪŋ] not expected (*überraschend*)
prominence *n* [ˈprɒmɪnəns] the state of being important and easily noticed
stranger *n* [ˈstreɪndʒə] sb that you do not know or have never met before
skill *n* [skɪl] the ability to do sth well
painful *adj* [ˈpeɪnfl] sth that hurts (*schmerzhaft*)
embarrassing *adj* [ɪmˈbærəsɪŋ] *peinlich*
humiliating *adj* [hjuːˈmɪlieɪtɪŋ] shameful
misfortune *n* [ˌmɪsˈfɔːtʃuːn] bad luck
willingness *n* [ˈwɪlɪŋnəs] *Bereitschaft*
stem from *v* [ˈstem frəm] to come from
empathize *v* [ˈempəθaɪz] to be able to understand how another person is feeling
sympathy *n* [ˈsɪmpəθi] feeling sad about other people's misfortunes
unscripted *adj* [ʌnˈskrɪptɪd] without a script
contrived *adj* [kənˈtraɪvd] clearly artificial or invented, not natural
footage *n* [ˈfʊtɪdʒ] filmed material
rating *n* [ˈreɪtɪŋ] a measurement of how popular sth is
executive *n* [ɪgˈzekjətɪv] boss
suffering *n* [ˈsʌfərɪŋ] *Leiden*
merely *adv* [ˈmɪəli] only, just
glory *n* [ˈglɔːri] fame or honour (*Ruhm*)
question *v* [ˈkwestʃən] *in Frage stellen*
attracted (to) *v* [əˈtræktɪd] interested in
65 **participant** *n* [pɑːˈtɪsɪpənt] *Teilnehmer/in*
66 **set up** *v* [ˌset ˈʌp] here: to deliberately invent, stage (*aufsetzen*)
ensure *v* [ɪnˈʃʊə] to make sure of sth, to guarantee
unique *adj* [juˈniːk] very special (*einmalig*)
67 **predict** *v* [prɪˈdɪkt] to say what will happen in the future

tʃ	dʒ	ʃ	ʒ	θ	ð	ŋ	s	z	v	w
chips	jet	ship	garage	thing	the	ring	ice	as	very	wet

be glued to sth *v* [bi 'gluːd tə] to be absolutely fascinated by sth

68 **broadsheet** *n* ['brɔːdʃiːt] a serious newspaper

subscription *n* [səb'skrɪpʃn] *Abonnement*

print issue *n* ['prɪnt ɪʃuː] printed version of a newspaper (i.e. not the online version)

advance *n* [əd'vɑːns] *Fortschritt*

quote *v* [kwəʊt] to repeat exactly what sb else has said (*zitieren*)

69 **handle** *v* ['hændl] to deal with or control

circulation figures *n* [ˌsɜːkjə'leɪʃn fɪgəz] the number of copies of a newspaper, magazine, etc. that are sold each time it is printed

current affairs *n* [ˌkʌrənt ə'feəz] important political or social events that are happening at the present time

encourage *v* [ɪn'kʌrɪdʒ] to give hope, support or confidence to sb

UNIT 7 JUSTICE

70 **violent** *adj* ['vaɪələnt] brutal

decline *v* [dɪ'klaɪn] to become less

property *n* ['prɒpəti] all the things that belong to sb, here: especially houses and land

overall *adv* [ˌəʊvər'ɔːl] including everything

juvenile *adj* ['dʒuːvənaɪl] *jugendlich*

victimization *n* [ˌvɪktɪmaɪ'zeɪʃn] punishing or making sb suffer unfairly

probation n [prə'beɪʃn] *Bewährung*

parole *n* [pə'rəʊl] *bedingter Straferlass, Bewährung*

71 **shoplift** *v* ['ʃɒplɪft] to steal things from a shop

sheet *n* [ʃiːt] *Bettlaken*

mall (AE) *n* [mɔːl] big shopping centre

sentence *n* ['sentəns] the punishment given by a judge to sb who has been found guilty of a crime

commit a crime *v* [kəˌmɪt ə 'kraɪm] *eine Straftat begehen*

convict *v* ['kɒnvɪkt] to declare in a court of law that sb is guilty of a crime

conviction *n* [kən'vɪkʃn] a case when sb is found guilty of committing a crime

incident *n* ['ɪnsɪdənt] *Vorfall*

purse snatching *n* ['pɜːs snætʃɪŋ] the act of robbing or stealing sb's purse/bag

burglary *n* ['bɜːgləri] *Einbruch*

honour *n* ['ɒnə] *Ehre*

be sentenced *v* [bi 'sentənst] *verurteilt werden*

retired *adj* [rɪ'taɪəd] having stopped work permanently, usually after having reached a certain age

appeal *n* [ə'piːl] a formal request to sb in authority to change a decision

slim *adj* [slɪm] here: small

suffer a stroke *v* ['sʌfər ə strəʊk] *einen Schlaganfall haben*

notify *v* ['nəʊtɪfaɪ] to tell sb, to let sb know

wheelchair *n* ['wiːltʃeə] *Rollstuhl*

strong-featured *adj* [ˌstrɒŋ 'fiːtʃəd] *mit markanten Gesichtszügen*

tentatively *adv* ['tentətɪvli] shyly, not confidently

mock *adj* [mɒk] not real or genuine

gravestone *n* ['greɪvstəʊn] *Grabstein*

vigil *n* ['vɪdʒɪl] *Mahnwache*

72 **case history** *n* [keɪs 'hɪstri] *Vorgeschichte*

glove *n* [glʌv] *Handschuh*

cash *v* [kæʃ] to exchange a cheque for money

forged *adj* [fɔːdʒd] *gefälscht*

possession *n* [pə'zeʃn] *Besitz*

application *n* [ˌæplɪ'keɪʃn] *Antrag*

razor blade *n* ['reɪzə bleɪd] *Rasierklinge*

proposition system *n* [ˌprɒpə'zɪʃn sɪstəm] type of voting system used in California

electorate *n* [ɪ'lektərət] all the people who are allowed to vote in a country or region

policy *n* ['pɒləsi] *Politik*

restrict *v* [rɪ'strɪkt] to limit

imprisoned *adj* [ɪm'prɪznd] in prison

petty theft *n* [ˌpeti 'θeft] stealing things that are not worth a lot of money

offender *n* [ə'fendə] a person who commits a crime

outnumber *v* [ˌaʊt'nʌmbə] to be greater in number than sth else

iː	ɪ	e	æ	ɑː	ɒ	ɔː	ʊ	uː	ʌ	ɜː	ə
see	sit	ten	bad	arm	got	saw	put	too	cut	bird	about

rape *n* [reɪp] *Vergewaltigung*
assault *n* [ə'sɔ:lt] a sudden attack on sb
estimate *v* ['estɪmeɪt] to calculate the cost, size, etc. of sth
roughly *adv* ['rʌfli] about, approximately
support *v* [sə'pɔ:t] here: to agree with the aims or ideas of sb
purpose *n* ['pɜ:pəs] the reason/motivation for doing or making sth
oppose *v* [ə'pəʊz] to be against sth
73 **unlawful** *adj* [ˌʌn'lɔ:fl] against the law
act *n* [ækt] here: *Tat*
punishment *n* ['pʌnɪʃmənt] *Strafe*
court *n* [kɔ:t] *Gericht*
enforce *v* [bi ɪn'fɔ:s] to make sure a law or rule is obeyed
lock sb up *v* [ˌlɒk 'ʌp] to put sb in prison (*jmdn einsperren/wegsperren*)
permission *n* [pə'mɪʃn] *Erlaubnis*
behave *v* [bɪ'heɪv] to act in a certain way
currently *adv* ['kʌrəntli] at present
74 **rule of thumb** *n* [ru:l əv 'θʌm] *Faustregel*
usage *n* ['ju:sɪdʒ] the way that words are used in a language
underage *adj* [ˌʌndər'eɪdʒ] too young to be allowed to do sth
tackle *v* ['tækl] here: to solve, to deal with
raise *v* [reɪz] to increase
75 **steer** *v* [stɪə] to control the direction a vehicle is going in (*lenken*)
rumble *v* ['rʌmbl] to make a deep heavy sound
rain-soaked *adj* ['reɪn səʊkt] very wet from the rain
dull *adj* [dʌl] boring, uninteresting
beat *v* [bi:t] to be better than
damp *adj* [dæmp] a little wet
crummy (AE) *adj, infl* ['krʌmi] boring, not fun (*lausig*)
cut off *v* [ˌkʌt 'ɒf] to interrupt
flatten *v* ['flætn] *platt machen*
swing open *v* [ˌswɪŋ 'əʊpən] to open quickly
knock *v* [nɒk] to hit sb
can (AE) *n, infl* [kän] bottom (*Po*)
kinda *abbr, infl* [kaɪndə] kind of (*irgendwie*)
nuts *adj, infl* [nʌts] mad, crazy
chicken out *v, infl* [ˌtʃɪkɪn 'aʊt] *einen Rückzieher machen*

blurred *adj* [blɜ:d] unclear (*verschwommen*)
weave *v* [wi:v] *sich schlängeln*
fool around *v* [ˌfu:l ə'raʊnd] to joke or do silly or stupid things
swerve *v* [swɜ:v] to change direction suddenly
grab *v* [græb] to hold onto
scared *adj* [skeəd] frightened
headlights *n* ['hedlaɪts] *Scheinwerfer*
squeal *n* [skwi:l] loud, high noise
slick *adj* [slɪk] smooth, here: wet and slippery
hollow *adj* ['hɒləʊ] with an empty space inside; here: a sound that seems to be coming from a hollow place
thud *n* [θʌd] the low sound that is made when sth heavy falls down
hurl *v* [hɜ:l] to throw sth with great force
roof *n* [ru:f] *Dach*
speed *v* [spi:d] to go very (or too) fast
76 **blob up** *v* [ˌblɒb 'ʌp] here: to develop, to collect
jerk (AE) *n, infl* [dʒɜ:k] idiot
get nailed *v, infl* [get 'neɪld] to be sentenced for sth
manslaughter *n* ['mænslɔ:tə] *fahrlässige Tötung, Totschlag*
shiver *v* ['ʃɪvə] to shake (*zittern*)
rear view mirror *n* [ˌrɪə vju: 'mɪrə] *Rückspiegel*
lunge forward *v* [ˌlʌndʒ 'fɔ:wəd] to move forward suddenly
pick up speed *v* [ˌpɪk ʌp 'spi:d] to go faster
yard *n* [jɑ:d] a measurement of length; 1 yard = 0.914 m
hang a sharp right *v* [ˌhæŋ ə ˌʃɑ:p 'raɪt] to turn right quickly
narrow *adj* ['nærəʊ] not very wide
hardly *adv* ['hɑ:dli] almost none
turn into *v* ['tɜ:n ɪntə] here: *abbiegen*
winding *adj* ['waɪndɪŋ] with a lot of bends or curves
hit and run *n* [ˌhɪt ənd 'rʌn] *Unfall mit Fahrerflucht*
out in the sticks *phr, infl* [aʊt ɪn ðə 'stɪks] in the countryside (*in der Pampa*)
close fast *v* [kləʊz 'fɑ:st] *schnell aufholen*
sharply *adv* ['ʃɑ:pli] *scharf, heftig*

tʃ	dʒ	ʃ	ʒ	θ	ð	ŋ	s	z	v	w
chips	jet	ship	garage	thing	the	ring	ice	as	very	wet

relieved *adj* [rɪ'li:vd] *erleichtert*
pace *v* [peɪs] to walk with slow regular steps
fault *n* [fɔ:lt] *Schuld*
coward *n* ['kaʊəd] sb with no courage, who is afraid in dangerous or unpleasant situations
low *adv* [ləʊ] here: quietly
get away with sth *phr v* [ˌget ə'weɪ wɪð] to not be caught
brick *n* [brɪk] *Ziegel(stein), Backstein*

77 **narrator** *n* [nə'reɪtə] the person who tells a story
roar *v* [rɔ:] to make a deep, loud noise, like a lion
aimlessly *adv* ['eɪmləsli] without aim, direction or purpose
puddle *n* ['pʌdl] *Pfütze*
dissuade *v* [dɪ'sweɪd] to persuade sb not to do sth

78 **robber** *n* ['rɒbə] a person who steals things, e.g. from a bank
boot (BE) *n* [bu:t] *Kofferraum*
convict *n* [kən'vɪkt] a person who has been found guilty of a crime and put in prison
end up *v* [ˌend 'ʌp] to find yourself in a certain place/situation

79 **juvenile delinquency** *n* ['dʒu:vənaɪl dɪ'lɪŋkwəsi] *Jugendstraffälligkeit*
dropout *n* ['drɒpaʊt] a person who leaves school, university, etc. without finishing his/her studies
sensibly *adv* ['sensəbli] responsibly, intelligently
sentence *v* ['sentəns] *verurteilen*
truancy *n* ['tru:ənsi] the act of staying away from school without permission
peer pressure *n* ['pɪə preʃə] *Gruppenzwang*

UNIT 8 PRESERVING THE PLANET

80 **coal** *n* [kəʊl] *Kohle*
renewable *adj* [rɪ'nju:əbl] recyclable, sth that can be used again
tidal power *n* [ˌtaɪdl 'paʊə] energy produced from the regular change in the level of the sea

81 **cabin** n ['kæbɪn] a small wooden house or hut
porch *n* [pɔ:tʃ] *Veranda*
rugged adj ['rʌgɪd] rough and rocky
gladly *adv* ['glædli] happily
lock horns with sb *phr* [lɒk 'hɔ:nz] to be in disagreement with sb
claim *v* [kleɪm] to say that sth is true
view *n* [vju:] *Aussicht*
disturb *v* [dɪ'stɜ:b] here: to change sth from its natural condition
countryside *n* ['kʌntrisaɪd] land which is away from towns and cities
affluent *adj* ['æfluənt] rich, having a lot of money
perspective *n* [pə'spektɪv] the way you think about sth, a point of view
urgency *n* ['ɜ:dʒənsi] sth that needs immediate attention
humanity *n* [hju:'mænəti] all the people in the world
face sth *v* [feɪs] to have to deal with sth unpleasant, to confront
intention *n* [ɪn'tenʃn] a plan or purpose (*Absicht*)
undergo sth *v* [ˌʌndə'gəʊ] to have a difficult or unpleasant experience
pollution *n* [pə'lu:ʃn] *(Umwelt-, Luft-)Verschmutzung*
habitat *n* ['hæbɪtæt] the natural home of a plant or an animal
downside *n* ['daʊnsaɪd] the negative side of sth
erect sth *v* [ɪ'rekt] to build sth
migratory route *n* ['maɪgrətri ru:t] route that birds fly in winter to get to warmer countries
spring up *v* [ˌsprɪŋ 'ʌp] to be built quickly, to appear or develop quickly or suddenly
subject to sth *adj* ['sʌbdʒɪkt tə] depending on sth as a condition
impact assessment *n* [ˌɪmpækt ə'sesmənt] evaluation of the effect of sth
blanket approach *phr* [ˌblæŋkɪt ə'prəʊtʃ] one solution
not in my backyard *phr* [ˌbæk'jɑ:d] *Bitte nicht vor meiner Tür*
hypocritical *adj* [ˌhɪpə'krɪtɪkl] *scheinheilig, heuchlerisch*
counterproductive *adj* [ˌkaʊntəprə'dʌktɪv] *kontraproduktiv; die gegenteilige Wirkung haben*

82 **make sense** *v* [meɪk 'sens] *sinnvoll sein*
operate *v* ['ɒpəreɪt] to work or to make sth work
improve *v* [ɪm'pru:v] to make sth better

i:	ɪ	e	æ	ɑ:	ɒ	ɔ:	ʊ	u:	ʌ	ɜ:	ə
see	sit	ten	bad	arm	got	saw	put	too	cut	bird	about

smokestack (AE) *n* ['sməʊkstæk] chimney (*Schornstein*)
belch out *v* ['beltʃ aʊt] to send out, to produce
concerned about *adj* [kən'sɜːnd əbaʊt] worried or anxious about
pride *n* [praɪd] the feeling of pleasure when you do sth good or are proud of sth (*Stolz*)
pour *v* [pɔː] to flow out of or into sth quickly and steadily
acid rain *n* [ˌæsɪd 'reɪn] *saurer Regen*
harness *v* ['hɑːnɪs] here: to control an energy source so that you that you can use it to produce electricity
spin *v* [spɪn] to turn around quickly
curse *v* [kɜːs] to use rude language to express your anger
object *v* [əb'dʒekt] to not like or to be against sb/sth
dispose of sth *v* [dɪ'spəʊz əv] to throw sth away

83 **valuable** *adj* ['væljuəbl] worth a lot (of money) (*wertvoll*)
chimney *n* ['tʃɪmni] *Schornstein*
emit *v* [ɪ'mɪt] to send out sth (e.g. a smell, a sound, smoke, etc.)
equation *n* [ɪ'kweɪʒn] *Gleichung*

84 **tend to** *v* ['tend tə] to often or normally do or be sth
trust *n* [trʌst] the feeling that you have when you know that you can rely on sb/sth (*Vertrauen*)
culprit *n* ['kʌlprɪt] a person who has done sth wrong
petrol *n* ['petrəl] *Benzin*
downward *adj* ['daʊnwəd] towards a lower level

85 **carrier bag** *n* ['kæriə bæg] *Plastiktüte*
furious *adj* ['fjʊəriəs] very angry
blow sth *v, infl* [bləʊ] to waste an opportunity of succeeding in sth
return flight *n* [rɪ'tɜːn flaɪt] a flight to a destination and back again
mushroom *v* ['mʌʃrʊm] to grow or increase in number very quickly
aviation *n* [ˌeɪvi'eɪʃn] the flying of aircraft
mode *n* [məʊd] type
unless *conj* [ən'les] if … not; except if
be capped *v* [bi kæpt] limit, to stop at a certain level
vapour trails *n* ['veɪpə treɪlz] *Kondensstreifen*
tiny *adj* ['taɪni] extremely small
altitude *n* ['æltɪtjuːd] the height of sth above sea level
choke *v* [tʃəʊk] to be or make unable to breathe
trap *v* [træp] to keep sb/sth in a place from which he/she/it cannot escape
enhance *v* [ɪn'hɑːns] to improve
give rise to *v* [gɪv 'raɪz tə] to cause
prevent *v* [prɪ'vent] to stop sth from happening
heat *n* [hiːt] warmth, the feeling of sth hot
drought *n* [draʊt] a long period with very little or no rain
sea level *n* ['siː levl] *Meeresspiegel*
swamp *v* [swɒmp] to cover or fill sth with water; to flood
olive grove *n* ['ɒlɪv grəʊv] place where olive trees grow

86 **layer** *n* ['leɪə] *Schicht*
cause *v* [kɔːz] to make sth happen
solely *adv* ['səʊlli] only
thoughtlessly *adv* ['θɔːtləsli] not thinking about what other people want or need
revenue *n* ['revənjuː] income
conquer *v* ['kɒŋkə] to take control of an area, to defeat sth or sb
gist *n* [dʒɪst] the general meaning of sth
swamp *n* [swɒmp] an area of soft wet land
arise *v* [ə'raɪz] to come up, to appear, to happen
at risk *adj* [ət 'rɪsk] in danger

87 **account for** *v* [ə'kaʊnt fə] to explain or give a reason for sth
melt *v* [melt] *schmelzen*
device *n* [dɪ'vaɪs] a (usually quite small) machine or piece of equipment
plug into *v* ['plʌg ɪntə] to connect sth to the electricity supply
mains *n* [meɪnz] the electricity supply from sockets in the wall

88 **logger** *n* ['lɒgə] sb whose job it is to cut down trees
chop *v* [tʃɒp] *hacken*
impurity n [ɪm'pjʊərəti] *Unreinheit*
soil *n* [sɔɪl] earth
photovoltaic *adj* [ˌfəʊtəʊvɒl'teɪɪk] *photoelektrisch*
scrap *n* [skræp] rubbish

tʃ	dʒ	ʃ	ʒ	θ	ð	ŋ	s	z	v	w
chips	jet	ship	garage	thing	the	ring	ice	as	very	wet

UNIT 9 HIGH TECH

90 **drawback** *n* ['drɔ:bæk] a negative side of sth (*Nachteil*)
available *adj* [ə'veɪləbl] *erreichbar*
91 **humanoid** *n* ['hju:mənɔɪd] a robot that looks and behaves like a human
relate to *v* [rɪ'leɪt tə] here: to deal with; to be able to understand how sb feels
robotocist *n* [ˌrəʊ'bɒtəsɪst] sb who makes robots
hug *n* [hʌg] *Umarmung*
happily complied *adv, pp* [ˌhæpɪli kəm'plaɪd] willingly agreed
plop down *v, infl* ['plɒp daʊn] to sit down
nap *n* [næp] a short sleep
approach *v* [ə'prəʊtʃ] to come near to sb
strike up a conversation *phr* [straɪk ˌʌp ə ˌkɒnvə'seɪʃn] to start talking to sb
sit up *v* [ˌsɪt 'ʌp] *sich aufsetzen, sich gerade hinsetzen*
interact *v* [ˌɪntər'ækt] to communicate with sb, to have an effect (on each other)
get sb upset *v* [get ˌʌp'set] to make sb unhappy
grin *v* [grɪn] to smile
jealous *adj* ['dʒeləs] *eifersüchtig*
engineer *n* [ˌendʒɪ'nɪə] *Ingenieur/in*
task *n* [tɑ:sk] a piece of work
salvage *n* ['sælvɪdʒ] here: the act of rescuing sth from a damaged ship or building
obsessed *adj* [əb'sest] *besessen*
squarely *adv* ['skweəli] firmly, well
playmate *n* ['pleɪmeɪt] friend that you play with as a child
social worker *n* ['səʊʃl wɜ:kə] *Sozialarbeiter/in*
come up with sth *v* [ˌkʌm 'ʌp wɪð] to invent sth, to have an idea
speech *n* [spi:tʃ] the act of speaking
gesture *n* ['dʒestʃə] *Geste*
awareness *n* [ə'weənəs] knowledge, consciousness or interest
current *adj* ['kʌrənt] happening now (*derzeitig*)
advances *n* [əd'vɑ:nsɪz] Annäherungsversuche, *Anmache*
92 **artificial** *adj* [ˌɑ:tɪ'fɪʃl] *künstlich*
lung *n* [lʌŋ] *Lunge*
draw *v* [drɔ:] here: to attract
sell-out *adj* ['sel aʊt] *ausverkauft*
clunky *adj* ['klʌŋki] *klobig*
draft *n* [drɑ:ft] an unfinished version of sth (*Entwurf*)
sense of touch *n* [ˌsens əv 'tʌtʃ] *Tastsinn*
formidable *adj* ['fɔmədəbl] difficult to deal with, needing a lot of effort
converse *v* [kən'vɜ:s] to talk, to have a conversation
take into account *v* [ˌteɪk ɪntu ə'kaʊnt] to consider sth
variety *n* [və'raɪəti] a number of different things
supplement *v* ['sʌplɪmənt] to add sth to sth else
frown *v* [fraʊn] *die Stirn runzeln*
acquire *v* [ə'kwaɪə] to get sth
trial *n* ['traɪəl] the act of testing sth (*Probelauf*)
elementary school (AE) *n* [ˌelɪ'mentri sku:l] *Grundschule*
joyfully *adv* ['dʒɔɪfəli] full of happiness
recall *v* [rɪ'kɔ:l] to remember sth
sixth-grader *n* ['sɪksθ greɪdə] *Sechstklässler*
researcher *n* [rɪ'sɜ:tʃə] *Wissenschaftler/in, Forscher/in*
feel sorry for sb/sth *phr* [fi:l 'sɒri fə] to feel sympathy or pity for sb
regard *v* [rɪ'gɑ:d] to view, to think of sth/sb in a certain way
unthreatening *adj* [ʌn'θretnɪŋ] unlikely to do anything unpleasant
root *n* [ru:t] *Wurzel*
inanimate *adj* [ɪn'ænɪmət] sth that is not living (in the way that humans, animals or plants live)
range *v* [reɪndʒ] here: to stretch from one thing to another quite different thing
make up for *v* [ˌmeɪk 'ʌp] *ausgleichen*
labor (AE) *n* ['leɪbə] workers (as a group)
shortfall *n* ['ʃɔ:tfɔ:l] loss, shortage (*Ausfall*)
application *n* [ˌæplɪ'keɪʃn] *Anwendung*
have your way *phr* [həv jɔ: 'weɪ] to get or do what you want
93 **be way ahead** *phr* [bi ˌweɪ ə'hed] to be very far in front of sb, to be a lot better than sb

i:	ɪ	e	æ	ɑ:	ɒ	ɔ:	ʊ	u:	ʌ	ɜ:	ə
see	sit	ten	bad	arm	got	saw	put	too	cut	bird	about

comprehend *v* [ˌkɒmprɪ'hend] to understand
impertinent *adj* [ɪm'pɜːtɪnənt] rude, not showing respect
hitherto *adv* [ˌhɪðə'tuː] until now
inclination *n* [ˌɪnklɪ'neɪʃn] a feeling that makes you want to behave in a certain way
suspicious of sb/sth *adj* [sə'spɪʃəs əv] not trusting sb/sth

94 **leading** *adj* ['liːdɪŋ] *führend*
acute *adj* [ə'kjuːt] very great, strong
shortage *n* ['ʃɔːtɪdʒ] *Mangel*
manpower *n* ['mænpaʊə] the people that you need to do a certain job

95 **inject** *v* [ɪn'dʒekt] *spritzen*
icecap *n* ['aɪskæp] *Eisdecke*
sustain *v* [sə'steɪn] here: to keep sth alive or healthy
habitable *adj* ['hæbɪtəbl] *bewohnbar*
propose *v* [prə'pəʊz] to suggest
surface *n* ['sɜːfɪs] *Oberfläche*
issue *n* ['ɪʃuː] here: *Ausgabe*
proliferate *v* [prə'lɪfəreɪt] to increase quickly in number
revert *v* [rɪ'vɜːt] to return to a previous state
dormant *adj* ['dɔːmənt] not active for a long time
revive *v* [rɪ'vaɪv] to make sth strong or healthy again
note *v* [nəʊt] to notice sth
artificially *adv* [ˌɑːtɪ'fɪʃəli] *künstlich*
detrimental *adj* [ˌdetrɪ'mentl] harmful or damaging
retain *v* [rɪ'teɪn] to keep or continue to have
lifespan *n* ['laɪfspæn] length of time that sb/sth lives, works, lasts, etc.
back up *v* [ˌbæk 'ʌp] *unterstützen*
fluorine *n* ['flʊəriːn] *Fluor*
readily *adv* ['redɪli] easily, without difficulty
approximately *adv* [ə'prɒksɪmətli] about, around
spark *v* [spɑːk] to cause sth
instantaneous *adj* [ˌɪnstən'teɪniəs] happening at once or immediately
self-perpetuating *adj* [ˌself pə'petʃueɪtɪŋ] constantly continuing
sheet *n* [ʃiːt] here: *Decke*
evaporate *v* [ɪ'væpəreɪt] to disappear (into the air/atmosphere)
release *n* [rɪ'liːs] here: *Austreten (von Gasen)*

96 **pressure** *n* ['preʃə] *Druck*
restore *v* [rɪ'stɔː] to fix, to put sth back into a previous condition
conclude *v* [kən'kluːd] to reach a belief or opinion as a result of study or research
feasible *adj* ['fiːzəbl] possible to do
sprinkle *v* ['sprɪŋkl] to drop small pieces of sth over a surface
absorb *v* [əb'sɔːb] to take in and hold sth (heat, a liquid, etc.)
have in mind *phr* [həv ɪn 'maɪnd] to be thinking of sth, to remember
immediately *adv* [ɪ'miːdiətli] straight away, at once

97 **curious** *adj* ['kjʊəriəs] *neugierig*

98 **desirability** *n* [dɪˌzaɪərə'bɪləti] how much or how badly sth is wanted
keep tabs on sb/sth *phr, infl* [kiːp 'tæbz ɒn] to watch sb/sth carefully
administer *v* [əd'mɪnɪstə] to give sb sth (especially medicine); to control or manage sth
on the spot *phr* [ɒn ðə 'spɒt] immediately

99 **retire** *v* [rɪ'taɪə] to stop working, usually because you have reached a certain age
surveillance *n* [sɜː'veɪləns] *Überwachung*
exhibition *n* [ˌeksɪ'bɪʃn] *Ausstellung*

100 **be faced with sth** *phr* [bi 'feɪst wɪð] *mit etwas konfrontiert sein*

UNIT 10 THE DEVELOPING WORLD

101 **inhabitant** *n* [ɪn'hæbɪtənt] *Bewohner*
makeshift shelter *n* [ˌmeɪkʃɪft 'ʃeltə] *Notunterkunft*
sanitation *n* [ˌsænɪ'teɪʃn] *Abwassersystem*
illiterate *adj* [ɪ'lɪtərət] unable to read or write
undernourished *adj* [ˌʌndə'nʌrɪʃt] *unterernährt*
starving *adj* ['stɑːvɪŋ] suffering very badly or dying from hunger

102 **eight-foot-square** *adj* [ˌeɪt fʊt 'skweə] eight feet by eight feet
shack *n* [ʃæk] a small, roughly built hut
ankle-high *adj* ['æŋkl haɪ] *knöchelhoch*

tʃ	dʒ	ʃ	ʒ	θ	ð	ŋ	s	z	v	w
chips	**jet**	**ship**	**garage**	**thing**	**the**	**ring**	**ice**	**as**	**very**	**wet**

drain *n* [dreɪn] a pipe or hole that dirty water etc. goes down to be carried away
sewage *n* ['su:ɪdʒ] *Abwasser*
smoulder *v* ['sməʊldə] to slowly burn without a flame
dump *v* [dʌmp] to leave or put down sth that you do not want anymore
payment *n* ['peɪmənt] *Bezahlung*
stretch *v* [stretʃ] here: to cover a large area
unhealthy *adj* [ʌn'helθi] bad for your health or well-being
stilts *n* [stɪlts] *Stelzen*
volatile *adj* ['vɒlətaɪl] likely to change suddenly
growth *n* [grəʊθ] *Wachstum*
share *v* [ʃeə] to have or use sth together with sb else
tenant *n* ['tenənt] *Mieter/in*
access *n* ['ækses] the chance or right to use or have sth (*Zugang zu etwas haben*)
staggered by *v* ['stægəd baɪ] very surprised, shocked by
take office *v* [teɪk 'ɒfɪs] to start a (very important / senior) job
pledge *v* [pledʒ] to promise to give or do sth
waste *n* [weɪst] rubbish (*Abfall*)
abandoned *adj* [ə'bændənd] left alone
debt relief *n* [det rɪ'li:f] *Schuldenerlass*
owe *v* [əʊ] to have to pay money to sb for sth (*schulden*)
dreadful *adj* ['dredfl] very bad, awful
transmit *v* [træns'mɪt] *übertragen*
disease *n* [dɪ'zi:z] illness
community worker *n* [kə'mju:nəti wɜ:kə] here: social worker
bright *adj* [braɪt] light, here: positive
stabbing *n* ['stæbɪŋ] *Messerstecherei*
pregnancy *n* ['pregnənsi] *Schwangerschaft*
abortion *n* [ə'bɔ:ʃn] *Abtreibung*
chemist *n* ['kemɪst] *Apotheker/in*
103 **trickle** *n* ['trɪkl] a thin stream of liquid
drip *v* [drɪp] (used about liquid) to fall in small drops
crack *n* [kræk] a line on the surface of sth where it has broken
stall *n* [stɔ:l] a small shop with an open front or table
wander *v* ['wɒndə] to walk around
shanty *n* ['ʃænti] a small town or part of a town where poor people live in bad conditions
malnourished *adj* [ˌmæl'nʌrɪʃt] not getting the right or enough food to keep you healthy
tell-tale *adj* ['tel teɪl] giving information about sth secret or private (*preisgeben*)
swollen *adj* ['swəʊlən] *angeschwollen*
belly *n infl* ['beli] stomach (*Magen*)
drag (on) *n* [dræg] *Belastung (für)*
attempt *n* [ə'tempt] *Versuch*
poverty *n* ['pɒvəti] *Armut*
endemic *adj* [en'demɪk] *endemisch*
life-expectancy *n* ['laɪf ɪkspektənsi] *Lebenserwartung*
exceed *v* [ɪk'si:d] to be greater than sth
unpaid *adj* [ˌʌn'peɪd] not yet paid, not receiving money for work done
queue *v* [kju:] to stand in a line of people that are all waiting for sth (*sich anstellen*)
war-ravaged *adj* [ˌwɔ: 'rævɪdʒd] destroyed or damaged by war
patiently *adv* ['peɪʃntli] calmly, not getting angry, especially when waiting for sth
clutch *v* [klʌtʃ] to hold onto very tightly
dole out sth *v* [ˌdəʊl 'aʊt] to give out sth to a group of people
maize *n* [meɪz] corn (*Mais*)
gruel *n* ['gru:əl] *Haferschleim*
ladle *n* ['leɪdl] *Kelle*
shade *n* [ʃeɪd] *Schatten*
educate *v* ['edʒukeɪt] to teach
soup kitchen *n* ['su:p kɪtʃɪn] *Suppenküche*
provide *v* [prə'vaɪd] to give or supply sth to sb
nourished *adj* ['nʌrɪʃt] *ernährt*
104 **greedy** *adj* ['gri:di] wanting more food, money, power, etc. than you need
loan *n* [ləʊn] money that you borrow
unfit *adj* [ʌn'fɪt] unsuitable, not good enough for sth
abominable *adj* [ə'bɒmɪnəbl] extremely unpleasant, extremely bad
root cause *n* ['ru:t kɔ:z] main or underlying reason

i:	ɪ	e	æ	ɑ:	ɒ	ɔ:	ʊ	u:	ʌ	ɜ:	ə
see	sit	ten	bad	arm	got	saw	put	too	cut	bird	about

honest *adj* ['ɒnɪst] telling the truth, not deceiving people or stealing
debt *n* [det] money that you owe sb
run-down *adj* [ˌrʌn 'daʊn] in bad condition
bloated *adj* ['bləʊtɪd] *aufgeschwemmt, geschwollen*
widespread *adj* ['waɪdspred] affecting a large number of people
squander *v* ['skwɒndə] to waste time, money, etc.
physical appearance *n* [ˌfɪzɪkl ə'pɪərəns] the way sb's body looks
willing *adj* ['wɪlɪŋ] prepared to do sth (*bereit*)
aware *adj* [ə'weə] knowing about or realizing sth
prerequisite *n* [ˌpriː'rekwəzɪt] *Bedingung*

105 **case study** *n* ['keɪs stʌdi] *Fallstudie*
desperation *n* [ˌdespə'reɪʃn] *Verzweiflung*
stream *n* [striːm] a small river
serving spoon *n* ['sɜːvɪŋ spuːn] *der Vorlegelöffel*
equality *n* [ɪ'kwɒləti] the situation in which everybody has the same rights (*Gleichberechtigung*)
apparent *adj* [ə'pærənt] clear, obvious, easy to see
surpass *v* [sə'pɑːs] to do or be better than sb/sth else
birth rate *n* ['bɜːθ reɪt] *Geburtenrate*
lack *v* [læk] to have too little or none of sth
saint *n* [seɪnt] *Heiliger*

106 **relief organization** *n* [rɪˌliːf ˌɔːgənaɪ'zeɪʃn] *Hilfsorganisation*
investigate *v* [ɪn'vestɪgeɪt] to try to find out all the facts about sth
be supposed to do sth *v* [bi sə'pəʊzd tə du] to be expected to or to have to do sth
various *adj* ['veəriəs] more than one, several
invention *n* [ɪn'venʃn] *Erfindung*
guess *n* [ges] an attempt to give the right answer when unsure about the facts
usefulness *n* ['juːsfəlnəs] *Nutzen, Nützlichkeit*

107 **set off** *v* [ˌset 'ɒf] to leave on a journey
self-confident *adj* [ˌself 'kɒnfɪdənt] feeling sure about your own value and abilities
anticipate *v* [æn'tɪsɪpeɪt] to expect sth to happen
load *n* [ləʊd] sth heavy that is carried/transported
pawpaw (AE) *n* ['pɔːpɔː] papaya (BE)
reluctantly *adv* [rɪ'lʌktəntli] unwilling to agree to do sth
ache *v* [eɪk] to hurt
grand *adj* [grænd] seeming to be important
hoop *n* [huːp] a large ring of wood or plastic (*Reifen*)
bunch *n* [bʌntʃ] a number of things, usually of the same type, put together
change *n* [tʃeɪndʒ] *Wechselgeld*
mule *n* [mjuːl] an animal that has a horse and a donkey as its parents (here: *Packesel*)
bundle *n* ['bʌndl] a number of things tied or wrapped together
screw up your eyes *phr* [ˌskruː 'ʌp jɔːr aɪz] *die Augen zusammenkneifen*
room for sb/sth *n* ['ruːm fə] space, enough space
twine *n* [twaɪn] *Schnur*
pile *n* [paɪl] a number of things lying on top of each other
mind *v* [maɪnd] here: (used as a command) to be careful of/about sth
sigh *v* [saɪ] to let out a long, deep breath that shows you are tired, sad, etc.
sweat *n* [swet] *Schweiß*
gasp *n* [gɑːsp] a quick breath
farther *adj* ['fɑːðə] more distant in space or time
cluck *v* [klʌk] *glucken*
crossly *adv* ['krɒsli] angrily
presently *adv* ['prezntli] after a short time
ahead of sb/sth *adv* [ə'hed əv] in front of sb/sth
crossness *n* ['krɒsnəs] the feeling of being angry, in a bad mood
mere *adj* [mɪə] nothing more than; here: even
pack mule *n* ['pæk mjuːl] *Packesel*

108 **rib** *n* [rɪb] *Rippe*
joint *n* [dʒɔɪnt] *Gelenk*
shuffle *v* ['ʃʌfl] to walk by sliding your feet along instead of lifting them off the ground
wobble *v* ['wɒbl] to move quickly from side to side in an unsafe way

tʃ	dʒ	ʃ	ʒ	θ	ð	ŋ	s	z	v	w
chips	jet	ship	garage	thing	the	ring	ice	as	very	wet

topple over *v* ['tɒpl əʊvə] to fall over
waver *v* ['weɪvə] to become uncertain, to wobble
suffer *v* ['sʌfə] to experience sth unpleasant, e.g. pain, sadness, difficulty, etc.
severely *adv* [sɪ'vɪəli] seriously, strictly
peel *v* [piːl] *schälen*
overlook *v* [ˌəʊvə'lʊk] here: to have a view over sth
squat *v* [skwɒt] *hocken*

109 **treat** *v* [triːt] *behandeln*
hop *v* [hɒp] to jump while standing on one leg
excitement *n* [ɪk'saɪtmənt] a feeling of pleasure, happiness, looking forward to sth
hatch *v* [hætʃ] *schlüpfen*
talk sb into doing sth *v* ['tɔːk ɪntə] to persuade sb to do sth
squint *v* [skwɪnt] to look at sth with your eyes almost closed
flash *v* [flæʃ] here: to give
gaze up *v* [ˌgeɪz 'ʌp] to look up at sth
glaring *adj* ['gleərɪŋ] too strong and bright
uncertain *adj* [ʌn'sɜːtn] not sure about sth

110 **fetch** *v* [fetʃ] to go and get
burden *v* ['bɜːdn] to make things difficult for sb/sth (*aufbürden, belasten*)
poverty trap *n* ['pɒvəti træp] *Armutsfalle*
destitution *n* [ˌdestɪ'neɪʃn] state of not having the things that are necessary in life, like money, food etc
rural *adj* ['rʊərəl] *ländlich*
resident *n* ['rezɪdənt] a person who lives in a place
reluctant *adj* [rɪ'lʌktənt] not willing to do sth
trade barrier *n* ['treɪd bæriə] *Handelsschranke*
vital *adj* ['vaɪtl] very important or necessary
necessity *n* [nə'sesəti] *Notwendigkeit*
power station *n* ['paʊə steɪʃn] factory where electricity is produced
power grid *n* ['paʊə grɪd] *Energieversorgungsnetz, Hochspannungsnetz*
establish *v* [ɪ'stæblɪʃ] to start sth, to set sth up
lasting *adj* ['lɑːstɪŋ] continuing for a long time
relationship *n* [rɪ'leɪʃnʃɪp] *Beziehung*

111 **struggle** *v* ['strʌgl] to try very hard to do sth that is difficult
aid *n* [eɪd] money, food, etc. that is sent to a country or people in order to help them
lift *v* [lɪft] to move sb/sth to a higher position or level
elsewhere *adv* [ˌels'weə] in another place
publish *v* ['pʌblɪʃ] *veröffentlichen*
due to *adj* ['djuː tə] caused by or because of sth
midwife *n* ['mɪdwaɪf] *Hebamme*
contain *v* [kən'teɪn] *enthalten*
tariff *n* ['tærɪf] *Zoll*
peasant *n* ['peznt] (poor) farmer
weed *v* [wiːd] *(Unkraut jäten)*
sparse *adj* [spɑːs] small in quantity or amount
bribe *n* [braɪb] *Bestechung*
deteriorate *v* [dɪ'tɪəriəreɪt] to get worse
basin *n* ['beɪsn] *Becken*
enlightened *adj* [ɪn'laɪtnd] knowing the truth (and/or danger) of sth
curb *n* [kɜːb] here: limit
logging *n* ['lɒgɪŋ] the act of cutting down trees

112 **expectancy** *n* [ɪk'spektənsi] *Erwartung*
preventable *adj* [prɪ'ventəbl] can be stopped from happening
visible *adj* ['vɪzəbl] *sichtbar*
starvation *n* [stɑː'veɪʃn] the act of dying because there is not enough food
healthcare *n* ['helθkeə] medical help
be out of the question *phr* [bi ˌaʊt əv ðə 'kwestʃən] to be impossible
prevalence *n* ['prevələns] being common in a particular place at a particular time
grant *v* [grɑːnt] to give sb sth that he/she has asked for, to allow

UNIT 11 ENGLISH SPOKEN HERE

113 **project** *v* [prə'dʒekt] to estimate or calculate
reach *v* [riːtʃ] here: to affect, influence

iː	ɪ	e	æ	ɑː	ɒ	ɔː	ʊ	uː	ʌ	ɜː	ə
see	sit	ten	bad	arm	got	saw	put	too	cut	bird	about

release *v* [rɪ'li:s] to make a film, record, etc. available so the public can see or hear it
match *v* [mætʃ] to find sth/sb that is suitable for sth/sb else
114 **pleasure** *n* ['pleʒə] the feeling of being happy or satisfied
straightforward *adj* [ˌstreɪt'fɔ:wəd] easy to do or understand, simple
law *n* [lɔ:] *Gesetz*
directive *n* [də'rektɪv] an official order to do sth
translate *v* [træns'leɪt] *übersetzen*
at best *phr* [ət 'best] taking the most hopeful/optimistic view
use *n* [ju:s] *Verwendung*
in view of this *phr* [ɪn 'vju: əv ðɪs] because of sth; as a result of sth
agriculture *n* ['ægrɪkʌltʃə] *Landwirtschaft*
development *n* [dɪ'veləpmənt] *Entwicklung*
desirable *adj* [dɪ'zaɪərəbl] wanted, often by many people; worth having
environmental protection *n* [ɪnˌvaɪrənˌmentl prə'tekʃn] *Umweltschutz*
happen to be *v* ['hæpən tə bi:] to be somewhere or sth by chance
native speaker *n* [ˌneɪtɪv 'spi:kə] *Muttersprachler/in*
insulting *adj* [ɪn'sʌltɪŋ] rude
flourishing *adj* ['flʌrɪʃɪŋ] developing in a successful way
proposal *n* [prə'pəʊzl] suggestion, idea
apologize *v* [ə'pɒlədʒaɪz] to say sorry
have a lot going for it *phr* [həv ə ˌlɒt 'gəʊɪŋ fə] to have a lot of advantages
get rid of *v* [get 'rɪd əv] to remove sth that is unpleasant or not wanted
unworkable *adj* [ʌn'wɜ:kəbl] not possible
indisputably *adv* [ˌɪndɪ'spju:təbli] undeniably, definitely true, sth that cannot be proved wrong
115 **speech** *n* [spi:tʃ] a formal talk (*Rede*)
116 **English immersion camp** *n* [ˌɪŋglɪʃ ɪ'mɜ:ʃn kæmp] camp where only English is spoken
subsidized *adj* ['sʌbsɪdaɪzd] given money by the government to help keep prices low
fake *adj* [feɪk] not real or genuine
conduct *v* [kən'dʌkt] to carry out or do sth
capable *adj* ['keɪpəbl] having a lot of skill, good at doing sth
front line *n* [ˌfrʌnt 'laɪn] *Front*
empowerment *n* [ɪm'paʊəmənt] the act of giving power to sb
engine *n* ['endʒɪn] *Motor*
deaf *adj* [def] not able to hear
dumb *adj* [dʌm] not able to speak
fluency *n* ['flu:ənsi] being able to speak a language easily
middle school *n* ['mɪdl sku:l] school found in some parts of GB for pupils between nine and thirteen years old
common denominator *n* [ˌkɒmən dɪ'nɒmɪneɪtə] *gemeinsamer Nenner*
hammer out *v* [ˌhæmər 'aʊt] to make a plan or agreement after a lot of difficulty (*entwerfen*)
emerge *v* [ɪ'mɜ:dʒ] to appear or to become known (*entstehen*)
exchequer *n* [ɪks'tʃekə] *Finanzministerium*
acquire *v* [ə'kwaɪə] here: to learn
bustling *adj* ['bʌslɪŋ] busy
eager *adj* ['i:gə] very interested and motivated
117 **unequivocal** *adj* [ˌʌnɪ'kwɪvəkl] clear (*eindeutig, unmissverständlich*)
prized *adj* [praɪzd] considered to be very valuable
pick up *v* [ˌpɪk 'ʌp] here: to learn (the language)
draft *v* [drɑ:ft] to make a first or early version of a piece of writing
be advised by *v* [bi əd'vaɪzd baɪ] to be informed by, helped by
spell check *n* ['spel tʃek] *Rechtschreibprüfung*
shrink *v* [ʃrɪŋk] to become smaller
emulate *v* ['emjuleɪt] to copy, to try to do sth as well as sb/sth else
advance *n* [əd'vɑ:ns] *Fortschritt*
brand *n* [brænd] a particular type of sth
lose out (on sth) *v* [ˌlu:z 'aʊt ɒn] to be at a disadvantage
insist on *v* [ɪn'sɪst ɒn] to say or demand that you must have or do sth
giggle *n* ['gɪgl] *Kichern*

tʃ	dʒ	ʃ	ʒ	θ	ð	ŋ	s	z	v	w
chips	**jet**	**ship**	**garage**	**thing**	**the**	**ring**	**ice**	**as**	**very**	**wet**

blank *adj* [blæŋk] here: without feelings, understanding or interest
jabber on *v, infl* ['dʒæbə ɒn] to keep on talking about sth for a long time
miss the point *v* [mɪs ðə 'pɔɪnt] to not understand sth
erode *v* [ɪ'rəʊd] to destroy sth slowly
118 **lure** *v* [lʊə] to attract or tempt sb/sth
base sth on sth *v* ['beɪs ɒn] to form or develop sth from a particular starting point
disgusted *adj* [dɪs'gʌstɪd] disliking or disapproving (*angewidert*)
terrified *adj* ['terɪfaɪd] very scared
miss out on sth *v* [ˌmɪs 'aʊt ɒn] to not be included, to lose a chance to gain sth
119 **yearn** *v* [jɜːn] to want sth very badly or strongly
aspire to *v* [ə'spaɪə tə] to try to achieve sth, to have a strong desire to do or achieve sth
dedication *n* [ˌdedɪ'keɪʃn] willing to give lots of your time and energy to sth
devote *v* [dɪ'vəʊt] to give a lot of time, energy, etc. to sth/sb
decisive *adj* [dɪ'saɪsɪv] *entscheidend*
hold office *v* [həʊld 'ɒfɪs] to have a certain job (*ein Amt innehaben*)
gratify *v* ['grætɪfaɪ] to give sb pleasure
prospect *n* ['prɒspekt] *Aussicht*
abhor *v* [əb'hɔː] to hate sth very much
creep *v* [kriːp] to move forward slowly
120 **not go down well with sb** *phr* [nɒt ˌgəʊ 'daʊn wel wɪð] here: to not be liked by sb
royalty *n* ['rɔɪəlti] *Honorar*
presenter *n* [prɪ'zentə] a person who introduces a radio or television programme
121 **command** *n* [kə'mɑːnd] here: the ability to speak a language well
take its toll *phr* [teɪk ɪts 'təʊl] to cause loss, damage, suffering
shrinking *adj* ['ʃrɪŋkɪŋ] becoming smaller
accomplish *v* [ə'kʌmplɪʃ] to achieve or finish sth, to succeed in doing sth

UNIT 12 SETTLING DOWN IN OTHER CULTURES

122 **settle down** *v* [ˌsetl 'daʊn] to begin a quieter way of life, e.g. by staying in the same place or getting married
ranking *n* ['ræŋkɪŋ] Reihenfolge (*sortiert nach Wichtigkeit*)
earning potential *n* [ˌɜːnɪŋ pə'tenʃl] maximum amount of money that you can possibly earn
soulmate *n* ['səʊl meɪt] *Seelenverwandte/r*
123 **have in store for sb** *phr* [həv ɪn 'stɔː fə] to plan for sb
get the hang of sth *v, infl* [get ðə 'hæŋ əv] to learn how to use or do sth
arranged marriage *n* [ə'reɪndʒt 'mærɪdʒ] a marriage in which the parents find the husband/wife for their child
chunky *adj* ['tʃʌŋki] made of thick material or pieces
strap *v* [stræp] *umbinden*
have sth in common with sb/sth *v* [həv ɪn 'kɒmən wɪð] to share sth with sb/sth else
influence *v* ['ɪnfluəns] to have an effect on sb/sth
close-knit *adj* [ˌkləʊs 'nɪt] *eng (verbunden)*
require *v* [rɪ'kwaɪə] to need, to have to
in secret *phr* [ɪn 'siːkrɪt] without other people knowing
recover *v* [rɪ'kʌvə] to get back to normal again after a bad experience
be whisked away *v* [biˌwɪskt ə'weɪ] to be taken somewhere quickly
change into *v* ['tʃeɪndʒ ɪntə] to put on different clothes (*sich umziehen*)
suit *n* [suːt] *Anzug*
sit sb down *v* [ˌsɪt 'daʊn] *jdn hinsetzen*; here: to have a serious talk with sb
124 **complexion** *n* [kəm'plekʃn] the natural colour and quality of the skin or face
counter *v* ['kaʊntə] to answer
burgeoning *adj* ['bɜːdʒənɪŋ] growing, expanding

iː	ɪ	e	æ	ɑː	ɒ	ɔː	ʊ	uː	ʌ	ɜː	ə
see	sit	ten	bad	arm	got	saw	put	too	cut	bird	about

compound *v* ['kɒmpaʊnd] to make sth worse
heady *adj* ['hedi] here: *berauschend*
endure *v* [ɪn'djʊə] to suffer sth painful or uncomfortable for a period of time
dump *n, infl* [dʌmp] here: *Bruchbude*
replete *adj* [rɪ'pli:t] filled
resent *v* [rɪ'zent] to feel angry about sth
slob *n, infl* [slɒb] a very lazy or untidy person
indulge *v* [ɪn'dʌldʒ] to allow yourself to have a lot of sth for pleasure
fight tooth and nail *phr* [faɪt ˌtu:θ ənd 'neɪl] to do everything in your power
prepared to do sth *phr* [prɪ'peəd tə du:] willing to do sth
dare *v* [deə] here: *herausfordern*
occur *v* [ə'kɜ:] to think of sth, to come into sb's mind
be beyond sb *phr, infl* [bi bɪ'jɒnd] to be impossible for sb to do or understand
voraciously *adv* [və'reɪʃəsli] here: *sehr eifrig*
in exchange *n* [ɪn ɪks'tʃeɪndʒ] giving or receiving sth in return for sth else
East Enders [ˌi:st 'endəz] British soap opera
throw in *v, infl* [ˌθrəʊ 'ɪn] to add
do the dishes *phr* [du: ðə 'dɪʃɪz] to wash up all the plates, cups, etc. that have been used for a meal
bank loan *n* ['bæŋk ləʊn] *Kredit bei der Bank*
flaw *n* [flɔ:] downfall, mistake
common *adj* ['kɒmən] here: *gemeinsam*
bond *n* [bɒnd] attachment or link between two (or more) people
roller-coaster *n* ['rəʊlə kəʊstə] *Achterbahn*
125 **lad** *n, infl* [læd] boy, young man
mend your ways *phr* [ˌmend jɔ: 'weɪz] to improve your behaviour
distinct *adj* [dɪ'stɪŋkt] clearly different
host *n* [həʊst] a person who receives and entertains visitors
comply (with) *v* [kəm'plaɪ wɪð] to do what you are told, to obey an order or request
upbringing *n* ['ʌpbrɪŋɪŋ] *Erziehung*
desolate *adj* ['desələt] alone, very unhappy and without hope
innermost *adj* ['ɪnəməʊst] here: the most secret or private
by and large *phr* [ˌbaɪ ənd 'lɑ:dʒ] mostly
take sb by surprise *v* [teɪk baɪ sə'praɪz] to do sth when sb is not expecting it
sibling *n* ['sɪblɪŋ] a brother or sister
bluntly *adv* ['blʌntli] saying exactly what you think in a not very polite way
shudder *v* ['ʃʌdə] to shake with fear
senseless *adj* ['sensləs] having no meaning or purpose
126 **disapprove** *v* [ˌdɪsə'pru:v] to think that sth/sb is bad, foolish, etc.
bias *n* ['baɪəs] opinion, feeling, attitude that is not fair and not based on facts
struggle *n* ['strʌgl] a fight
disability *n* [ˌdɪsə'bɪləti] *Behinderung*
127 **surreptitiously** *adv* [ˌsʌrəp'tɪʃəsli] secretly
rouse *v* [raʊz] here: to get up (out of a chair)
clue *n* [klu:] *Hinweis*
bewilder *v* [bɪ'wɪldə] to confuse
tangle *n* ['tæŋgl] a confused mass (*Unordnung*)
cricket bat *n* ['krɪkɪt bæt] *Cricketschläger*
outgrow *v* [ˌaʊt'grəʊ] to become too old or too big for sth
torn *adj* [tɔ:n] ripped (*zerrissen*)
contain *v* [kən'teɪn] to have inside (*enthalten*)
part from sb/sth *v* ['pɑ:t frəm] to leave sb/sth, to separate from sb/sth
remark *n* [rɪ'mɑ:k] comment
elicit *v* [ɪ'lɪsɪt] to get information, facts, a reaction, etc. from sb
conclusive *adj* [kən'klu:sɪv] showing that an idea is definitely true or real
eccentricity *n* [ˌeksen'trɪsəti] behaviour that is strange or unusual
injustice *n* [ɪn'dʒʌstɪs] *Ungerechtigkeit*
pitfall *n* ['pɪtfɔ:l] an unexpected danger, a mistake that can be easily made
bear *v* [beə] here: to show
mark *n* [mɑ:k] a spot or line

tʃ	dʒ	ʃ	ʒ	θ	ð	ŋ	s	z	v	w
chips	**jet**	**ship**	**garage**	**thing**	**the**	**ring**	**ice**	**as**	**very**	**wet**

imperative *adj* [ɪm'perətɪv] very important or urgent
cabbie *n, infl* ['kæbi] taxi driver
practical joke *n* [ˌpræktɪkl 'dʒəʊk] *Streich*
lewd *adj* [luːd] with sexual content and rude

128 **truant** *v* ['truːənt] to stay away from school without permission
excel *v* [ɪk'sel] to be very good at sth
scholar *n* ['skɒlə] a person who studies
busted *adj, infl* ['bʌstɪd] broken, damaged, old
pour out your account *v* [ˌpɔːr 'aʊt jɔːr əˌkaʊnt] *jdm sein Herz ausschütten*
glance *n* [glɑːns] *Blick*
grave *adj* [greɪv] serious, sad
scrupulously *adv* ['skruːpjələsli] very carefully, paying a lot of attention
severe *adj* [sɪ'vɪə] strict, mean
stagger out *v* ['stægə aʊt] *hinaustaumeln*
bare *adj* [beə] here: empty
supervisor *n* ['suːpəvaɪzə] *Vorgesetzter/in, Betreuer/in*
failure *n* ['feɪljə] a person or thing that is unsuccessful
alongside *prep* [əˌlɒŋ'saɪd] together with
develop a sharp tongue *v* [dɪˌveləp ə ˌʃɑːp 'tʌŋ] to start being rude, angry, severe

129 **grid** *n* [grɪd] *Tabelle*

UNIT 13 GOING GLOBAL

133 **in charge of sth/sb** *phr* [ɪn 'tʃɑːdʒ əv] in control or command of sth/sb; responsible for
port *n* [pɔːt] harbour
patch *n* [pætʃ] area

134 **supplier** *n* [sə'plaɪə] *Lieferant*
remote *adj* [rɪ'məʊt] far away from where other people live
heifer *n* ['hefə] young female cow
dairy *adj* ['deəri] here: for producing milk products
uncommon *adj* [ʌn'kɒmən] unusual, not normal or standard
require *v* [rɪ'kwaɪə] to need
premium *n* ['priːmiəm] here: an extra payment
differentiate *v* [ˌdɪfə'renʃieɪt] to treat one person, group or thing differently from another
facility *n* [fə'sɪləti] building, here: factory
close sth down *v* [ˌkləʊz 'daʊn] to stop all work or business permanently
hem sewer *n* ['hem səʊə] *Saumnäher/in*
retraining *n* [ˌriː'treɪnɪŋ] *Umschulungsmaßnahme*
benefit *n* ['benɪfɪt] advantage
ease *v* [iːz] to make sth easier
dental insurance *n* [ˌdentl ɪn'ʃʊərəns] *zahnärztliche Versicherung*
willing *adj* ['wɪlɪŋ] happy to do sth
benefit *v* ['benɪfɪt] to have an advantage because of sth

135 **serve** *v* [sɜːv] *bedienen*, here: *beliefern*
rock lobster *n* ['rɒk lɒbstə] *Hummer*
fishery *n* ['fɪʃəri] part of a river or sea where large numbers of fish are caught (*Fischfanggebiet; Fischerei*)
devastated *adj* ['devəsteɪtɪd] completely destroyed
literally *adv* ['lɪtərəli] *wortwörtlich*
outcome *n* ['aʊtkʌm] how an event, action or situation ends
staple food *n* ['steɪpl fuːd] basic food, the food that people eat the most
license (AE) *n* ['laɪsns] *Lizenz*
beyond *prep* [bɪ'jɒnd] out of reach of sb
handsomely *adv* ['hænsəmli] here: generously
venture *n* ['ventʃə] project
depleted *adj* [dɪ'pliːtɪd] reduced (*aufgebraucht*)
raise (children/kids) *v* [reɪz] *(Kinder) aufziehen*
minimum wage *n* [ˌmɪnɪməm 'weɪdʒ] *Mindestlohn*

136 **purity** *n* ['pjʊərəti] *Reinheit*
on top of *phr* [ɒn 'tɒp əv] here: in addition to sth else
underestimate *v* [ˌʌndər'estɪmeɪt] *unterschätzen*
cause *v* [kɔːz] to make sth happen
restock *v* [ˌriː'stɒk] to refill, to fill up the supply of sth
relocate *v* [ˌriːləʊ'keɪt] to move sth/sb somewhere else

iː	ɪ	e	æ	ɑː	ɒ	ɔː	ʊ	uː	ʌ	ɜː	ə
see	sit	ten	bad	arm	got	saw	put	too	cut	bird	about

firmly *adv* ['fɜ:mli] here: strongly
grow used to *v* [grəʊ 'ju:st tə] to become familiar with, accustomed to
thereby *adv* [ˌðeə'baɪ] in that way
jack up *v* [ˌdʒæk 'ʌp] to raise sth, to make sth higher
prosperous *adj* ['prɒspərəs] wealthy, rich and successful
outstrip *v* [ˌaʊt'strɪp] to overtake, to be more than
137 **income bracket** *n* ['ɪnkʌm brækɪt] *Einkommensklasse*
relate to sth *v* [rɪ'leɪt tə] here: to be concerned with sth, to have sth to do with sth
average *n* ['ævərɪdʒ] *Durchschnitt*
service sector *n* ['sɜ:vɪs sektə] *Dienstleistungssektor*
point sth out to sb *v* [ˌpɔɪnt 'aʊt tə] to make sth clear to sb
disturbing *adj* [dɪ'stɜ:bɪŋ] causing sb to worry
cite *v* [saɪt] *zitieren*
138 **impose** *v* [ɪm'pəʊz] to make sth be accepted because you are the person with power
tax revenue *n* ['tæks revənju:] income received (in the form of taxes) by a government
entrepreneur *n* [ˌɒntrəprə'nɜ:] *Unternehmer/in*
transfer to *v* [træns'fɜ: tə] to send, to move from one place to another
remarkable *adj* [rɪ'mɑ:kəbl] unusual or noticeable
139 **semiconductor** *n* [ˌsemikən'dʌktə] *Halbleiter*
affordable *adj* [ə'fɔ:dəbl] when sth is cheap enough for you to buy
assembly line *n* [ə'sembli laɪn] *Fließband*
line *n* [laɪn] here: telephone line
churn sth out *v, infl* [ˌtʃɜ:n 'aʊt] to produce large numbers of sth very quickly
fraction *n* ['frækʃn] a small part of sth (*Bruchteil*)
epitomize *v* [ɪ'pɪtəmaɪz] to be typical of sth
grinding *adj* ['graɪndɪŋ] crushing
edge *n* [edʒ] *Rand*
chances are *phr* ['tʃɑ:nsɪz ɑ:] it is probable that
come up with sth *v* [ˌkʌm 'ʌp wɪð] to find an answer or solution to sth

self-sufficient *adj* [ˌself sə'fɪʃənt] being able to produce or provide everything that you need for yourself
irrespective of *prep* [ɪrɪ'spektɪv əv] not affected by
man *v* [mæn] to operate sth or to provide people to operate sth
dutiful *adj* ['dju:tifl] willing to respect and obey
instruct *v* [ɪn'strʌkt] to teach, to tell sb what to do
get in *v* [ˌget 'ɪn] to reach a place, here: to be allowed/accepted to work there
applicant *n* ['æplɪkənt] *Bewerber/in*
recruit *n* [rɪ'kru:t] here: a person who has recently joined a company/organization
140 **per capita income** *n* [pə ˌkæpɪtə 'ɪnkʌm] *Pro-Kopf-Einkommen*
return *v* [rɪ'tɜ:n] to give back or to come back
mother-in-law *n* ['mʌðər ɪn lɔ:] *Schwiegermutter*
debt *n* [det] *Schulden*
remind *v* [rɪ'maɪnd] *erinnern*
debtor *n* ['detə] sb who owes sb else money
impact *v* ['ɪmpækt ɒn] to affect
scale *n* [skeɪl] degree, amount (*Maß*)
dazzle v ['dæzl] here: to impress sb very much
hire (AE) *v* ['haɪə] to employ
stock *n* [stɒk] *Wertpapier*
tax *n* [tæks] *Steuer*
national pride *n* [ˌnæʃnəl 'praɪd] *Nationalstolz*
make its mark *v* [meɪk ɪts 'mɑ:k] to make a lasting impression
workforce *n* ['wɜ:kfɔ:s] group of employees
labor pool (AE) *n* ['leɪbə pu:l] group of employees
equivalent to *adj* [ɪ'kwɪvələnt tə] equal in amount, meaning, value, importance, etc.
141 **catch up** *v* [ˌkætʃ 'ʌp] to reach sth/sb that is ahead of you
fellow-citizen *n* [ˌfeləʊ 'sɪtɪzn] *Mitbürger/in*
unbearable *adj* [ʌn'beərəbl] too unpleasant, painful, etc. to accept
humidity *n* [hju:'mɪdəti] *Feuchtigkeit*

tʃ	dʒ	ʃ	ʒ	θ	ð	ŋ	s	z	v	w
chips	jet	ship	garage	thing	the	ring	ice	as	very	wet

Gross Domestic Product (GDP) *n* [ˌgrəʊs dəˌmestɪk 'prɒdʌkt] *Bruttoinlandsprodukt* (*BIP*)
thick *adj* [θɪk] here: strong
get a grip on sth *phr* [get ə 'grɪp ɒn] to start dealing with a problem in an effective way
142 **low-wage** *adj* [ˌləʊ 'weɪdʒ] *Niedriglohn*
sweatshop *n* ['swetʃɒp] a company or factory that exploits its employees (*Ausbeuterbetrieb*)

UNIT 14 DEALING WITH TERRORISM

144 **fortify sth** *v* ['fɔːtɪfaɪ] to make sth stronger and ready for an attack
public appearance *n* [ˌpʌblɪk ə'pɪərəns] *öffentlicher Auftritt*
strike at will *v* [straɪk ət 'wɪl] to attack when you want
reel *v* [riːl] to move in an unsteady way; here: almost out of control
turmoil *n* ['tɜːmɔɪl] a state of great excitement, noise or confusion
take to doing sth *v* [teɪk tə 'duːɪŋ] to begin doing sth regularly
assassinate *v* [ə'sæsɪneɪt] to kill
boil over *v* [bɔɪl 'əʊvə] here: to become more serious or angry
heir *n* [eə] *Erbe*
trigger *v* ['trɪgə] to cause sth to start or happen (*auslösen*)
political ends *n* [pə'lɪtɪkl endz] political goals, aims
blackmail *v* ['blækmeɪl] *erpressen*
alter *v* ['ɔːltə] to change
blood-curdling *adj* ['blʌd kɜːdlɪŋ] horrible and frightening
weapons of mass destruction *n* [ˌwepənz əv 'mæs dɪstrʌkʃn] *Massenvernichtungswaffen*
breed *n* [briːd] here: type
fearsome *adj* ['fɪəsəm] frightening
means *n* [miːnz] a method of doing sth
call sth off *v* [ˌkɔːl 'ɒf] to cancel sth
spare *v* [speə] here: to not hurt or damage sb
innocent *adj* ['ɪnəsnt] *unschuldig*
indiscriminate *adj* [ˌɪndɪ'skrɪmɪnət] not carefully chosen, random
immoral *adj* [ɪ'mɒrəl] *unmoralisch*
unwise *adj* [ˌʌn'waɪz] not wise, not clever or sensible
inhibition *n* [ˌɪnhɪ'bɪʃn] *Hemmung*
incite *v* [ɪn'saɪt] to encourage
145 **vanguard** *n* ['vængɑːd] front
operate *v* ['ɒpəreɪt] to do business
faith *n* [feɪθ] belief
believer *n* [bɪ'liːvə] *Glaubender/in, Gläubiger/in*
engaged *adj* [ɪn'geɪdʒd] involved in, busy or occupied with sth
oppressive *adj* [ə'presɪv] allowing no freedom, unjust, controlling by force
misconception *n* [ˌmɪskən'sepʃn] wrong idea or understanding of sth
despair *n* [dɪ'speə] *Verzweiflung*
dare *v* [deə] to have the courage to do sth you are scared about (*sich trauen*)
supporter *n* [sə'pɔːtə] sb that supports or agrees with sth/sb
suffocate *v* ['sʌfəkeɪt] to die because there is no air to breathe
defuse *v* [ˌdiː'fjuːz] here: to make a situation calmer or less dangerous
in the meantime *phr* [ɪn ðə 'miːntaɪm] in the time between two events
harm *n* [hɑːm] damage or hurt
defy imagination *phr* [dɪˌfaɪ ɪˌmædʒɪ'neɪʃn] to be impossible to imagine
prevail *v* [prɪ'veɪl] to win or gain control, to continue to exist
146 **flourish** *v* ['flʌrɪʃ] to develop in a successful way, to grow
inhibit *v* [ɪn'hɪbɪt] to prevent sth or make sth happen more slowly
147 **deed** *n* [diːd] sth that you do, an action
harsh *adj* [hɑːʃ] difficult, severe, cruel
subject sb to sth *v* [səb'dʒekt] to make sb suffer sth painful or unpleasant
dissatisfied *adj* [dɪs'sætɪsfaɪd] not satisfied, not pleased, unhappy
carry out *v* [ˌkæri 'aʊt] *ausführen*
civil liberties *n* [ˌsɪvl 'lɪbəti] *Bürgerrechte*
enable *v* [ɪ'neɪbl] to make sb/sth able to do sth, to make possible, to allow
give in *v* [ˌgɪv 'ɪn] *nachgeben*
148 **get it** *v, infl* ['get ɪt] to understand sth
message *n* ['mesɪdʒ] *Nachricht*

iː	ɪ	e	æ	ɑː	ɒ	ɔː	ʊ	uː	ʌ	ɜː	ə
see	sit	ten	bad	arm	got	saw	put	too	cut	bird	about

cover *v* ['kʌvə] to put sth on or in front of sth
cheek *n* [tʃiːk] *Wange*
caller ID *n* [ˌkɔːlər ˌaɪ 'diː] *Anruferkennung*
cell phone (AE) *n* ['sel fəʊn] mobile phone
scoot *v* [skuːt] to slide
instantly *adv* ['ɪnstəntli] at once, immediately
crackling *adj* ['kræklɪŋ] *knackend, knisternd*
whispering *n* ['wɪspərɪŋ] the act of speaking very quietly (*Flüstern*)
pick up (the phone) *v* [ˌpɪk 'ʌp] *(den Telefonhörer) abnehmen*
149 **squeeze** *v* [skwiːz] to hold tightly (*drücken*)
shake your head *phr* [ʃeɪk jɔː 'hed] *den Kopf schütteln*
forgive sb *v* [fə'gɪv] to stop being angry towards sb or about sth
have a hard time *v* [həv ə ˌhɑːd 'taɪm] to have problems or difficulties
151 **resist** *v* [rɪ'zɪst] to stop yourself from having or wanting to do sth
conquest *n* ['kɒŋkwest] an act of taking control of an area
casualty *n* ['kæʒuəlti] a person who is killed or hurt in a war or accident
irreversible *adj* [ˌɪrɪ'vɜːsəbl] impossible to stop or change
152 **bullet-proof** *adj* ['bʊlɪt pruːf] *schuss-sicher*
negotiator *n* [nɪ'gəʊʃieɪtə] *Verhandlungsführer/in*
settlement *n* ['setlmənt] agreement

UNIT 15 INTO THE FUTURE

153 **fertilizer** *n* ['fɜːtəlaɪzə] sth that is put on land to make plants grow better (*Dünger*)
extinct *adj* [ɪk'stɪŋkt] *ausgestorben*
breed *v* [briːd] *züchten*
crop *n* [krɒp] *Ernte*
eradicate *v* [ɪ'rædɪkeɪt] to delete or destroy sth completely
154 **cuddly** *adj* ['kʌdli] soft and nice to hug
ewe *n* [juː] a female sheep
watershed *n* ['wɔːtəʃed] an important event or point which marks the beginning of sth new
redesign *v* [ˌriːdɪ'zaɪn] to invent, plan or develop sth again
announcement *n* [ə'naʊnsmənt] a statement, the act of telling people about sth
spark sth off *v* [ˌspɑːk 'ɒf] to cause or start sth
heated *adj* ['hiːtɪd] here: angry or excited
feat *n* [fiːt] achievement (*Leistung*)
voice *v* [vɔɪs] to express
slippery *adj* ['slɪpəri] *rutschig*
bring about *v* [ˌbrɪŋ ə'baʊt] to cause sth to happen
resolve *v* [rɪ'zɒlv] here: to find a solution to a problem or dilemma
turn out *v* [ˌtɜːn 'aʊt] to appear, here: to breed
row *n* [raʊ] *Reihe*
calf, calves *n* [kɑːf, kɑːvz] *Kalb, Kälber*
confer *v* [kən'fɜː] to discuss sth with sb before making a decision
eerily *adv* ['ɪərəli] strange and frightening
extension *n* [ɪk'stenʃn] continuation
demagogy *n* ['deməgɒgi] *Demagogie*
impose *v* [ɪm'pəʊz] to make sth be accepted because you are the person with power
fanciful *adj* ['fænsɪfl] unimaginable, unrealistic
notion *n* ['nəʊʃn] idea
foresee *v* [fɔː'siː] to know or guess that sth is going to happen in the future
undesirable *adj* [ˌʌndɪ'zaɪərəbl] not wanted
bound to do sth *adj* ['baʊnd tə duː] certain to do sth
cheer *n* [tʃɪə] a loud shout to show that you like or want to encourage sth/sb
fault *n* [fɔːlt] mistake
subsequent *adj* ['sʌbsɪkwənt] coming after or later
hail *v* [heɪl] to say in public that sth is very good
breakthrough *n* ['breɪkθruː] *Durchbruch*
unlock *v* [ˌʌn'lɒk] to open sth with a key; here: to find
cure *n* [kjʊə] a medicine or treatment that makes sb healthy again

tʃ	dʒ	ʃ	ʒ	θ	ð	ŋ	s	z	v	w
chips	jet	ship	garage	thing	the	ring	ice	as	very	wet

inherited *adj* [ɪn'herɪtɪd] *vererbt*
discard *v* [dɪs'kɑːd] to throw away
lend themselves to *v* ['lend tə] *sich eignen für*
155 **burn victim** *n* [bɜːn 'vɪktɪm] sb who has been hurt in a fire
trial *n* ['traɪəl] an act of testing sth
gamut *n* ['gæmət] variety, range
tissue *n* ['tɪʃuː] *Gewebe*
array *n* [ə'reɪ] a large collection of different things
inject *v* [ɪn'dʒekt] *spritzen*
dearth *n* [dɜːθ] a lack of sth, not enough of sth
donor *n* ['dəʊnə] *Spender/in*
forge ahead *v* [ˌfɔːdʒ ə'hed] to go forward quickly and strongly
manner *n* ['mænə] *Art und Weise*
ban *n* [bæn] officially forbidden (*Verbot*)
miraculous *adj* [mɪ'rækjələs] impossible to explain or understand
unbridled *adj* [ʌn'braɪdld] uncontrolled
undeniably *adv* [ˌʌndɪ'naɪəbli] clear, true, certain
immeasurable *adj* [ɪ'meʒərəbl] not measurable (*nicht messbar*)
irreparable *adj* [ɪ'repərəbl] not able to be repaired or fixed
maintain *v* [meɪn'teɪn] here: *behaupten*
sorcerer *n* ['sɔːsərə] magician (*Zauberer/in*)
overly *adv* ['əʊvəli] far too
apprentice *n* [ə'prentɪs] *Auszubildende/r*
resolution *n* [ˌreʒə'luːʃn] a decision to do or not to do sth
paramount *adj* ['pærəmaʊnt] most important
enforceable *adj* [ɪn'fɔːsəbl] *durchsetzbar*
re-emergence *n* [ˌriː ɪ'mɜːdʒəns] re-appearance
inferior *adj* [ɪn'fɪəriə] low or lower in quality, importance, etc.
156 **cure** *v* [kjʊə] to heal, to make sb healthy again
ban *v* [bæn] to forbid sth officially, by law
rule sth/sb out *v* [ˌruːl 'aʊt] to say that sth/sb is not possible
inherit *v* [ɪn'herɪt] *erben*
contagious *adj* [kən'teɪdʒəs] *ansteckend*
pass sth on to sb *v* [ˌpɑːs 'ɒn tə] to give sth to sb else
157 **solve** *v* [sɒlv] to find an answer or solution to a problem
remainder *n* [rɪ'meɪndə] the rest
159 **poised** *adj* [pɔɪzd] not moving but ready to move
beam *v* [biːm] here: to send a signal
palm *n* [pɑːm] *Handfläche*
recognition *n* [ˌrekəg'nɪʃn] *Wiedererkennung*
command *n* [kə'mɑːnd] *Befehl*
curtain *n* ['kɜːtn] *Vorhang*
await *v* [ə'weɪt] to wait for sth
remote control *n* [rɪˌməʊt kən'trəʊl] *Fernbedienung*
smoothly *adv* ['smuːðli] here: without any difficulty
node *n* [nəʊd] *Knotenpunkt*
scroll *v* [skrəʊl] here: to move text up or down on your computer screen
embedded *adj* [ɪm'bedɪd] sth that is fixed firmly and deeply in sth else
tag *n* [täg] a label
drawer *n* [drɔː] *Schublade*
light up *v* [ˌlaɪt 'ʌp] to switch the lights on (*erleuchten*)
dry clean *v* [ˌdraɪ 'kliːn] to clean clothes using special chemicals, without using water
due *adj* [dju.] expected or planned to happen or arrive
collection *n* [kə'lekʃn] *Abholung*
laundry basket *n* ['lɔːndri bɑːskɪt] *Wäschekorb*
granny *n* ['græni] grandmother
habitually *adv* [hə'bɪtʃuəli] doing sth very often, usually, frequently
in advance *phr* [ɪn əd'vɑːns] before a particular time or event
bug *n* [bʌg] here: bacteria
roast *v* [rəʊst] to cook in an oven
spoil *v* [spɔɪl] to ruin, here: to go off (*schlecht werden*)
kick in *v, infl* [ˌkɪk 'ɪn] to start, to turn on
delivery service *n* [dɪ'lɪvəri sɜːvɪs] *Lieferservice*
bulletin board *n* ['bʊlətɪn bɔːd] *Pinnwand, Anzeigetafel*
unlikely *adj* [ʌn'laɪkli] not likely to happen, unexpected

iː	ɪ	e	æ	ɑː	ɒ	ɔː	ʊ	uː	ʌ	ɜː	ə
see	sit	ten	bad	arm	got	saw	put	too	cut	bird	about

supply *n* [sə'plaɪ] *Vorrat*
derive from *v* [dɪ'raɪv] to get sth from sth
fireplace *n* ['faɪəpleɪs] *Kamin*
flood *n* [flʌd] *Überschwemmung*
text message *n* ['tekst mesɪdʒ] *SMS*
immediate *adj* [ɪ'mi:diət] happening at once or without delay
avert *v* [ə'vɜ:t] to avoid, to prevent, to stop
wade *v* [weɪd] to walk with difficulty through relatively deep water
rescue *v* ['reskju:] to save
stranded *adj* ['strændɪd] left in a place which you cannot get away from
160 **leakage** *n* ['li:kɪdʒ] when gas or liquid comes through a hole in its container
mattress *n* ['mætrəs] *Matratze*
peg *n* [peg] *(Wäsche-)Klammer*
remotely *adv* [rɪ'məʊtli] from a distance
alert *v* [ə'lɜ:t] to warn sb
screen *n* [skri:n] *Bildschirm*
a host of *n* [ə 'həʊst əv] a large number of
groceries *n* ['grəʊsəriz] food (everyday foods like milk, bread, fruit, vegetables, etc.)
run low *v* [ˌrʌn 'ləʊ] to only have a little of sth left
appliance *n* [ə'plaɪəns] *Gerät*
schedule *n* ['ʃedju:l] a plan
suspicious *adj* [sə'spɪʃəs] that makes you feel or believe that sth is wrong
161 **pile up** *v* [ˌpaɪl 'ʌp] to increase in quantity
related *adj* [rɪ'leɪtɪd] connected with sth/sb
jumble *v* ['dʒʌmbl] to mix

tʃ	dʒ	ʃ	ʒ	θ	ð	ŋ	s	z	v	w
chips	jet	ship	garage	thing	the	ring	ice	as	very	wet

ALPHABETISCHES WÖRTERVERZEICHNIS

Dieses Wörterverzeichnis enthält in alphabetischer Reihenfolge alle Wörter, die in der chornologischen Liste enthalten sind. Die Zahl nach dem Stichwort bezieht sich auf der Seite, auf der das Wort zum ersten Mal erscheint. Für eine Erklärung des jeweiligen Wortes auf Englisch können Sie im chronologischen Wörterverzeichnis unter der entsprechenden Seite nachsehen.

A

abandoned *adj* 102 *aufgegeben, verlassen*
abhor *v* 119 *verabscheuen*
ability *n* 39 *Fähigkeit*
abominable *adj* 104 *grässlich*
abortion *n* 102 *Abtreibung*
abroad *adv* 21 *im/ins Ausland*
absorb *v* 96 *aufnehmen, absorbieren*
access *n* 102 *Zugang (zu etw haben)*
accompanied *adj* 62 *begleitet*
accomplish *v* 121 *schaffen, erreichen*
according to *prep* 10 *laut, nach*
account *n* 60 *Darstellung, Bericht;*
pour out your ~ *phr* 128 *sein Herz ausschütten;*
take into ~ *v* 92 *berücksichtigen;*
~ for *v* 87 *verantwortlich sein für*
accountant *n* 52 *Buchhalter/in*
accuse *v* 60 *beschuldigen, vorwerfen*
ache *v* 107 *schmerzen, wehtun*
achieve *v* 15 *erreichen, erzielen*
acid rain *n* 82 *saurer Regen*
acquire *v* 92 *erlangen; v* 116 *erwerben, lernen*
act *n* 73 *Tat*
action, take ~ *v* 46 *Schritte unternehmen*
ad *abbr* 29 *Anzeige, Reklame*
adapt (to sth) *v* 12 *(sich) anpassen (an etw)*
addicted *adj* 33 *süchtig, abhängig*
additional *adj* 10 *zusätzlich*
adept *adj* 9 *geschickt*
administer *v* 98 *ausführen, anwenden*
admit *v* 22 *zugeben*
advance *n* 68 *Fortschritt; n* 117 *Vormarsch;*
in ~ *phr* 159 *im Voraus, vorher;*
advances *n* 91 *Annäherungsversuche*
advantage over *n* 39 *Vorteil gegenüber*
advantageous *adj* 53 *vorteilhaft*
advertising lines *n* 29 *Werbesprüche*
advised by *v* 117 *beraten durch*
advocate *n* 29 *Befürworter/in*
affect *v* 54 *betreffen*
affluent *adj* 81 *wohlhabend*
afford *v* 20 *(es) sich leisten (können)*
affordable *adj* 139 *erschwinglich*
afterthought *n* 42 *(nachträglicher) Einfall*
age *v* 49 *altern;*
come of ~ *v* 39 *erwachsen werden*
agitated *adj* 33 *aufgeregt*
agree *v* 11 *übereinstimmen, zustimmen*
agreement, reach an ~ *v* 34 *zu einer Übereinstimmung kommen*
agriculture *n* 114 *Landwirtschaft*
ahead of *adv* 107 *vor*
aid *n* 111 *Hilfe; v* 60 *unterstützen, helfen*
aim at *v* 39 *ausrichten auf*
aimlessly *adv* 77 *ziellos*
air *v* 43 *übertragen (werden)*
alert *v* 160 *alarmieren*
alertness *n* 29 *Aufmerksamkeit*
alike *adv* 52 *in gleicher Weise*
all-too-sober *adj* 44 *allzu nüchtern*
alongside *prep* 128 *neben*
alter *v* 144 *(ver)ändern*
altercation n 60 *Streit, Auseinandersetzung*
altitude *n* 85 *Höhe*
amass *v* 49 *anhäufen*
ambiguous *adj* 38 *zweideutig*
amount *n* 24 *Menge*
ankle-high *adj* 102 *knöchelhoch*
announce *v* 33 *verkünden*
announcement *n* 154 *Nachricht, Ankündigung*
annoying *adj* 38 *lästig, störend*
anticipate *v* 107 *vorhersehen, erwarten*
apologise *v* 114 *sich entschuldigen*
apparent *adj* 105 *offensichtlich, deutlich*
appeal *n* 71 *Berufung;*

~ **to sb** *v* 42 *jdn ansprechen*
appealing *adj* 38 *ansprechend*
appear *v* 45 *erscheinen;*
~ **to do sth** *v* 61 *ew zu tun scheinen*
appearance *n* 44 *Aussehen, (äußere) Erscheinung*
appendix *n* 12 *Anhang*
appliance *n* 160 *Gerät*
applicant *n* 139 *Bewerber/in*
application *n* 72 *Antrag;* *n* 92 *Anwendung*
apply for *v* 25 *sich bewerben um*
apply to *v* 23 *gelten für*
appreciate *v* 53 *würdigen, zu schätzen wissen*
apprentice *n* 155 *Lehrling*
approach *n* 32 *Methode, Ansatz;* *v* 91 *sich wenden an*
appropriate *adj* 15 *geeignet, passend*
approximately *adv* 95 *ungefähr, etwa*
arch-rival *n* 52 *Erzfeind*
argument *n* 14 *Streit, Auseinandersetzung*
arise *v* 86 *entstehen, sich ergeben, auftreten*
arranged marriage *n* 123 *arrangierte Ehe*
array *n* 155 *Ansammlung, Reihe*
artificial *adj* 92 *künstlich;*
artificially *adv* 95 *künstlich*
ashtray *n* 13 *Aschenbecher*
aside, set ~ *v* 12 *einplanen, erübrigen*
aspire to *v* 119 *anstreben*
assassinate *v* 144 *ermorden, ein Attentat verüben auf*
assault *n* 72 *Überfall, Körperverletzung*
assembly line *n* 52, 139 *Fließband*
assume *v* 44 *annehmen, glauben, übernehmen*
assure *v* 22 *zusichern, versprechen*
astounding *adj* 42 *erstaunlich*
at best *phr* 114 *bestenfalls*
attack *v* 3 *angreifen, überfallen*
attempt *n* 103 *Versuch*
attend *v* 32 *teilnehmen*
attracted (to) *adj* 64 *angezogen, angelockt*
audible *adj* 60 *hörbar*
audience *n* 44 *Publikum, Zuschauer*
Austrian *adj* 29 *österreichisch*
availability *n* 30 *Erhältlichkeit, Vorhandensein*
available *adj* 90 *erreichbar, (am Telefon) zu sprechen*
average *adj* 9 *durchschnittlich;* *n* 137 *Durchschnitt*
avert *v* 159 *verhindern*
aviation *n* 85 *Luftfahrt*
avoid *v* 21 *(ver)meiden*
await *v* 159 *erwarten*
aware *adj* 104 *bewusst;*
be ~ that *v* 9 *sich bewusst sein, dass*
awareness *n* 91 *Bewusstsein*

B

back up *v* 95 *unterstützen*
balance *v* 52 *in Übereinklang bringen*
ban *n* 155 *Verbot;* *v* 156 *verbieten*
be banned *v* 34 *ausgeschlossen werden*
bandage *v* 52 *etw verbinden, bandagieren*
bang *v* 60 *schlagen*
bank loan *n* 124 *Bankkredit*
bare *adj* 128 *nackt, bloß*
based, be ~ on *v* 118 *basieren auf*
basin *n* 111 *Becken*
be in *phr* 13 *zu Hause sein*
beam *v* 159 *strahlen*
bear *v* 127 *tragen*
beat *v* 75 *besser sein als, übertreffen, schlagen*
behave *v* 73 *sich verhalten, sich benehmen*
behaviour *n* 21 *Verhalten, Benehmen*
belch out *v* 82 *ausstoßen*
believer *n* 145 *Gläubige/r, Glaubende/r*
belly *n* 103 *Bauch*
belongings *n* 49 *Hab und Gut*
beloved *adj* 49 *geliebt*
benchmark *n* 52 *Maßstab*
benefit *n* 134 *zusätzliche Leistung, Vergünstigung;* *n* 22 *Vorteil, Nutzen;* *v* 134 *profitieren*
bewilder *v* 127 *verwirren*
beyond *prep* 135 *jenseits, außerhalb;*
be ~ sb *phr* 124 *über jds Horizont hinausgehen*
bias *n* 126 *Neigung, Vorliebe*
birth rate *n* 105 *Geburtenrate*
bitterness *n* 14 *Bitterkeit*
blackmail *v* 144 *erpressen*
blank *adj* 117 *leer, verständnislos*
blanket approach *n* 81 *pauschale/ generelle Herangehensweise*
blend *v* 29 *(ver)mischen*
bloated *adj* 104 *aufgeschwemmt, geschwollen*
blob up *v* 76 *sich sammeln*
block out *v* 41 *unterdrücken, ausblenden*
bloke (GB) *n, infl* 14 *Kerl, Typ*
blood-curdling *adj* 144 *Grauen erregend*
blotto *adj, infl* 29 *besoffen*
blow sth *v* 85 *etw vermasseln, verpatzen*
bluntly *adv* 125 *direkt, unverblümt*
blurred *adj* 75 *verschwommen*

boast *v* 58 *prahlen, angeben, sich rühmen*
boil over *v* 144 *überkochen*
bond *n* 124 *Band, (Ver-)Bindung*
boost *v* 9 *erhöhen, verstärken, steigern*
boot (BE) *n* 78 *Kofferraum*
booze *n, infl* 29 *Schnaps, Alkohol*
border *n* 23 *Grenze*
borrow sth from sb *v* 11 *sich von jdm etw ausleihen*
bouncer *n* 60 *Türsteher*
bound to do sth *adj* 154 *etw sicher/ bestimmt tun*
brackets *n* 17 *Klammern*
brainpower *n* 29 *Gehirn, Verstand*
brand *n* 117 *Marke, Typ*
breadwinner *n* 52 *Ernährer*
breakthrough *n* 154 *Durchbruch*
breed *n* 144 *Typ*
~, bred, bred *v* 39 *hervorrufen;* *v* 153 *züchten*
bribe *n* 111 *Bestechung*
brick *n* 76 *Ziegel(stein), Backstein*
bright, from the ~ side *phr* 102 *positiv*
brim with *v* 19 *voll sein mit, überborden*
bring about *v* 154 *herbeiführen*
bring forth *v* 32 *hervorbringen, auslösen*
brisk *adj* 52 *lebhaft, kräftig*
broadcast *v* 11 *übertragen, senden*
broadsheet *n* 68 *großformatige Zeitung, seriöse Tageszeitung*
bug *n* 159 *Bazillus, Bakterium*
bulletin board *n* 159 *Anzeigetafel*
bullet-proof *adj* 152 *schuss-, kugelsicher*
bump *n* 60 *Stoß, Schlag*
bunch *n* 107 *Bündel*
bundle *n* 107 *Bündel, Paket*
burden *n* 49 *Belastung, Last;* *v* 110 *aufbürden, belasten*
burgeoning *adj* 124 *aufkeimend*
burglary *n* 71 *Einbruch(sdiebstahl)*
burn victim *n* 155 *Brandopfer*
bury *v* 60 *vergraben, verbergen*
busted *adj* 128 *kaputt*
bustling *adj* 116 *voller Leben*
by and large *phr* 125 *im Großen und Ganzen*

C

cabbies *n* 127 *Taxifahrer*
cabin *n* 81 *Ferienhaus*
caffeine *n* 29 *Koffein*
calf, calves *n* 154 *Kalb, Kälber*
call sth off *phr* 144 *absagen, abblasen*
caller ID *n* 148 *Anruf-Erkennung*
can *n* 29 *Dose;* *n* 75 *Po, Hintern*
capped, be ~ *v* 85 *nach oben begrenzt, gedeckelt*
capability *n* 32 *Fähigkeit*
capable *adj* 116 *fähig*
caption *n* 18 *Bildunterschrift*
captive *adj* 19 *gefangen*
care for *v* 19 *sorgen für, pflegen*
careful *adj* 38 *vorsichtig*
caricature *v* 44 *karikieren*
caring *adj* 60 *sozial (eingestellt), verantwortungsvoll*
carrier bag *n* 85 *Plastiktüte*
carry out *v* 147 *aus-, durchführen*
case *n* 32 *Fall;*
~ history *n* 72 *Vorgeschichte;*
~ study *n* 10 *Fallstudie*
cash *v* 72 *einlösen;*
~ machine *n* 48 *Geldautomat*
casualty *n* 151 *Opfer, Verletzte/r*
catch up with *v* 141 *einholen*
cause *v* 40 *veranlassen;* *v* 86,136 *verursachen*
~ harm *v* 22 *schädlich sein, Schaden anrichten*
caution *n* 39 *Vorsicht*
cavort *v* 60 *sich tummeln, herumtreiben*
cell phone (AE) *n* 148 *Handy, Mobiltelefon*
challenge *n* 33 *Herausforderung;* *v* 32 *herausfordern*
chances are *phr* 139 *(es ist) wahrscheinlich*
change *n* 107 *Wechselgeld;*
~ into *v* 123 *anziehen*
charge *v* 61 *(Preis) fordern;*
in ~ of sth/sb *phr* 133 *verantwortlich für etw/jdn*
charity *n* 22 *wohltätiger oder gemeinnütziger Verein*
charming *adj* 25 *reizend, bezaubernd*
chase *v* 60 *verfolgen, jagen*
cheat *v* 60 *mogeln, schummeln*
check out *v* 23 *sich (etw) anschauen*
cheek *n* 148 *Wange*
cheer *n* 154 *Beifall*
chemist *n* 102 *Apotheker/in*
chicken out *v, infl* 75 *einen Rückzieher machen*
chimney *n* 83 *Schornstein*
choke *v* 85 *ersticken*
chop down *v* 88 *fällen*
chunky *adj* 123 *dick, klobig*
churn sth out *v, infl* 139 *etw am Fließband produzieren*
cigarette butt *n* 14 *Zigarettenkippe*
circle *n* 42 *Kreis*
circulate *v* 32 *zirkulieren*
circulation figures *n* 69 *Auflage(nzahlen)*
cite *v* 137 *zitieren*
civil liberties *n* 147 *Bürgerrechte*

claim *v* 81 *behaupten*
clash *n* 63 *Streit, Auseinandersetzung*
climax *n* 46 *Höhepunkt*
climb *v* 52 *klettern, aufsteigen*
clock, right around the ~ *phr* 29 *rund um die Uhr;*
ticking back on the ~ *phr* 32 *die Zeiten werden schlechter;*
~ up *v* 32 *zurücklegen, erreichen, schaffen*
close fast *v* 76 *schnell aufholen*
close sth down *v* 134 *etw schließen*
close-knit *adj* 123 *eng (verbunden)*
cluck *v* 107 *glucken*
clue *n* 127 *Hinweis*
clunky *adj* 92 *klobig*
clutch *v* 103 *umklammern*
coal *n* 80 *Kohle*
coincidence *n* 11 *Zufall*
coke *n* 55 *Cola*
collapse *v* 29 *zusammensinken*
collection *n* 159 *Abholung*
college crammer *n, infl* 29 *übereifrige/r Student/in*
come up with sth *v* 91 *erfinden, sich ausdenken; v* 139 *etw vorschlagen*
command *n* 121 *Beherrschung; n* 159 *Befehl*
commercial *n* 44 *Werbespot*
commit a crime *v* 71 *eine Straftat begehen*
common *adj* 43, 124 *gemeinsam;*
~ denominator *n* 116 *gemeinsamer Nenner;*
~ ground *n* 19 *gemeinsame Basis, Übereinstimmung;*
have sth in ~ with *v* 123 *etw gemeinsam haben mit*
commonplace *adj* 43 *alltäglich, normal*
community *n* 49 *Gemeinde;*
~ worker *n* 102 *Gemeindearbeiter/in*
comparable to *adj* 40 *vergleichbar*
compete *v* 33 *konkurrieren, sich messen*
competitive spirit *n* 32 *Wettkampfgeist*
competitively *adv* 32 *aus Wettbewerbsgründen*
competitor *n* 32 *Wettbewerber/in*
complaint *n* 39 *Klage*
complexion *n* 124 *Gesichtsfarbe, Teint*
comply (with) *v* 125 *nachkommen*
compound *v* 124 *verbinden*
comprehend *v* 93 *verstehen*
compulsive *adj* 32 *zwanghaft*
concern *n* 29 *Sorge, Besorgnis; v* 23 *Wert legen (auf)*
concerned *adj* 39 *besorgt;*
~ about *adj* 82 *besorgt um/wegen;*
be ~ about *v* 58 *besorgt sein über, interessiert sein an*
concession *n* 52 *Zugeständnis, Konzession*
conclude *v* 96 *zu dem Schluss kommen*
conclusive *adj* 127 *überzeugend*
concoction *n* 29 *Mischung, Gebräu*
conduct *v* 116 *durchführen*
confer upon sb *v* 154 *jdm verleihen*
confident *adj* 52 *sicher*
conflict *v* 61 *sich widersprechen*
connect with *v* 42 *ansprechen*
conquer *v* 86 *erobern*
conquest *n* 151 *Eroberung*
conscious *adj* 38 *bewusst*
conservation *n* 19 *Schutz, Erhaltung*
consider *v* 22 *betrachten*
considerably *adv* 54 *beträchtlich*
considering *participle* 62 *bedenkt man*
consist of sth *v* 42 *bestehen aus etw*
consume *v* 30 *verzehren, konsumieren*
contagious *adj* 156 *ansteckend*
contain *v* 60 *zurückhalten, unterdrücken; v* 111, 127 *enthalten*
continually *adv* 9 *ständig*
contrast, in ~ to *phr* 32 *im Gegensatz zu*
contribute *v* 49 *beitragen, beisteuern*
contrived *adj* 64 *gestellt, gekünstelt*
converge (on) *v* 61 *sich zusammendrängen (um)*
converse *v* 92 *sich unterhalten*
convertible *n* 53 *Kabrio(lett)*
convict *n* 78 *Strafgefangene/r; v* 71 *verurteilen*
conviction *n* 71 *Verurteilung*
convince *v* 22 *überzeugen*
cookery *n* 19 *Kochen*
cooler (AE) *n* 43 *Kühlbox*
cope with sb/sth *v* 33 *fertig werden mit*
cops *n* 75 *Polizisten, Bullen*
copycat *n, infl* 29 *nachgeahmtes Produkt*
corporate ladder *n* 52 *Unternehmensleiter*
corporate philosophy *n* 54 *Unternehmensphilosophie*
corresponding *adj* 33 *entsprechend, passend*
cottage *n* 19 *Ferienhaus*
counter *v* 29 *bekämpfen; v* 124 *entgegnen*
counterpart *n* 58 *Gegenstück*
countryside *n* 81 *Landschaft*
court *n* 73 *Gericht*
cover *v* 29 *zurücklegen; v* 148 *(ab)decken*
coward *n* 76 *Feigling*
crack *n* 103 *Spalt(e)*
crackling *adj* 148 *knackend, knisternd*

crave *v* 52 *sich sehnen nach*
crawl away *v* 55 *langsam wegziehen*
creep into *v* 119 *sich einschleichen*
cricket bat *n* 127 *Kricketschläger*
crop *n* 153 *Ernte*
crossly *adv* 107 *ärgerlich*
crossness *n* 107 *Verärgerung*
crummy (AE) *adj* 75 *lausig*
crushing *adj* 49 *niederdrückend*
cuddly *adj* 154 *kuschelig*
culprit *n* 84 *Schuldige/r, Übeltäter/in*
curb (on) *n* 111 *Eindämmung, Begrenzung (einer Sache)*
cure *n* 154 *Heilmittel, -verfahren;* *v* 156 *heilen*
curious *adj* 97 *neugierig*
current *adj* 91 *derzeitig;*
~ **affairs** *n* 69 *Tagesereignisse, -politik, Zeitgeschehen*
currently *adv* 73 *momentan, gegenwärtig*
curse *v* 82 *verfluchen*
curtain *n* 159 *Gardine, Vorhang*
cut off *v* 75 *unterbrechen*
cycling *n* 28 *Radfahren*

D

dairy *adj* 134 *Milch-*
damage *v* 23 *beschädigen*
damn, not matter a ~ *phr* 14 *gar nichts ausmachen*
damp *adj* 75 *feucht, klamm*
dampen *v* 29 *dämpfen*
dare *v* 124 *auffordern;* *v* 145 *sich trauen*
dawn *n* 29 *(Morgen-)Dämmerung, Sonnenaufgang*
dazzle *v* 140 *blenden*
deaf and dumb *adj* 116 *taubstumm*
deal with *v* 34 *sich befassen mit*
dearth *n* 155 *Mangel (an)*
debt *n* 104 *Schuld(en);* *n* 140 *Schulden*
~ **relief** *n* 102 *Schuldenerlass*
debtor *n* 140 *Schuldner/in*
decade *n* 52 *Jahrzehnt*
decent *adj* 14 *anständig*
decisive *adj* 119 *entscheidend*
decline *n* 56 *Niedergang;* *v* 70 *sinken, zurückgehen*
decrease *v* 32 *zurückgehen, sich verringern*
dedicated *adj* 45 *engagiert*
dedication *n* 119 *Hingabe, Engagement*
deed *n* 147 *Tat*
defuse *v* 145 *entschärfen*
defy imagination *phr* 145 *die Vorstellungskraft übersteigen*
degree *n* 14 *(akademischer) Grad*
deliberately *adv* 60 *absichtlich*
delight *n* 19 *Entzücken*
delivery service *n* 159 *Lieferservice*
demand *n* 52 *Nachfrage;* *v* 28 *erfordern*
dental insurance *n* 134 *zahnärztliche Versicherung*
depend on *v* 14 *sich verlassen auf*
depleted *adj* 135 *aufgebraucht, leer gefischt*
deposit *v* 32 *(sich) ablagern*
derive *v* 61 *stammen;*
~ **from** *v* 159 *ableiten von*
desirability *n* 98 *Notwendigkeit*
desirable *adj* 114 *wünschenswert*
desire *n* 38 *Wunsch, Sehnsucht*
desolate *adj* 125 *trostlos, verzweifelt*
despair *n* 145 *Verzweiflung*
desperation *n* 105 *Verzweiflung*
despite *prep* 52 *trotz*
destitution *n* 110 *Armut*
deteriorate *v* 111 *(sich) verschlechtern*
detrimental *adj* 95 *nachteilig, schädlich*
devastated *adj* 135 *zerstört*
develop a sharp tongue *v* 128 *ein freches Mundwerk bekommen*
Developing World *n* 23 *Entwicklungsländer*
development *n* 114 *Entwicklung*
device *n* 87 *Gerät, Apparat*
devise *v* 45 *ausarbeiten, entwerfen*
devote *v* 119 *widmen*
devoted *adj* 52 *hingebungsvoll*
diaper (AE) *n* 52 *Windel*
differentiate *v* 134 *unterscheiden*
din *n, infl* 29 *Lärm*
directive *n* 114 *Richtlinie, Anordnung*
disability *n* 126 *Behinderung*
disadvantage *n* 52 *Nachteil*
disagree 11 *widersprechen, nicht zustimmen*
disappointment *n* 13 *Enttäuschung*
disapprove (of) *v* 126 *ablehnen, missbilligen*
discard *v* 154 *ausrangieren*
discomfort *n* 32 *Unbequemlichkeit, Schmerz*
disease *n* 102 *Krankheit, Erkrankung*
disgusted *adj* 118 *angewidert*
dishes, do the ~ *phr* 124 *das Geschirr spülen*
dislike *v* 40 *nicht mögen*
dismiss *v* 49 *aufgeben*
display *v* 53 *aufweisen*
dispose of sth *v* 82 *etw entsorgen*
dissatisfied *adj* 147 *unzufrieden*

dissuade *v* 77 *abbringen*
distinct *adj* 125 *deutlich, klar erkennbar*
disturb *v* 81 *stören, beeinträchtigen;*
disturbing *adj* 137 *beunruhigend, alarmierend*
division *n* 23 *Unterscheidung, Unterteilung*
dole (GB) *n, infl* 14 *Arbeitslosengeld;*
~ **out sth** *v* 103 *etw verteilen*
donor *n* 155 *Spender/in*
doorbell *n* 76 *(Tür-)Klingel*
dormant *adj* 95 *schlummernd, ruhend*
downside *n* 81 *Nachteil*
downtown (AE) *adv* 29 *Innenstadt*
downward *adj* 84 *abwärts*
dozen *n* 52 *Dutzend*
draft *n* 92 *Entwurf; v* 117 *entwerfen, abfassen*
drag (on) *n* 103 *Belastung (für)*
drag sb out *v, infl* 32 *jdn herauslocken*
drain *n* 102 *Abfluss(rohr), Kanalisation(srohr)*
draw *v* 92 *anziehen;*
~ **to** *v* 46 *erreichen*
drawback *n* 90 *Nachteil*
drawer *n* 159 *Schub(lade)*
dreadful *adj* 102 *schrecklich, furchtbar*
drip *v* 103 *tropfen*
drive *n* 32 *Antrieb*
drop *v* 48 *fallen lassen;*
~ **out of sth** *v* 15 *(die Schule) abbrechen*
dropout *n* 79 *Aussteiger/in*
drought *n* 85 *Dürre(periode)*
drunk *adj* 62 *betrunken*
dry-clean *v* 159 *chemisch reinigen*
due *adj* 159 *fällig;*
be ~ to sth *phr* 111 *auf etw zurückzuführen sein*
dull *adj* 75 *trüb, langweilig*
dump *n* 124 *Bruchbude; v* 102 *abstellen, zurücklassen*
dutiful *adj* 139 *pflichtbewusst, gehorsam*

E

eager *adj* 116 *eifrig, bestrebt*
earn *v* 47 *verdienen;*
earning potential *n* 122 *Verdienstmöglichkeit(en)*
earth-shaking *adj* 29 *ohrenbetäubend*
ease *v* 134 *lindern, erleichtern*
East Enders 124 *brit. TV-Serie, spielt im Londoner East End*
eccentricity *n* 127 *Überspanntheit*
eclipse *v* 29 *übertreffen*
ecological *adj* 23 *ökologisch*
edge *n* 139 *Rand*
editor *n* 49 *Herausgeber/in*
educate *v* 103 *erziehen, ausbilden;*
educated *adj* 29 *gebildet*
eerily *adv* 154 *unheimlich*
effectively *adv* 54 *hier: erfolgreich*
effort *n* 32 *Anstrengung*
eight-foot-square *adj* 102 *acht Fuß im Quadrat (ca. 6 Quadratmeter)*
eightfold *adv* 52 *achtfach*
electorate *n* 72 *Wählerschaft, die Wähler*
elementary school (AE) *n* 92 *Grundschule*
elicit *v* 127 *entlocken*
eliminate *v* 33 *beseitigen, abschaffen*
elsewhere *adv* 111 *anderswo*
embarrassing *adj* 64 *peinlich*
embedded *adj* 159 *eingebettet*
embrace *v* 52 *(bereitwillig) übernehmen*
emerge *v* 61 *(auf)treten, entstehen; v* 116 *entstehen*
emission *v* 38 *Abgas*
emit *v* 83 *ausstoßen*
empathize (with) *v* 64 *mitfühlen (mit), sich hineinversetzen (in)*
emphasis *n* 49 *Betonung, Wert*
emphasize *v* 23 *betonen, hervorheben*
employ *v* 42 *anwenden*
employee *n* 25 *Angestellte/r*
empowerment *n* 116 *Management, Führungskräfte*
emulate *v* 117 *nachahmen*
enable *v* 147 *(es) ermöglichen, in die Lage versetzen*
encounter *n* 49 *Begegnung; begegnen*
encourage *v* 69 *motivieren, verleiten*
end up *v* 78 *landen;*
~ **(as sth)** *v* 13 *enden (als etw)*
endanger *v* 50 *gefährden*
endemic *adj* 103 *endemisch*
ending *n* 15 *Ende (der Geschichte)*
endure *v* 124 *aushalten, erdulden*
enduring *adj* 52 *fest, andauernd*
enforce *v* 73 *durchsetzen*
enforceable *adj* 155 *durchsetzbar*
engaged *adj* 145 *engagiert*
engaging *adj* 39 *fesselnd*
engine *n* 116 *Motor*
enhance *v* 85 *erhöhen, steigern;*
enhancer *n* 9 *Verstärker*
enlightened *adj* 111 *aufgeklärt*
ensure *v* 66 *sicherstellen, gewährleisten*
entertaining *adj* 41 *unterhaltsam*
enthusiastic *adj* 28 *begeistert*
entire *adj* 46 *ganz, vollständig*
entitle *v* 35 *berechtigen;*
be entitled to *v* 50 *berechtigt sein zu, Anspruch haben auf*
entrepreneur *n* 138 *Unternehmer/in*
environment *n* 22 *Umwelt*

environmental protection *n* 114 *Umweltschutz*
epitomize *v* 139 *verkörpern*
equal *adj* 51 *gleich*
equality *n* 105 *Gleichberechtigung*
equation *n* 83 *Gleichung*
equipment *n* 36 *Geräte (im Fitness-Studio)*
equivalent, be ~ to *v* 140 *entsprechen*
eradicate *v* 153 *ausrotten*
erase *v* 32 *auslöschen*
erect sth *v* 81 *etw (er)bauen, errichten*
erode *v* 117 *austrocknen, abtragen*
especially *adv* 56 *besonders, insbesondere*
establish *v* 110 *herstellen, begründen*
estimate *v* 72 *(ein)schätzen*
eternal *adj* 38 *ewig*
evaporate *v* 95 *verdunsten*
evil *adj* 22 *schlecht, böse; n* 144 *(das) Böse*
evolve *v* 52 *sich entwickeln*
ewe *n* 154 *(Mutter-)Schaf*
exaggerate *v* 23 *übertreiben;*
  exaggerated *adj* 38 *übertrieben*
exam preparation *n* 12 *Vorbereitung auf eine Prüfung*
exceed *v* 103 *übersteigen, -schreiten*
excel *v* 128 *übertreffen, hervorragen*
exchange, in ~ *n* 124 *zum Ausgleich*
exchequer *n* 116 *Finanzministerium*
excitement *n* 109 *Aufregung*
exclude *v* 23 *ausschließen*
executive *n* 64 *Manager/in*
exertion *n* 32 *körperliche Anstrengung*
exhausted *adj* 30 *erschöpft*
exhibition *n* 99 *Ausstellung*
expectancy *n* 112 *Erwartung*
expenditure *n* 39 *Ausgabe(n)*
expense, at the ~ of *phr* 32 *auf Kosten von*
experienced *adj* 61 *erfahren*
explanation *n* 10 *Erklärung*
exploraholic *n* 22 *Entdeckungssüchtige/r*
explore *v* 20 *erforschen, erkunden*
express *v* 8 *ausdrücken, äußern*
  expressly *adv* 40 *ausdrücklich*
extension *n* 154 *Verlängerung*
extensive *adj* 25 *umfassend, umfangreich*
extinct *adj* 153 *ausgestorben*
extra-curricular *adj* 48 *außerlehrplanmäßig*
eye *v* 52 *beobachten*
  ~ sb/sth warily *phr* 52 *jdn misstrauisch beobachten*

F

face sth *v* 81 *sich etw gegenübersehen, entgegensehen*
  faced with *v* 42 *angesichts*
  be faced with sth *phr* 100 *mit etw konfrontiert sein*
facility *n* 44, 134 *Einrichtung, Betrieb*
factual *adj* 62 *sachlich*
fail *v* 15 *keinen Erfolg haben, scheitern*
failure *n* 128 *Misserfolg, Fehlschlag, Versagen*
fair game *phr* 61 *Freiwild*
faith *n* 145 *Glaube;*
  have ~ *v* 12 *Vertrauen haben*
fake *n* 116 *Attrappe*
familiar *adj* 61 *vertraut, bekannt*
family values *n* 12 *Familienwerte*
fanciful *adj* 154 *unrealistisch, fantastisch*
fancy *v* 9 *gefallen, mögen*
far side *n* 61 *Beifahrerseite*
faraway *adj* 20 *weit entfernt*
farther *adj* 107 *weiter*
fashionable *adj* 60 *modern, schick*
fastest-growing *adj* 22 *am schnellsten wachsend*
fast-forward *adj* 29 *überdreht*
fatherhood *n* 52 *Vaterschaft*
fathering *v* 52 *bevatern, Vater sein für*
fatigue *n* 29 *Müdigkeit*
fault *n* 76 *Schuld; n* 154 *Fehler, Defekt*
favour *v* 43 *bevorzugen;*
  be in ~ of *phr* 30 *befürworten*
fearsome *adj* 144 *Furcht einflößend*
feasible *adj* 96 *machbar, möglich*
feat *n* 154 *Leistung*
feel sorry for sb *phr* 92 *jd leidtun*
fellow-citizen *n* 141 *Mitbürger/in*
fertilizer *n* 153 *Dünger*
fetch *v* 110 *holen*
fieldwork assistant *n* 22 *Feldforschungshelfer/in*
fifth, one ~ *n* 25 *ein Fünftel*
fight tooth and nail *phr* 124 *mit allen Mitteln kämpfen*
fine-tune *v* 43 *genau abstimmen*
fireplace *n* 159 *Kamin*
firmly *adv* 136 *fest*
fishery *n* 135 *Fischerei*
fizzy *adj* 29 *sprudelnd, spritzig*
flash *v* 109 *signalisieren*
flatten *v* 75 *platt machen*
flaw *n* 124 *Mangel, Fehler*
flood *n* 159 *überschwemmen*
flourish *v* 146 *gedeihen, blühen;*
  flourishing *adj* 114 *blühend*
flow chart *n* 28 *Flussdiagramm*
fluency *n* 116 *fließende Sprachkenntnisse*
fluorine *n* 95 *Fluor*
focus on sth *v* 23 *sich auf etw konzentrieren*
fool around *v* 75 *herumalbern*

foot, ft; feet *n* 60 *Fuß*
footage *n* 64 *Filmmaterial*
force *v* 33 *zwingen*
forecast *n* 39 *Vorhersage, Prognose;* *v* 22 *vorhersagen*
foresee *v* 154 *vorhersehen, voraussehen*
forge ahead *v* 155 *schnell vorangehen*
forged *adj* 72 *gefälscht*
forgive sb *v* 149 *jdm verzeihen*
formidable *adj* 92 *gewaltig*
fortify sth *v* 144 *etw verstärken*
fortune, pay a ~ *v* 47 *ein Vermögen ausgeben*
fraction *n* 139 *Bruchteil*
frantic *adj* 49 *wild, verzweifelt*
freelance *adj* 60 *freiberuflich, freischaffend*
frequent *adj* 49 *häufig;*
frequently *adv* 44 *oft, häufig*
fresco *n* 49 *Wandgemälde, Fresko*
fries *n* 48 *Pommes (frites)*
frightened by *adj* 30 *erschreckt durch*
fringe benefit *n* 49 *freiwillige Sozialleistung*
front line *n* 116 *Front*
frown *v* 92 *die Stirn runzeln*
fuel *v* 39 *anregen, anheizen*
fume *v* 60 *wütend sein, (vor Wut) kochen*
funpark *n* 52 *Vergnügungspark*
furious *adj* 85 *wütend, böse*
fuss *n* 30 *Getue, Aufhebens*

G

gaggle *n* 61 *Schar, Horde*
gain *v* 40 *gewinnen*
gamut *n* 155 *(die ganze) Bandbreite*
gap year *n* 26 *Pausenjahr*
gapped *adj* 44 *mit Lücken*
gasps, in ~ *phr* 107 *stoßweise*
gaze up *v* 109 *aufblicken*
genius *n* 12 *Genie*
gentle *adj* 49 *sanft, leicht*
gesture *n* 91 *Geste*
get *v, infl* 148 *verstehen, begreifen;*
~ away with it *phr* 76 *ungestraft davonkommen;*
~ in *v* 139 *einsteigen;*
~ it *v* 148 *etw verstehen*
giant *n* 49 *Riese*
gig *n* 16 *Auftritt*
giggle *n* 117 *Kichern*
gist *n* 86 *Kern, Wesentliche(s)*
give in *v* 147 *nachgeben*
gladly *adv* 81 *gern, bereitwillig*
glance *n* 128 *Blick*
glaring *adj* 109 *gleißend*
glide *v* 29 *gleiten*
globe *n* 40 *Erdball, Globus*
glory *n* 64 *Ruhm, Glanz*
glove *n* 72 *Handschuh*
glow *n* 32 *Glühen*
glued, be ~ to sth *v* 67 *an etw kleben, gebannt auf etw starren*
go, try and make a ~ of it *v, infl* 14 *es mal versuchen;*
~ down well with sb *phr* 120 *gut bei jdm ankommen, jdm gefallen*
goal *n* 32 *Ziel*
grab *v* 48, 75 *packen, (er)greifen*
gradually *adv* 33 *allmählich, nach und nach*
graduate *n* 53 *(Hochschul-)Absolvent/in, Schulabgänger/in*
grand *adj* 107 *großartig*
granny *n* 159 *Oma*
grant *v* 112 *gewähren, einräumen;*
take for granted *phr* 9 *als selbstverständlich ansehen*
gratify *v* 119 *erfreuen*
grave *adj* 128 *ernst, traurig*
gravestone *n* 71 *Grabstein*
greasy *adj* 161 *fettig*
greedy *adj* 104 *(hab)gierig*
grid *n* 129 *Tabelle*
grin *v* 91 *lächeln, grinsen*
grinding *adj* 139 *zermürbend*
grip, get a ~ on sth *phr* 141 *etw in den Griff bekommen*
groceries *n* 160 *Lebensmittel*
Gross Domestic Product *n* 141 *Bruttoinlandsprodukt (BIP)*
growth *n* 102 *Wachstum*
gruel *n* 103 *Haferschleim, Grütze*
grunt *v* 60 *grunzen, ächzen*
guarantee *v* 19 *garantieren*
guess *n* 106 *Schätzung, Vermutung, Annahme;* *v* 25 *(er)raten*
guide *n* 52 *Führer, Vorbild*
guilt *n* 52 *Schuld*
guilty *adj* 32 *schuldig*
gym *n* 36 *Fitness-Studio*

H

habit *n* 16 *Gewohnheit, Angewohnheit*
habitable *adj* 95 *bewohnbar*
habitat *n* 81 *Lebensraum*
habitually *adv* 159 *wie gewohnt*
hail *v* 154 *feiern, begrüßen*
hammer out *v* 116 *entwerfen*
hamper *v* 40 *(be)hindern, hemmen*
hand down *v* 55 *weitergeben, vererben*
handle *v* 69 *umgehen mit, fertig werden mit*
handsomely *adv* 135 *ansehnlich*

I

ingredient *n* 29 *Bestandteil, Zutat*
inhabitant *n* 101 *Bewohner/in*
inherit *v* 156 *erben;*
inherited *adj* 154 *vererbt, Erb-*
inhibit *v* 146 *hemmen, hindern*
inhibition *n* 14 *Hemmung*
initiate *v* 52 *starten, in die Wege leiten*
inject *v* 95, 155 *spritzen*
injured *adj* 34 *verletzt*
injustice *n* 127 *Ungerechtigkeit*
innermost *adj* 125 *innnerst*
innocent *adj* 144 *unschuldig;*
innocently *adv* 32 *unschuldig*
innovative *adj* 44 *innovativ*
insignificant *adj* 39 *unbedeutend*
insist on *v* 117 *bestehen auf*
instant *adj* 53 *sofortig;*
instantaneous *adj* 95 *unmittelbar*
instruct *v* 139 *ein-, anweisen*
insulting *adj* 114 *beleidigend*
insured *adj* 57 *versichert*
intend *v* 26 *beabsichtigen, vorhaben;*
intended *adj* 44 *gewollt*
intense *adj* 33 *intensiv, angespannt*
intent *n* 40 *Anliegen*
intention *n* 81 *Absicht*
interact *v* 91 *kommunizieren*
interrupt *v* 46 *unterbrechen*
intoxicated *adj* 32 *berauscht*
invent *v* 23 *erfinden*
invention *n* 106 *Erfindung*
investigate *v* 106 *untersuchen*
invigorated *adj* 19 *gestärkt, angeregt*
involve *v* 52 *engagieren*
involvement *n* 52 *Beteiligung*
ironically *adv* 42 *paradoxerweise*
irreparable *adj* 155 *irreparabel*
irrespective of *prep* 139 *ohne Rücksicht auf*
irresponsible *adj* 22 *unverantwortlich*
irreversible *adj* 151 *unwiderruflich, unumkehrbar*
irritable *adj* 32 *reizbar, gereizt*
issue *n* 23 *Frage, Problem, Thema, Anliegen;* *n* 95 *Ausgabe*

J

jabber on *v* 117 *plappern*
jack up *v* 136 *in die Höhe treiben*
jealous *adj* 91 *eifersüchtig*
jerk (AE) *n, infl* 76 *Trottel*
job profile *n* 48 *Stellenbeschreibung*
joint *n* 108 *Gelenk*
jolt *n, infl* 29 *Schuss*
joyfully *adv* 92 *freudig*
jumble *v* 161 *durcheinander werfen, kunterbunt vermischen*
justified *adj* 40 *berechtigt*
juvenile *adj* 70 *jugendlich;*
~ **delinquency** *n* 79 *Jugendstraffälligkeit*

K

keen *adj* 28 *(sehr) interessiert*
keep, it's hard to ~ a good man down *phr* 55 *der Tüchtige lässt sich nicht unterkriegen*
kettle *n* 13 *Wasserkocher*
kick *n, infl* 33 *anspornen, kicken;*
~ **back** *v* 49 *sich zurückziehen;*
~ **in** *v, infl* 159 *einsetzen, angeben*
kinda *abbr, infl* 75 *irgendwie*
knock *v* 75 *klopfen, schlagen*

L

labor (AE), labour (BE) *n* 92 *Arbeitskräfte;*
~ **force** *n* 49 *arbeitende Bevölkerung;*
~ **pool (AE)** *n* 140 *Arbeitskraftreservoir*
~ **relations** *n* 52 *Beziehungen zwischen Arbeitgebern und Arbeitnehmern*
lack *v* 105 *mangeln an, fehlen;*
~ **of** *n* 40 *Mangel an, Fehlen von*
lad *n* 125 *Junge, Bursche*
ladle *n* 103 *(Schöpf-)Kelle*
lash out (at/against sb/sth) *v* 60 *um sich schlagen, (jdn/etw) angreifen*
lasting *adj* 110 *dauerhaft*
laugh, have a ~ *phr* 9 *lachen, sich amüsieren*
laundry basket *n* 159 *Wäschekorb*
law *n* 114 *Gesetz*
lay, be laid off *v* 54 *entlassen werden*
layer *n* 86 *Schicht*
leading *adj* 94 *führend*
leakage *n* 160 *Leck*
learning type *n* 12 *Lerntyp*
lecture *v* 58 *Vorträge halten*
legacy *n* 52 *Erbe*
legion *n* 29 *Legion*
leisure *n* 49 *Freizeit*
lend (sth to sb) *v* 11 *(jdm etw) ausleihen;*
lend themselves to *v* 154 *sich anbieten für*
length *n* 36 *(eine) Länge, Bahn (im Schwimmbad)*
lengthen *v* 49 *verlängern*
lewd *adj* 127 *anzüglich*
license (AE) *n* 135 *Lizenz*
life-expectancy *n* 103 *Lebenserwartung*
lifeguard *n* 49 *Rettungsschwimmer/in*
lifespan *n* 95 *Lebenszeit, -dauer*
lift *v* 111 *heben;*
~ **sb's mood** *phr* 10 *jds Stimmung heben*
light up *v* 159 *aufleuchten*
likes, the ~ of *phr* 29 *Konkurrenten wie*
limitation *n* 32 *Grenze*
line *n* 139 *(Telefon-)Leitung,*

literally *adv* 135 *buchstäblich*
living, make a ~ *v* 48 *seinen Lebensunterhalt verdienen*
load *n* 107 *Ladung*
loan *n* 104 *Kredit, Darlehen*
local *adj* 22 *örtlich*
lock horns *phr* 81 *mit jdm in Streit geraten*
lock sb up *v* 73 *jdn weg-, einsperren*
logger *n* 88 *Holzfäller*
logging *n* 111 *Abholzung*
lonely *adj* 19 *einsam*
long-term *adj* 9 *langfristig, Langzeit-*
looks *n* 12 *Aussehen*
lose out (on sth) *v* 117 *den Kürzeren ziehen, schlecht wegkommen (bei etw)*
low *adj* 76 *leise*
low-wage *adj* 142 *Niedriglohn-;*
~ countries *n* 49 *Niedriglohnländer*
lung *n* 92 *Lunge*
lunge (at) *v* 60 *sich stürzen (auf);*
lunge forward *v* 76 *vorschnellen*
lure *v* 118 *(an)locken*

M

mains *n* 87 *(Strom-)Netz*
maintain *v* 155 *behaupten*
maize *n* 103 *Mais*
major *adj* 32 *bedeutend, größer*
make the world go round *phr* 9 *die Welt regieren*
make up *v* 18 *bilden;*
~ for *v* 92 *ausgleichen*
makeshift shelter *n* 101 *Notunterkunft*
mall (AE) *n* 71 *Einkaufszentrum, (Einkaufs-)Passage*
malnourished *adj* 103 *unterernährt*
man *v* 139 *besetzen*
mandate *v* 52 *anordnen*
mandatory *adj* 49 *obligatorisch*
manifestation *n* 29 *Ausdruck, Erscheinung*
mankind *n* 29 *Menschheit*
manner *n* 155 *Art und Weise*
manpower *n* 94 *Arbeitskräfte, Personal*
manslaughter *n* 76 *Totschlag, fahrlässige Tötung*
mark *n* 127 *Fleck;*
make its ~ *v* 140 *sich profilieren*
marketer *n* 39 *Vermarkter*
masses, the ~ *n* 22 *die große Masse (der Bevölkerung)*
match *v* 32 *erreichen; v* 113 *zuordnen*
matter *v* 9 *von Bedeutung sein*
mattress *n* 160 *Matratze*
mean *v* 48 *bedeuten*
means *n* 144 *Mittel, Möglichkeit*
meantime, in the ~ *phr* 145 *in der Zwischenzeit*
measure *n* 53 *Maßnahme; v* 39 *messen*
melt *v* 87 *schmelzen*
mention *v* 30 *erwähnen;*
not to ~ *phr* 29 *ganz zu schweigen (von)*
mere *adj* 107 *bloß;*
merely *adv* 64 *bloß, lediglich*
mess *n* 48 *Chaos, Durcheinander*
message *n* 13 *Nachricht*
middle school *n* 116 *Mittelschule*
midwife *n* 111 *Hebamme*
migratory route *n* 81 *Vogelzugroute*
mind *v* 107 *aufpassen;*
get their minds off sth *phr* 45 *sich von etw lösen;*
have in ~ *phr* 96 *denken an*
minder *n* 60 *Leibwächter/in*
mindset *n* 52 *Denkart, Mentalität*
minimum wage *n* 135 *Mindestlohn*
minor *adj* 40 *gering, unbedeutend*
miraculous *adj* 155 *erstaunlich*
misconception *n* 145 *falsche Annahme*
misfortune *n* 64 *Unglück*
miss out on sth *v* 118 *etw verpassen, sich etw entgehen lassen*
mobility *n* 38 *Beweglichkeit, Mobilität*
mock *adj* 71 *simuliert, nachgemacht*
mode *n* 85 *Form, Art*
modest *adj* 39 *mäßig, gering; adj* 58 *bescheiden*
mood *n* 9 *Stimmung, Laune;*
put sb in a good ~ *phr* 11 *jdn in gute Laune versetzen;*
~-altering *adj* 29 *stimmungsaufhellend*
mop *n* 48 *Wischmopp*
mortal *adj* 32 *Sterbliche/r*
most, make the ~ of 19 *das Beste aus etwas machen*
mother-in-law *n* 140 *Schwiegermutter*
motorbike *n* 21 *Motorrad*
mule *n* 107 *Maultier, -esel*
muscle into *v* 49 *drängen zu*
muscle tone *n* 32 *Muskeltonus*
mushroom *v* 85 *sprunghaft ansteigen*

N

nailed, get ~ *v* 76 *kriegen, geschnappt werden*
nap *n* 91 *Schläfchen, Nickerchen*
narrator *n* 77 *Erzähler/in*
narrow *adj* 76 *eng, schmal*
national pride *n* 140 *Nationalstolz*
native speaker *n* 114 *Muttersprachler/in*
neat *adj* 58 *ordentlich*
necessary *adj* 33 *nötig, notwendig*

necessity *n* 110 *Notwendigkeit*
negotiate *v* 52 *verhandeln, aushandeln*
negotiator *n* 152 *Verhandlungsführer/in*
night out on the town *phr* 9 *Stadtbummel bei Nacht*
node *n* 159 *Knotenpunkt*
note *v* 95 *anmerken;*
take notes *v* 12 *(sich) Notizen machen, protokollieren*
notify *v* 71 *benachrichtigen*
notion *n* 154 *Vorstellung, Idee*
nourished *adj* 103 *ernährt*
nurture *v* 49 *ernähren*
nuts *adj* 75 *verrückt*

O

object to *v* 82 *ablehnen*
obligatory *adj* 33 *obligatorisch*
observe *v* 39 *beobachten*
obsessed *adj* 91 *besessen*
obvious *adj* 41 *offensichtlich;*
obviously *adv* 43 *offensichtlich*
occasional *adj* 10 *gelegentlich, ab und zu*
occur to sb *v* 124 *jdm einfallen*
odds, be at odds *phr* 60 *nicht übereinstimmen*
offender *n* 72 *Straftäter/in*
offer *v* 22 *(an)bieten*
olive grove *n* 85 *Olivenhain*
on-site *adv* 19 *vor Ort*
open, out in the ~ *adv* 20 *im Freien*
operate *v* 82 *antreiben; v* 145 *operieren, tätig sein*
opinion, voice your ~ *v* 63 *seine Meinung äußern*
opportunity *n* 22 *Gelegenheit, Chance*
oppose *v* 72 *sich widersetzen, opponieren*
opposite *adj* 24 *gegenüberliegend*
oppressive *adj* 145 *repressiv*
ordinary *adj* 33 *gewöhnlich, normal*
organism *n* 30 *Organismus*
originate from *v* 43 *stammen aus*
ounce *n* 29 *Unze*
outcome *n* 135 *Resultat, Ergebnis*
outdated *adj* 45 *überholt, veraltet*
outgrow *v* 127 *herauswachsen (aus)*
outnumber *v* 72 *übertreffen*
outstanding *adj* 54 *hervorragend*
outstrip *v* 136 *übertreffen*
outweigh *v* 52 *überwiegen, wettmachen*
overall *adj* 70 *total, Gesamt-*
overcome *v* 32 *überwinden*
overexert *v* 33 *überanstrengen*
overlook *v* 108 *überblicken*
overly *adv* 155 *allzu*
overshadow *v* 60 *überschatten*
overtime *n* 52 *Überstunden*
owe *v* 102 *schulden*
oxygen *n* 32 *Sauerstoff*

P

pace *n* 49 *Tempo;*
~ around *v* 76 *herumlaufen*
pack mule *n* 107 *Packesel*
package holiday *n* 22 *Pauschalreise*
pact, make a ~ *phr* 32 *einen Pakt abschließen*
painful *adj* 64 *schmerzhaft*
palm *n* 159 *Handfläche*
parachuting *n* 28 *Fallschirmspringen*
paramount *adj* 155 *vordringlich*
parole *n* 70 *bedingter Straferlass, Bewährung*
part from sb/sth *v* 127 *sich von jdm/etw trennen*
participant *n* 65 *Teilnehmer/in*
participate *v* 19 *teilnehmen, sich beteiligen*
particular *adj* 12 *bestimmt, speziell;*
particularly *adv* 39 *insbesondere*
party set *n* 61 *Schickeria*
pass *v* 13 *(Examen) bestehen;*
~ sth on to sb *v* 156 *etw an jdn weiterleiten*
patch *n* 133 *Fleck, Stück*
paternity leave *n* 52 *Vaterschaftsurlaub*
patiently *adv* 103 *geduldig*
pattern *n* 55 *Muster*
pavement *n* 60 *Bürgersteig*
pawpaw (AE) *n* 107 *Papaya*
pay *n* 51 *Lohn, Gehalt, Bezahlung*
payment *n* 102 *Bezahlung*
peak *v* 14 *gipfeln, den Höhepunkt erreichen*
peasant *n* 111 *Bauer/Bäuerin*
peel *v* 108 *schälen*
peer pressure *n* 79 *Gruppenzwang, -dynamik*
peg *n* 160 *(Wäsche-)Klammer*
per capita income *n* 140 *Pro-Kopf-Einkommen*
performance bonus *n* 53 *Leistungsprämie*
permission *n* 73 *Erlaubnis, Genehmigung*
permit *v* 40 *erlauben, zulassen*
personal protection officer *n* 60 *persönliche/r Leibwächter/in*
personal success *n* 12 *persönlicher Erfolg*
perspective *n* 81 *objektive Betrachtung*
pervasiveness *n* 29 *Vorherrschen*
petrol *n* 84 *Benzin*
petty theft *n* 72 *kleinere Diebstähle*
photovoltaic *adj* 88 *photoelektrisch*
physical *adj* 29 *körperlich;*
~ appearance *n* 104 *Aussehen, Äußeres, (äußere) Erscheinung*

pick *v* 45 *auswählen*
pick up *v* 117 *lernen, erwerben;*
~ **(the phone)** *v* 148 *(den Telefonhörer) abheben;*
~ **speed** *v* 76 *schneller werden;*
pick-up *n* 9 *Verbesserung, Anstieg*
pile *n* 107 *Haufen, Stapel;*
~ **up** *v* 161 *(sich) anhäufen*
pin (sb against sth) *v* 60 *(jdn gegen etw) drücken, pressen*
pint *n* 29 *Pint*
pitfall *n* 127 *Gefahr*
place, put in *v* 52 *beschließen*
plainly *adv* 63 *klar, deutlich*
plant *n* 52 *Werk, Betrieb*
playmate *n* 91 *Spielkamerad*
pleasure *n* 10, 114 *Vergnügen, Freude*
pledge *v* 102 *geloben*
plenty *adv* 14 *viel, genug, reichlich*
plop down *v, infl* 91 *sich hinplumpsen lassen*
plug into *v* 87 *anschließen an, verbinden mit*
point, miss the ~ *phr* 117 *an der Sache vorbeigehen;*
~ **sth out to sb** *v* 137 *hinweisen auf*
poised *adj* 159 *stationiert*
poisonous *adj* 57 *giftig*
policy *n* 72 *Politik*
political ends *n* 144 *politische Ziele*
poll *n* 42 *Umfrage*
pollution *n* 81 *(Umwelt-, Luft-)Verschmutzung*
porch *n* 81 *Veranda*
port *n* 133 *Hafen*
portray *v* 60 *darstellen*
pose *v* 33 *darstellen*
possession *n* 72 *Besitz*
pour out *v* 82 *ausströmen*
poverty *n* 103 *Armut;*
~ **trap** *n* 110 *Armutsfalle*
power blackout *n* 43 *Stromausfall*
power grid *n* 110 *Stromnetz, Hochspannungsnetz*
power station *n* 110 *Kraftwerk*
practical joke *n* 127 *Streich*
practice, put into ~ *v* 12 *in die Praxis umsetzen*
praise sth/sb *v* 42 *jdn/etw loben*
predict *v* 67 *vorhersagen*
pregnancy *n* 102 *Schwangerschaft*
prejudiced, be ~ against sb/sth *v* 40 *Vorurteile haben gegen jdn/etw*
premium *n* 134 *Prämie*
prepared to do sth *phr* 124 *bereit, etw zu tun*
prerequisite *n* 104 *Bedingung*
presenter *n* 120 *Moderator/in*
presently *adv* 107 *gleich darauf*
press charges (against sb) *v* 60 *(jdn) anzeigen*
pressure *n* 50, 96 *Druck*
pretend *v* 48 *so tun als ob*
pretty *adv, infl* 14 *ziemlich, recht*
prevail *v* 145 *siegen, sich durchsetzen*
prevalence *n* 112 *Verbreitung*
prevent *v* 85 *(ver)hindern;*
preventable *adj* 112 *vermeidbar*
previous *adj* 58 *vorherig, früher*
pride *n* 82 *Stolz*
print issue *n* 68 *Druckauflage*
privacy *n* 61 *Privatsphäre*
private health insurance *n* 57 *private Krankenversicherung*
privileged *adj* 23 *privilegiert*
prized *adj* 117 *angesehen, hochgeschätzt*
probation *n* 70 *Bewährung*
proclaim *v* 29 *verkünden*
production facilities *n* 53 *Produktionsanlagen*
profit margin *n* 52 *Gewinnspanne*
progress *n* 32 *Fortschritt(e)*
project *v* 113 *prognostizieren, voraussagen*
proliferate *v* 95 *sich vermehren*
prominence *n* 64 *Bekanntschaft, Berühmtheit*
promise *v* 29 *versprechen;*
promising *adj* 42 *vielversprechend*
promote *v* 44 *anpreisen, bewerben, Werbung machen für*
promotion *n* 52 *Beförderung*
prompt *v* 13 *Stichwort geben*
proper *adj* 49 *richtig, angemessen*
property (crimes) *n* 70 *Eigentum(sdelikte)*
proposal *n* 114 *Vorschlag*
propose *v* 95 *vorschlagen*
proposition system (AE) *n* 72 *Vorschlagssystem zur Gesetzesänderung oder -ergänzung*
prospect *n* 119 *Aussicht*
prosperity *n* 58 *Wohlstand*
prosperous *adj* 136 *reich, wohlhabend*
prove *v* 53 *sich erweisen als*
provide *v* 103 *zur Verfügung stellen, (an)bieten*
public appearance *n* 144 *öffentlicher Auftritt*
publish *v* 111 *veröffentlichen*
puddle *n* 77 *Pfütze*
pull up *v* 61 *vorfahren*
punishment *n* 73 *Strafe*
purchase *v* 45 *kaufen*

pure *adj* 22 *rein*
purity *n* 136 *Reinheit*
purpose *n* 72 *Zweck, Ziel*
purse snatching *n* 71 *Handtaschendiebstahl*
pursue *v* 12 *verfolgen, nachgehen*
pursuit *n* 49 *Streben*
push yourself very hard *v* 33 *sich sehr anstrengen*

Q

question *v* 64 *in Frage stellen;*
be out of the ~ *phr* 112 *außer Frage sein*
queue *v* 103 *sich anstellen*
quick fix *phr* 9 *rasche Lösung*
quote *v* 68 *zitieren*

R

rain-soaked *adj* 75 *durchnässt, regennass*
raise *v* 74 *anheben;*
~ (children/kids) *v* 135 *(Kinder) aufziehen*
range *n* 28 *Auswahl, Bandbreite;*
~ (from … to) *v* 92 *liegen (zwischen … und), sich erstrecken (von … bis)*
rank *v* 29 *einstufen, zählen zu;*
ranking *n* 122 *Reihenfolge (sortiert nach Wichtigkeit)*
rape *n* 72 *Vergewaltigung*
rating *n* 64 *(Einschalt-)Quote(n)*
razor blade *n* 72 *Rasierklinge*
reach *v* 113 *erreichen*
readily *adv* 95 *leicht, ohne weiteres*
ready yourself (for) *v* 61 *sich fertig machen, sich vorbereiten (auf)*
rear view mirror *n* 76 *Rückspiegel*
re-brand *v* 22 *umbenennen*
recall *v* 92 *sich erinnern an*
receipt *n* 24 *Quittung*
receiver *n* 13 *(Telefon-)Hörer*
reckoned, be ~ with *v* 41 *rechnen mit*
recognition *n* 159 *Wiedererkennung*
recognize *v* 49 *anerkennen*
recommend *v* 62 *empfehlen*
recover *v* 123 *sich erholen*
recovery time *n* 32 *Erholungszeit*
recreational activities *n* 54 *Freizeit-, Erholungsaktivitäten*
recruit *n* 139 *Neueinstellung von Mitarbeitern; einstellen, anwerben*
redesign *v* 154 *neu entwerfen, umstrukturieren*
reel *v* 144 *erschüttern*
re-emerge *v* 60 *wieder aussteigen;*
re-emergence *n* 155 *Wiedergeburt*
refer to *v* 44 *erwähnen, hinweisen auf*
refreshed *adj* 19 *erfrischt*
refuge, take ~ *v* 29 *sich eine Auszeit gönnen*
regard *v* 92 *ansehen, betrachten*
rehearse *v* 14 *proben, üben*
relate to *v* 91 *sich beziehen auf;*
relate sth to sb *v* 44 *jdm etw erzählen;*
relate to sb/sth *v* 137 *auf jdn/etw Bezug haben*
related *adj* 161 *verwandt, bezogen*
relationship *n* 110 *Beziehung*
release *n* 95 *Austreten (von Gasen); v* 45 *veröffentlichen; v* 89 *ausstoßen; v* 113 *herausbringen, veröffentlichen*
relief organization *n* 106 *Hilfsorganisation*
relieved *adj* 76 *erleichtert*
relocate *v* 136 *verlegen*
reluctant *adj* 110 *zurückhaltend;*
reluctantly *adv* 107 *widerwillig, -strebend*
rely on *v* 61 *sich verlassen auf*
remainder *n* 157 *Rest(bestand)*
remark *n* 127 *Bemerkung;*
remarkable *adj* 138 *bemerkenswert*
remind *v* 140 *(jdn an etw) erinnern*
remote *adj* 134 *abgelegen;*
remotely *adv* 160 *aus der Ferne;*
~ control *n* 159 *Fernbedienung*
renewable *adj* 80 *erneuerbar*
repeal *v* 49 *widerrufen, aufheben*
replete *adj* 124 *prall gefüllt*
request *v* 52 *bitten um*
require *v* 134 *erfordern, verlangen;*
be required to do *v* 123 *tun müssen*
rescue *v* 159 *retten*
research *n* 43 *Untersuchung, Analyse;*
researcher *n* 92 *Forscher/in, Wissenschaftler/in*
resent *v* 124 *sich ärgern über*
resident *n* 110 *Einwohner/in*
resist *v* 151 *Widerstand leisten (gegen), sich wehren (gegen)*
resolution *n* 155 *Lösung*
resolve *v* 154 *auflösen*
resort to *v* 44 *ergreifen, anwenden*
respect, with ~ to *phr* 54 *hinsichtlich*
respond *v* 39 *reagieren*
responsibility, take ~ *v* 12 *Verantwortung tragen*
responsible, be ~ towards *v* 23 *verantwortlich umgehen mit*
rest *n* 32 *Ruhe, Erholung;*
~ with/on *v* 9 *ruhen auf, liegen bei*
restlessness *n* 56 *Ruhelosigkeit*
restock *v* 136 *wieder auffüllen*
restore *v* 96 *wiederherstellen*

S

make ~ *v* 82 *sinnvoll sein, Sinn ergeben; Sinn machen;*
make ~ of sth *phr* 40 *den Sinn verstehen*
senseless *adj* 125 *sinnlos*
sensibly *adv* 79 *vernünftig*
sensitive *adj* 60 *sensibel*
sentence *n* 71 *Strafe;*
sentence *v* 79 *verurteilen;*
be sentenced *v* 71 *verurteilt werden*
serve *v* 135 *beliefern;*
serves you right *phr* 14 *geschieht dir recht*
service sector *n* 137 *Dienstleistungssektor*
serving spoon *n* 105 *Vorlegelöffel*
set off *v* 107 *aufbrechen, losgehen*
set up *v* 66 *aufbauen*
settle down *v* 122 *häuslich werden, eine Familie gründen*
settlement *n* 152 *Entscheidung*
severe *adj* 58 *ernst, schwer; adj* 128 *streng;*
severely *adv* 108 *streng*
sewage *n* 102 *Abwasser*
shack *n* 102 *Hütte, Baracke*
shade *n* 103 *Schatten*
shaken up *adj* 61 *verstört, geschockt*
shanty *n* 103 *Hütte, Baracke*
shape *n* 40 *Form*
share *v* 102 *(sich) teilen, gemeinsam benutzen*
sharply *adv* 76 *scharf, heftig, schnell, stark*
sheer *adj* 42 *rein, bloß*
sheet *n* 71 *Bettlaken; n* 95 *Platte*
shelter *n* 30 *Schutz*
shift *n* 52 *Wandel*
shiver *v* 76 *zittern*
shoplift *v* 71 *Ladendiebstahl begehen*
shortage *n* 94 *Mangel*
shortfall *n* 92 *Ausfall*
shortly *adv* 15 *in Kürze, bald*
short-term *adj* 9 *kurzfristig, Kurzzeit-*
shot, have a pretty good ~ *phr* 55 *eine ziemlich gute Chance haben*
shrink *v* 117 *schrumpfen, zurückgehen;*
shrinking *adj* 121 *sinkend*
shudder, I ~ *v* 125 *mir graut*
shuffle up *v* 108 *heranschlurfen*
sibling *n* 125 *Geschwister*
sigh *v* 107 *seufzen*
sight, lose ~ of *phr* 32 *aus den Augen verlieren*
sin *n* 49 *Sünde*
sit sb down *v* 123 *ein ernstes Wort mit jdm reden*
sit up *v* 91 *sich aufsetzen, sich gerade hinsetzen*
sixth-grader *n* 92 *Sechsklässler/in*
skill *n* 64 *Fertigkeit, Fähigkeit, Geschicklichkeit*
slammer *n* 60 *Drink, Cocktail*
slender *adj* 29 *schlank*
slick *adj* 75 *glatt*
slim *adj* 71 *gering, klein*
slippery *adj* 154 *rutschig*
slob *n, infl* 124 *fauler Sack*
smart (AE) *adj, infl* 53 *intelligent*
smokestack *n* 82 *Schornstein*
smoothly *adv* 159 *ruhig, glatt*
smoulder *v* 102 *schwelen*
snap *v* 60 *ausflippen, ausrasten*
snatch *n* 61 *günstige Gelegenheit, große Chance*
social worker *n* 91 *Sozialarbeiter/in*
soil *n* 88 *Erde, (Erd-)Boden*
solely *adv* 86 *(einzig und) allein*
solid *adj* 29 *ordentlich*
solve *v* 157 *lösen*
sophisticated *adj* 40 *raffiniert*
sorcerer *n* 155 *Zauberer*
sore *adj* 2 *schmerzhaft, wund*
soulmate *n* 122 *Seelenverwandte/r*
soup kitchen *n* 103 *Suppenküche*
source *n* 9 *Quelle*
span, over the ~ of a year *phr* 33 *im Laufe eines Jahres*
spare *v* 144 *verschonen;*
go ~ *phr, infl* 14 *durchdrehen, verrückt werden*
spark *n* 14 *Funke; v* 95 *auslösen;*
~ sth off *v* 154 *etw auslösen*
sparkling *adj* 19 *glitzernd, funkelnd*
sparse *adj* 111 *spärlich*
speak out against *v* 23 *sich gegen etw aussprechen*
special *adj* 32 *besonders*
speech *n* 91 *Sprache; n* 115 *Rede*
speed *v* 75 *rasen, schnell fahren*
spell check *n* 117 *Rechtschreibprüfung*
spell racing doom *v* 32 *das Ende des Laufens bedeuten*
spending power *n* 42 *Kaufkraft*
spider *n* 21 *Spinne*
spin *v* 82 *sich schnell drehen*
spire *n* 19 *Turm*
spirit *n* 53 *Geist*
splash the cash *phr* 9 *eine Menge Geld ausgeben*
spoil *v* 159 *schlecht werden*
spokesperson *n* 9 *Sprecher/in*
spot *n* 42 *Werbespot; v* 16 *(heraus)finden, bemerken;*
on the ~ *phr* 98 *auf der Stelle, vor Ort*
spread *n* 39 *Ausbreitung*

T

take office *v* 102 *das Amt übernehmen*
take over *v* 32 *sich durchsetzen, überhand nehmen*
take to doing sth *v* 144 *dazu führen, etw zu tun*
talk sb into doing sth *v* 109 *jdn überreden, etw zu tun*
tangle *n* 127 *Unordnung*
tap *v* 52 *anzapfen*
target *v* 43 *zielen auf;*
~ **market** *n* 29 *Zielgruppe;*
~ **shooting** *n* 28 *Scheibenschießen*
tariff *n* 111 *Zoll*
task *n* 91 *Aufgabe, Arbeit*
tax *n* 140 *Steuer;*
~ **revenue** *n* 138 *Steueraufkommen, -einnahmen*
tell-tale *adj* 103 *verräterisch, charakteristisch*
temper, lose one's ~ *v* 60 *die Geduld verlieren*
tempt *v* 52 *locken*
tempting *adj* 49 *verführerisch, verlockend*
tenant *n* 102 *Mieter/in*
tend to *v* 84 *dazu neigen*
tension *n* 61 *Spannung*
tentatively *adv* 71 *vorsichtig, zaghaft*
term *n* 22 *Ausdruck;*
come to terms with *phr* 40 *umgehen mit;*
in terms of *phr* 39 *in Bezug auf*
terrified *adj* 118 *erschrocken, ängstlich*
text message *n* 159 *SMS(-Nachricht)*
thereby *adv* 136 *damit, dadurch*
thick *adj* 141 *stark*
thoughtlessly *adv* 86 *gedankenlos, unüberlegt*
threat, be under ~ *v* 49 *bedroht sein*
threatened *adj* 19 *bedroht*
thrill *n* 32 *Nervenkitzel, Eregung;*
thrilling *adj* 46 *packend, spannend*
throw in *v* 124 *einwerfen*
thud *n* 75 *(dumpfer) Aufprall*
thus *adv* 45 *so, dadurch*
tidal power *n* 80 *Gezeitenenergie*
tidy *adj* 58 *aufgeräumt*
tighten *v* 34 *verschärfen*
till *prep* 29 *bis*
time, have a hard ~ *v* 149 *Probleme (mit etw) haben;*
on ~ *adv* 58 *pünktlich;*
take ~ off *phr* 52 *sich frei nehmen*
time-slot *n* 12 *Zeitfenster*
tiny *adj* 85 *winzig, klein*
tip sb off *v* 61 *jdm einen Tipp/Wink geben*
tissue *n* 155 *Gewebe*
toddler *n* 52 *Kleinkind*
toll *n* 49 *Opfer, Schaden;*
take its ~ *phr* 121 *seinen Tribut fordern*
top *v* 42 *übertreffen;*
come tops *phr* 12 *die Nummer eins sein;*
on ~ of *phr* 136 *über hinaus*
topple over *v* 108 *umkippen*
torn *adj* 127 *zerrissen*
touch, get in ~ *phr* 13 *(sich) in Verbindung setzen*
tough *adj* 13 *schwierig*
tour operator *n* 25 *Reiseveranstalter*
track, keep ~ *v* 48 *die Übersicht behalten*
trade barrier *n* 110 *Handelsschranken*
trait *n* 43 *Eigenschaft*
trampled, get ~ on *v* 14 *geschurigelt werden*
tranquil *adj* 19 *ruhig*
transfer to *v* 138 *versetzen nach*
translate *v* 114 *übersetzen*
transmit *v* 102 *übertragen*
trap *v* 85 *speichern*
travel experience *n* 25 *Reiseerfahrung*
tray *n* 48 *Tablett*
treasure *n* 19 *Schatz*
treat *n* 10 *Freude, Hochgenuss* *v* 34, 109 *behandeln*
trembling *adj* 29 *bebend*
trial *n* 92 *Probelauf;* *n* 155 *Versuch, Test*
tribe *n* 23 *Stamm*
trickle *n* 103 *Rinnsal*
trigger *v* 144 *auslösen*
trivia *n* 68 *Belanglosigkeiten*
truancy *n* 79 *(Schule-)Schwänzen, unentschuldigtes Fehlen*
truant *v* 128 *(Schule) schwänzen, unentschuldigt fehlen*
trust *n* 84 *Vertrauen*
truth *n* 13 *Wahrheit*
truthful, be ~ *v* 53 *die Wahrheit sagen*
turmoil *n* 144 *Aufruhr*
turn, do sb a good ~ *phr* 12 *jdm einen Gefallen tun;*
~ **in** *v* 29 *schlafen gehen;*
~ **into** *v* 14 *(sich) verwandeln in, werden zu;* *v* 76 *ein-, abbiegen;*
~ **out** *v* 154 *herstellen, produzieren;*
~ **to** *v* 42 *sich wenden an*
Tuscany *n* 49 *Toskana*
twine *n* 107 *Schnur*

U

unbearable *adj* 141 *unerträglich*
unbridled *adj* 155 *ungezügelt, zügellos*
uncertain *adj* 109 *unsicher*
uncomfortable *adj* 21 *unwohl, unbequem*
uncommon *adj* 134 *ungewöhnlich, unüblich*

undeniable *adj* 42 *unbestreitbar, nicht zu übersehen;*
undeniably *adv* 155 *zweifellos*
underage *adj* 74 *minderjährig*
underdog *n* 44 *Unterlegene/r, Schwächere/r*
underestimate *v* 136 *unterschätzen*
undergo sth *v* 81 *etw erfahren, erleben*
undernourished *adj* 101 *unterernährt*
underprivileged *adj* 61 *unterprivilegiert*
undesirable *adj* 154 *unerwünscht*
unequivocal *adj* 117 *eindeutig, unmissverständlich*
unfit *adj* 104 *ungeeignet*
unfortunately *adv* 20 *unglücklicherweise, leider*
unhealthy *adj* 102 *ungesund*
unintentionally *adv* 33 *unabsichtlich, unbeabsichtigt*
(trade) union *n* 49 *Gewerkschaft*
unique *adj* 66 *einmalig*
unlawful *adj* 73 *rechtswidrig, ungesetzlich*
unless *conj* 85 *wenn nicht*
unlikely *adj* 159 *unwahrscheinlich*
unlock *v* 154 *entschlüsseln*
unpaid, go ~ *v* 103 *kein Gehalt bekommen*
unprecedented *adj* 42 *beispiellos*
unscramble *v* 17 *entschlüsseln, in die richtige Reihenfolge bringen*
unscripted *adj* 64 *ohne Drehbuch*
unspoiled *adj* 38 *unzerstört, unberührt*
unsympathetic *adj* 52 *verständnislos, kein Verständnis haben*
unthreatening *adj* 92 *nicht bedrohlich*
unwise *adj* 144 *unklug*
unworkable *adj* 114 *undurchführbar*
upbringing *n* 125 *Erziehung*
upset *adj* 60 *verärgert, aufgeregt;*
get sb ~ *v* 91 *jdn verwirren, aufregen*
urgency *n* 81 *Dringlichkeit*
usage *n* 74 *(Sprach-)Gebrauch, Verwendung*
use *n* 114 *Verwendung*
used, get ~ to *v* 9 *sich gewöhnen an;*
grow ~ to *v* 136 *sich gewöhnen an*
usefulness *n* 106 *Nutzen, Nützlichkeit*
utmost *adj* 30 *äußerst*

V

vacant *adj* 25 *frei, offen*
vacation *n* 49 *Urlaub, Ferien*
vain, in ~ *phr* 13 *vergebens*
valuable *adj* 83 *wertvoll*
value *n* 42 *Wert;* *v* 12 *schätzen, Wert legen auf*
vanguard *n* 145 *Spitze, Vorhut*
vapour trails *n* 85 *Kondensstreifen*
varied *adj* 19 *abwechslungsreich*
variety *n* 92 *Abwechslung, Vielfalt*
various *adj* 106 *verschieden*
vary *v* 12 *wechseln, variieren*
vast *adj* 32 *riesig, ungeheuer*
vendor *n* 49 *Verkäufer/in*
venture *n* 135 *(gewagtes) Unternehmen*
vice versa *phr* 32 *und umgekehrt*
victimization *n* 70 *Schikanierung, ungerechte Behandlung*
view *n* 81 *Aussicht;*
in ~ of sth *phr* 45 *angesichts;*
in ~ of this *phr* 114 *angesichts dessen*
viewer *n* 43 *Zuschauer/in*
vigil *n* 71 *Mahnwache*
vigorous *adj* 29 *energisch;*
vigorously *adv* 29 *kräftig, energisch*
violent *adj* 70 *gewalttätig, Gewalt-*
virtually *adv* 41 *praktisch, nahezu*
visible *adj* 112 *sichtbar*
visit, pay sb a ~ *v* 14 *jdn besuchen*
vital *adj* 110 *wesentlich, unerlässlich*
voice *v* 154 *zum Ausdruck bringen*
volatile *adj* 102 *provisorisch, unbeständig*
volunteer *n* 22 *Freiwillige/r*
voraciously *adv* 124 *sehr eifrig*
vote *v* 53 *wählen*
vulnerable *adj* 19 *schutzlos*

W

wade *v* 159 *waten*
wander *v* 103 *(ziellos) herumlaufen, schlendern*
war-ravaged *adj* 103 *kriegszerstört*
waste *n* 102 *Abfall, Müll;*
~ of time *n* 97 *Zeitverschwendung;*
~ time *v* 15 *Zeit verschwenden*
wastefully *adv* 89 *verschwenderisch*
watershed *n* 154 *Wendepunkt*
waver *v* 108 *flimmern, tanzen*
way, be on their ~ out *phr, infl* 40 *aus der Mode kommen;*
be ~ ahead *phr* 93 *weit voraus sein;*
they have their ~ *phr* 92 *es geht nach ihnen;*
mend your ways *phr* 125 *sich bessern*
wealth *n* 49 *Reichtum, Vermögen*
wealthy *adj* 57 *wohlhabend, reich*
weapons of mass destruction *n* 144 *Massenvernichtungswaffen*
wear off *v* 9 *nachlassen*
weave *v* 75 *sich schlängeln*
wedding *n* 123 *Hochzeit*
weed *v* 111 *(Unkraut) jäten*
weigh up *v* 49 *abwägen*

welfare *n* 22 *Wohlergehen;*
~ **benefits** *n* 49 *soziale Vergünstigungen*
well, do ~ *v* 13 *gut abschneiden*
well-being *n* 9 *Wohlergehen*
wheelchair *n* 71 *Rollstuhl*
whisk away *v* 123 *(schnell) entführen*
whisper *v* 13 *flüstern;*
whispering *n* 148 *Flüstern*
whistle *v* 14 *pfeifen*
white-collar workers *n* 52 *(Büro-)Angestellte*
whitewater rafting *n* 28 *Wildwasserfahren*
wide awake *adj* 30 *hellwach*
widespread *adj* 104 *weit verbreitet*
will, strike at ~ *phr* 144 *nach Belieben zuschlagen*
willing *adj* 104 *bereit (sein); adj* 134 *gewillt (sein), bereit(willig);*
willingness *n* 64 *Bereitschaft*
win over *v* 42 *(jdn) gewinnen*
winding *adj* 76 *gewunden*
wing *n* 29 *Flügel*
withdraw *v* 52 *abheben*
wobble *v* 108 *wackeln*
wonder *n* 19 *Wunder*
workforce *n* 140 *Arbeitskräfte(potential)*
workload *n* 48 *Arbeitsbelastung*
world, do sb the ~ **of good** *phr, infl* 9 *jdm unwahrscheinlich gut tun*
worth *n* 32 *Wert*
written excuse *n* 16 *Entschuldigungsschreiben*

Y

yard *n* 76 *Yard (91 cm)*
yearn *v* 119 *sich sehnen;*
~ **(for)** *v* 38 *sich sehnen (nach)*
yobbo (GB) *n infl* 14 *Halbstarker, Rowdy*

Quellenverzeichnis

Titelfoto:Getty Images RF (1); Corbis RF (2,3); Caro/Ruffer (4)
Corel Lib: S.45/3;
Corbis: S.8/1/A.Inden; S.8/3/M.Keller; S.8/4/Grace; S.8/5/M.Prince; S.8/6/L.Manning; S.19/RF; S.19/2/P.Souders; S.20/1/Grace; S.20/2/J.Feingersh; S.20/3/J.Pelaez; S.20/4/J.Feingersh; S.20/5/R.Morsch; S.29/P.Fisher; S.45/J.Westrich; S.52 Caro/Korth.; S.55/J.Stettenheim; S.56/T.Soqui; S.71/D.Butow; S.74/1/D.Galante; S.74/2/R.Schultheiss; S.74/4/RF; S.74/4/M.Prince; S.74/6/M.Prince; S.75/Turbo; S.81,82/G.Marx; S.91/E.Sugita; S.92/Y.Nakao; S.101/B.Vikander; S.103(2)G.Mendel; S.105/M.Pelletier;S.122/1/J.Fisher; S.122/2/K.Mitchell; S.123/B.Krist; S.127/N.Feanny-Hicks; S.135/1/T.Stewart; S.135/2/C.Carroll; S.138/1/RF; S.144/RF; S.145/C.Collins; S.148/Emely;
Comstock: S.74/3RF; S.90/1RF;
Fotofinder: S.34/Argum; S.90/vario-images/B.Lauter; S.95/Bildagentur-online; S.114/M.Egbert; S.130/Agentur Focus/J.Jin; S.138/Plus 49/N.Cornet; S.139/agenda/J.Boethling; S.153/plainpicture/Bussenius;
Getty Images: S.8/2/RF; S.42/PM Images; S.32/Yellow Dog Productions; S.13/RF, S.14/RF; S.138/2RF;
D.Graham: S.63;
Picture Alliance: S.65/Rtl S. Menne; S.143(2)dpa; S.153/2/dpa; S.153/4/dpa; S.153/1/P.Pleul; S.153/3/J.Büttner; S.154/dpa;
C.Pycraft: S.62(2);
Austin: S.101/2

Mit freundlicher Unterstützung folgender Unternehmen:
S.133; Exxon Mobil: S.38; Nissan: S.38; Nokia: S.38; Singapore Airlines: S.38; Volvo: S.39; Siemens: S.59;
Sony: S.90/2/3/4;

Illustrationen/Cartoons: Oxford Designers & Illustrators, Oxford, England
Landkarten: Carlos Borrell, Berlin
Language Check Jokes, Bernard Brown, Bad Tölz

Texte: S.13: In A Dry Season/P. Robinson/Macmillan; S.22: The Guardian; S.29: National Geographic; S.32: The joy of running/http://www.shelterpub.com; S.42:The International Herald Tribune; S.42: Newsweek; S.49: The New York Times; S.52: Newsweek; S.55: Allentown, Billy Joel; S.60/S.61: The Daily Express;
S.64: Reality TV/http://atheism.about.com; S.71: The Guardian; S.76: Just Along for the Ride/D. Kurumada; S.81: The New Scientist; S.85: The Observer; S.91: Newsweek; S.95:Using global warming to create conditions for life on Mars/www.spaceref.com;
S.102: The Guardian; S.103: The Independent; S.107: Fesito goes to market/N. Mandela's Favourite African Folktales/Tafelberg Publishers; S.113: Doing a Number on English/http://daphne.palomar.edu/jquintero/does/doing/a/Number/English.doc; S.114: A talk given at the European Parliament; S.116: Newsweek; S.123: The Observer; S.127:H. Kureishi/Love in a Blue Time/Faber and Faber; S.131: Frankfurter Rundschau; S.135:http://geoc.uconn.edu/ViasCourse.htm; S.135: http://www.earthwindow.com/grc2/SaraSamson; S.139: http://www.cbsnews.com; S.144: National Geographic, S.148:J. Safran Foer/Extremely Loud and Incredibly Close/Houghton Mifflin Company; S.150: Süddeutsche Zeitung; S.154: www.bbc.co.uk; S.158: Der Tagesspiegel; S.159: www.bbc.co.uk and www.technology.com

THE BRITISH ISLES